feet first

feet first

A Memoir

To Joseph Zazyczny
with my best wishes.

Spring 2006

Walter Baran

Walter A. Baran

Walter Baran
87 Country Club Road
Ashland, Pa 17921

waltb@verizon.net

To order additional copies of this book, contact:
Xlibris Corporation
1-888-795-4274
www.Xlibris.com
Orders@Xlibris.com
18744

CONTENTS

This book is dedicated to
My friend, Irene
Who has; for the past few years
Has patiently corrected my grammer,
and :punctuation's
Made sure that I did not leave any dangling
Participles, or tripling consonants,
corrected any solecism's she found
And espicaley her invaluable help with my spelling.

HOW TO BE REMEMBERED

If you would not be forgotten,
as soon as you are dead and rotten,
either write things worth the reading,
or do things worth the writing.

Benjamin Franklin

FORWARD

Originally, it was my intention to record and recapture some of my boyhood memories—a story of what I hoped would be of some interest to my family and grandchildren. For me, this was an easy and pleasant task. I asked some friends to critique what I had written, and I expected my family to correct some of the dates and challenge some of the stories.

In writing my "Memoirs," while everything I wrote was true, it was written with a flippant, frivolous and occasionally humorous way. Since I had not planned to have my story published, most of what I wrote was not written in a serious vein. As an example, the story about my visits to the White House. It was a great honor that a first generation American actually sat at a conference table with the President of the United States, Ronald Reagan. I had three separate occasions to personally speak with him. I also met with President Bush in the White House. On that occasion, I was interviewed by a member of his staff to be appointed as a member of the "Enterprise Fund for Poland" (I was on the short list) After the interview, President Bush came into the room and spoke to each of us individually. I decided not to rewrite the article on the White House since it was a true recollection of my experience.

A few friends have suggested (actually insisted!) that I write about my work history and my time spent in Pennsylvania Government. This turned out to be pure Sisyphean labor!

In my attempt to add both of these subjects to what was to be only my childhood memories it required occasional repetition, and a couple of awkward flashbacks or leaps forward. I feel that I have not been very successful accomplishing this task. I will leave it to you, the reader, to make that decision.

In putting together this story, I have sometimes used language that is not part of my normal vocabulary. Certain four letter words, a scatological or an occasional profane one may offend some readers. Please understand why these words are used: they are an accurate expression of the times and situations pictured, to change or omit them would not be historically honest.

With some small exceptions, I did have a happy childhood.

WAB

Cover
Summer vacation on the farm 1930
Brandonville, Pennsylvania

Rear: Two unidentified Bible salesmen
Front: Left to right-Marie Sczypyn,
Walter Baran age 7, Florence Klein

ALPHA

O n Wednesday, June 18, 1924. I entered this world with my feet first. I was a very *"przeciwny"* (contrary/ mischievous) child. All of my friends were born headfirst. I figured that if I am to be different, I have to start at the beginning of things. Ergo, my entrance into this world. I was born in our home at 114 North Broad Mt. Avenue, Frackville, PA. My mother's name was Antonina Gibowicz Baranowska of Suwalki, Poland and my father was Waldyslaw Baranowski. He was born in the Polish City of Plosk. The first thing I remember was the fact that here I am in the United States of America and everyone around me was speaking "Polish!" I was taken to the Annunciation B.V.M. Lithuanian Church on Broad Mt Avenue to be baptized. What was I doing in a Lithuanian Church? Well you see, the congregation of St. Ann's was in formation and the church building was not yet built. (Actually it was built, but it was in a small town in Indiana, being loaded on railway cars to be shipped to Frackville.) **Circle-A-Unit Buildings & Co.** of Newcastle, Indiana built the church. While the church was being built, St Ann's parish paid a rental fee of $20.00 per month to the Annunciation B.V.M. Church for the use of their church. A newly ordained priest, Father Stanislaus J. Garstka, was sent to Frackville as the first pastor of the newly organized parish named St. Ann's. (The one without a building). It was on its way from Indiana

In the REGISTRUM BATISMORUM IN ECCLESIA DIOECESIS of St. Ann's Church, the first two children in the new parish were baptized on the same day. June 29, 1924. Irene

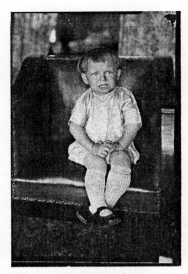

Age two. My mother gave me this haircut

Golabiewska and Ladislaus Baranowski. Of course I was a gentleman even then, and allowed Miss Golabiewska to go first. I was given the name of Wladyslaw Antoni Baranowski. A wartime army friend of my father's, Stanislaus Kosierp, and Anna Ziolowska were my Godparents. I enjoyed being born and especially the fact that I came into this world feet first. That meant a lot to me. (More on this topic later.) The next entry was Veronica Dzwingle (Swingle) August 31, 1924, and on September 7, 1924, Peter Baran (no relation) was baptized.

THE CHRISTENING

I have always been very curious, questioning, *przeciwny*, and just plain inquisitive.

As an example: June 29, 1924. It is about 11:00 am on a Sunday morning and some strange lady is giving me a bath in the kitchen sink. I was dried with a towel that felt very rough on my tender, eleven-day-old skin. I was dressed only in a cloth diaper and wrapped in an old but very clean gray blanket. There was a lot of activity in the house. All were strangers (at least to me). I did not recognize any of the voices, but I do remember that everyone was speaking Polish. At about 1:00 o'clock in the afternoon, my diaper was changed, it was not soiled but it was changed anyhow. The new diaper was new and it was very soft. Once again it was the same strange lady that gave me my morning bath that was dressing me. I thought, "This lady whoever she is, is alright! When she was washing me, she did not get any soap in my eyes; I forgave her for using an old and very rough towel on my eleven-day-old body. Now she is dressing me with my first set of all new clothes." Every thing was going fine until I noticed that she was, GASP, putting a girls slip over my head. Things were going from bad to very, very bad because she now was dressing me in a GIRL'S DRESS! I didn't give a damn if it was brand new. I began with what was to be my first real tantrum; I screamed, I cried, I kicked my legs, I tried moving my arms about but they dicdn't seem to work. I think it was because I was born feet first. I even peed in my brand new diaper. None of this bothered the strange lady that was dressing me. Lucky for me, or rather lucky for my tender bottom, this strange lady brought a package of three very soft 100% cotton diapers. I did not want to be dressed in a girl's dress for what for me was my very first trip out of the house and into the wide, wide new world with all the marvelous sights and sounds and every thing that I would begin to discover.

Well, like it or not, I was wrapped in a new, lightweight, white, 100%, wool blanket. Even though it was a wonderful and bright sunny day, the new, 100% wool blanket was covering my face. I couldn't see a thing. I knew it was not my mother; she would not try to hide my face. At first I thought, am I that ugly that my face is covered? I knew that I was not ugly since a lot of the old ladies that came to our house to see me use these words, *Piekny, Sliczny, Wspanialy* Beautiful, Pretty, Handsome. And then I thought, maybe it's a good thing that my face is covered, so no one will know that I am wearing a dress. I could tell by her voice that the strange lady that bathed and dressed me was now taking me out the front door. Much later in life, I found out that we lived at 114 North Broad Mountain Avenue (I told you I was and still am very observant) First, my older sister Frances, age five, holding the hand of my older brother Leonard, age seventeen months. My real old sister Veronica who was fifteen followed them. She had to pick him up carry Leonard since he was holding up the parade.

Veronica was working in a rectory in a large Polish Church in Philadelphia that had six priests assigned to the parish. She used to help the cook in the kitchen and she also worked in the laundry. She came home to help when the stork visited my mom. In Poland there are lots of storks. The special kind and bring babies. Well anyhow, following Frances was a friend of my mother's from the old Country, Poland, named Mrs. Anna Ziolkowska who was to be my godmother. Next were my mother, Antonina Baranowska and my father, Wladyslaw Baranowski. Then my Godfather, Stanislaw Kosierp, an army buddy of my father's with his wife, Anna. Mr. Jozef Ziolkowski was next followed by my older (not the oldest) brother, Peter Nielubowicz age ten. My oldest brother, Charlie Nielubowicz aged 12 1/2, could not attend. He was caught smoking a "stumpy" he found in the street and was being punished by having to kneel down in the kitchen and say *"Ojcze nasz"* (Our Father) fifteen times, and *"zdrowas Maryjo"* (Hail Mary) sixty times.

Fortunately for me, the strange lady that was carrying me switched arms while carrying me with the result that the 100% wool blanket only covered half of my face. The very first thing I saw was that we were under a real tall maple tree. It was the first tree I ever saw. In the tree way up high, was a bird. It had a sort of blue color, but the most important thing about this bird was that it was singing! No one in our group saw or heard the bird but me! Heck they did not even see the tree. It was June and the leaves were a wonderful dark green color. The leaves were still very young and fresh.

Walking down the street, I saw the cemetery on our left, almost a block long and I thought to myself, I am the Alpha and across the street was the Omega. The right side of the street had many homes, one very close to another. Yup, Life and Death.

We arrived at the Annunciation B.V.M. Lithuanian Church right on time; it was, if my memory serves me well, exactly 1:57 PM. Next thing I saw was that we were gathered around what looked like a sink without faucets. It smelled real nice in church which I found out later came from the incense used a few hours earlier at high Mass. Lots of little candles were burning in small red glass cups, and there were windows that had a lot of dark pictures on them. There was a lot of mumbling going on, (it sure wasn't Polish.) by a man who was wearing what looked to me like a dress. I didn't feel so bad since I was also wearing a dress. More mumbling in some foreign tongue. Then the same strange lady, who dressed me, started to take off my cap! By this time, you the reader should have figured out, that the strange lady was Mrs. Ziolkowska, my Godmother! The next thing that happened was that the guy wearing the dress started to pour water on my head. No one told him that I had a bath a couple of hours earlier. After he put some oil in my ears, he shook hands with all the big people. And we walked the block and a half to our home. We called our house, "The Brown House" I found out eight years later, why we gave all the houses that we lived in a name.

When we returned to the house, that's when the party began. I was in a little bed with sides on it, pretending that I was asleep. More strange people came in. First all the ladies and one man, came to look at me wearing a dress. All the ladies speaking in Polish used all the words *(In italics)* that I wrote in the third paragraph on the first page of this story. The man looked at me but he didn't say a word.

It wasn't much of a party. Most of the people were in the kitchen. A large pot of soup and a smaller pot with kielbasa were simmering on the kitchen coal stove. The kitchen table held some bowls for the soup and assorted dinner plates, some of which actually matched. A large loaf of dark rye bread and two jars of *Krzan* (horseradish) one white and the other red. There were two quarts of white lightning moonshine on a small cabinet near the sink. That completed the *Buffet*.

At about 5:30, the party really began when they started to sing, *Sto Lat, Sto Lat, niech zyje zyje nam;* 100 years, 100 years, may he live 100 years. While they were singing and drinking, Charlie tried to sneak out the back door so that he could have a smoke. He had a few stumpies hidden under the back porch. My mom caught him and asked him if he finished his prayers or did he want to say them over again. He was saved at the last minute because Stanley Kosierp and his wife Anna began an awful fight. This is one time that we were happy that we did not own a player piano. Mrs. Kosierp would throw piano rolls at Stanley when they had a fight at home.

After the fight, it became awfully quite. As I was sound asleep, I really cannot tell you how the evening ended.

Mom and her Progeny. Christmas 1949

POLAND

M y mother, Antonina Gibowicz, was born on June 7, 1887 in a small village called Wizajny in the county of Suwalki, Poland. She was the eldest of six children. She was married in Poland to Franciszek Nielubowicz, who was born October 5, 1883, in the village of Kuporny. A child, Veronica, was born and shortly thereafter her husband sailed to America from the port of Hamburg Germany Feb. 20, 1909 on a ship named "Victoria" arriving at Ellis Island March 1, 1909. In the great migration of the early 1900's many men left Poland for economic reasons. It was common for the husband to come first, work in the coalmines and save enough dollars to pay passage for his family to come to the United States. In some cases this took many years since the husband had to send funds to his family in Poland until arrangements were made for them to come to America. In my mother's case this took about two years. Not only was money needed for the fare, but also additional dollars were needed to pay for a guide to illegally cross the border from Poland, which was in control of Russia at the time.

In my mother's words: "There were twelve people making the trip across the border. I was the only one with a child. We traveled at night through the deep forest. The guide told me 'your child must not make any noise. If it does, you must hold your hand over its mouth or we will all be captured.' Fortunately it was a very dark moonless night and we made it safely into Germany where we were met by a Polish-speaking German and taken by train to the Port at Hamburg. Before boarding, we were all given a large yellow tag attached to a string to wear around our necks; my tag said SHENANDOAH, PENNSYLVANIA. After what seemed like months we arrived at Ellis Island in New York. We were given good food and after a few days, we were put on a train for Shenandoah were I was met by my husband."

In the years that followed, my mother gave birth to three additional children. Charles, Peter and Frances. November 10, 1918, during the great flu, her husband died. She was pregnant with Frances at the time. So many died during this time that there were not enough vehicles or horses to carry the coffins to the cemetery about three miles up the hill to the Shenandoah Heights cemetery. Her husband's casket was carried by some of his friends on their shoulders with my mother and the children walking behind. The Priest wanted to have the burial on Nov. 12th since he had many funerals every day. My mother told him that she felt that she would give birth very soon and she insisted that the burial should take place as soon as possible. While walking to the cemetery she had birth pains but continued to walk. Later at about 5:00 PM on the same day, she told the children to go out to play and my mother gave birth to Frances in the living room of her home. One of the neighbors who was a pallbearer, came in and found her on the sofa. She asked him to hand her a blanket that was on a chair. She used the blanket to cover the child. She also asked him to get a pair of scissors from the kitchen and she herself cut the cord. He arranged to get a doctor to look in on her. The doctor came and took care of the child and the mother. She then was aided by some of the women from the neighborhood. The doctor called in a few days (He was Irish, everyone that spoke English was called Irish.) He told her that he and his wife could not have any children and he asked her if she would give them the child. He also said that he would help her financially. He offered her $500. She thanked him but said that she would manage. The doctor said that she might starve. Mom said, "If we starve we will all starve together."

She was now a widow with four children with no means of support. Fortunately, her late husband had two brothers with their families living in Shenandoah, George and Joseph Nielubowicz, who were able to assist her. Many of the neighbors brought food and they helped with other expenses. Without their help, the family would not have survived.

My father was born in the city of Plock in Poland. We do not have much information about him. I do know that he immigrated to America sometime before the First World War. When World War 1 began, he joined the American army and met my uncle, Joseph Gibowicz, while serving in France. He also met another Pole who immigrated to the US, Mr. Stanley Kosierp. Both my father and Mr. Stanley Kosierp lived in Philadelphia. Since they both were Polish, they stayed together throughout the war. My uncle used the time they were together to convince them to move to Shenandoah to the "hard coal regions" and work in the coal mines where wages were high.

None of these men ever worked in a coal mine since both came from the farming area of Poland. Mr. Kosierp was married and had two children. My father was *single!* And I'm sure that my uncle Joe had this in mind when he convinced these two guys to move "upstate" soon after they returned to the U.S.

LIFE IN THE COAL TOWNS

IN THE EARLY 1900'S

The great migration to the United States from Europe, especially Eastern Europe, consisted mostly of single young men and a few who were married. As mentioned previously, they had to earn enough dollars in order to send for their families. All of these men lived as "boarders" in homes that were already established. When a newly arrived miner sought living quarters he was often asked by the woman of the house, "Are you on day or night shift?" A typical home would have two or possibly three bedrooms and at least five children so space was at a premium.

Having the men sleep in shifts was a practical and profitable way to earn extra dollars. With this system, the beds never had time to cool off! Of course meals came with the bed. The lady of the house was quite busy, packing lunches, making meals, doing the miners laundry at all hours of the day and most of the nights.

Most of the coal collieries did not have shower facilities for the miners when they came up from the mine. This also was true with the men and boys who worked in the coal preparation plant called by the miners "The Breaker." Since the coal miners lived close to the mine, they all walked home still wearing the clothes they wore in the mine. Their faces were all black with the exception of their eyes. They carried their water can and lunch pail. When the mine whistle blew signifying the end of the shift, the children would walk towards the mine to meet their father. He always saved part of a sandwich or an apple in his lunch pail to give to his child who approached him and said "did you leave anything for me."

It's not that the child was hungry, but this little ceremony gave proof to his son that his father loved him. It was not manly for the father to occasionally tell his son, "Son I love you."

A large percentage of the miners were not married. They lived as boarders in the home of a widow whose husband was killed in a mine accident. With the death of her husband, her income stopped. None of the miners carried life insurance

My Parents Wedding Day

even if it was available. The cost would be prohibitive since their occupation was very hazardous. The only income that would be available to her was to open her home to boarders. Some homes had four or even six of these men. Not only did she have to supply room and board, she also had to wash the miners working clothes. She also had another duty to perform. She had to wash their backs. During the summer every home had a wooden tub in the basement. Heated water was placed in the tub and a bar of soap and a towel were placed nearby. The miner stripped to his waist he would then call the woman or one of her older children to come down and wash his back. He then undressed completely and washed the rest of his body. They used the basement until the weather became very cold. During the winter they would bathe in the kitchen. This caused quite a problem since everyone in the house had to vacate the kitchen. If three or four boarders lived in the home it took quite a while till they all had their bath.

A few years ago, during a discussion about the good old days (?) A friend of mine was explaining how his widowed mother with seven children managed to feed and clothe them when there were no food stamps, welfare, or heating allotments, Medicaid or mother's assistance. When I asked him how in the world she managed, he said "Why, she took in boarders!"

While most of these boarders were single, there were a few that were married, with a wife and children in Europe. Eventually, most of these married men would earn enough money to bring their family to the United States. The single men had a problem, as I wrote previously, there were very few women of their same background available for to marriage. They did not date any English, Welsh, Irish, or German even if they were available since they could not communicate with them. Their only recourse was to write to a girl in their native land or better yet, to write to a father in his native country to ask for the hand of one of his daughters and inform him that he would be responsible for her passage and other expenses. Occasionally this would end successfully. Since many miners were killed in accidents in the mine, there were also many widows who after a full year of mourning would be available for marriage. Many of the young miners married widows with children.

Most of these young miners had other things on their mine besides marriage and that was sports, especially the great American sports of baseball and football. Language was not too important in sports. Each village and occasionally each colliery would have a team. It was great to see a football game where many languages were used. Lithuanian, Slovak, Italian, Polish, Ukrainian, Hungarian and yes even English speaking Irishmen. (The Irish often served as referees.) After working a full shift in the mines they found some time to relax to enjoy sports. They had all the equipment they needed to play football. All they needed was a ball that held enough air to last to the half of the game. The owner of the ball also owned a small air pump. During halftime, the air pump was used until the football was firm. Baseball was another matter. Two or three bats and at least four baseballs were required before the start of any game. At least one bat was broken during a game not because it was a cheap bat, but some of the batter's were very strong. The reason for having at least four baseballs before the start of the game was because a few teenagers would be stationed beyond the home run line so that they would either catch or pick up a ball and run home with it! I guess you could call it "stealing home." Since they did not have any money, that was the only way the young players could acquire a baseball. The rest of the equipment was a catcher's mitt, a glove for the first baseman and if possible a glove for the shortstop. The pitcher rarely wore a glove. The games between towns were always played at about 1:30 PM on Sunday's. Since doing any type of work on the Lord's Day was frowned on, the whole town turned out to see the game. Even a few of the wives were in attendance.

We now at last, I come to the reason for the comments made about my Father. Why else would a young man marry a widow with four children? A widow who was eight years older than he and her youngest child a bit less than two years old? They were married and lived in Shenandoah, and about a year later my brother, Leonard, was born. At this time my father decided to move to Frackville. Uncle Joe Gibowicz already lived there and was responsible for Mr. Kosierp and my father moving to a more civilized and spacious town with plenty of room to grow. There the Nielubowicz/ Baranowski family lived and grew and Wladyslaw Antoni (born feet first) and Helen were born. The family now consisted of a Mother, Father and seven children. Veronica, Charles, Peter and Frances Nielubovicz and Leonard, Walter, and Helen Baranowski.

The summer of 1928, my brother Leonard was six years old, I was four and my sister Helen, was two. My father took his bimonthly salary that he received from the colliery where he worked and deserted his family. His decision changed my life. From that date on, he never gave a single dollar of support to my mother or his children.

FIRST GRADE

At the age of six, my mother enrolled me in the first grade in the Franklin Elementary School located on South Broad Mt. Ave. My teacher's name was Mrs. Ivy Kershner. She was very kind to me. She always helped me with my writing. I had difficulty holding a pencil because of my birth injury and had some difficulty with my wrists. She spent much more time with me than she did with the other children. I had a problem in taking my coat off and even more in putting it back on.

Mrs. Kershner My first grade teacher

She helped me with my coat and always made sure that I buttoned it properly. I had a hell of a time putting on my hat. I would hold the hat in my right hand and then I would swing my arm in an arc, then quickly swing it to my head. I got so good at this that I was successful three out of four times. This was the first time that anyone outside my home took a special interest in me. I knew long ago that being born feet first would be a great advantage. It was even better than being born rich. Mrs. Kershner taught me when I was six years old, that is, in 1930, and I never forgot her.

In August of 1969, the Frackville Chapter of the Senior Citizens Club came to our grove to hold their summer picnic. Among the senior citizens present was my first grade teacher *Mrs. Kershner!* I could not believe my eyes. She was still in good health and she said that she remembered me. First I thought that she was just being kind but then I thought, "Gee, she must remember me." While I know she helped thousands (well maybe hundreds) of first graders to put on their coats, I don't believe there was any other kid that put his hat on like I did. She certainly would remember that! It was a very happy day for me. We had our picture taken and I really believe that this would never have happened if it weren't for the fact that I was born feet first.

My mother brought me to school each morning and came for me after school. Some of the other mothers brought their children to school for the first week and later the children came to school alone. But my mother came for me every day. In the winter she would pull me on my brother's sled. I don't remember my mother taking my brother or sister to school on a sled. Yet another advantage of being born feet first.

TONSILS

Each year during the month of June after the school year was finished, the Ashland State Hospital became very busy. All the mothers made arrangements for their children to have their tonsils removed. Since all of the families were quite large, the children who reached the age of eight or nine were taken to the hospital for the operation. In our case there were three, Leonard, Helen, and me.

It didn't seem to matter that we did not have any problems with our tonsils; Mom said that it would save us trouble later in life and besides all the kids in our neighborhood went through this ritual.

Mom did not tell me that it was going to hurt, but I sort of figured out myself even though I was only seven years old. The day before the operation mom told me that I could have a whole can of cling peaches for myself and all the ice cream that I wanted. Now I sure loved canned peaches, the peach slices were packed in a can in heavy sweet syrup. The peaches would just slide down your throat. We rarely had canned peaches in our house. I remember one year when I was about six years old, and we had canned peaches three times in that year. I also dearly loved ice cream that we had quite a few times during the summer. The ice cream came in second to canned peaches.

It got me to thinking, why is Mom telling me that I could have a whole can to myself? And then she also mentioned that I could have ice cream every day when I came home.

My brother Charlie drove me and my mother to the Ashland Miners Hospital located in Fountain Springs. We arrived early in the morning. I was taken to a large room called "The Children's

Ward." The room was filled with children who in turn filled most of the children's hospital beds that were located there. My mother undressed me and put on a small gown that the nurse gave her.

In about a half-hour, I was placed on a small rolling bed that did not have side railings but it had two belts. One belt was buckled on my ankles and the other was buckled at my chest. I was wheeled into the operating room. The doctor and the nurses were all wearing masks. When I looked up I saw a very large light fixture that looked like a big mirror with a small light bulb in the center. A nurse came holding a rubber mask that fit over my nose and mouth. They told me to take a deep breath. When I did, I thought they that they were killing me! I fought with all my might. One nurse was holding my head and the other one was choking me with the mask.

Sometime later, I don't know if it was a few hours or a few days later, I awoke in a strange room. I was lying flat on my back and I looked up at the ceiling. I could see the sky that was very blue and some small clouds that were drifting by. I kept looking at the clouds to see if I could see any Angels. I was sure that I died and I was in heaven! Each cloud that passed by did not have any Angels sitting about. After a while I decided that I was not in heaven at all because when I was preparing to receive first holy communion, I was told that in heaven there was no pain or suffering. Well, I was in pain and I was suffering. I tried to call out but my throat was sore. In a little while, a nurse came to see me. I told her that I wanted to see my mom. In fact I insisted upon it. She said I would have to wait until visiting hours in the afternoon. When the nurse came in, she was carrying a small sort of half round tray. I soon found out why she had this tray. I started to "Throw Up." The only time I ever had to "throw up" was when I ate eleven very green apples last summer. The only difference was that this time there was **"Blood"** mixed with a lot of spit. I thought that it was odd since when I threw up the apples, there was some spit and a little bit of oatmeal that came out. This time it was only spit and blood. I later found out why my mother did not give me any breakfast that morning or even a glass of milk. After about an hour I was moved back to the children's Ward and placed in a large white crib.

When my mother came to see me, I thought she looked a little guilty but she kissed me and held my hand. I'm glad she didn't tell me that I could have all the ice cream and peaches that I wanted. I didn't feel like eating anything. The next morning the nurse brought me some Jell-O and I could take a few sips of water. I began feeling better.

I asked the nurse the reason why I was in this huge round room with a glass ceiling. She said, "That room is being temporarily used as the children's recovery room. It's called the Solarium and was used for children who had tuberculosis." I found out what it meant when my brother Charlie came with my mother.

By the second day I was ready to go home. My mother told me that she and my brother Pete would come for me the next morning.

During that day, a boy about my age was walking around the ward with a cast on his arm. He came to my bed and asked me if I lived in Girardville. I told him that I lived all my life in Frackville. He then asked me, "Are you a medical or a surgical?" I told him I did not know what that meant. He said, "Well, were you sick when you came in here or did they make you sick after you got here?" That's when I found out that I was a surgical patient.

LIST OF FRACKVILLE HOUSES WHERE WE LIVED

1923   131 North 4th Street
1923   114 North broad Mountain Avenue, the home where I was born.
1925   226 North broad Mountain Avenue
1928   315 South Line Street
1930   235 South Wylam Street.
       422 South Broad Mountain Avenue.
1938   Gilbert Street, Shenandoah.
1939   201 South Broad Mountain Avenue
       438 South Middle Street
1941   233 Spencer Street
1942   220 Casa Loma Apt. Wylam Street
1945   246 North Nice Street

After our marriage.

1949   222 South Centre Street, Frackville
1959   200 Butler Road, Frackville
1994   87 Country Club Road, Ashland

I researched the dates and addresses from St. Ann's Church records. I may be off a year or two. If any family member could confirm or correct the dates or locations, the author of this one-inch thick book will appreciate it.

My mother lived in Shenandoah when she arrived from Poland. Her home was *"Na Kamieni"* (on the rocks). All the homes in the south end of Shenandoah were built on an outcropping of rocks. It had more Poles in town than even Suwalki had. She lived there until she married my father and shortly thereafter the family moved to Frackville.

This moving business bothered me so much that when I was thirteen and a half years old, I promised myself that I would not marry until I had a brand new house with a toilet *inside* the house and that it was built in the center of Frackville, on the best street in town, and damn if I didn't do it. More on this later.

226 NORTH BROAD MT. AVE.

O ur family moved into this house in 1929. It was a "double block" house. We got the side with the large yard. The yard had many fruit trees, a few different varietys of cherry trees, a few apple, pear and plum trees. The yard also had two very large geese that competed with the police dog that protected the Nielubovicz/Baranowski family. The geese would stick out their long necks and emit a loud hissing sound. Our dog did not have to worry about protecting the family as long as the geese were around. He spent his time getting his kicks by killing the neighborhood chickens. This caused my mother a lot of grief. She tried communicating with the aggrieved neighbor without much success. She spoke Polish while the neighbor spoke in

Sister Verna and John Matusick

some foreign tongue. These negotiations that lasted some hours really did not resolve anything. She decided to once again patch the holes in the fence that surrounded the yard. This fence was something to behold. I suppose that in the present time, it would be considered a work of art. The fence was originally built in the last century, circa 1894 or thereabouts. It had an assortment of pickets, all-different colors and sizes, placed haphazardly. Not one picket assumed an upright position. In some areas the pickets were overlapped so often that it was impossible to see the original pickets.

My mother would warn us kids to be careful when we played a little too rough. She would warn us that if we lost a tooth or two, our teeth would look like "Arciszewski's fence." After all the repairs made to this fence, the dog would somehow leave the yard in search of chickens.

There was a barn-like building in the backyard. It had a large room under the roof that was accessible by a ladder built into the wall. It was a great place for a ten-year-old kid to play "cops and robbers."

Each spring my mother purchased a piglet from a farmer. It became a family pet. Every Saturday she would give it a bath and bring it into the house. This is one pig that was house trained. It also was quite a performer. Mom would put a record in the victrola and this pink pig would dance around in circles. If mom stopped the record, the pig would stop his dance. The neighbors were often invited in to see the dancing pig. The pig had another trick. We had long carpet runners from the front door to the kitchen. This pig would lie down at the end of the carpet, put the tassels on the end of the carpet in his mouth, and roll himself halfway to the front door. This was a damn funny pig.

The family loved this pig. After a few months the pig was no longer a little pig. The neighbors (the ones without the chickens that they used to have) complained to the town officials, and so, the pig was sent to the Paskiewicz's to spend the rest of the year there since they lived in Butler township where keeping farm animals was permitted.

Sometime in late October mom sent Charlie and Pete to bring the pig back to its home where it spent its piglet childhood. I remember it was a Saturday. The pig was lying on its back; its back legs tied with a sturdy rope. Pete was holding its front legs while Charlie was holding the back legs. My sister Frances ran up to her bedroom. I don't know who made the most noise, her crying or the pig's squealing. Mom had a real big butcher knife in her hand. She placed her left hand on the pig's belly, and when she found the heart, she spread her middle and index fingers apart and the knife's blade disappeared from view. After a minute or two, she said "Hoist him up." The rope at its back legs was led up to a hook on the second floor of the barn. Mom got a big pot, placed it under the hanging head, and calmly slit its throat.

When my mother lived in Shenandoah, she found work in The Shenandoah Abattoir. Her job was butchering pigs. Well not exactly butchering, what she did was, well, like taking the pig apart. She would cut open the belly and she took out the various parts, the liver, kidneys, lungs and especially the intestines. They were used to make casings for *Kielbasa*. The pigs came by her on a chain conveyor with their heads hanging down. The unit where she worked was covered with a roof but one wall was completely open. That meant she worked in the winter outdoors. She told me that she wore boots but the water would get in her boots and would practically freeze.

Another of my mother's talents was the making of soap. My mother only had a forth grade education in Poland. In spite of that, I was amazed at her knowledge. Making soap was a very complicated process. I will try to explain:

CHEMISTRY OF SOAP

All fatty oils and fats are mixtures of triglycerides; are compounds (esters) and some fatty acid such as palmitic acid, etc. The chemistry involved in soap making may be expressed in the following equation: $C_3 H_5 (OCOC_{15} H_{31})_3 + 3 NAOH = 3 NAOCOC_{15} H_{31}$

Pallmitin caustic soda soap which consists of (fat) and (sodium palmitate).

The reaction of the fat with the aqueous caustic solution is termed saponification. (The term may also refer to the action of the water on a fat to produce fatty acid) As seen in the equation, the saponification reaction produces soap.

How in the world did my mother know all this? I came to the decision that all women who were born in Poland are super smart, even if they only completed fourth grade. The soap was only used for washing clothes. She saved all the fat and grease from cooking and she bought some suet from the butcher and farmer. She began by melting down the fat in a large boiler on the kitchen coal stove. Water was added after the fat liquified (water was important in the soap making process). After boiling for about eight hours, the water would evaporate leaving a heavy liquid. The soap-making season was in early spring when all the windows and doors could be open in the house. The aroma was something that a person should try to avoid at all costs.

A wooden tub (which also served as our bathtub when not used for making soap) was placed outdoors and the fat was poured in and a few cans of Lye were added. Then the mixing began. Francis was the mixer. She had a wooden paddle and she had to continually stir the mixture until it began to solidify. If the reader plans to make soap, please be advised that you should never use a metal implement to stir the concoction. Not only would the metal dissolve in the mixture within twenty minutes, but also the iron would subsequently leave rust marks on your best white shirts if you used this soap. It would be wise for you to make this soap when your neighbors go away for a long weekend.

After the soap would dry out, which would take seven or eight days, the tub was turned over and the soap would drop out. A beautiful white/gray large round tub size piece of soap. Next the soap must be cut into usable sections. This must be done as soon as the tub is turned since it will harden very fast and would be impossible to cut. A large butcher's knife (like one used to kill pigs) should be used. After the pieces are cut they are placed on boards to completely dry out. (They were usually placed on the back porch in case of rain.)

After the soap is completely dry, it becomes very hard. On washday, mom used a special grater (similar to one used for grating cheese) to grate the soap, and it had the look of grated cheese. Meanwhile in the kitchen, mom filled the copper boiler with all the white bedclothes. While they boiled she added about two cups of grated soap and after about an hour the clothes were ready to be removed from the tubs. She used a broomstick to remove the hot steaming clothes. These were then placed into a tub with cool clean water.

Since the draft on the kitchen coal stove was wide open she did not waste the heat so she often baked bread on washday. While mom was a miracle worker with food, she made the lousiest bread in Frackville. The crust was hard on the day it was baked and real, real hard about three days later. She managed to feed us for pennies a day. As an example, mom would send my sister Helen to Wagner's butcher shop on Spring Street, for a soup bone. She was given instructions to ask the butcher for one with some meat on it. A big good soup bone cost 5 cents. Since Helen was about six years old, the butcher looked at this small waif and gave her a nice size bone. Mom said "I'll always send you to the butcher."

MOONSHINE WHISKEY

W hen we lived in Arciszewski's house we had free rent. Well not exactly. Mom made a good grade of Moonshine whiskey. The Arciszewski's had a (speakeasy) saloon on Chestnut Street, (always use the back door, prohibition you know) which was frequented by a high class of hard liquor drinkers. They demanded the best and mom made a high quality superb whiskey. The Arciszewski's had an agreement with mom, two gallons of whiskey a week and no rent for a month! (If I keep repeating Arciszewski's name, I'll be much closer to reaching my goal of a one-inch thick book) Arciszewski's customers never knew who produced this very high-class whiskey. It was a well-kept secret, and thank God for that!

Mom had a beautiful still. I will try to explain the process as I remember it.

It was shiny, made in the USA, 100% copper, 10-gallon still that was purchased at "Abrachinsky's Hardware Store" in Shenandoah, PA. There was a large opening at the top. It had copper half-inch coil from the top of the boiler to the bottom. At the bottom of the coil, was a very small spigot that could be opened a little or all the way. A person has to have a lot of patience to make whiskey. It would come out of the little spigot very, very slowly. In the beginning a few drops at a time, then a small stream of pure white lightning. As the mixture boiled it formed a vapor that would cling to the sides of the tubes as it returned to a liquid state, it would run round and round and it (as the old song goes) came out here.

Mom would fill a water glass with the new whiskey and would proceed to test its alcohol content. She had a tester that looked like a test tube but was sealed both top and bottom.

There were little round beads in the tester that looked like buckshot. The bottom of the tester had a sort of bulb filled with mercury and there were grading lines on the tube. If she was not satisfied with the reading, she would open the top and pour the whisky back in the boiler.

The contents consisted of water, rye grain, and sugar. The sugar was sold openly in most of the small grocery stores in town. It was sold in large 50 lb. brown bags, and the pieces were as large as a man's fist and had a yellowish / brown color. And lastly mom put in the special ingredient that made it so famous.

I am about to reveal for the first time since the winter of 1930, the ingredient that made her whiskey so special. It was *"Apples, Real Green apples."*

This is what made all the customers at Arciszewski's Saloon coming back for this high quality whiskey.

The still sat on the kitchen stove all night with cold water running on a coil that was attached to the small coil on the boiler. This was done to cool the lower coil to change the vapor to a liquid form. She was concerned that the neighbors would hear the water running all night, (water was not metered in those days) so she tied a washcloth to the kitchen faucet so the water would not splash and make noise. Of course anyone could hear the water coursing through the plumbing.

Mom did not sell any of her products to anyone; she just bartered it in lieu of paying rent. We were able to stay in this wonderful house with the big yard with all the apple, cherry and plum trees. Our dog, Prince, loved to hop over the fence to get at the neighbors chickens and the geese were happy, they did not know that they soon were to contribute their fine feathers for a new *"pierzyna"* (feather tick comforter) mom was planning to make for my bed! I couldn't wait since the only time it was warm in our house was when she was making soap or whiskey!

Mom did not sell any of the whiskey. She kept a quart in the kitchen cabinet. I say cabinet because there was only one. It held, besides the one quart of whiskey, the butcher book, Church dues

book, a jar of Vaseline, mom's good scissors, and other odds and ends.

Occasionally, Mom would take down the quart she had in the cabinet. When Uncle Joe Gibowicz or Mr. And Mrs. Stanley Kosierp or other friends would visit, she would offer them a *"Kieliszek"* (a very small glass that is used to serve whiskey). She would also have a little with her friends.

I don't know why she drank it since she always made a face as if she just drank a glass of lemon juice, Brrr . . . yuck . . .

One day a neighbor asked mom to sell him a pint. She refused; she thought he was going to report her to the "Revenuers".

MOMS SHOE REPAIR

M om was a true renaissance woman, which was very fortunate for us children during the Depression.

Whether it was making soap, curtains, clothing, or making an occasional meat dinner stretch to feed six, we could always count on having clean clothes and an almost full stomach!

She really excelled when it came to repairing shoes. She had a metal shoe repair stand that was used to nail on the .29-cent soles that were available at Alexander's 5 & 10-cent store. She would not use a .19-cent glue-on type since she never was successful in getting us boys not to walk through rain puddles! After spending a small fortune on .29-cent quasi leather soles, she decided to make her own using the tread from some old "Goodyear" tires. My Sister Francis was the one selected to be the first girl on our block to have wear-out proof soles. This did not make her very happy. It was not too bad wearing them to school, but when she knelt down in church there was a debate with the boys in the choir loft if indeed they were "Goodyear" or "Firestone." After pleading with mom to no avail, my mother (she was also a philosopher) said, "listen, it would teach you humility and also do wonders for your soul!"

With a mother like we had, it may have been the depression but we were never depressed.

315 SOUTH LINE STREET

June 1934, Mom was in the Ashland State Hospital with appendicitis. While she was recovering, my brother Peter and sister Frances decided to surprise mom by moving to a large house *with a toilet that was inside the house!* They found such a house on Line Street in Frackville. They made arrangements with Mrs. Pamalavage who thought that they were a newly married couple. They did not tell her and she did not ask and they certainly did not try to mislead her. The rent was $18.00 per month paid in advance. Later in the week we moved in, **all of us,** with the exception of mom who was still in the hospital. Charles, Pete, Frances, Leonard, Wally, Helen, and later mom.

Every thing went well except we no longer had a big dog and we had to get rid of the geese. I missed the big yard, all the fruit trees, and the wonderful and very colorful neighbors.

Of course television was not yet invented but every Saturday afternoon and evening we had a live version of "soap operas." Mr. Kosierp would come home very happy and quite inebriated and the fight started. They had a piano that played rolls. About 3:30 in the afternoon the piano rolls would come flying out the front door (and occasionally) out the open front window. Actually loud arguments would start first and then the rolls would follow. After a few hours, things would get quiet which meant that Mr. Kosierp was taking a nap. We then carefully picked up the rolls from the street and placed them on the porch near the front door.

We picked them up so that later in the week we would ask Mrs. Kosierp to play the piano for us. She would sit down in the evening and start to pump the pedals. We would look with fascination at the keys automatically moving up and down as if some unseen hands were playing the piano. Most of the rolls were Polish songs, with a few classics like, The Blue Danube Waltz and some Strauss waltzes. We had many other interesting people who lived in our neighborhood. Those stories will appear in volume II.

Line Street was in West Mahanoy Township, which meant, that in September, I would have to attend the township school. I had to make new friends and would have to put up with some brand new bullies.

Our landlady and neighbor was Lithuanian. The family consisted of one son a year older than Frances and two younger daughters. Her son, Joseph, would visit our house occasionally. Frances thought he came to see Pete since he never said a word to Frances. Mrs. Pamalavage began teaching Frances the Lithuanian language, just in case they would marry! It took a while until Frances realized that Mrs. Pamalavage. Was telling her son Joseph that he is falling in love with my sister! He didn't know it until his mother told him so. After about seven months it appeared that Frances had other ideas, and so, Mrs. Pamalavage refused to take the rent money and asked us to move. We received a notice from Squire Connelly who had his office on the first floor of the present Law Building on Frack Street. Mom tried to pay the Squire but he told her he could not accept it. That's when we moved to 235 South Wylam Street, Actually all of us did not move to 235 Wylam since brother Peter ran off and got himself married to Amy Bretz of Frackville.

MOVING

When I was about six years old, I thought that moving to a new house was great fun. It certainly was exciting. For one thing I was asked to carry only the small boxes. And that was because I was born Feet First.

My big brothers, Charlie and Pete would arrange to borrow a coal truck to move our furniture and all our worldly possessions. First, my mother would sweep out the truck. Next the sides were covered with old bed sheets or big pieces of cardboard. I was allowed to ride in the back of the truck. It was great fun since the truck made a few trips. We would start very early in the morning and by the evening we were again sleeping in our own beds in a new, (not brand new) different house. As I got older, I knew when we were going to move. My mother began saving all the newspapers she could find. When we moved, we took along all our rugs and yes, the kitchen floor linoleum. In those days plywood was not invented. The floors used wood floorboards that sort of curled up on the sides, as they got older. (We only moved into older houses.) That's where the newspapers came in.

The day before moving, mom would go to the new house and sweep it out. She also mentally placed all the furniture for the bedrooms and the rest of the house. She would fill the first truck with all the upstairs furniture. Next came the newspapers. All the paper was spread out very evenly on the floors in the "Parlor" and kitchen.

The purpose of the newspapers was to prevent the linoleum from wearing out at the ridges and forming black stripes It did not look good since my mother always purchased linoleum with pretty pink and blue flowers in the center and a blue four inch solid border all around.

After she was satisfied she told the boys "Bring the carpets, linoleum, the Heatrola, and the kitchen coal stove in the next load." (She was careful to use up all the coal in the bin before moving.) Finally came the rest of the furniture and our wooden icebox. She told the boys "Don't forget the pan." It seems that on one of the other moves they misplaced or lost the pan and she would not let them forget it.

When I was six years old, it was fun but when I became a teenager, it was pure hell! My friends (?) would tell me, "Where are you living this month?" "Why doesn't your mother buy a house so you don't have to keep moving." "I bet its hell on your furniture moving so often." Etc.

Another problem was that we would live in the township a few years (occasionally a few months) and then in the borough, which meant that I had to change schools again, sometimes in the middle of the school year. During my freshman year in high school, we moved to Shenandoah. That was not too bad since the kids did not know that we were known for moving on a regular basis. It's not that we were not satisfied with the house we were living in. It was because my mother could not pay the rent. No one had a "credit" rating in those days and paying a deposit was not heard of. So the new landlord was happy that he had a new tenant. We were always clean. Our hair was combed, and when we went to church our shoes were always polished, especially in summer when we wore white shoes.

THE STUDENT

At the age of ten, I was a student in the fourth grade at the Franklin School on Broad Mt. Avenue. We were told by our teacher, "Next Wednesday, the photographer will be at our school to take photographs of all the children, please wear your best clothes." I explained to my mother that I should wear my Sunday go-to-mass clothes. My mother of course did not care for me wearing my best pair of trousers since I might tear them during recess. So we compromised! She had me wear my best white, freshly pressed, long sleeved, shirt and my only, and therefore my best, red rayon tie. To complete the outfit, I wore my two year old, fraying pair of "Keds" sneakers with about eight knots in the shoelaces and my freshly washed **Bib Overalls.** These were purchased after much discussion, *actually very heavy* bargaining, by mom and Mr. Charles Abeloff of **"Abeloff's The Working Man's Store."**

Fourth Grade. Ten Years Old

Mom gave me the following order. "As soon as you are seated, unhook the straps and fold the bib down since they only take a picture from the waist up" All these instructions were given to me in Polish.

After I brought the picture home (we bought only one). I showed mom how the bib overalls looked at the bottom of the picture. She told me *"My kupimy papierowe ramkie od*

53

*Alexander's 5 & 10 sklepu za dziesiec centy to nikt nie zobaczy!" **

*We will buy a paper frame from Alexander's 5 & 10-cent store for ten cents and no one will see the overalls!

THE TUBELESS WONDER

W hen I was in sixth grade in the West Mahanoy Township School, our teacher decided to have a "show and tell day." We were all instructed to bring in items that pertained to our hobbies. When the day arrived, all the kids brought in various items. Some boys had homemade slingshot's, wooden pistols made from an eight inch piece of wood and a wooden spring loaded clothespin that shot large rubber bands that were made from automobile inner tubes. Some of the girls brought in items that they crocheted, an arrangement of wildflowers that were dried, some artwork done both with crayons and some pencil sketches etc.

Of course since I was born feet first, I had to bring something very special. All my young life, I was fascinated by radio. In those days there was a company called Johnson and Company, in Chicago IL. They mailed a small catalog to any one requesting this most marvelous catalog. This catalog had many items for sale that would thrill a young boy's heart. One item was a machine with two rollers and a small handle to turn. If you inserted a piece of paper the size of a $1.00 bill between these rollers, and turned the handle, it would crank out a five-dollar bill! This money making machine cost $1.25 plus postage. Of course the five-dollar bill was not included. It also had a handshake buzzer machine; after it was wound up you would shake hands with someone and give a mild shock to the person on the receiving end. It had all sorts of puzzles, games, plus a lot of other items that were all under $2.50. One of the items was a crystal radio. I knew all about crystal radios but I never actually saw one. After visiting a few of the (garbage) dumps in Frackville to collect some old rags, a few pots made from aluminum, and some iron that someone foolishly threw out, I waited until Saturday to sell these items to the junk dealer (we called them "sheenies." We did not then know that it was a derogatory term.) so that I would have enough money to purchase a crystal radio kit.

I feel that I should write about the junk dealers that came to Frackville and other small towns. They came to town during the week in the summer. When school started, they came on Fridays after school and on Saturdays. I remember one of the dealers came with a large cart pulled by a horse. Most had a small truck. They all had an old brake drum from a car attached to the side of the driver's door. They used a small hammer or a piece of iron to hit the drum to give notice that the junk man was coming down your alley. Since the break drums came from various cars, they all gave a different sounding ring. By the sound it was easy to know which of the dealers was approaching. Most kids would sell their junk to the first junk man that they saw, but not me! I waited for the one who paid top Dollar for my junk! They had regular prices that changed every few weeks. Copper, five cents a lb., aluminum, three cents, brass, eight cents! Clean rags, three cents, dirty rags, one cent. Some of the dealers also bought bones and clear glass. I usually sold my junk to a black man who was from Pottsville; he gave, by far, the highest prices. He said even though I drove a hard bargain, I was his best customer.

The crystal radio kit consisted of a coil of copper wire that was as thin as the hair on my head; it also included two small connectors that were used to attach the antenna and the ground wire.

The main part was a crystal contained in a small metal case that was as large as an Indian head nickel. Attached to this case was a little lever that was arranged in such a way that when moving it, (now get this!) a small piece of wire that was black and rather stiff, and made from some special material touched the crystal stone when attached to this lever. It was called a *cat's whisker*. Using the lever moved the cat's whisker in different parts of the crystal until a station was heard. This corresponded to the tuning knob on a regular radio. After my crystal radio kit came in the mail, I found a thin board that was approximately five inches wide and eight inches long. I then had to get a cardboard tube that once held about 800 separate sheets of toilet paper. Since our house consisted of four rooms and a path, we used a Sears Roebuck catalogue. If we didn't have one, we would use a Spiegel catalog that was somewhat thinner but worked just as well. I had to ask a friend who had a toilet inside the house (they used store-bought toilet paper) to save me the cardboard tube after they were finished with the roll. I then followed the instructions and wound the thin copper wire around this tube very carefully and evenly, round and round until the wire covered the tube within ¾ inch on both ends of the tube. I had to paste two strips of heavy cardboard inside the tube folding those strips down at an angle. I used small nails to mount it on the board in a horizontal position. I then had to mount the crystal to the board and attach both ends of the wire on the tube that was called the coil. After attaching the clips to the board, I also attached the clips that were used to plug in the earphones

The antenna for this radio had to be very long. It reached from the bedroom window on the second floor and was attached to the top back end of the pole that held our clothesline. The antenna had insulators at both ends. I attached a wire about 8 feet from the end of the antenna and ran a wire through my (our) bedroom window. This wire had to enter beneath the window while being protected by a porcelain tube. It also required a ground wire. It had to be attached to an iron rod that was at least four feet long and driven into the ground.

After the kit was assembled I was ready to try to receive a radio signal. The only station that I would probably receive was station WAZL Hazleton. I tried to pick up this station for a few evenings without success. I discussed my problem with my older brother Charlie. He informed me that the station lowered its sending power during the evening hours and suggested that I try it in the morning. So, the first Saturday I was up before dawn wearing earphones, which of course did not come with the kit but Charlie allowed me to use his. Well, I started moving the cat's whisker all over the crystal. Occasionally I thought I heard a bit of static that was probably my imagination since I wanted this crystal set to work so badly. Finally the next day on Sunday morning, I received the sound of a preacher giving his sermon from a Hazleton church. I was never, but never so interested in hearing that sermon. I also have to admit that I was both shocked and surprised that my radio worked.

I disconnected the ground and aerial wire, put the radio and the earphones in a small cardboard box, and took everything to school for show and tell time. This action caused me problems for many years.

Could you picture me explaining the radio that did not have any tubes or even batteries and the fact (and this brought the most laughs) that it was tuned with a cat's whisker! Even though the teacher told the children that it's possible to have a crystal radio, that it would only work if you were near a powerful radio station, many of my friends thought it was impossible that it would work. One kid by the name of Joseph "Zuity" Kalaburda, who was one of the bullies of the class, teased me terribly. During recess and lunchtime the called me, **"THE TUBELESS WONDER."** I invited him to my home for the next Saturday morning so that he could hear the tubeless radio in operation. He of course refused my invitation even though some of my friends did hear the radio and it really worked. He was having too much fun. He did not want to hear if it indeed worked. I know this is a very long story but I feel it must be told.

Many years later I was driving my 1931 Chevrolet and I stopped at a gas station where my friend, Joe Swingle worked. I had a date that evening with a girl that lived in Morea. My lifelong antagonist, "Zuity," pulled up his car behind me to get gas. He was married and his wife was sitting in his car. He came to my car and said to any one who was in earshot of his loud voice, "look it's the **TUBELESS WONDER."** He turned to his wife and said, "He has your kid sister in the car with him." He asked his sister-in-law (my date) if she knew that she was dating the wild inventor of a tubeless radio. Whenever we met in town or at dance, he would shout, "Look! Here comes the tubeless wonder."

A few years later before I was married, I was building a new house on Centre Street in Frackville. Since I worked in Mt. Carmel while the carpenters were building the house, I couldn't wait to come home and see how much progress was made that day. I noticed that a trench was being dug for the water and sewer lines. The sewer line ran diagonally down the street and it was about six-foot deep. During those days, most of these trenches were dug by hand. A backhoe was used only on big jobs. As I approached the trench, I saw a lot of dirt being shoveled out. I looked in the trench and lo and behold, it was my old friend "Zuity" Halaburda. It was the first time since we were both in fourth grade that he called me **"Wally."** I asked him, "How are you doing, Zuity?" That was the end of our conversation. I did feel like informing him that as soon as my home was finished I was going to move my television set from my mother's home on North Nice Street to my new home. I also decided not to tell him that the TV worked and, that, by the way, was the FIRST television in a private home in Frackville.

In May of this year 1998, "Zuity" Kalaburda died of cancer. I attended his viewing and without any malice on my part, I forgave him and said a prayer for the happy repose of his soul.

RADIO

S ince early childhood, I was always fascinated by radio. I
was very fortunate to have two older brothers, Charlie and
Pete. Charlie was about thirteen years older than me. They also
loved radios. The first radio that Charlie had at home was an
"Atwater Kent." I found out much later that it was called an
"Atwater Kent" when we had some "remember the old day's talk"
while we were eating supper. The radio came in two parts, a wooden
frame which held four large batteries. They were the size of truck
batteries. The radio was placed on top of the frame. There were
many dials on the front. The radio case was made of wood. The
case was about 36 inches long, 10 inches wide and 12 inches high.
The lid was attached with a piano hinge that, when lifted, all the
vacuum tubes and the aluminum variable condensers were in full
view. Earphones were normally used. The radio also had a large
horn shaped loudspeaker which worked quite well when tuned to a
strong station.

My brothers played a trick on Uncle Joe Gibowicz when he
came to visit mom. They had another or loudspeaker in their
bedroom. The loudspeaker acted as a microphone and when
attached by a pair of wires to the radio that was located in the
"Parlor," it worked much like a public address system. Pete,
who played a concertina waited in their bedroom until Charlie
prepared Uncle Joe. Uncle Joe, asked, "Does that radio really
work." Of course it does, in fact in a few minutes a new Polish
program will come on the air." Charlie turned on the radio turning
the dial to the extreme end and the radio program began with a
Polish melody played on a concertina. Uncle Joe brought two

of his friends with him to visit with mom. Actually they came to sample some of mom's famous "Apple-flavored Moonshine Whiskey." Everything was going well until Pete, acting as the announcer of this Polish program, dedicated the next tune to "Joseph Gibowicz, brother of Mrs. Baranowski of Frackville! The tune was an old Polish drinking song, *Goralu czy cie nie zal?* This song would bring an abundance of tears to anyone listening especially the men even if they were only on their second "kieliszek" of mom's wonderful apple-flavored moonshine. The song that caused a copious flow of tears, told how the men were leaving the beautiful mountains and valleys of Poland to immigrate to America.

When mom finally put the bottle back in the cupboard, Uncle Joe and his friends decided that they spent enough time visiting with her.

Before they left, Uncle Joe played a little game with me that he did only if he had an audience. He placed a dime and a nickel in the palm of his hand and asked me to choose one. I always took the nickel that caused Uncle Joe to look at his friends with a big grin. After he left, Charlie asked me, "Why do you always take the nickel?" I said, "Because if I took the dime he would never play that game with me again."

About twenty pages or even possibly thirty pages back in this book, I wrote a chapter on "The Tubeless Wonder." It dealt with the time that I brought to school my crystal set radio. I could repeat the whole story at this point since it would bring me much closer to fulfill my plan to write a one-inch thick book.

Since I want you, the reader, to read this book to the end, I will ask you to go back the twenty or so pages and reread the chapter on "The Tubeless Wonder." There is a lot more good stuff in the last few chapters of this one-inch thick book, so continue reading.

THE ACCIDENT!

During the spring of 1935, I was in fifth grade at the Franklin School. During recess, the boys and some of the girls in the lower grades amused themselves running up and down the concrete steps on the front of the school building that led to the main entrance. There were twelve steps on the east side and sixteen on the west side. We would run up on the east side and down the west side. While I was at the top ready to run down, an eighth grader put his foot out and I went down much faster than I wanted or expected to, with the result that I had a great deal of pain in my right arm. After three days it was decided that a doctor should see me. My mother took me to see Dr. Hartman who had an office on Balliet Street. No one ever made an appointment in those days. We waited an hour and he called us into his office. The doctor gave me a checkup. He looked in my ears, throat and eyes. He then used the stethoscope to check my heart. He listened again and again. He told me to squat down, listened, and listened some more. After a while my mother spoke to me in Polish, "Tell him it's your arm that hurts." I told him how I fell. He felt my arm and announced that I had a fracture in my lower arm. Even though there were a few people in the waiting room, he filled a basin with hot water and unrolled some cotton bandages into the basin then added some white powder. After mixing the bandage with the white powder, he began winding the bandage on my arm. After he was done, he took a towel and sort of padded the bandage to take off the excess water. He did all this with people waiting in his office. All this was done without an x-ray or having it done when his office hours were over. When he was finished, my mother took a dollar bill out of her purse.

He looked at it and said "Missus, put it back in your purse. Bring the boy back in four weeks." I told my mother what he said after we left his office. Walking back home I thought, "Boy, am I lucky that this happened to me in the springtime when it's warm outside and I don't have to wear a hat." There was no way that I could swing my arm with the heavy cast on it to put my hat on. Four weeks later my mother took me back to see Dr. Hartman. He had a big pair of tin shears and proceeded to remove the cast. He then put on his stethoscope and again began listening to my heart. When he was finished, he told me that I have a heart murmur. He asked me if I ever had Rheumatic fever. I asked my mother and she said that I had a few colds in the winter just like my brother and sister had. He then told me that one of the best baseball players on the New York Yankees baseball team has a heart murmur and that I should not worry about it.

*   *   *Warning to the reader*   *   *

If you are still with me, I am giving you fair warning that I will stop at nothing until I write this book that will measure at least one inch thick when finished, even if I have to use thick paper or fill it with minutiae like the above true story. I also cannot promise not to keep using the phrase "born feet first" throughout the rest of this one-inch book.

TEACHERS

I don't remember some of my teachers. However I do remember the teacher I had in the sixth grade. During our history lesson the teacher spoke about Martin Luther. She said that he was a great reformer and a great church leader. She told us that the Catholic Church demanded that to be forgiven your sins, you had to pay money to the priest. She spent the whole history lesson on the Reformation. This continued for a few days. During recess my friend and I sat on the curb with our feet in the street. The street was not paved and during a rainstorm it was very muddy. My friend who was not Catholic asked me if was true that you must pay the priest or you won't go to heaven. I told him that it must be true, because the teacher said it, and the teacher knows everything and, I also know that when our priest comes to our house each month, my mother gets her purse and gives him money. He then marks it in a book that she keeps in the cupboard. I know that she paid him .25 cents a month. My mother told me that if my father were living with us, we would have to pay .50 cents a month. I did not realize that my mother was paying dues to the church. When I attended Saturday catechism class, I asked Father Garska why we had to pay money to have our sins forgiven and to get to heaven. He told me that the money he was collecting was church dues and that my mother did not have to pay them if she could not afford to. Many pay so that they have a sense of belonging.

MUSIC

When I was in fifth grade Miss Speidel, our music teacher, came to our school every Thursday morning for class. She brought a victrola. Today, it's called a phonograph. She drew a music scale on the blackboard and we then sang the scale.

"Do re me fa so la ti do" After what seemed like an hour of singing the scale, she opened the small case that held the victrola, wound it up, and put on a record. I now know that it was an aria from one of Verdi's operas, La Traviata. All of the boys and some of the girls could not keep from giggling. During recess, my friends would laugh and tell me how stupid it was. I did not tell them that I thought the singing was very pleasant. I knew why they thought it was stupid and that I thought, "Hey, this is great!" The reason they did not appreciate good serious music was the fact that they were not born feet first like I was.

Many years later, I was about eighteen years old and working in Mt. Carmel at Pre-vue Sportswear, I would go to Stecker's Stationary Store to pick up supplies for the office. I noticed that the store also carried classical records. Each Sunday we bought the *Philadelphia Inquirer.* The entertainment section of the paper had a column listing the program of a radio station that played only classical music. I would listen to the program with a pencil in hand. When I heard something I liked, I would put a check mark at the name of the piece. On Monday, I would visit Stecker's carrying the newspaper article and I would hear the clerks say, "Here he comes again to order more records." I had a rather large collection of twelve-inch classical records at home.

I knew nothing about the composers or the artist performing. I just knew what sounded good to my ear. One of my first purchases was *Puchinelli's "Dance of the Hours."* I drove my mother crazy by playing it constantly. A few years later I became a member of the *Anthracite Concert Association of* Pottsville and a member of a similar group in Mt. Carmel. Before I married, I would take my good friend, Irene, who later became my wife to the concerts. We still attend concerts at home and when we travel. All this because of Ms. Speidel's victrola!

Each morning, the school day began with the pledge of allegiance to the flag and a student that read well would read a few verses from the King James Version of the Bible.

This was great for me since in St Ann's Church we heard readings from the Old Testament and the gospel for the day read in Polish. I did not understand most of what was said since my Polish was used mostly for communication.

During the class day, we sang a lot of Protestant hymns. I liked to sing them especially *"Lead Kindly Light"* and *"In The Garden,"* *'I walk in the garden alone, while the dew is still on the roses and he walks with me and he talks with me and he tells me I am his own etc.'* Our music book had many different songs and a few Protestant hymns. We sang more hymns than the regular songs. All my life in Church, all I heard were Polish and some Latin Hymns. Now we sing all those Protestant hymns that I was taught in fourth and fifth grade. I guess all the Protestant hymns are now Catholic hymns. Now we rarely hear any Latin Hymns and I miss them.

The only time I hear a Latin hymn is when I am attending a wedding and some lady with a shaking and trembling voice sings *Ave Maria.* There are many Polish hymns that I love. My favorite is *Serdeczna Matko.* I could list at least twenty more but I don't know how to spell them. I keep asking Irene to spell all the Polish words I need but I can't keep asking her. You see, I try not to be *"przeciwny"* (contrary) when it comes to Irene. When I get some time, I'm going to find my Polish hymnbook and make a list of my favorites to give to my friends and any one else that may be interested. The main reason I'm spending so much time on this is to write a book that is at least an inch thick requires a lot of words and stories and I just may run out of memories. Dr. Weber tells me that as a person grows older he forgets things.

One day in school we were taught a very beautiful song. It was called, *"April."* It had a very pleasant and delightful melody. I still remember the words, *Smile a while April and tell me please whether you'll weep or smile April, or do them both together etc.* I was very engrossed looking at the words and following the teacher that I did not notice that on the upper right hand side of the page were written these words, **"A Polish Melody."** **Wow!** I must say honestly that I did not know this before I fell in love with this song, honest. I was so happy and could hardly wait to come home to sing it for my mother. I was disappointed that she did not know it. I told her that I would teach her. She said, "I don't have time to sing." She said it in such a manner that I knew that I should not bring it up again, but since I have been born not only feet first, but also *"przeciwny."* (Contrary) I kept on singing it whenever Mom was within earshot. She didn't say anything but after about three and a half weeks of my singing, she told me, "If you want to continue singing that song, go outside and sing it."

MOM

My mother was a very tiny woman. She probably never weighed more than 115 pounds. Her brown hair was shiny and it was worn in a bun at the back of her head. She never had a gray hair and couldn't understand why some of the younger mothers in the church had gray hair. God knows, my mother with all the problems she suffered should have had pure white hair! She was farsighted. She purchased her eyeglasses (now called corrective lenses) at Alexander's 5 & 10-cent store. They worked fine when she could find them.

When she saw a nearsighted person hold a letter right up to his or her nose, she remarked to anyone who would listen, "Why is she holding the paper so close to her nose? everyone knows that a person could see much better if they held the paper at arms length." No one could convince her that some people (like me) are nearsighted while others are farsighted and the lucky ones in the in-between are neither.

She was very religious. She made sure that all the kids were very religious as well. We attended **all** the services that the church held. Sundays,

Sister Helen and Mom

71

Wednesdays, Fridays and Saturdays and sometimes every day of the week!

She had a very hard and sad life but she had a very good sense of humor.

She often told me about her life in Poland. Her father owned a large forest, was a lumberman selling timber, and also did some farming. She had a normal childhood with the exception of attending school for only four years, She worked hard, but food was plentiful and the house was warm in the winter.

Her father was working alone in the forest when he had a fatal accident. He was loading lumber on his horse drawn wagon when the horse kicked him in the stomach. As mom told me, his intestines were out of his body, he held them and managed to get on the wagon and somehow drove to their home where he died within a few hours. When I was about twelve years old my mother told me of the trips her mother took to the forest carrying some lunch for the kids and her husband. It was like a grand picnic. She described that there were filbert nut trees, a cool stream of pure clear water where they waded and looked for crawfish. Her mother would spread out a cloth and call the children and their father for lunch.

Many years later on one of our trips to Suwalki, I asked if we could visit the forest and the location of the farmhouse that my uncle Casimir still owned. We rented a Russian car in Warsaw. After we left the cobblestone road, we had no problem driving on narrow sandy roads in the forest. It was a very small car but we all managed to fit. Our boys, Tony and Joseph, were about ten and twelve years old at the time so it was a great adventure for them (and for me). We found the foundation of the farmhouse. I was surprised at how small it was. Tony found an old rusty hinge and I took a small plastic container of soil that I still have.

The priest usually pours sand on the casket during a burial. Me? I probably will be the only one in town to have good Polish soil poured on my casket.

When we arrived at the forest that was a short distance away, my Aunt opened the trunk of the car. I don't know when she put the items in the trunk, but she removed a blanket that was soon covered with cold chicken, lettuce, some pickles, and bread. I nearly flipped! We found the stream and the filbert nut trees. It was a beautiful sunny day that I'll never forget. Yup, It was de-ja vu all over again.

CHURCH

Early spring brought the holy season of lent. We had Mass on Sunday morning, *Gorzkie Zale* (bitter lamentations) at four o'clock, one full hour of very sad songs followed By Benediction. Wednesday evening the rosary, and Friday the Stations of the Cross followed by Benediction. Saturday afternoon confessions were held. Of course Mass was offered each morning. During holy week we went to church every day.

St. Ann's Church. 1932
(In 1941, the building was covered with a light red brick)

During the church year, Saint Ann's Church held many special services. Since St. Ann, the mother of Mary was the patroness of our Church, a novena was held which lasted nine days. It always began nine days before her saint's day. It began with mass every morning and the recitation of prayers to St. Ann and the singing of the litany to St. Ann. We also had a "Mission" every two or more years. It usually lasted seven days. A missionary from Africa, the Philippines, or China was invited to "Give the Mission." He would read the mass each morning and preach the gospel each evening. He would always begin with a brief description of the country and the people he served but most of his homily dealt with how we should live as good Christians. All of the evening services always concluded with the Benediction of the Holy Sacrament. The entire service was held in the Polish language with the exception of the Benediction, which was in Latin. On the rare occasions when there were no evening Devotions, The Benediction was held after the High Mass on Sundays. There were two masses held every Sunday. The 8 AM Low mass and the 10:30 AM High Mass. Every mass had congregational singing, but during a high mass, the choir sang the full Latin mass.

Lent began with Ash Wednesday. After we received the ashes on Wednesday morning, my mother held a ritual as soon as we returned to our home. She went into the living room and moved the radio away from the wall. She then put her hand in the back and pulled out one of the tubes. She placed the tube in the unlocked cabinet. She did not say a word to us. I suppose actions really do speak better than words

FORTY-HOUR DEVOTIONS

The church was packed. I did not have to worry about getting a seat since I sang in the youth choir. We had about twenty-five kids in the choir and we all stood, girls in the front. Sopranos on the left side, altos on the right. Tenors on the left and baritones were on the right. We were taught to sing four-part Harmony and sometimes it worked. Our organist and music teacher was Miss Tessie Waleska was very patient with us. She was also very powerful. She selected who was to sing the solo parts at the Forty Hours Devotions sung in Latin. I looked forward to the forty-hour devotions.

The devotions began with mass on Friday morning. After mass the Holy Sacrament was exposed for the entire day. Throughout the day many church members would visit the Sacrament until the hour of 7 PM when the evening service began. This was repeated on Saturday. The "Closing of the Forty Hours" was held Sunday at 7 PM. The church would be filled to capacity. The young men stood in the side aisle and completely filled the back vestibule of the church. All of the Polish priests from the area attended the closing. Each year 30 or 40 priests attended. The local Lithuanian and Irish priest from Frackville also attended. Three priests, the Celebrant and two co-celebrants were vested and sat in the sanctuary. The rest of the priests wore their cassocks with white surplices and sat in the front rows. The "Senior Choir" consisting of 30 to 35 members sang the Latin vespers that lasted for about 35 minutes. There was great competition to sing the solo parts. Actually there was no competition since miss Tessie Waleska would never change her mind after she made the selections. Famous composers wrote the Latin vespers. Bach, Mozart and other composers. I particularly liked when we sang the vespers by Walenty Bonk. The vespers began when the celebrant intoned, *Deus in adjutorm meum intende.* And the entire choir responded with,

> *Domine ad adjuvaandum me festina*
> *Gloria Patri, et Filo, et Spiritui Santo*
> *Sicut erat in principo, et nunc et semper, et in saecula*
> *saeculorm Amen, etc.*

There were many altar boys in the sanctuary. Four very tall boys wore black cassocks and white surplices. During the 8 AM Low Mass on Sundays, six acolytes served. During the 10:30 AM High Mass, occasionally 12 altar boys were in the sanctuary

It was a custom for the St. Cecilia Choir of St. Ann's Church to visit all the homes on Christmas day to sing Polish Christmas carols. The town and the Choir would be divided in half.

The south half group would also have to visit the homes in Maizeville and Gilberton since there were not many Polacks living on the other side of the tracks. We all spoke fairly good Polish and the families would greet us with a small glass of white moonshine whiskey or good homemade grape wine. (The white stuff was also homemade) After we sang all the families favorite Kolendys (Christmas carols) we were treated to some Polish sausage, *kielbasa,* (It tasted different in each house, of course the white stuff may have had something to do with it.) Since I had a wonderful and mellow baritone voice, I was always selected to join the East side of Frackville where most of the more refined Poles lived.

Naturally quite a few of the homes we visited were homes that I had lived in my youth. I would comment, "When did you put in the open stairway? When we lived here we had a Heatrola in the living room, I see that you installed a bathroom etc."

When I married I did a terrible thing, I left Irene and our two young boys at home on Christmas day to sing *Kolendys*. It was for me the natural thing to do. I started when I was in my teens and continued after I was married. I realize now that it was a selfish thing to do.

THE ANGELUS

A summer morning in August would find my mother, brother Lenny, sister Helen and me leaving our home (wherever it was at the moment) so early that it was quite dark. We were heading for Morea, a town about four miles east of Frackville. We followed the Morea road and made a right turn to a coal-stripping pit that was abandoned a few years previously. There was still some coal located mostly at the bottom of the pit mixed with a lot of slate. The site was called "The number 100 job." Lucky for us, back in the thirties, the coal mining technology was sort of primitive. There was so much coal that the coal company just selected the "easy" clean stuff and they left the coal that was mixed with some rock for us to find and pick up.

The purpose of our visit to this site was to pick as much coal as would fill a two and a half ton dump truck. Mom came prepared; she had four empty burlap bags, a cloth bag containing sandwiches, a few bottles of water and no watch. We marked the time by the sun. By the time we reached the pit, it was just light enough to make our way to the bottom of the pit. We all wore old overalls (now called jeans) except for mom. She always wore one of her old dresses. Come to think of it, she never had a "new" dress. Well anyway, we began picking the pieces of coal, without gloves. The hard anthracite coal was very sharp and we often had cuts on our hands, but not to worry! Mom was always prepared for any contingency. The evening before (she was always too busy to do it during the day) she prepared strips of old sheets or any clean rags (she never used any new or dirty rags) to be used as bandages. These bandages were kept in the same bag as the sandwiches and the water. Mom would fill her bag and Lenny would fill his almost to the top. After all he was almost thirteen years old. Helen would have less than half a bag full and I would have almost as much as Helen. Mom said, "Don't put too much in your bag since you might hurt your arms." Another advantage of being born feet first. Lenny did not think it was fair that I did not have to carry as much coal as he and he complained to mom about this obvious favoritism being shown to me.

When we got to the top, we emptied our coal bags on a pile that was near the dirt road where we entered. After many, many, many trips down and up the pit, a distance of about 200/300 feet, we kept looking at the sun to see if it was high in the sky so we could stop for lunch. Mom would say, "Lets make one more trip and we will have lunch."

At noon we had lunch. The sandwiches were made with "white" store bought bread. (As I previously wrote, my mother made lousy bread. Since it crumbled a lot, it could not be used for sandwiches.) I had a peanut butter sandwich since that was my favorite food. The other sandwiches were mince baloney with mustard. Since we had no water to wash our hands, our sandwiches did not have fingerprints, they had black marks from our dirty hands. Mom said that it wouldn't hurt to eat a little dirt. We also had an apple for dessert and some warm water to drink with the food. When we first came, mom covered the water bottles with some large stones to try keeping the sun from heating the water. It didn't work.

After lunch, we again began to carry more coal to the top of the pit. All morning I planned to make my job easier.

I only filled my bag as much as Helen did, but I then picked up smaller pieces as I was going up. With this modus operandi, when I reached the top, I had almost as much coal as Lenny had.

Of course, I had to walk (actually sort of crawl) up a different path each time since the smaller pieces were scattered all along the stripping pit. Mom said what are you doing? I told her that I developed a way to get my bag filled with less labor. She said we have a path made to go up down and it is much safer to use the path and not get hurt. I told her that a person must find new ways to work, there may be more risk but the rewards are greater. In fact it was much easier on my back since the bag only got heavy when I was near the top. I did not want to tell my mother that the fact that I was born feet first, I did have an advantage over my friends so that I was always thinking, "How can I make this job easier?"

Late in the afternoon, our pile of coal was quite large and I again was hungry. When mom was getting our evening sandwiches ready, we heard the bells of St. Ann's Church pealing. The bells were made of iron and could be heard at a great distance. It was the Angelus that rang at 6:00 am, 12:00 noon and 6:00pm.

We all knelt on our knees and faced St. Ann's Church and mom recited the Angelus "The angel of the Lord declared unto Mary and she conceived of the Holy Spirit." *Hail Mary* "Behold the handmaid of the Lord. Be it done to me according to your word." *Hail Mary,* etc.

Even though I was just a kid, I looked at my mom, her hands folded in prayer, her knees on the rocky soil, her dress was black with coal dust, hands that were raw and cut from the sharp coal and I thought, why is she praying? She should be at home in the kitchen preparing the evening meal for her family, and later in the evening sewing a new dress for Helen. Many other thoughts entered my head. Is God looking at this scene? What does He think? Is it fair? While I was thinking these thoughts, mom said, "We will eat our food and we will soon be finished." This scene was so set in my mind, that I never forgot it. I have an oil painting at my home, of an elderly farmer and his wife standing in a farm field with their sacks of potatoes on a wheelbarrow. In the distance could be seen a church. It is dusk, the sun is setting, the man has his cap off, and the woman her hands folded in prayer. They are praying the Angelus. They are both standing with bowed heads. Even today when I look at this painting, I say to myself, "They have soft soil to kneel on but my mom did not stand, she knelt on the hard sharp rocks and prayed."

As planned, at about 8:00 PM Mr. Gorski came with his truck to pick up the coal. This coal was not to heat our home. It was to earn money to buy food. He had three shovels and Mr. Gorski, mom, and Lenny shoveled the coal on the truck. We did not walk home. Mom sat inside the truck and we kids sat in the back on top of the coal. Mr. Gorski who was a member of St.Ann's and a wonderful man would deliver the coal to a coal breaker which purchased all the coal mined in "bootleg coal mines." This was done the next day. After the coal was weighed he would give mom the money less the cost for hauling. Our day's work would be about $3.00 to 5.00 dollars, We repeated this a few times during the summer. Mr. Gorski owned a small gas station on the Morea road and also delivered prepaired coal to the people who could afford to buy it.

FRESH COAL

During the 30's my brothers, Charlie and Pete had a Plymouth Coupe with a rumble seat in the back. They removed the seat and used it to haul coal. I was about eight years old and I was allowed to make a coal trip with them. They always went after work about 6:00PM.

The coalmine was about one mile west of Mahanoy Plane. The mine breaker crossed the road to Girardville, and all the traffic passed under part of the breaker. It was called "East Bear Ridge Colliery."

While a new section of the mine was being opened, it was necessary to drill and blast through a wall of rock, to get at the next vein of coal. The refuse rock to be hauled to the surface had some large pieces of coal. If there was more rock than coal, it was loaded on large trucks and hauled to the spill bank.

Each evening there were many men and boys picking out the coal as the trucks dumped it. This was a very dangerous job. The rock mixed with coal came tumbling down a distance of about 200 feet. Charlie made me sit in the car that was located about fifty feet away from the spill bank. The trick was, after the truck unloaded and before another one took it's place, the men would rush to the bank and pick out the largest chunks of freshly mined coal and put it on a pile until they had a enough to fill the car. This was an amazing scene.

Each night about thirty men with cars or old beat up trucks were lined up at the bottom of the spill bank, getting all this free coal. Pete told me that a lot of men and boys were hurt because they did not wait for the truck to finish dumping and were hit by large rocks that were rolling down the bank.

You may ask, were you allowed to take this coal? The answer is "sort of." The Coal & Iron Police who worked for the Reading Coal Co. would appear and inform every one that **"You are trespassing on private ground and we order you leave the premises immediately!"**

Some of the men looked at them without responding and others would keep on working. Since there were a lot of us and only two of them, before leaving they informed us **"The Company has no responsibility if you are injured."**

After we returned home, we unloaded the coal in the back yard and the next day we began cracking the coal with hammers to break it to the size of a beat up tennis ball. This size is called appropriately enough "stove coal." All the neighbors had coal in the back yard that needed cracking. A small piece of rail about one foot long was placed on a large block of wood and using gloves you would pick up a large piece of coal and keep hitting it into small pieces. This work was done by any one in the family, Mothers, boys and yes even the girls.

If you haven't guessed by know, that is where the term **"Coal Cracker"** came from! If you were not known by your coal cracker accent, the people from Philly could tell just by looking at your hands that you came from **"The coal regions."** There was another way to be able to keep your house warm on those real cold Frackville nights. Of course coal was needed all the months of the year since all the kitchen cook stoves used the coal to bake bread and fry the mince baloney.

The local clergy and even some lay people frowned upon this method as well. It worked this way; all the coal mined in the Mahanoy Valley was prepared in the coal breaker (Coal preparation plant) to various sizes, stove, nut, pea, and buckwheat, and was shipped from the collieries, that is Maple Hill near Shenandoah, Gilberton Coal Co, East Bear Ridge Colliery, Mahanoy Plane, Reading Coal Co, Near Mahanoy City and other collieries were shipped via the **"PLANE"**, a very large Stationary Steam Engine that pulled the cars from the valley, to the top of the mountain in Frackville.

The cars were all loaded with prepared coal for shipment to

Philadelphia, New York, Boston etc. The cars were piled in high peaks to save freight cars.

As the cars were moving very slowly through town, the men & boys with shiny large shovels would get up on the cars and begin shoveling coal down on the tracks. They shoveled mostly the stove size, but I did see other sizes being shoveled down. It was very exciting, just like a "Cops And Robbers" movie. About six Reading Coal & Iron Police would try to chase the men off the cars. Again there were more robbers than cops. Occasionally they did apprehend some of the men who had to eat their next few meals in very small rooms that were divided with steel bars. After the trains were on their way down the mountain to St. Clair, the women and kids and some of the men who were not apprehended, would began filling their bags with freshly mined and cleaned coal. This went on for years!

THE BARAN BROTHERS

COAL HAULING CO.

After Charlie and Pete were married, it was the job of Lenny and me to supply the coal for the winter. We had a small steel wagon that I found on a garbage dump, I couldn't figure out why someone would throw it out just because one wheel was broken.

It worked fine except it only had three good red wheels. I found a same sized wheel that worked very well except the new but used wheel was painted green.

I had a friend from school who lived on what was then the last house leaving Frackville on the Morea Road, whose name was Wassil Niemick. His parents were immigrants from Russia. Like most men in the area, Mr. Niemick worked in the mines. While visiting my friend, I saw a wagon that his father made. He used oak saplings to make the spokes for the wheels. He would cut the small oak trees the size of a broomstick handle, and would trim them to size and heat them in scalding hot water, then bent them to a round shape in a form that he made. He made the entire wagon, steel axles, bed, sides, and the steering handle. He covered the wheels with steel rims. Wassil told me that his Pop (no one called their father Dad in those days) made large horse drawn wagons when he lived in Russia.

I told my mother about the wagon and asked her if she would ask him to make us a large wagon to haul coal from the small strip mines near the "Whippoorwill Dam." We went to see Mr. Niemick, Mom spoke in Russian/Polish, and Mr. Niemick spoke in a sort of Polish/ Russian. Mr. Niemick told mom that he would make us a wagon according to my (our) specifications. He said the cost would be $5.00 dollars, and that he would make in during the winter. Mom wanted to pay him in advance, but he told her that she should pay when it is done and built to her liking!

In the early spring, we took possession of a beautiful large wagon; he even painted it a dark shade of green. Would you believe Lenny and I could hardly wait to go to the spoil bank at "Whippoorwill" to bring home our first load of coal?

Our first "Job" demanded a decision. The floor of the new wagon was made of heavy oak planks painted green. We knew that the first load of coal would mark and dirty the beautiful wood. Should we put the coal in Bags? Line the wagon with heavy cardboard? We asked mom to make the decision. As usual she used common sense, she said, "Is this a sport wagon, or a working wagon?"

That settled it. We filled the wagon full, we even put a "cope" * on it. It looked like one of the overloaded coal freight cars that were such a temptation to the guys with the shiny shovels that were rolling through Frackville. Because of the steel rims, mom knew when to put our supper on the table since she could hear us coming home when we were a block and a half away.

Of course it was now a used wagon. The resale value dropped about 47% after it's first trip. The wagon performed well, it took the hills with ease. I was pulling and Lenny provided most of the power from the rear. It really excelled on the sharp turns. And best of all, it carried five and a quarter times more coal than our previous wagon, the one with the three red and one green wheel. I was able to sell my old wagon to a kid from across the railroad. Unlike the new wagon, my old one appreciated in value 100% since it did not cost me a cent. He paid me 87 cents and a bag of marbles (including three glass knucklers and a "STEELY")**. Later he wanted to trade a baseball instead of the glass knucklers. He did not know that I was born feet first and couldn't play baseball. I was pretty good at marbles though. I remember that I owned over 325 marbles before I was thirteen years old, and I was far from a champ.

Cope (fr. Latin *cappa* peaked Bishops hat).
** A much sought after, steel ball bearing

THE HOUSE ON BROAD MOUNTAIN AVENUE

E very house on the street seemed identical. We called them double blocks. Three rooms down, three up, plus an attic and of course a basement. (Only we called it a "cellar") The homes were on a lot 35 feet wide with an entryway between houses that measured 4 feet. All the homes had electricity that consisted of a single bulb hung from a cord in the center of the room. There were no receptacles. Those lucky enough to have a radio used a "double socket" in the light cord. There were practically no other appliances in the home. Each month we received "The Light Bill". If it was over $3.50, the lights would go on later and go off sooner for the next 3 months!

One of the most important rooms was not even in the house. It was located in the back yard about 30 feet from the back porch. It did not have any outstanding architectural features. It was more practical than beautiful. The interior consisted of a seat with two holes, one large and one small. I liked to use this facility best in the spring and fall. Of course it was a year around facility, but woe to the one who occupied it on February 12, at about 11:00 PM with the temperature at-02 Fahrenheit, and to have to use a page from last year's copy of the Sears Roebuck catalogue on one of the most delicate parts of the human anatomy. During the summer it served another purpose. It kept most of the flies out of the kitchen. All children 6 years old and under had the privilege to "use a potty." It was kept under the bed and had to be deposited in the *"WYCHODEK"* * by an older member of the family with the instruction "make sure you use the small side so that it would be more even."

Each Saturday morning my mother would scrub the seats and the floor, so I would try to use it every Saturday afternoon at about 3:00. It smelled from Lysol. Of course it was not Lysol but my mothers homemade lye soap, 180 percent stronger than Lysol, and caused the seat to be bleached almost white but it really was a dull shade of gray.

For those who have never had the opportunity of experiencing this room, I will go into detail of its construction and use. To begin with, a hole must be dug about 4 by 8 feet and 5 or 8 feet deep. It all depended how many were in the family. Next it was necessary to construct a wooden building. Since there was no foundation the building was placed on four sills, called by the more educated "railroad ties." These sills were perfect for the job since they were coated with creosote, which served as a natural deodorant. These sills were to be "found" near the railroad tracks either very early in the morning or late at night. After they were in place, the main structure was raised. A roof was constructed and covered with tarpaper and the door was installed. To complete the unit, a door lock had to be installed. This could be a six-inch board with a nail driven in the center. By turning this ingenious board you were sure that you would have perfect privacy. Some of my friends whose parents were quite wealthy had a metal hook that could be purchased from Hack's hardware store. I could not see the reason for the metal hook since it did not provide any additional privacy.

*Polish for the French "la toilet."

MY FIRST JOB AS AN ADULT

In the summer of 1939, I was all of 14 years old and was called upon to do a man's job. My brother, Lenny, a bit older than me had a summer job at an independent coal mine we called a "Bootleg coal hole."

One day my brother was ill and could not go to work. Since we could not inform the "Boss" that Leonard could not come to work, and since we needed the money, my Mother looked at me and said, "Put on your worst pair of overalls and that plaid shirt you hate. You are going to take your brother's place today". After she prepared my lunch can, off I went towards the village of Morea, a distance of about 2 miles to the "coal hole." I knew where it was because one Sunday, Lenny proudly showed me where it was located.

"Who the hell are you?" "I'm Lenny's brother and I came to take his place today because he is sick." After the laughter subsided, they discussed their predicament. Now I was not only thin, I was downright skinny. I stood there with my lunch pail (which was about three inches from the ground) in hand and said, **"I COULD DO IT!"**

The mine employed a total of three men and Lenny. After some discussion I was told, "get in the buggy" I was given an oversized cloth cap with a carbide lamp attached and down we went.

My job was to sit in the "Chute" The chute was a wooden box about the size of the box on a pickup truck. It was located at the bottom of a slope and the coal came from above and ran down to the holding box. A wooden lever opened the door. When the lever was pulled down, the coal would rush down to the coal buggy that was directly under the chute box. Sometime the coal would get stuck and I had to sit on the coal and kick it with my feet to get it moving, the coal would run in to the buggy. When it was filled I would press the signal button three times. The operator at the top would then haul it to the surface.

I was alone in this area of the mine. All was very quiet while the buggy was going up or down. After about two hours I heard a very loud noise and heard a lot of rock and, I suppose coal falling, together with a rush of air. My carbide light went out. My first thought was that my cap fell down over my eyes because the cap was too large and I came to work without a safety pin. Then it became very quiet. I came to the conclusion that we were, as miners would say, "caved in." I decided to save as much oxygen as I could by not lighting my lamp. I was surprised that the buggy came down and the bell rang two times which was the signal for me to fill it. But I just sat there in the dark hoping that I would be rescued.

Many thoughts ran through my head. I thought about my mother blaming Lenny for getting sick. I thought, "Gee, now I don't have to go to school anymore," and I wondered what was in my lunch pail since I could not find it in the dark.

After a while, I saw a light coming towards me. One of the miners called me and said, "Why the hell are you sitting in the dark and why did you stop filling the buggy?" I told him that it was no use to fill it since we are "caved in." After he used some words that I cannot repeat here, he said "Stupid, there was no cave in. We set off a dynamite blast at the "face" and the concussion always blows the carbide lamp out. Put your light on and start filling the damn buggy." After we came up to the surface after the shift, I pleaded with them not to tell my friends of the incident. "It all depends whether your brother comes to work tomorrow."

That was my first experience working in the mines. And no, I did not receive any pay for the day. It was added to Lenny's pay.

HUCKLEBERRIES

V ery early in the morning about 5:30 AM the huckleberry pickers began entering the forests, actually in our case it was the bushes. My older sister Frances, my brother Leonard, and my younger sister Helen and I began walking to the area now occupied by the Schuylkill Mall. Mom was wearing a dress and she was carrying three 10-quart buckets. Frances was wearing her older brother's bib overalls. Since this was 1932, wearing jeans was not in fashion. Frances was very upset that she had to wear overalls and was concerned that her friends might see her. We walked on the street and she followed us by using the alleys behind the homes. Before leaving home mom would check if we were dressed properly for the woods. We were instructed to wear shoes that covered our ankles just in case we would be surprised by a rattler or even a copper head snake. In all the years that I picked huckleberries I never did see a snake. That is not to say there were no snakes in the woods. We occasionally saw a dead "rattler" that someone killed and was lying on the path.

There is another item I would like to tell that is rather gross but true. We have never heard of the "Society for the prevention of cruelty to animals." While walking through the woods we would occasionally see the skeleton of a dead dog with a rope around its neck and tied to a small tree. In the fall of the year, the family's faithful dog "Shep" who had an advanced case of rheumatism had difficulty walking. The mother of the house would tell one of her older boys "I can't stand to see him suffer through another winter. You will have to put him out of his misery before the winter." The dog collar would be removed and replaced with a small length of old clothesline rope and led to the woods with his master who was carrying a rifle or small pistol. This was a common occurrence. No one would take a sick animal to the veterinarian to put the animal out of it's misery, since in our area they only treated farm animals, and besides a bullet was cheaper than paying the vet. It is not my intention to upset the reader any further with what seems like cruelty to animals but you may wonder what could be done with the old, blind, family cat. The sick old cat was placed in a burlap bag and placed in a large can filled with water with a heavy rock holding him down. Sad to say when a cat had kittens an effort was made to give the kittens away. Those who were left were treated the same way as the old blind and sick cat. This was a normal and humane way to send these animals to animal heaven.

When we finally reached the area where we were going to pick the huckleberries, the sun was beginning to rise. Even though it did not rain during the night, the bushes were wet from the dew with a result that we were wet from the waist down. There were many huckleberry pickers on the Mountain. We heard the mothers and occasionally a father speaking different languages, Russian, Ukrainian, Polish, Lithuanian and occasionally even English. Instructions were given especially to the small children. "Be careful to pick only the ripe berries and make sure you do not get any leaves or small twigs in your can." All the children spoke English among themselves except when speaking to their mother. After only a few weeks of the picking season the buyers could tell which family picked the best berries. The buyers occasionally refused to buy berries from some families whose berries were not clean.

I'll explain some of the equipment that was needed to pick berries properly. Everyone wore a belt. The younger children used a small coffee can that held about one quart. Two holes were punched into both sides of the coffee can with a nail and a wire was attached to make a handle. We call the small cans "starters." The belt went through the handle and hung at the waist. In this manner you could pick berries with both hands. When the can was full, it would be poured into mom's or Frances's bucket. Of course the older people did not "use starter cans" but placed the berries directly into the 10 quart bucket. One problem that the children had would be having their berries spilled on the ground. This often happened. They would trip on a root or a stone. If mom was not looking we would try to put the berries back in the can without getting any small stones or twigs mixed with the berries. Of course Mom would pour our berries into her bucket very slowly so she could pick out any twigs or green berries.

There were many varieties of huckleberries. The most common true huckleberry grew on a plant about 8 two 12 inches high. We called them "Grounders" The ripe berries would be in small clusters and a good picker could sort of "tickle" the cluster and get eight or ten ripe berries without any stems. Another less common berry called "stonies" by us and was called "June berries" by the more educated. Most good pickers would not pick these berries. These berries grew on plants that were 12 to 18 inches high. Another type of berry that was colloquially called "Swampers" grew in low-lying areas containing water. These plants grew to a height of four and occasionally five feet high. The berries were three times the size of the normal blue huckleberry and were much sought-after.

Mom instructed us to stay within talking distance to each other not only to prevent us from getting lost, but also informing each other when you found a "Kutch" that contains many berries. "I found a good kutch. Come on over here." Another reason for keeping within talking distance was that you did not have to walk too far to put your berries in mom's big bucket. Yet another reason was that mom was carrying the bottle of water and more importantly the sandwiches. After a bucket was filled, mom would cover it with a piece of cloth and tie it around the bucket with a piece of string. It was difficult for mom to carry the bucket full of berries with her as she continued picking berries with another empty big bucket.

Finally, our three buckets and three small one-quart cans were completely full and we began leaving the woods. We were accompanied by many other families (I estimate that usually about 200 and as much as 300 people) heading our way to where the berry buyers parked their trucks. The trucks were parked on a large dirt area on the left side of Route 122 (now called Route 61) going south. Motel 6 now occupies this site. There usually were three and occasionally four trucks set up to buy and box the berries. Mom would try to pick the buyer who did not put an extreme "cope" in the small square wooden one quart box even if that was the longest line of berry pickers. The buyers would pour the berries into the one-quart boxes that were placed on top of the large wooden boxes that looked like large egg crates. After the one-quart box was filled it would be covered with a square of cellophane. The cellophane would be printed with the words "Mountain Blueberries" and occasionally would have a store's name printed in small letters.

In the beginning of the season when the berries were just beginning to ripen, the highest price per quart as I remember it, was about 27 cents. As the season progressed the price went down by a few cents and at the end of the season it was as low as four cents a quart. When the price got as low as 10 cents, many pickers would not sell to the commercial buyers and instead would assign a member of the family to sit by the side of the highway and sell their berries to motorists who stopped. They were equipped with small brown paper bags and a square one quart wooden box to use as a measure. Even though they had to wait a few hours to sell their berries, it was worth the time spent since many of the motorists who stopped paid on occasion as much as 50 cents! a quart. This usually happened if the most beautiful young daughter of the family was the salesperson.

The picking of berries went on every day of the week with the exception of Sunday or a day of heavy rain. If it were only a light drizzle you would find mom and the kids picking berries. Mom would say, "it's only a small drizzle, and that means that it won't be as hot as it was yesterday." All other work around the house was put on hold. On Monday evening after picking berries for about nine hours, mom would wash the family clothes after she prepared and we ate the supper. If there was coal to be cracked we did it in the evening. This is one time that mom would allow us to turn on the back porch light so that we could crack the coal and not our fingers.

At the end of the berry-picking season, the young men of the town would set the woods on fire. They would burn the scrub oak and the berry bushes. In the evening you could see the glow of the fires in the areas where we picked berries all summer. This would guarantee a good crop of berries for the next year.

When the berry prices were extremely low mom did not send us out to sit by the side of the road to sell our berries to the motorists. Instead she would bake seven or eight delicious blueberry pies and we were allowed to eat as much as we wanted.

At the end of the berry-picking season, Lenny and I would take our wagon to the Wipperwill strippings to pick enough coal to last the coming winter. If we could convince mom that we had enough coal for the year she would allow us to play some baseball. She also gave us money to see a cowboy movie at the Victoria Theater. We did not have an "allowance." The term allowance was not in our vocabulary; in fact it was unknown in our day. It was a more of a hit and miss arrangement that mom used. Whenever mom had some extra change (which was very rare) and if nothing upset her and she was in a good mood, it was good chance that you were going to see a movie or even buy a "Babe Ruth" candy bar. There was a time when mom was very upset because the price of margarine went up a few pennies. I did not see a movie for the next three weeks.

SPRING-CLEANING

Two eleven year old boys + summer = Happiness.

M y best friend, Joe Kosierp, and I had a few wonderful adventures early in the summer. The plans were made during the last week of school. We both knew that we had chores that would be assigned to us in our respective homes. All the chores would be done during the daylight hours, but the hours after supper were often free.

All the mothers in the neighborhood seemed to select the same time to begin their spring-cleaning. I often thought all the mothers held a secret meeting to set plans to get the spring cleaning finished before the huckleberries were ready to be harvested and when the coal supply was diminished and had to be replaced. Mom would say, "The winter will be upon us before we know it." I said to Joe, "I don't understand it, the last snow just melted in our back yard and my mom is telling us that the winter will soon be upon us!" How else could it be explained that practically every family in a four-block area decided to put the kids to work.

The first order from mom would be, "Boys, first straighten up the cellar" (no one on our block had a basement, we all had cellars.) She never said clean the cellar, always straighten up the cellar. This meant rearrange the old boxes, hang up the tools. If she was not watching, we would throw out the old shoes she was saving for us to wear when picking blueberries. "They are high tops, they will come in handy if we meet up with some rattlesnakes when we are in the bush." It didn't matter that the shoes belonged to my older brothers and in addition to being worn out, they were three sizes too big! After about two days of hard work, mom held an inspection, and would say, "It's a lot better, but I'll finish the job next week when I get some time."

Next came rug and carpet beating time. The entire neighborhood seemed to beat the rugs about the same time. The rugs and carpets were taken up, hung on the wash line (most of the lines were made of aluminum and could take the weight of the heavy carpets) then they were beaten on both sides with a "rug beater." Every family had a beater; most were handsome works of art. It had a small wooden handle and was four feet long. It had various designs on the business end of this appliance. In the past few years, I have been trying to find a beater whenever we visit an antique shop or when we stop at a flea market. I don't understand it, we see a lot of old washboards, a rolling pin, butter churns, and cast iron frying pans but we never could find an old "rug beater." We beat the 9 by 12 living room rug on both sides for what seemed like hours. Meanwhile mom and my sister Helen removed and replaced all the newspapers after sweeping the floors. This kept up until all the small rugs and runners were beaten up! Mom kept all the windows closed until the entire neighborhood was finished beating the rugs. For a while it looked like an Oklahoma sandstorm was in progress. (Boy, I sure have beaten this story to death!)

Next we were told to "RAKE" the yard. Most of the backyards in our neighborhood were basically the same, 25 feet wide and about 60 feet long. Somewhere, back about 30 feet from the back porch, stood as the English say "the necessary." Some yards had a small shed at the back fence that once was home for a few chickens or occasionally some ducks, or more likely geese.

Most of the yard was used as a vegetable garden. Tomatoes, cucumbers, carrots, potatoes, dill and other herbs and lots and lots of cabbage were planted.

All the moms in the block always had room for flowers in their garden. Even though they never purchased fertilizer, they had the most beautiful flowers in town. In late April and for the rest of the summer, all the moms in the neighborhood would prepare bouquets of flowers each Saturday morning and assign one of the girls to take them to the church for Sunday Mass. Since we had three services each Sunday, 8:00am Low Mass, 10:30 High Mass and 4:00 p.m. vespers, the flowers were enjoyed by everyone. There was only a small problem; all the mothers would compete to see who had the most, best, different varieties of flowers. Occasionally it was hard to see the altar. In those days all Catholic churches had three altars, two side and a main altar. Everyone wanted to have his or her flowers on the main altar. The women would approach the priest and ask, "Why weren't my flowers on the main altar? Mrs. Kolakowski's flowers were on the main altar for the last three weeks!" Father Garstka would always solve the problem to their satisfaction. He blamed it on Mr. Bialecki the sexton! It was part of his job to place and remove the flowers each week. A few busybody women did not intimidate Mr. Bialecki.

Mr. Bialecki who was also the janitor was responsible for the *hand fired anthracite coal furnace*. When we boys were working on the grounds of the church, or were waiting to attend the Saturday morning catechism classes, we occasionally ran about, made a lot of noise, and acted like normal nine-year-old kids. Mr. Bialecki got us together and announced (in Polish of course) that he would like to share something with us. He led us to the furnace room under the church, the entrance of which was accessible only from outside the building. It was dark with only a 20-watt bulb as the only light. After we were gathered in front of this large furnace, he opened both large doors exposing the bed of hot burning coal. He asked each of the boys to get up close and look at the burning coals. He then announced "You boys have been taught about hell in your catechism classes, well I'm here to tell you that **HELL** is much hotter, the flames are much higher in hell that what you are looking at in this furnace. That is my lesson for you boys today." After this experience, we were on our best behavior, which lasted a full three or four weeks!

All the above was not exactly happiness for the boys. NOW comes the happiness part! Joe Kosierp and I knew all the great and interesting areas surrounding Frackville. Just a few yards south of the present interstate 81 highway and route 61, a spring with cool, clear, delicious water can still be seen. It bubbles up from the sandy ground to a height of twelve inches, (well maybe about seven inches.) It reminded us of the water fountain on the first floor hallway at the Franklin Building School. When we pressed the button the water would bubble up except that the water at school was warm and had a horrible taste. We would lie on the ground and drink from this pure, crystal clear, delightful and delicious natural water fountain. There was a small problem drinking this way. The fountain would carry some fine pieces of sand up with the water and of course would end up in our mouths. We did not mind this since we were able to spit out most of the sand. I must tell the reader about this sand. I would examine the sand being disturbed by the flow of the water. Each piece of sand was washed a hundred times. Each piece of sand sparkled in the sunlight. I don't believe I saw a real diamond at the age of ten, but some of the sand pieces sparkled and looked like I believed a diamond should look like.

There were other colors of sand, pink, red, gray and most of the colors that could be seen on a rainbow! It was great, lying on the ground, taking sips of cool water and in-between times studying the sand.

This spring is actually the headwater of the south branch of the Schuylkill River! The town can honestly place a sign at the entrance, **"Frackville—where the mighty Schuylkill River begins."** A few yards south, it was a very small stream, a quarter mile further downstream, it merges with the overflow water from the Mud Run Dam (Pottsville water dam) where it begins to look like a small river. This stream was and still is located between highway 61 leading to Saint Clair and the bed of the old Reading Railroad line. Frackville had two railroad lines, the Reading and the Pennsylvania Line. The Pennsy line was a passenger and freight line, while the Reading was for the most part, the coal shipping line. Now for the happiness part. Joe and I would follow the tracks about a quarter of a mile south of town. We would leave our homes at dusk hoping to see if any hobos were in camp. This was an evening that luck smiled on us. Just ahead we could see the glow of a campfire between the railroad tracks and the stream.

We left the tracks and approached very quietly. Seated around the fire were five "Hobos." Some people called them bums but Joe and I never called them bums. Some of the town folk called them bums and thieves. The way I looked at it, whenever some damage was done in town, the hobos were always blamed. I remember when a few outhouses were pushed over and some back yard gates were torn off the hinges. The hobos were blamed. I am not saying that the hobos were the most honest temporary citizens of the town. Occasionally a chicken was missing and a few heads of almost ripe cabbage were pulled out of the ground, but these were minor problems. Could you imagine if it was necessary to use the "necessary" and you had to wait for your father and your big brothers to come home from work so that they could "right" the outhouse. Now that's a problem.

As we cautiously approached we could smell food. A large tin can that once held a gallon of tomatoes was set upon a few stones and was steaming away. They were making what some people called "Bum's soup." While waiting for their dinner, they entertained themselves, Joe, and me. We were only a few yards away from them, hiding in the dense undergrowth. When I think back on it now, they probably knew that we were there. One hobo had a harmonica. We called it a mouth organ. It was a mouth organ until I was about eighteen years old. Another was playing a Jew's harp. They sang many railroad songs such as *"The Wabash Cannonball" Listen to the jingle, the rumble and the roar, riding thru the woodlands, to the hill and by the shore; hear the mighty rush of engines, hear the lonesome Hobo squall, riding thru the jungles on the Wabash Cannonball.* Most of the songs they sang were sad songs. *The Wreck of Old Number Nine, Casey Jones, Call of the Whippoorwill, etc.*

We were fascinated listening to them sing and watching a few of them enjoying what smelled like the best soup in the world. Since we did not own a watch and since the moon was high in the sky, we had to make plans on what we would tell our mothers where we had been and why we were so late coming home. We rehearsed the story we'd tell since we knew our mothers would compare notes. Walking home by moonlight, the moon was shining on the railroad tracks, and the light on the tracks looked like ribbons of silver.

The hobos for the most part were loners, they did not travel in groups, so what we were seeing, five hobos, was a rare occurrence. Since it was the time of the great depression, there were many "Knights of the Road" visiting Frackville. They came into town usually walking the alleys at the edge of town. We boys from St. Ann's church often helped Father Garstka with the church grounds, pulling weeds, raking leaves and other small chores. The hobos often came to Father for a meal. He would make a sandwich and other food that he had in the kitchen. He never refused them a meal. He asked us not to torment them or call them names because they may have a family somewhere and that times are hard and they should be helped. He told us that we should pray for them and others who cannot find work. The hobo would sit on the steps of the garage to eat his meal.

BULLIES

O ne of the things that were not pleasant when a child is growing up has to put up with "bullies." I, like many other kids had to suffer their taunts and an occasional beating, but what hurt me most was that there was no defense against a bully. If you are walking home from school with some school friends and are being picked on by one of these characters, your friends cannot come to your aid since they would be next on the list. Occasionally an older person passing by would say, "Let the kid alone" this was a signal for more abuse from the ruffian. One of the worst was Mike W . . . . When my school friends left for their homes, I had to walk alone past this kids house. I would walk three blocks away from his house because he scared the shit out of me. He taunted me because I was skinny, I had "funny" arms and I wore heavy corduroy pants even when the weather was warm. My mom would ask me why it took so long to get home from school. I told her that I had to walk a few blocks out of my way because of this kid. When I told her his name, she said he does that because he is a Russian. When she lived in Poland she had many Russian neighbors since she lived close to the Russian border and she was taunted all her life. For them, this was normal behavior. She said that I should get used to it since they will never change. I could have asked my older brothers to beat this kid up, but had they done that, I would not be alive today to write this long story.

THE BUTCHER BOOK

E very family in our neighborhood had a butcher book. We did not have grocery stores in those days, they were all called the "butchers" even though they all sold groceries. Most of the butchers (now called mom-and-pop stores) also sold large bags of sugar for making "moonshine whiskey." This type of sugar was not sold at the local A&P stores (Frackville had two A&P stores, one on the north side the other on the south side of town) since they were a part of a chain and moonshine whiskey was made in the coal region towns. Since purchasing ice for the icebox was very expensive, most of the housewives made purchases every day except during the winter when they bought food enough for two or three days. Some of the butcher shops also sold dynamite and exploding caps for use by the coal miners. I don't know if this was true but I heard it while attending a "Wake" for my friend's father who died from injuries in a coal mine. During those days no one in our neighborhood was buried from a funeral parlor. A small floral bouquet tied with a purple ribbon was placed near the front door of the home. The entire "Parlor suite" and other large pieces of furniture were stored with the family next door. Chairs were borrowed from the neighbors that were placed along the wall in the front room (when we had company, it was called the Parlor.) During the day, the neighbors would bring in a lot of food and cakes. This food was only for the family and the relatives from out-of-town who came in for the funeral.

Most homes had a large (Grandmother) clock. The frame was carved from wood. It had a large pendulum, which made a loud ticking sound and had to be wound every eight days. During the funeral, the clock was stopped at the exact moment of death. The downstairs mirror was covered with a white cloth. It was a custom for a few men, and occasionally ladies, to sit with the body until the time of the burial. There were usually two days of viewing. Mourners would come in beginning early in the morning until about 9 PM. I decided to stay up all night with my friend Joe. We sat in a corner in the parlor. A few men played cards in the kitchen. That is when I heard one miner telling his friend where he purchased the dynamite.

Where was I? Oh yes. I was writing about the butcher book. Of course my mom had a butcher book. Occasionally she gave the book to one of the kids with instructions to purchase a pound of sugar and a pound bag of flour. When I was sent to the store I was tempted to buy some penny candies. The candies were sold loose and there was a whole tray full in the glass display case. One day I gave in to temptation and I bought 10 cents worth of assorted candies. I thought that my mom would not notice this item in the butcher book. I only did this once in my entire childhood. Even though I was wearing my heavy corduroy pants, I occasionally think about this day and I could feel the sting of the belt on my bottom.

When a purchase was made at the butcher shop, the butcher's wife listed all the items in a small sales book. A sheet of carbon paper made a duplicate. I then would hand her the butcher book and she would enter all the items and the date of purchase. When Charlie and Pete gave mom their weekly pay envelopes, the next day mom would take the butcher book and pay at least part of the balance due.

My friend Stanley from Shenandoah once told me a story that he swears is true. The sisters at St. Casmir's Elementary School in Shenandoah asked all the children to bring to the school their father's prayer book. All of the children brought the books to school. All were printed in the Polish language except for one, and it was printed in Lithuanian. I suppose it was a Lithuanian man that married a strong-willed Polish girl who must have been in charge of the household. One boy brought in the family's butcher book. The sister thought that he was playing a joke on her. "Why do you bring in the butcher book?"

He replied, "Every evening when my father came home from work, even before he has his supper, he would open the kitchen cabinet located above the sink, look at it and exclaim **"O Jesu, O moj Jesu** (Oh Jesus, Oh my Jesus!).""

BILL BOROWSKY

B ill had one leg. When he was a small child, he ran behind his father's car when the car was backing out of the garage resulting with the car running over his leg. His right leg was amputated above the knee. While he had a "peg leg" he never used it. He used only one crutch and he managed very well. He was a neat guy, he didn't mind if some of his friends called him "Peg" he was about five years older than I was.

He loved to sing "Cowboy songs." Often, in the early evening, just about dusk, a few of us would sit in the alley behind Broad Mt. Avenue, and listen to him sing.

"Home in the West."
With someone like you, a pal good and true
I'd like to leave it all behind and go and find
A place that's known to God alone
Just a spot to call our own
We'd build a little nest, somewhere out in the West
And let the rest of the world go bye.

He often told us that he wanted to get married and move out West and spend his life quietly, living in his little home in the wide-open spaces, he did not care if his nearest neighbor lived forty miles away. With his wife at his side, he would spend every evening looking at the setting sun. He never got his wish. He never married and died in 1995 spending his last years as a recluse; he did not leave his house for the last six years of his life even though he was not bedridden.

Bill had a job. He was the movie projectionist for the Victoria and Garden Theaters in Frackville. He worked part-time in the beginning; later in life he was a full-time employee.

His chief occupation was gambling. He ran the crap games every Sunday beginning at about 10:30 AM until dusk. The crap games were played in the same alley where he entertained us with his singing. The alley (and many of the streets) was not paved in those days. The ground was well packed and smooth and made a perfect spot to throw the dice. I remember that the guys were dressed in their Sunday slacks and clean well-starched white long sleeved shirts. The shirts cuffs were folded up just one turn. I wondered if their mothers knew that they were kneeling on the ground wearing their Sunday pants.

Sometimes there were about twelve or more guys kneeling in a big ring. Of course I was too young to play and besides, I did not have any money that I could spare. I was most impressed with seeing all the guys with their left-hands open and a role of quarters laying neatly in a row between their index and third finger. They also had some piles of quarters stacked neatly in front of them. Bill controlled the game. He had a few sets of dice, most of which were colored green or red, but occasionally he had white dice with black dots. The shooter would ask for a certain color dice since they were his "lucky" dice. I know all this because we younger kids were allowed to watch if we kept quiet. We were able to see everything since the guys playing were kneeling and we were standing. Most of the players smoked "Lucky Strikes" but some smoked "Camels." All the guys smoked including many of the young kids watching.

The shooters were allowed to make any comments that they pleased, "come on seven, baby needs a new pair of shoes." Sometimes a guy would shout, "snake eyes" when a shooter was about to throw the dice. This rarely happened since a guy like that was lacking in "couth." Besides it was in very poor taste. Since Bill ran the game (and since he was the owner of the dice) he would take a percentage from each "pot."

We kids always stood around while the high rollers were playing.

We would also "shoot craps," but we used wooden matches for money. Nearly everyone used wooden matches to light their cigarettes. Cigarettes cost 18 to 20 cents a pack in those days. As soon as we were about twelve years old, we bought cigarettes at any corner grocery store for two cents each. When we were nine or ten years old, we smoked corn hair wrapped in dry grape leaves.

If cigarette prices were too high, many guys bought a pack of "Bugler" tobacco. A pack cost 10 cents and came complete with a pack of "rolling paper." To make a cigarette, a paper is held in the left hand, some tobacco is placed in the paper and it is "rolled" until a good example of a cigarette was made. The edge of the paper contained some glue and was licked with the tongue and you're ready for a good "Smoke." My brother Pete purchased a "Cigarette-making machine." It was sold by the Brown and Williamson Tobacco Co. the same company that produced "Bugler Tobacco." It worked very well and made professional looking cigarettes. A cigarette paper was placed in the machine, tobacco was placed on the paper, a small lever was moved forward and a perfect cigarette was made. The paper still had to be sealed by wetting the edge of the paper with your tongue. Pete would make 20 or more at a setting, placing them in fancy silver (?) Cigarette case.

DR. MENGEL

By now, the reader should know that I was born feet first. While I have treated this subject with some humor, all the stories are true. Throughout my entire life not a day passed, that I was not reminded in some way that I was a breech birth. Like most children in those days I was born at home. A midwife delivered most of the babies in our neighborhood. In my case a doctor delivered me. In the 20's and 30's, all the doctors in our community delivered babies. Called general practitioners, they treated colds, stitched open wounds, set bones, put on plaster casts, removed cinders from your eye, and on occasion they treated mental illness and oh yes, they delivered lots of babies.

I was the sixth child born to my mother. The date was June 18, 1924. I was born in our home at 124 North Broad Mountain Avenue, Frackville, PA.

1948—During this year I was building a new home at 222 South Center Street. I was engaged to Irene Saukaitis of Mt. Carmel. We did not set a wedding date; the date would be set when the house was finished. During this period there were a lot of decisions to be made. Since I was raised without a father in the house, I made up my mind to be first, a good father and a good husband. I had one problem; I was not covered by life insurance. I applied for a $5000.00 policy with the Metropolitan Life Insurance Company. Dr. Dougherty of Frackville was the doctor assigned by Metropolitan to give me the required medical examination. I responded honestly to all his questions and after his examination he told me that I had infantile paralysis as a child. I informed him that I did not, I was a breech birth. While he was a good doctor he was wrong in this case and I could see that I would get nowhere arguing with him. He gave me the medical report to sign. He listed infantile paralysis as the reason for my underdeveloped arms and shoulders. Before I signed, I specifically asked him, "Would this cause the insurance company to reject my application?" He was emphatic when he said "Absolutely not." Within a week, I received notification from Metropolitan that I was rejected. This was not good news. I asked for and received an appointment at the Metropolitan Life Insurance office in Shenandoah to discuss my report. I asked them for another doctor to give me a physical. I was told that the decision was made at their office in New York City and that their decision was final.

I was extremely upset that I would not be able to purchase life insurance. I found the girl that I wanted to spend my life with, our home was under construction, I had a very good job, and was paid very well for a job that I enjoyed.

I decided to discuss my problem with Mr. Jacobs the new owner who purchased the former New Cumberland Dress Co. Inc. The factory where I worked was now called Mitzi Frocks Inc. I only knew Mr. Jacobs about two months. During a meeting with him, I told him that the Metropolitan Insurance Company rejected me for life insurance. And I thought, "How could I marry Irene when the Metropolitan Insurance Company would not take the risk that I would live at least a few years?" The thought that came to my mind was that the Metropolitan Insurance Company was in the risk business and they would not take a risk on me. Their agents were very aggressive when selling life insurance policies. They want the business and yet they turned me down. I was very depressed and I thought, "Why should this young girl take a risk on me?" Mr. Jacobs asked, "Did you tell Irene?" I replied in the affirmative, "She told me, we would manage somehow." And I thought, "You should never trust anyone who is in love."

The next week when Mr. Jacobs returned from Philadelphia, he told me that he made arrangements with a doctor friend from Jefferson University Hospital to give me a complete physical in the hospital and I would be there for two days. I told Irene, "I did not change my mind and I am not running away. Mr. Jacobs arranged a full physical examination so that I could put my mind at ease about my health. I will call when I have some news."

We left Mt. Carmel after lunch on Wednesday and he drove me to his home in suburban Philadelphia. He lived in an absolutely beautiful home. His wife was not at home. She was spending a few days with their daughter at boarding school. The guest bedroom where I stayed reminded me of a movie I once saw. The bedroom was large, the adjoining bath had gold plated faucets (at least they looked like gold), the towels were huge and had a large "J" embroidered on the hand and bath towels. I had my choice of "Designer soaps." I chose the one that had a scent that women would like. The light blue satin bed sheets and pillowcase were very sensuous. Getting between those sensuous light blue satin bed sheets was a real pleasure. I made a mental note to ask Irene to let me know when she intended to buy new sheets for our bed. In those days, many young men wear their hair crew cut style. This of course means that you have to use a pomade to keep your hair standing up. I used "Brill Cream." It was advertised, as "A little dab will do ya." I was never cheap, I use a few dabs.

When I awoke in the morning, the first thing I saw when I lifted my head off the pillow was a huge circle of grease right in the middle of the light blue satin pillowcase. The only thing I thought of doing was to leave a $5 dollar bill attached with a note to the maid and asking her not to say anything to the lady of the house. My wallet only contained a few one's and four $20 bills, so I turned the pillow clean side up. I made my way down to the kitchen where I smelled coffee brewing with the hope that Mr. Jacobs was doing the brewing.

Mr. Jacobs made our breakfast. Orange juice, toast with blueberry jam, and a cup of very strong coffee. After breakfast we left for the Jefferson Hospital in Center City Philadelphia. I thanked him and told him that I would be discharged on Saturday, and I would take the bus home to Frackville. He usually came to Mt. Carmel on Tuesday or Wednesday. That gave him plenty of time to forget about the grease on the light blue satin pillowcase, the one with a lot of grease on it.

I was given a complete examination that included a few x-rays and a lot of blood tests. Various specialists examined me. Neurologist, cardiologist, optometrist, and other doctors with "gist" at the end of their specialty.

All they found was a small area on my left arm just below my shoulder that did not have any feeling. And this was because I was born feet first and some of the nerves were damaged. This area without feelings on my arm was another advantage of being born feet first. I decided that I would tell my doctor back home that whenever I see him with a syringe and a long needle in his hand I will show him where to put it!

The doctor said that in spite of having a birth injury, I should expect to live a long life only if I drive very carefully.

Saturday arrived and so did Irene. I was very happy and surprised to see her. The nurse told me that I would be discharged about 2 PM. I shared my hospital lunch with Irene, this would be the supreme test that she loved me by eating one-half of my hospital food.

When I was dressed the nurse gave me a large brown grocery bag and told me to take the following items: a toothbrush and a very small tube of toothpaste, an almost full bar of soap, a small black comb, a half filled box of tissues and a male urinal.

Irene was looking out the window down on the street when she saw an ambulance with the words "St. Clair Ambulance" painted on the side and back. Right then and there I knew that she would be a very good wife and hopefully a mother. We hurried down the street and I asked the driver of the ambulance if he was going back to St. Clair preferably without a patient. He said he was, so I asked if he would take me and my friend to St. Clair. He waited until his partner came out of the hospital. I told Irene to join me in looking very sad. After consulting with his friend, we were told that they would take us as far as Pottsville. They did not want to take the risk of some busybody in St. Clair writing a letter to the editor at the *Pottsville Republican* complaining that these two volunteers were breaking the law by carrying two very healthy people from Philadelphia to St. Clair. I thought of giving them a tip but I remembered that my wallet held only a few $1 dollar bills and a few 20's. They let us off at the Pottsville bus station. It was very convenient and the bus to Frackville ran every half-hour.

I did not receive a bill from the Jefferson hospital nor the doctors who examined me. I suppose Mr. Jacobs paid for all my expenses.

After I left Mitzi Frocks to begin my own business, Mr. Jacobs called me a few times with a question about a problem he was having with certain machines. I did not hear from him since he sold Mitzi Frocks and began a new business in the Philadelphia area.

Approximately 10 years later, I met him in Chattanooga, TN while attending the "Bobbin Show." All of the various manufacturers of sewing machines and other supplies for the garment manufacturing business gave demonstrations on the new equipment that was available. Industrial engineers also held seminars. The show lasted a full week.

While walking through this enormous exhibit, I saw a stand exhibiting some automated equipment for the garment industry. I could not believe my eyes, the sign said "Jacobs Engineering." Standing in the middle of this exhibit was Mr. Herbert Jacobs. When I worked for him at Mitzi Frocks in Mt. Carmel, he was always experimenting in my workshop with gadgets to be used not only in the garment factory but items that could be used in the home. He did not seem to be too successful in this area.

Many years later in 1979, when I was appointed by the governor of Pennsylvania to be the Secretary of General Services in Harrisburg, I received a call from Herbert Jacobs. During the first months in my new position I received many calls of congratulation and offers of help from the heads of other agencies in the government. His call was different. He asked if he could see me as soon as possible. He told me he was in Harrisburg and would like to see me on an urgent matter later in the same day. I checked with my secretary who told me that I did not have any appointments after 3 PM. He arrived in my office at 4:00. I was very happy to see him but I could read in his face that he was very troubled. I felt very awkward. My former boss who was very good to me was coming to me as he said, for a big favor.

He began by telling me that his wife died from cancer. He took her to the finest doctors that he could find in Philadelphia, New York, and Baltimore. His new business was not successful and he spent his entire savings to find a cure for his wife. "I was broke." He asked his friend, Pennsylvania Governor Milton Shapp, if he could get him a job with the state. He knew Milton Shapp of Philadelphia who ran a large manufacturing business producing large television towers and antennas that were necessary before cable TV was invented. Mr. Jacobs was very interested in television in those early days. He arranged for me to buy the first television set that I had in my home.

Governor Shapp arranged for him to work at the Department of Environmental Resources (DER) He worked at the department for the two terms that Milton Shapp was governor that is eight years. When Pennsylvania elected Dick Thornburgh, a republican governor. Many changes were made in personnel who were not under the civil service umbrella. Since Herbert Jacobs did not have civil service protection he most probably would have been removed from his position with DER.

The problem that Mr. Jacobs had was an employee of the state had to work a minimum of 10 years to be able to collect a pension check plus health benefits. He asked me if I could save his job until he became eligible to retire with a pension. I assured him that I could do it. I called the Secretary of DER and asked him for an appointment so that I could make sure that the Secretary would keep Mr. Jacobs on board. I was successful in having him keep his position. I only saw him once in the two years he was in Harrisburg. A few days after he was assured that he would be held on, he asked if Irene and I would come to his apartment in Harrisburg for dinner so that we could meet his new wife. After dinner we discussed our lives since we last met many years ago. I felt very awkward because I knew it was difficult for him to come to me to save his job. But I was very happy that I was able to help him.

I have not heard from him since both he and I left government service.

And now back to the life insurance business.

I spoke to a friend who was an insurance agent for the Home Life Insurance Company. I told him about my rejection by Metropolitan. He informed me that his company would give me life insurance. After completing the application form, I answered the question "have you been rejected for insurance from any company," with a yes. Within a few days, I was seated in the office of Dr. Mengel of Frackville for the required physical examination. I told the doctor that I was rejected a few weeks ago by the Metropolitan Insurance Company because the doctor listed on the form that I had infantile paralysis as a child. Dr. Mengel said it was very obvious that I had an injury during birth. Then he said that some doctors did not have enough training to deliver babies. He had seen other children that were injured during birth etc. etc.

I tried to interrupt him without much success until I almost shouted **"Dr. Mengel you delivered me!"** I did not say this with any malice on my part but I did not want him to be embarrassed.

He then spent the next 45 minutes explaining the difficulty with a breech birth. He told me that the doctor attending a breech birth must work quickly because with the baby halfway out of the birth canal, it would try to breathe since the cooler air on the child's body would start the child breathing. He went into great detail on how the doctor must pull the child out as fast as he can. In the process, occasionally the arms go above the head and as in my case an injury occurred at the shoulder. I again tried to interrupt him without much success. I told him that I understood and that I was not blaming him. "Your office is filled with sick people and you should attend to them." I then asked if the insurance company would accept me as a client. He assured me that the report that he would send explained the reason why Metropolitan Insurance Company rejected me, and that he was the attending physician at my birth.

Within a week, I was notified that the insurance policy would be sent to my home within a few days. At this time I was very much in love, concerned with the construction of a new home, and my duties at my place of work in Mt. Carmel. After a few months, I read the policy and found out that I was "rated" which meant that my monthly premium was much higher than a normal policy would cost. A few years later, I joined the Knights of Columbus and applied for a large insurance policy that I was able to purchase at the normal rate. A few examples on how being born "feet first" affected my life: As a child, I had difficulty in dressing myself. I had very little movement and could not lift my arms. At about the age of five, I had quite a bit of movement in my right arm and was able to feed myself.

The Schuylkill County Crippled Children's Society held a clinic at the Ashland State Hospital each month. A pediatrician and other physicians and nurses would see many children with various problems. This clinic was held with no charge for their services. Each month my mother would take me to this clinic. My older brother Charles was both the driver of the car and the translator for my mother.

After a few months of these visits, the doctors informed my mother that, unlike other bone problems where leg braces or special crutches were prescribed, in my case nothing could be done. My mother specifically asked if an operation could be performed on my shoulders. She was told that the only thing that would help me was physical therapy. Upon returning home, my brother Charlie would hang me on the top of a door for as long as I could bear it to stretch my muscles. Gradually I was able to have a little more movement especially in my right arm.

GAMES AND SPORTS

After supper, we boys would meet at an empty neighborhood lot for a game of baseball. The baseball was not white because no one had a new ball. We always had an old used ball that was taped round and round with black electricians tape. We could only play if we had the following: a catcher's mitt, pitchers glove, a glove for the first baseman, and a shortstop glove. If we were lucky, someone would have an outfielders glove. The most important item was the bat. We could, if necessary, play without some gloves but a proper bat was essential. We also had to have at least seven players on each side. Sometimes we had a full field of nine players on each side, it really did not matter, and we had fun playing.

Having assembled enough players and at least the minimum amount of equipment the pre-game ritual began. Two of the bigger kids began "picking sides." A coin was tossed to decide who would pick first. "I pick Frankie," said the winner of the toss. "I pick Stash," "I pick Cotton head" :I pick big Joe" "I pick Lil Joe" "I pick Bull," and so it went until there were no more kids left. Everyone knew who was going to be picked last, including me. I was always picked last because I could not throw a ball more than a few feet. (Now you know why it was so critical to win the toss.) You see, I was born feet first and my shoulders and arms didn't work so well. I was always assigned to the same position, right field. When the guys saw me coming, someone would say, **"Here comes the right fielder."** I did not mind since everyone knew my limitations. I was just happy that they allowed me to play. In fact we had another player, Bill Borowsky who also had a problem. When he was about twelve years old, his right leg was amputated above the knee. He had a prosthesis (it was a regular peg leg made of wood and had a large rubber pad on the base) but he rarely used it. It was great to see him make a hit and run to first base. He used only one crutch. I don't know this for a fact but the outfielder's seemed to make a lot of errors whenever Bill was at bat. Bill did not play every game but he did play. And now back to "Waldziu." I don't know if it was true, but the guys always tried to hit the ball to right field since a single always became a double when I was at my permanent position. In fact, so I heard, the guys actually trained to hit the ball into right field! But somehow I was really good when it was my turn at bat. They called me "Dlugi Wladziu" (long ball Wally) since I hit many singles and occasionally a double.

The games rarely lasted a full nine innings, and I know for a fact that we never had to play extra innings because of a tie. One of the biggest problems was, the small sister of "Yash," the kid that owned the catcher's mitt, would appear at the field and say those dreadful words, **"Mom sez that you have to come home right away."** That's one of the reasons that some games were over at the forth inning.

We did not have a referee. Whoever shouted the loudest "That was a ball" was in fact called a ball. We did not play in any league ball because there was no league for what was called sandlot ball. Once in a while, the guys from South Broad Mt. Ave. would challenge the North Broad Mt Ave. kids to a game. The best players of each team were selected for this game.

This game always lasted the full nine innings. One of the reasons was that there were two catcher's mitts and almost all the outfielders had gloves. Of course, I was never picked to play in these games. This special game was played twice a year.

At one of these games I had a plan on how I could get into the game. It was the eighth inning we were behind 8 to 5, we had the bases loaded, with two-out. I went to the "Manager" (the biggest kid was always the manager) and said, "Do you want to win this game?" He said, "That's the most stupid question I ever heard in my whole life."

That's when I said, "Put me in as a pinch-hitter." He asked for timeout and shouted, "We're going to put in a pinch-hitter," and that's when the fight started. "The hell you are." Our manager shouted, "My brother who almost played for the semi pro Mt Carmel Reds told me that in these kind of games, a pinch-hitter could be used." By that time everyone was on the field. Some of the mothers came to see what was happening. They said, "Stop the fighting," and other said, "Yash, go home, I SAID GO HOME!" (In Polish of course.) That was the end of the game. I came home and my brother Pete asked, "Who won the game?" I told him what happened and he said "You're damn lucky you made it home safe, but I must say it was a good idea."

Our sons, Tony and Joe were not very interested in sports even when I told them stories of how I was a great hitter. I was so good that we won a few games because of my prowess with a bat. My, nephew, young Bernie Kiefer, excelled in all sports, especially in baseball. He was a star when he played in the Frackville Little League. A lot of the guys at the K of C told me that I should see him in action, I decided to attend a game. I went up to Little League Park and they were right. Young Bern played one hell of a game. It was a good game but the longer I watched the action the angrier I became. I always financially supported all the sports for children in town. In fact, it was the first time I saw the sign on the backfield fence that our company, Model Garment Co. Inc. sponsored for years. But what I saw during this game made me sick! While sitting in the stands, I heard one of the adults (?) Shout, "Hey, stupid, how could you drop that ball? It was right in your glove. How did you ever make the team? Etc." The kid left the field in tears. The worst thing I saw was when some of these fathers and mothers would scream at the boys who struck out. At a Lion's meeting, one of the coaches of the team that the club sponsors came to speak to the Lions about Little League baseball. Actually they always attended a meeting when the team needed new uniforms. I know I sound sarcastic, but I was, and still am upset on how organized sports for children are managed. Most of the members of the Lions Club are sport jocks. During the question period that followed after the dinner, a member said "Make sure that our team wins the championship this year." In talking with some of the guys at the K of C (who also sponsored a team) I asked them many questions since a lot of the guys at the club have sons, grandsons or nephew's that play Little League Baseball. I also read why Little League Baseball was organized. It was to teach fair play, sportsmanship, and team cooperation, to give all boys an opportunity to learn and play sports.

I found that the coaches, who gave their time to attend the endless meetings and spend hours at practice, etc., have forgotten or have not read the rules and regulations. It was my turn to ask questions from our coach. The purpose of the Little League is to give every child that wants to play, an opportunity to play. From my observation, most of the kids on the bench go home with a perfectly clean uniform after every game. Only the "stars" get to play.

The only time every member of the team participates, is when each year, the entire team marches in the annual Memorial Day Parade. This is the only time that the *entire* team goes home with a clean uniform.

One of the worst practices that the coach would follow during "trying out for the team" time is for some 10-year-old's a nightmare. These boys are perfectly healthy and probably all were born headfirst. After trying out for the team, some boys came home in tears; they have failed to make the team. A child ten years old cannot handle this psychologically. It seems the whole reason is only to win.

Had I been born during these times, I never would have been allowed to play and enjoy baseball.

CAN KICKING

To play "kicking the can" one would have to find a proper can. The can must have a bottom and a lid. I would look for a "Gold Seal" evaporated milk can. A Gold Seal can came in two sizes, a full pint and a half pint. A real can kicker will only use the pint size. The whole purpose in "kicking the can" is to set a record on how far you can kick the same can. My best record was kicking a can from fourth and Oak Street to within one block of my home at 223 Spencer Street. Since Spencer Street was not paved, actually it was paved by the WPA but with cobblestones. The cans hitting those cobblestones made one helluva racket. The reason for stopping a block from home was that my mother was blessed with terrific hearing. She would come out on the front porch to see if I was kicking a can even if I did wear my weekday shoes. I occasionally went kicking the can when I was wearing my sneakers but sneakers were used only for a few blocks because of the pain the can inflicted on my toes. As soon as she heard me walking up the steps to the back porch, she would say "Where you kicking a can today? I thought I heard someone can kicking in the next block." I did not respond to her question but I use the old ruse of answering a question with a question. I said "Is supper almost ready?" She responded "Make sure you wipe your shoes carefully before you come into the kitchen."

ETHNICS

There were more ethnics living in the east end of Frackville than the rest of the town. Hell, we had a lot of "ethnics" that lived on Railroad Avenue. Railroad Avenue was not really an Avenue, whenever I think of an Avenue, I think of "Park Avenue." Now that's an Avenue. Railroad Avenue was just a normal street where a lot of "hunky's" lived. That's what we were called by the high-class people of town. I did not mind if they called us "ethnics" but I guess they did not know that we were ethnics. I always thought that some of these people that called us Hunky's were not very smart. We did not know we're ethnics and we did not find out until we were much older. In my case I found out that I was an "ethnic" when I reached 13 years of age.

Well anyway, the ethnics (I really like the sound of the word) lived on Railroad Avenue and all streets going north. Broad Mountain Avenue, Line Street, Wylam Street, Spencer Street, and Green Street. There also were a lot of ethnics that lived in Gilberton, Maizeville, and the Englewood section of Frackville.

We "ethnics" are regular normal people whose parents came from Poland, Russia, Lithuania, Slovakia, Hungary,

The Baranowski Family

the Ukraine, Czechoslovakia and other East European countries. The more enlightened people of town called our parents who could not speak English, "Greenhorns." I always thought that people who were able to speak a few languages were educated. Many of our parents could speak at least two languages, some even spoke three. I never could figure it out why they were called greenhorns. All my friends, both boys and girls, spoke two languages, but we were not called greenhorns.

CCC CAMP

1 940. A year that I made an important decision. I was 16 years old and because there was very little food I was hungry most of the time. My mother, my sister, Helen, and I lived in an apartment above my brother Charles' garage. The only heat came from the kitchen coal stove. There was no bathroom, no commode, and no privacy (we used a neighbor's outhouse that was located three houses down the block (the family had installed indoor plumbing and no longer used the outhouse) but worst of all was the lack of food.

My brother Leonard was a member of the "Civilian Conservation Corps" serving in a CCC camp at Waynesboro, PA near the Maryland border. (He dropped out of high school when he was in the 10th grade. He went to night school in the town near the camp and received a high school diploma. He graduated with the students from the town. After serving in the Navy during the Second World War, he attended Scranton University and finished in the top four percent of the class.)

The CCC was founded during the depression for young men age 17 to 25 who were unemployed. Many camps were set up in State and Federal Parks where they worked on roads, built bridges, fought forest fires and many worthwhile projects. The pay was $30.00 per month. $25.00 was sent by check to the family home, leaving $5.00 for the member for small items such as cigarettes, candy and the price of a ticket for a movie show.

This was a big help to my mother. The term was for six months. My brother Leonard came home to find a job. After a few months without any luck, he decided to re-enlist for another term. I made the decision to "sign up." My mother would then receive the grand sum of $50.00. That was enough for my mother and sister to get by.

I had a few problems to overcome if I was to be accepted:

1. I was only 16 years old.
2. I did not meet the weight minimum.
3. I was born feet first which did a hell of job on my arms and shoulder.

I was not able to raise my left arm higher than my shoulder. My solution: First I took care of my age by using some ink eradicator on my baptismal certificate, the one that I received from the Lithuanian Church. I simply changed 1924 to 1923. It was a sloppy job (I still have the birth certificate). The clerk at the relief office knew it was changed, but let it pass since many boys did the same thing. He knew that things were tough so he looked the other way and marked the application "17 years old."

To enter the ranks of the CCC the following procedures must be followed:

1. Apply at the local relief office (assistance office and later called, welfare and now called Human Services Department.)
2. Fill out an application and be interviewed by a clerk. You will then be told when to come to the relief office for a physical, Tuesdays in the Shenandoah Office, Thursday at the Pottsville office.
3. I was told to report at 10:00 AM at the Shenandoah Office. At 9:00AM on Tuesday morning I spent .17 cents on bananas and upon arrival at the office I found the nearest water cooler and filled up. I knew I would pass the weight test.
4. We were told to strip to our underwear. I wore one of Lenny's good government issued underwear shorts that he got free when he was in the CCC's in

Waynesboro, PA, and got in line. The doctor listened to my heart, looked in my ears and eyes, and asked me to lift up my arms. That's when he handed me my file and instructed me to stand in the left line where the same clerk who interviewed me stamped, "FAILED" on my application and instructed me to dress and to leave the premises. It was about noon when I noticed that the doctor left with instructions to the boys that were left in line that he would be back in thirty minutes. That is when "Plan B" formed in my mind. I then applied at the Pottsville Office and once again I went through steps two through four.

I was told to appear for a medical examination on Thursday. I arranged to get into the line so that I would be one of the last to be examined before the lunch break. I don't remember if it was the same doctor, but I was not worried if it was since he was only interested in my heart, nose, eyes, and ears. Of course I again failed and was handed the file and told to give the file to the clerk. Fortunately he was busy and I managed to maneuver around and get in the "passed" line. I handed in my file to the clerk and he told me that I would receive travel instructions and a ticket in the mail within a week. Boy! Was I surprised that I passed!

On January 6, 1941, I found myself at the Pottsville Railroad Station that was located in the center of town. Even though I had visited the station, this was my first real trip on a train. (Or I should say, *in* a train. I had many short trips hanging on the ladder of a coal car) There were two steam engines inside the building. They looked *huge when* I saw them pass by; I never thought they were as big as they turned out to be. The engines were hissing and making other wonderful mechanical noises. There were quite a lot of boys that were leaving for the CCC camps. The Frackville contingent consisted of twelve boys, Shenandoah had about eighteen, and a few from Ringtown, Mahanoy City, and Giardville, etc.

We boarded the train early in the morning along with the regular passengers. We passed through Reading and arrived in New Cumberland, PA, (Harrisburg) before lunch. We were met by some CCC guys and transported to the camp in a few army trucks. We were at the CCC Reception Center for two days. January 9th we again boarded a train and arrived at Camp 322, NF-1 in Edinburgh, Virginia, where we stayed for ten days. We finally found where our final destination would be, Montesano, *Washington!*

Camp 322 in Virginia was closing and moving to the state of Washington. A few weeks before our arrival, preparations were being made to move all enrollees present in the camp plus the new enrollees to Washington. They took this time to prepare a troop train for the trip. There were about 12 passenger cars and 6 boxcars. The passenger cars were sleeping cars and the boxcars were used as kitchens and for storage. There was a dining car also. The boys in each passenger car took turns eating their meals in the dining car.

The trip took about eleven days to reach Washington. We headed west. As we were approaching the Mississippi River, some of the guys who made the trip before when they served in a CCC camp in Idaho, said that there is a custom for all CCC boys to piss in the Mississippi river when crossing for good luck.

The toilets were always locked when the train was in the station and opened only after we left the station and were about five miles out of town. When the commode was flushed a trap door opened and you could see the railroad ties. When we began to cross there were three guys at a time pissing in the river. We had to hurry because there was a line waiting. Since I was one of the lucky ones to piss in the Mississippi I did have good luck in the camp. When we reached the prairies, the captain had the train stopped. We were told to get off the train and run north. We were told to kept running until the whistle blew, which was the signal to stop and return to the train. I keep looking back, the train seemed to get smaller and smaller. The captain did this because the boys had too much energy and were causing problems in the cars. The whistle finally blew and we began the trip back. This was done a few times during the trip.

One of the guys from Frackville, George "Mutt" Locket, did not smoke, but he sure loved to chew tobacco. It amazed me to see him stuff a big wad of "Indian Brand Cut Tobacco" in his mouth, which of course required him to have to spit great volumes of tobacco juice. Crossing the country in a steam driven train with the windows open gave Mutt a chance to play his little game. He would wait until the train was going around a sharp curve. When the guys in the cars behind, (the lucky ones who had a window seat) would have their heads out of the window getting some fresh air, Mutt let go with a load of brown spit. About 2.4 seconds later, they not only got fresh air but they would also get hot tobacco juice spit in their face and hair. You could easily see the boys who were the recipients of Mutts copious generosity of tobacco juice because within a few minutes, they were in our car having removed some of the brown stain from their person looking for the kid with his cheeks filled with tobacco. "What the f—did you want me to do? When I spit on the floor my friends would get very angry." Spit out the f—window they shouted. If you have a problem, tell them about it, I only followed orders. Besides, when I spit out the window there was nobody in sight for miles and miles."

We arrived at Montesano, Washington a sleepy town, population about 4000. Our camp was on a high bluff overlooking the town that was about one mile from our camp. We were fortunate that we were close enough to town that we could walk to town on weekends.

We were issued sheets, pillow and blanket, and taught how to make the bed Army-style. I soon learned the necessity of a tight, neat bed, a properly hung barracks bag, a properly positioned foot locker, in order to be ready for open barracks inspection held every morning before work call. An improper made bed would be ripped apart and K.P. (kitchen Police) duty would be given. The camp had five barracks each holding 50 boys. These were wooden, barn-like structures without insulation. They were heated with wood burning stoves, three to a barrack. In its previous life, the stove was a large steel oil barrel. Both ends were cut out and a heavy cast iron door was attached to the front. The back consisted of a steel plate with a hole for the smoke stack that ran up through the roof. Since wood was plentiful, that was the only source of fuel.

Before lights out, the stove was filled with large pieces of wood. I loved to hear the wood crackling and it sure smelled good. The fire was so hot that after the lights were out, the entire stove, including about half of the smoke stack, was a ruby red color. The washroom and the latrines were located in an attached shed in the center of the building. During the night, all would be quite until Mutt Locket, returning to his cot after using the latrine, spit his tobacco juice on the hot stove from about thirteen feet away and it would sizzle, sizzle. We did not mind the noise it made but the guys next to the stove had to put up with the resulting extremely foul odor!

The Mess Hall was a building similar to a barrack. Another similar building held the recreation room and a small canteen with a jukebox, pool tables, ping-pong tables and other recreational games.

The mess hall contained large wooden tables, 12 men to a table. The food was filling and adequate. It was solid, substantial, filling and probably better (or more of it) than most of us had been getting at home. After everyone went through the food line, you could go back for seconds. How those boys from Philadelphia could eat! We were issued two sets of clothing, dress and work clothes. In this part of the state it rains for weeks at a time, we were issued special rain gear. When I received mine, the pants went up to my armpits. The issuing clerk said, "Don't issue this boy a vest." We also were issued a jacket and a hat. This rain outfit looked just like the clothes the whalers wore when they were harpooning whales, and it sure kept a person dry.

All enrollees were assigned a job. Some cut trees and others worked on building lumber roads through the forest. I was assigned to work on an erosion project. The Wenatchee River was eroding the banks of farms that held apple trees. It was a sad thing to see the trees loaded with beautiful Washington apples falling into the river. As can be seen in the photo below, we cut the riverbank on a slope and planted special trees with deep roots that held the soil in place.

A foreman supervised each crew of about thirty-five young men. The foremen were Army veterans from World War One. Mr. Frye served as a colonel in the army. He was a very impressive man. He stood ramrod straight, always wore riding jodhpurs and riding boots. He was stern but fair. He was a father figure to all the boys.

One day, Mr. Frye was watching me work. He called me and said, "Son did you hurt your arm? I see tha0t you are holding it in an odd position" I told him, "it's nothing, I fell and my arm is a bit sore." "Tomorrow do not report for work, I will arrange for the Doctor to see you. Report to the camp nurse at 9:00 AM." The next day the Doctor asked me, "How in the world did you pass the physical? You have a birth injury, are you sure the doctor examined you?" "Yes he gave me a thorough examination, he checked my ears, eyes. nose and listened to my heart and lungs. I gave my folder to the clerk and he told me that I should be ready to leave for camp in a week." I had to report to the Commanding officer and he told me that he would make arrangements to send me home. I spoke to Mr. Frye and asked him if I could stay with the crew until I had to leave.

He agreed and told me that I would not work, but he put me in charge of the toolbox. Each morning, I distributed the tools, shovels, twin blade axes, etc. I also was in charge of making coffee. A large farmers milk can was used. I poured two large bags of coffee in the can and set it on a few stones around the fire.

Before Mr. Frye discovered me, I was assigned a doubled bladed axe. During lunch I would place the axe in a tree and use a file to get it razor sharp. We were allowed to place our name on the tool we used since we took great care of it. Soon a lot of guys (especially the guys from Philly, I don't think they ever saw an axe) would say to me "Hey kid, would you sharpen my axe?" After a month had passed and I was still in the camp, the warehouse clerk in the camp was discharged and Mr. Frye arranged for me to be promoted to the position. He told the Captain that I was very knowledgeable, not only with tools, but with all the supplies that were on the job.

There were three ranks in the CCC, enrollee, assistant leader and leader. Enrollee was paid $30.00, assistant leader was paid $36.00 and a leader $45.00. I was made a **Leader and was paid $45.00!** All of this would not have been possible if I had not been born feet first. So once again being born feet first was a great advantage.

The first thing I did was to report to the supply room with my two dress and two work shirts in hand and turned them in for shirts that had **three stripes on the sleeves!** With my new rank came new responsibilities. I knew that I could handle the warehouse without any problems. I was responsible for tires and oil for the trucks, nails, tools, ropes and about 300 other items. The inventory I received from the guy leaving was in great shape so the job was right up my alley. What concerned me was the fact that now I was required to be in charge of one of the barracks! I had to see that the beds were made properly, settle any arguments that may occur, see that enough wood was available for the stoves and act as a **Leader.** Well, I did not have to worry about being a leader. As soon as I came in the barrack, wearing my shirt with the three stripes on my sleeve, I was approached by three big guys (I was assigned to a different barrack) and they said "Kid, lets get something straight. We are not taking orders from a 120-pound weakling. Them stripes don't mean shit to us. Just keep your place and we'll get along fine." I said "I have no problem with that," and so I spent the rest of my term giving orders only to the guys that would listen to me.

During my time in the camp, I noticed how all the boys worked hard without complaining. They, like me, appreciated the job; even the pay of $1.00 per day was a great help to my mother back home. We received all new clothes, complete from socks and shoes to two different hats! The trousers were **all wool!** The shoes were all leather and everything was made in the USA! We received all the toiletries needed, the laundry washed our clothes, and we had clean bedclothes each week.

The food was great; it was "Good and Plenty." No one complained that every Friday, we had fish for dinner and cheese sandwiches in our brown lunch bags. I was pleased with the arrangements. Even though only 43% of the boys were Catholic, everyone in the camp observed the no meat rule on Fridays. I suppose that the National Committee for Separation of Church and State was not active in the State of Washington.

When "Hot roast beef with rich brown gravy" was served for dinner, creamy mashed potatoes and creamy rich butter was always served. Also an assortment of vegetables, and sweet white bread baked by the cook that morning.

When I went through the buffet line, the kitchen worker would put the orange that we received for dessert, kurplunk! On top of the mashed potatoes (the ones with the rich brown gravy). I must say I did not care for that. We received oranges a few times a month so I really didn't mind. It did not bother me when he put the apples in the mashed potatoes because I did not have to wipe the apple, but oranges are a different matter, you have to peel the orange and they only gave one paper napkin with each meal

The truck drivers were among the most admired guys in the camp. They did not need any stripes to get respect. Every Saturday they could be found at the truck compound cleaning their truck, the engine compartment, the cab and especially the body.

They used the best car polish that they could find; occasionally they used some of their own money ($5.00 per month) and bought a special polish so that their truck was the cleanest, shiniest truck in the camp.

This work was not required of them Saturday was a day off. They treated their truck as if it was their own. This was true of all the guys in the camp. I never saw anyone misuse a tool or do damage to any building or any property belonging to the camp.

I remember one guy especially. He was the camp blacksmith named Fortunato Cardone. He was from Philadelphia and about twenty-one years old. His blacksmith shop was even cleaner than some of the trucks. The floor of his shop was painted a light gray. Keep in mind that the shop was a blacksmith shop with a charcoal forge, anvil, coal tongs, and other implements found in a smithy shop. He liked his work so much that many evenings after supper, he would change into his work clothes, go to his shop, fire up the forge, and go to work. The camp had only a few lights around the camp, most of the guys were in the recreation hall shooting pool, in the barrack writing letters or just loafing around.

Walking down to the blacksmith shop you would hear Fortunato singing Arias from Italian Opera's, *"Libiamo, libiamo ne' lieti calici,"* (Verdi's La traviata). *"La donna e' mobile, qual piuma al vento, muta d'accento e di pensiero"* (Puccini's Rigoletto ACT IV) for a while I closed my eyes and I felt like I was back in fifth grade and Ms. Speidel was playing a record on her portable victrola.

He had a great tenor voice. He reminded me of the great Italian tenor, Enrico Caruso. I really thought he sounded better than Caruso; of course the Caruso records I heard were made with the technology of the time that did not treat his voice kindly.

After turning the corner you could see his shop with all the lights on and the fire in the forge throwing shadows on the walls. He had a couple of pickaxes in the fire. He would take one out and began forming a fine point by hitting it with a small sledgehammer. That's when he began to sing the "Anvil Chorus."

MONTESANO CHURCH

There was one Catholic Church in Montesano. Mass on Sunday was at 8:00 and 10:00 AM. Most of the guys went to the late mass. It was a sight to behold, about 125 guys walking into town for mass, even in the rain. We were not exactly very welcome at the church by the town folks. It wasn't because we never dropped any money in the collection (at five bucks a month, we had no money for God) it was because some of the boys did not act as good Christians when they were in town on a Saturday night. They made life hell for the young girls in town. They were not careful where they disposed of the empty beer bottles. We all know that the boys at mass never did these things; after all, they were Catholic! (Oh yeh!) If we came in early, we took up a good number of seats. If we came in right before mass began, the good Catholics would not move in the pew for us. We did not mind this treatment. Besides when these guys attended mass at home, they always stood in the back of the church.

I was in the camp for two months and did not have my confession heard. In those years we went to confession every month.

We received communion during mass only if we were to confession. (In those days, you had to fast for 12 hours before receiving communion. This meant, no breakfast!) I did not go since I only knew how to confess in Polish. One Saturday some boys were going to confession so I decided to go. I told the priest (who was very kind, he liked to see the boys at mass) that I did not know how to confess in English.

He told me to say the prayers in Polish and my sins in English.

In those days we would say the Act of Contrition before asking for absolution. He asked me what the prayer was that I said at the end I did not know that the prayer was called "the act of contrition" so I said "It's a prayer of promise to God to tell him that I'm sorry." I must say he was much more lenient with my penance (by far) then Father Garska was!

A few weeks later I had a most marvelous experience. A large group of boys in our camp were from Philadelphia, and many were of Polish decent. One weekend one of these boys visited Grays Harbor, a small town on the Pacific coast about 25 miles west of our camp. While there he found the church of **St. Peter and Paul, a Polish church!** He made plans to ask the Commanding Officer if he would allow us to attend the church on the next Sunday. There were many boys of Polish decent in the camp. We would need a truck to take us to Grays Harbor The C. O. said, "Absolutely not! He said we only wanted to get a free ride to the city. He went alone to see him the first time. One evening he put Plan "B" into effect. We had about twenty guys appear at the C. O.'s office and again ask him for permission. We promised that we would return back to camp in time for Sunday dinner. He then gave his approval on a trial basis.

We wore our dress uniforms. We arrived at the church. The people did not know who we were or where we came from. We looked like we were in the Army, but we wore olive-green uniforms. The Mass, of course, was in Latin but the sermon and announcements were in English and Polish. They did not have a choir, but some of the people sang. When the organ played *"Serdeczna Matko"* (Loving Mother.) We all joined in the singing. All the people in church turned to us and smiled. Some of the ladies and a few men cried. We were seated in various pews throughout the church, wherever we found space, so it was not planned beforehand to sing.

After mass, the whole congregation surrounded us in front of the church. They wanted to know were we come from. They insisted that we speak in Polish. All but one guy spoke Polish. They asked us please to attend mass next Sunday. After the third Sunday, our leader went to see the Pastor after mass to ask him if we could come to confession next Saturday and could he would write a letter on church stationary asking our Commander to grant permission to use the camp truck. The reason for selecting this Sunday was that it was Mothers Day. He asked the priest if he could also give us a small card to send home to our mothers, stating that we attended mass and went to communion for our mothers. We again promised the Captain that we would be back for supper.

On Mothers Day, we arrived at church. The church was packed. The front pews had pink ribbons signifying "reserved." We decided to all stand in the back. Some guys went up to the choir loft.

The priest, Father Adolph Badran came out before he was vested and announced, "Boys, please come to the seats reserved for you." Now, it was time for us to cry and some of us did. During the sermon the priest spoke about Mothers Day and us.

I'll try to paraphrase what he said but I know I won't give justice to his sermon.

"Look at these boys in the front pews. They came to me to ask if they could come to confession yesterday to honor their mothers. It was their own idea. They are over 3000 miles from home. They were not prompted by anyone; they just followed their hearts.

This is a good example of how well their good Polish mothers taught and raised them." During the sermon the ladies were bawling and most of the men were using their handkerchiefs and crying. It was very emotional especially since it was Mothers Day.

After the last blessing, the priest announced that the whole church was invited to the Polish American Hall for breakfast and that we were the honored guests! The club was two blocks from the church on the same street. The Breakfast was on the second floor. We were seated in the center of the hall. The priest misled us, it was not a breakfast, and it was a banquet! Kielbasa, smoked ham, home made horseradish, boiled potatoes, (Polish style, sprinkled with parsley), string beans and other trimmings including pies for dessert. There were a few short speeches. We were asked to stand and give our name and the name of our hometown. Everything went well. There was only one guy that was embarrassed, Fortunato

Cardone, the blacksmith who was sort of adopted by the Polish guys. Now Fortunato had a dark Italian complexion, we all waited until it was his turn. He stood up and said, (very fast) "F.J. Cardone, Philadelphia" and sat down. All the guys and the entire congregation burst into laughter. For the rest of our term, we attended this church. And many boys were invited after Sunday Mass, to a home for dinner. My closest friend was Stanley Romanek from Shenandoah. The same family always invited us. The family consisted of the Mother, Father, and "Busia," the grandmother. They had two married children who moved to the big city, Spokane, Washington.

After the noon dinner, Stanley would play cards with them. I did not know to play pinochle so I just sat and listened to Stanley speaking fractured Polish. I must admit that my Polish was more fractured than his since I did not come from Shenandoah, PA.

The grandmother did not eat with us and I never heard her speak. One Sunday while they were playing cards, I was talking about my family and suddenly, "Busia" said, "You come from Suwalki." I said, "No, I was born in Frackville, PA." She said, "I could tell by your accent that you come from Suwalki." Since this is the first time she spoke to us, I was amazed that she could tell by my accent that my mother came from the north east section of Poland were I guess they spoke funny. This experience with the church and my adopted family is one of my fondest memories.

I was discharged June 10, 1941. I thought about signing up for another six months. After all, I was a leader and the $45.00 dollars, full board and food was a good deal. But I was homesick to see mom and the family. I returned to Frackville to look for work. There was no work available, even for .50 cents per hour. On January 20, 1941, I once again entered the CCC. My friend "Mutt Locket" who was in Montesano joined me and we were assigned to Camp Co. 13932 Luray, Virginia. Since we were both in the Corps before, we did not have to get a physical.

At Luray, we were assigned to work on the famous Skyline Drive, which was great except for the fact that we were on the top of the mountains in the month of January and February. I of course was an enrollee and paid $30.00 per month. Early in March, we were notified that we were going to be transferred to camp Co. 350 Corbin Va. We arrived in Corbin March 18, 1942.

I spent about two months in the camp at Luray, Virginia. The camp was located on the Skyline Drive. We did mostly maintenance work such as repairing the storm drains, repairing the stone safety walls etc.

We were suddenly transferred to Number 350 N.P. F-1 that was located on the A. P. Hill Military Reservation, Bowling Green, Virginia.

The United States was preparing for war. Our camp was a series of tents. Six men to one tent. It had a wooden floor and wooden sides. The sides were three foot high. A wood-burning stove was placed in the center of the square tent. Smokestack went up through a hole at the peak of the tent. Since it was the middle of winter, the woodstove was used only in the evening. We did have one electric light bulb that hung from the canvas roof. Whoever was first returning to the camp after today's work was in charge of building a fire in the stove.

Not only was it very cold lying in bed but sparks from the smoke pipe would drop on the canvas with the result that lying on our cot, we could see a small red circle a fire on the tent. We took turns in extinguishing this "ring of fire." When it was my turn, I would have to get up and poke my finger in the hole, and using a circular motion the fire was soon out. Occasionally no one noticed the spark igniting the tent with the result that one of the guys would wake up because of the smell, and eventually put out what was a small hole but sometimes turn out to be the size of a small plate.

While assigned to this camp, someone in the office, while looking through the records found my record that stated that I was in charge of the supply warehouse at the camp in Montesano. I was called to the office, and was told that I was now going to receive three stripes that meant that I was a "Leader", and my new duties would be in the camp in charge of all the supplies. Of course the most important thing was that my salary increased from $30 to $45 per month. This was also another piece of good luck for the fact that I was born feet first!

FIRST JOB

During the first week in June 1942, I received a letter from my brother Pete. I was a member of the CCC stationed in Boiling Green Virginia. In the camp I was a Leader, which is the highest rank a member can reach. The pay was $45.00 per month and included, housing (even though it was in a tent all year long) clothing and lots of good food. It even had a health plan, doctor, dentist and one very young pretty nurse.

The letter offered me a job. A real one, with a time card and pay every two weeks. The Civilian Conservation Corps was open for young men who could not find a job. If one was found, the member would be given an honorable discharge just by showing the Captain a letter listing the job offer.

I was discharged June 8, 1942. I was given a rail ticket to Pottsville, Pa. The next day June 9, I reported to the office of the Northumberland Dress Company located at Spruce Street, Mt.Carmel, Pa. This was the beginning of my life's work in the garment industry or as it was commonly called "The Rag Business."

My brother Pete was employed as the sewing machine mechanic. (It was really the sewing machine repairman). The floor lady, Jean Pekarick, interviewed me. There really was no interview. She said, "Give the office your name and address and they will give you a time card. You start tomorrow. I'll take you to your place of work and you can watch the girl sort the work. You will do the same thing tomorrow." When I got to the table, a girl was separating cut pieces by color, tying them in bundles, and attaching a tag. The tag had information such as "Style # 256, Lot # 4, sleeve, 2 4/12 dozen." I thought "Hell I could do that!" I soon found out why a boy was hired to help in the "Assorting Department." The cutwork came by truck from New York City in large canvas bundles weighing a few hundred pounds. They had four canvas straps attached. They looked like my CCC issued belt complete with a large belt buckle. I did not have to pick up this heavy bundle; I opened the straps and carried the cut pieces to the table. The skirts were very heavy; I weighed about 120 pounds. I was a lightweight, but I made up for that by being 5' 11 ½ inches tall.

Three days after I was on the job, the owner/boss arrived from New York. He walked through the plant. I did not pay any attention to him. After an hour or so, the forelady Jean, came to me to tell me that the boss told her to let me go. He said that I was too skinny and that I could not lift the heavy bundles etc. She told me that she spoke to him and received permission to try me out for a few weeks. A few weeks and a few months went by and I was still working. I was paid .25 cents per hour. Pennsylvania law allowed any firm that qualified to hire trainees to be paid .25 cents per hour for 120 working days. Since I received $2.00 for an 8-hour day, I said to myself, "Self, you just increased your pay by 100%." In the CCC's I was paid $1.00 a day. Of course, I received free lodging and free clothes and most importantly, free food! After a few weeks, I was given a big break! The belt boy joined the army. I became, in addition to my duties as an asorter, the belt boy.

I will explain the belt boy task. In those years an individual motor did not operate the machines. A row of sixteen sewing machines was driven by one 3 horsepower motor. A long drive shaft operated the row of eight operators facing each other. A long single shaft ran the distance of the row. Each machine had a 12-inch pulley on the shaft with a round leather belt about 40 inches in circumference attached to a small pulley on a clutch. There was also a small round leather belt about 20 inches in circumference that operated the machine. The belt boy's job was to repair these belts when they broke. The operation to repair a broken belt or to shorten a loose belt had to be done without shutting down the motor. The belts are made of leather, a new belt would stretch, and the machine would not run at full speed. Since the operators were paid piecework, the belt boy was constantly asked to "Tighten my belt, it's slipping." This was done with a special pair of pliers. A metal clip shaped like a "C" joined the belt. The clip was opened, one side, about ½ or ¾ inch of the belt, was cut and the belt was punched with the pliers making a small hole to accept the C clip.

In the early forties, all the women/girls wore dresses. I must explain why I bring up this subject. The only way to repair a belt and to replace it on the pulley was to get under the row of machines and using a long screwdriver, take the belt off the large pulley to shorten or repair it. All this was done without shutting off the motor. It was to say the least, a dangerous operation. It was possible to lose your grip on the screwdriver and the screwdriver could fly and strike the operator across the other side. The belt boy could easily be hurt if he got his arm caught in the fast spinning pulley. I also had to take a lot of ribbing from the girls about keeping my eyes on the floor.

My brother Pete, the sewing machine repairman, had a very short temper. Some of the girls hesitated to ask him for help. They would say to me "I don't want to bother Pete, would you change the folder on my machine?" Or "I can't seem to change the length of the stitches. Could you do that for me?" After a few months I was doing all the minor adjustments on the machines. Pete didn't mind. It gave him time to do the big repair jobs. When I had time he would teach me how to repair the specialized machines, buttonhole, button sewers and other special machines.

After about a year, I was given the title of "Assistant Sewing Machine Mechanic." I also trained a boy to take over my duties as "belt boy." One day, Pete had one of the buttonhole machines in the shop. It needed some of the gears changed and had to be "timed." It would take a few hours to do the job. The boss from New York was in that day. He went to the shop and told Pete "Why are you taking it all apart, you don't have to rebuild the entire machine."

Pete tried to tell him (as patiently as he could, the reason why it was taking so long) but the boss insisted that he get it back in production. "*Now!*" The machine was very large. Pete found a large wooden box, picked up the shell of the machine and all the loose parts placed them in the box and delivered the box to the office, put the box on the desk in front of the boss and said, "You fix it, I quit." That's how I became the "Head Sewing Machine Mechanic of Northumberland Dress Co Inc. "

After Pete left. I automatically became the head mechanic. It was quite a job. It was very difficult for me to fill Pete's shoes. With the help of both the shop manuals that I found and a lot of prayer, I was able to do the work required and the boss seem to be pleased. I even received a small raise in pay. It was an entirely new world for me. After awhile, I not only was able to repair the various machines but I also learned how to actually sew the garments. Normally I would use a scrap of cloth to test the machine. The operator would say, "Yes, it sure works good on that scrap of cloth but it doesn't work too well when I try to make these collars." I took this as a challenge. After running a machine with a scrap of cloth, I then attempted to do the operation that the operator was doing whether, it was making collars or pockets or sewing a side seam. I got quite good at it. This knowledge later paid me great dividends in my "career."

Unlike my brother Pete, I tried to listen to the operators, repair the machines so that they could produce more garments, and thus increase the money that they earned. By doing this, the operators sought my help in many ways. If they were working on a new style and the price set was a bit low, they would tell me, "It is no use to hurry since we'll never make our minimum at this price." I would then go to the boss and suggest that he add ½ of 1 cent to the price so that the operators would try harder, the girls would make more money, and you would get additional production. Of course I would make the suggestion only when I myself thought that the price was too low. After a few months, the boss asked me to set the piece rates on some new garments. That means I would set the piece rate for each operation. I was now part mechanic and part foremen and eventually assistant manager of the factory.

Beginning in 1942, most of the men working at Northumberland Dress Co. were being drafted into the service. Both of our cutters were drafted. Jeff Frye of Kulpmont was our head cutter. He took his "short knife" (a special knife to cut notches in the fabric. It had a heavy handle and very narrow blade about two inches long) and stuck it in one of the wooden posts that held up the roof, and announced, "Don't let anyone remove this knife. I will remove it when I return home from the war." And damned if he didn't do just that! Since Morris could not hire any cutter locally, he was able to hire an older man who looked about 65 years old from New York City. He was named Saul. He was an excellent cutter since he was in the trade most of his life. He did have one problem; he loved to drink Scotch, A lot of Scotch! He lived in the Marble Hall Hotel in Mt. Carmel and went home to New York on weekends. After working on and off for about a month, he went on a binge and didn't show up for four days. Mr. Wapner had one helluva problem. The four cutting tables were spread with fabric ready to be cut, the operators were running out of work, and Mr. Wapner was being pressured to ship the garments. During my work as a mechanic, I also had to repair the cutting machines occasionally. There were two cutting machines at each table, one that held a six-inch blade and the other a twelve-inch blade. It depended on how high the fabric was spread on the table. The lots were usually anywhere from four inches to nine inches high.

I was called to the cutting room. Morris told me, "*Valee*, you are going to have to cut the work until we find a cutter." I watched as Mr. Wapner was leaving the cutting room floor. As he was walking through the doors into the sewing area, he had both hands on his head (which was shaking) and I'm not positive, but I think he was praying. Now I did not have any experience in cutting. After repairing a cutting machine, I did try it in the area that did not contain any parts of garments. This was my total experience. After saying a short prayer, I turned on the machine and began cutting on the lines of the pattern. Each "lay" was about 30 feet long and the fabric was 48 inches wide. During this time, I would occasionally be interrupted because a sewing machine needed some repairs. This gave me a much-needed break. It would give my hands an opportunity to stop trembling. One miss-cut would cost up to $1000 and probably my job.

I know it is much too late to make a long story short, so I will continue to give all the particulars about this part of my "Career." The operators on the sewing machines told me "You're probably going to get much better after you cut the third lot." After the second day, Morris told me to try to repair sewing machines during the day, "Go the "Famous Lunch" for supper, then work overtime in the cutting room and finish at least one lot so that the girls could have work in the morning." This worked much better but I did not get home to Frackville until 9 or 10 PM.

When Mr. Wapner fired Saul, it looked like I was going to have a steady job cutting. The Northumberland Dress Co. was located in an old large substantial brick building originally built as a silk mill. On the second floor of the sewing department a "sickroom" measuring about 10 by 10 feet was located. It contained a sink with a cold-water faucet and a cot that was used in case one of the operators became ill. I made a decision to use this room instead of going home to Frackville, which meant that I would not have to get up at 5:30 AM to drive to Mt. Carmel.

I told mom of my plan. She gave me a nice soft pillow and a couple of heavy blankets and I moved in. The factory janitor who worked the night shift would wake me at 6 AM. I washed my face in the cold water, used my electric shaver, dressed, and drove to the "Famous Lunch" uptown for my breakfast. Every three days, I would drive home so that I could have a bath. I could not take a shower because it was impossible to attach a showerhead to the round galvanized tub that we used to take a bath. Even if I could arrange a showerhead I know that it would be very messy and there would be water all over the kitchen.

My cutting career lasted for exactly 23 weeks. Mr. Wapner was successful in convincing a cutter who worked in Shamokin to work in Mt. Carmel at the Northumberland Dress Co. He was an older man and was very pleased to have a substantial upgrade in his salary. I was pleased with this change since now I was able to continue with my other after work activities. Not only was there a great shortage of cutters, sewing machine repairman were also in great demand. My "after work activities" consisted of repairing sewing machines in parts of Schuylkill, Columbia and Northumberland County's. My normal schedule was as follows: I would normally leave my regular job in Mt. Carmel about 4:15 PM.

I would stop at a factory in Locust Dale. It was located in a former schoolhouse and had about 40 employees. The boss was still at work when I arrived. He would have one or two machines that needed adjusting. I then continued on to Girardville where another factory that was in a former school building the manager's name was Frank Leonforte. After adjusting and repairing a few machines, I would continue on to Frackville in time for supper that was held whenever I got home. My sister Helen, my mom and I enjoyed the evening meal. When Helen began doing the dishes, I would leave for Pottsville to again adjust a few machines at a factory on Laurel Street. Believe it or not this factory had a contract sewing ladies corsets. Yup, corsets. I always adjusted the same machine. It was a machine that attached the strip of hooks and eyes on the back of the corsets. This is such a fascinating machine that I must go into detail and explained its peculiarities. The feed on the machine had to be adjusted perfectly so that the needle would not strike the metal hook. The machine had a "walking foot" which pulled the fabric along in a perfectly measured speed. The operator of the machine always tried to make the machine work "better" resulting in quite a lot of broken needle's and damaged garments but most of all, the bane of all factory foremen, *lost production!* I feel that you the reader probably know by now that I had the machine working perfectly by the time I left.

Like St. Peter, I also had a bunch of keys to many factories in Mahanoy City, Tamaqua, and I even had a key for Martin's Dress Co. in Frackville. I would receive a telephone call at the factory in Mt. Carmel from these various factories when they needed some repairs done. I would arrive armed with my bag of tools, the key, and a flashlight so I could find the light switches. The girls would leave a small message on a piece of paper that was placed under the "foot" of the machine. The note would explain the problems she was having with the machine. Occasionally, a message was added asking a few questions. Most of these messages were very similar such as: Are you under 25 years old? Are you also lonely? If you are, please call 773-2580 after 9 PM on Wednesdays. If you can, please leave a picture of yourself. Do not leave it on top of the machine but put it in the drawer. I also received other messages that said, "This time fix the S O B of a machine so that it would work at least a few hours before it breaks. I don't know how much you are paid, but whenever it is you're getting it's too much." This happened quite a lot at most of the factories were I worked in the evenings. I know that you the reader would like to know how I responded. Actually I did not respond to any of them. I was so damn tired working day and night I was just happy to get home and get under my "Pierzyna" (feather tick filled with goose feathers) and get some rest so I could start all over again the next morning.

The best part of this job was that all the earnings I made from this extracurricular activity was mine *to keep!* I gave mom my entire pay envelope. She offered to give me a few dollars but I was happy that I did not have to take it. I made enough money for my lunch and for gas for the car. I began buying shares in the *Broad Mountain Building and Loan Association* I began saving to be able to buy a motorcycle, then a better car, and also a few dollars in the fund to purchase a lot in the center of Frackville where I was planning to build a brand new house when I got married.

Most Saturday mornings I spent repairing the machines at Northumberland Dress Company that needed a complete overhaul. Usually there were approximately 10 operators working overtime on operations that were behind the production. The afternoon I spent in other factories in the area repairing the machines. Occasionally, I received a telephone call from Siswein's Furniture Store in Shenandoah. Of the five furniture stores in Shenandoah, Siswein's sold the most carpets. They were cut to size that necessitated sewing on a 2 ½ inch wide border. It took two special sewing machines to do this work. First, the tape would first be stitched on with a large machine very similar to the ones that are used to make various types of garments. Except this machine use a needle that was the size of a 10-penny nail. The rug was on a roll and lay on a huge table next to the machine that consisted of long rollers so the rug could be placed in the machine. After this tape was attached it was sent to another table with long rollers with another huge machine that was similar to a "Blind stitch machine" the type that was used to hem dresses and the hems of ladies slacks. Again the needle was the size of a nail. Both of these machines are very easy to adjust since all the parts were so large.

Meanwhile back at the factory, (the one were I was the assistant manager) I was a part-time mechanic and part-time foreman, I was able to hire a mechanic and an assistant so that left me as a full-time assistant manager. Most of my time was spent in setting piece rates, and then a few months later I was also put in charge of production. How in the world I was able to do this I never figured out. At first I thought the reason was because I was born feet first. But my mother told me the fact that you can do this job is that you were born smart. Well I certainly was not going to argue with her on this point.

My boss, Morris Wapner gave me many new tasks to reform. "Valee," "When you get some time, please go to my home, my wife is having problems with the washing machine. Repair it and come back as soon as you can." (He had no doubts that I indeed could repair it). After Mrs. Wapner found out how bright I was, she no longer asked her husband Morris, when she needed something repaired. She simply called the office and asked them to tell me that she has a job for me. Sometimes a job would be babysitting since she had three young girls ages 2, 4 and 5. "I have to go to the drugstore to get a prescription filled. I should be back in a half-hour." This created quite a problem for me. I told my mother that I don't think that I'm very bright, since I don't know how to get out of this predicament.

Since sewing machine mechanics were difficult to find during the war years, I decided to make one. Next to the factory building was a small automobile repair garage. Since we had a one-hour lunch period, I would spend some time with the automobile mechanic. His name was Peter Repella. He spent 25 years working as a mechanic at "Kuzo Brothers Ford." He decided to open his own shop after he left Kuzo Brothers Ford. He was about 45 years old and he complained that he was tired of lying under cars especially during the winter. I told him that I could find him a job where it was always warm and that he could wear clean clothes and that it was very light work. He said that he was interested until I told him that the job was repairing factory sewing machines.

After a few weeks he decided to give the new job a trial. I did all of this on my own without telling Mr. Wapner. I gave him a few manuals on the basic Singer single needle machine. From these booklets he could see that sewing machines were much simpler than an internal combustion gasoline engine.

He came into my workshop on a Saturday morning and he watched as I put a machine "out of time" and then proceeded to put it "back in time." I then asked him to time the machine while I went and did other work. When I came back to the shop, he had the machine in proper working order. The basic Singer 95-1 single needle machine used a leather belt about one inch wide that was punched with holes so that the belt could ride on a sprocket to transfer power to the shaft that controlled the movement of the needle.

After a few months of use, the belt would stretch causing the machine to go out of time. I asked him to install a new belt using the instructions in the manual. I did not show him how it was done. I again returned after about an hour and was very surprised to see that the belt was installed in the proper manner. This gave him a lot of confidence. After about two months of Saturday's, I was ready to tell Mr. Wapner that I found a sewing machine mechanic that could be my assistant. He told me "Tell him to come in on a trial basis and if you feel that he can do the job, we will make the job permanent."

The rest is history. Since I was only 21 years of age, I always called him "Mr. Repella." He worked at Northumberland Dress Company and eventually became the head mechanic. Later, I went into business myself starting with 10 employees, a little later, 60 employees, and then moved into a much larger building with about 150 employees. It was at this time that I asked Mr. Repella to come work for "Model Garment Company" of Frackville, PA, as the head sewing machine mechanic. That is when I began calling him "Pete." He worked at Model Garment until he was 67 years old. When he retired, he made a little speech before he cut the cake. He explained how I talked him into becoming a sewing machine mechanic after he spent many years repairing cars. He said, "Wally (I just couldn't see him calling me "Mr. Baran") told me that it would be a great career change for me and that I would no longer have to lay under cars during the winter in an unheated garage and that I could wear clean clothes and have light work. He never mentioned that I would have to work in the extreme heat of summer!" He was one of the best employees I had.

About twenty pages or even possibly thirty pages back in this book, I wrote a chapter on "The Tubeless Wonder." It dealt with the time that I brought to school my crystal set radio. I could repeat the whole story at this point, since it would bring me much closer to fulfill my plan to write a one-inch thick book.

Since I want you the reader to read this book to the end, I will ask you to go back the twenty or so pages and reread the chapter on "The Tubeless Wonder." There is a lot more good stuff in the last few chapters of this one-inch thick book, so continue reading.

In the year 1940, I was a member of the CCC and I was stationed at Montesano, Washington. While there, I took advantage of taking a few correspondent courses one of which was, *"Practical Radio for Beginners."* Each week I would mail my *answer sheets* to:

> Correspondent Study Course Service.
> CCC District Educational Office
> Fort Lewis, Washington

I began the course on February 5, 1941, and my final examination was sent on May 28, 1941. I received a final grade of A-. The dates and my grades are correct because I still have a three ring binder that holds the text and the answer sheets that were returned to me after being graded.

A few months after returning home from our honeymoon, while visiting mom at her house on Nice St., she asked my bride to follow her upstairs to my former bedroom. On three sides of the room there were tables stacked with over thirty old radios. Mom pointed to the radios and said, "Now these are all yours. Please make arrangements with your husband to remove them." To this day I still have one short wave radio that remains from my bedroom collection.

VOTING

My mother was born and lived in a small village in Poland called Wiziany. She did not actually live in the village, but on a small farm next to a forest. The farm was used only to grow some food and to keep a few chickens and other farm animals for the use of the family only. Her father's main occupation was working as a lumberman in the forests.

At the time, Russia occupied Poland. The Polish language was forbidden to be taught in the schools. She attended elementary school for four years. She was taught to read and write by her mother who also was self-taught. She also received some schooling from the parish priest while preparing to receive Holy Communion.

I wrote previously how she was smuggled out of the country so that she may join her husband in America.

As a child of about five, I watched my mother hang the American flag on our front porch on all the national holidays. She was an early riser. She waited for the sunrise. She then placed a kitchen chair on the front porch and hung the flag on nails that were on the molding of the porch to hang the flag. In the evening as soon as the sun was setting, she took down the flag. I remember that she folded it very carefully as though it was a holy object and placed it in the special box she had for this purpose. She had a piece of white cotton fabric that she spread in the box. She then covered the flag with the white fabric. She would never hang the flag if it were raining. She taught us to respect the flag. As a child the flag seemed to me that it was about twelve foot long and about five feet wide. I now know that it was an average size flag about three by five feet.

Mom was very proud of the fact that she was an American

citizen she took her responsibilities very seriously. She could never understand why some of her neighbors did not go to the polls to vote just because it was raining. Or that they were busy or they just did feel up to it. She often told us that if they had lived under Russian or Prussian rule, they would realize how great America is.

Mom was a Democrat (as was just about everybody on our side of the town) she loved Franklin Delano Roosevelt. In her eyes, he was almost as important as Jesus! She never missed a vote whether it was the primary or general election. She had a small problem with the primary. Since all the candidates were Democrats, she would discuss the various candidates with her lady friends a few days before she entered the voting booth.

I became a Republican when I was in the eighth grade; I was not successful in getting my mother to at least split her vote. I told her that there are a few very good Republicans. She remained a staunch Democrat the rest of her life.

During the first campaign of Gen. Dwight Eisenhower, I used all my persuasive powers to get mom to vote for Eisenhower. I brought home a sample ballot and explained to her how she could mark her ballot. "Put a check mark next to Eisenhower so you would be giving a vote to a great man who helped liberate Poland and all of Europe. In this way you would be voting for all of the Democrat candidates but you will give vote for Eisenhower." I also told her, "Mom, I occasionally vote for a particular candidate who happens to be a Democrat if I feel he/she would do a better job than the Republican candidate. Voting in this way is what makes America the greatest country in the world."

I even told her that voting for Republican is not a sin and there's no need for her to confess that she indeed did vote for a Republican.

I spent about an hour trying to convince her to vote for Eisenhower. I did not try to get her to change her registration from Democrat to Republican. I did not even hint of such a possibility. She listened to me very carefully and did not try to interrupt me until I was finished. She then told me, "Son, that's what's so wonderful about this country, not even you could tell me how to vote." She got up from the table signifying that our conversation was over and that I should never bring it up again.

In my early 20s, I occasionally thought that since I felt so strongly in the Republican Party that I should become active and possibly even run for office. After this discussion with my mother, I knew then that I could never be a politician since I could not convinced even my own mother to vote for a single Republican. As a consequence of this experience I spent the next 42 years in lady pants.

Many years later, when I was named Secretary of General Services one of the deputies in the department was a very talented politician. Pat Solano was a resident of Pittston PA, a community near Scranton where 90 percent of the citizens were of Italian heritage. While I am not quite sure, I was told that 90 percent of them were registered Democrat.

Pat had a similar experience with his grandmother as I did. First a little history. He Served in the Air Force during the Second World War. He flew many combat missions and was a real hero to everyone in Pittston. After his return home after the war, a parade was held in his honor. He sat in a large Packard convertible sedan, his chest covered with metals, the high school band and the Italian band were followed by all of the fire trucks and other convertibles holding the borough and other high officials of Pittston. It was truly a grand parade.

Standing on the sidewalk was a man that paid special attention to this young hero. He was the Republican city chairman of Pittston. He had no office, no business card he worked from his home where his wife allowed him to use the telephone occasionally. He held the position as the Republican city chairman for twelve years and he was not successful in getting a single Republican to win any office in Pittston. He mentioned to his assistant who was standing at his side "We are going to register that kid as a Republican and run him for the school board. Everyone in this town will vote for him."

Pat Solano was the first Republican candidate in Pittston to serve on the school board. He quickly became chairman of the school board. He also found time to serve as the Assistant Chief of Police for Pittston Township. At the insistence of the Republican city chairman, he became the new Republican city chairman. Throughout all of these years he was able to reduce the Democratic majority by 22 percent of the voters in Pittston! The Pennsylvania Department of Transportation decided that they could no longer operate without having Pat Solano on board. He served with distinction at PENDOT for a few years and later he was appointed as a deputy in the department. Meanwhile, he became the Republican County Chairman for his County.

He advanced very fast and became a member of the Republican State Committee; in fact, he was selected as one of the candidates for the high post of Chairman Of the Republican State Committee.

Another prominent nominee for the post was Cliff Jones, a close friend of Pat's. During this time Pat, decided to talk to his grandmother and to tell her that he may be the next Chairman of the Republican Party in Pennsylvania. He found his Grandmother seated next to the kitchen coal stove saying her rosary. "Nonna, on Monday of next week the State Republican Convention will be held in Harrisburg. I have been selected by members of the committee from as far away as Erie and Pittsburgh, Allentown, Scranton, Wilkes Barre and even Philadelphia to be elected as the chairman. Throughout the years, all our relatives in Pittston and the County have changed their registration to Republican. Your daughters Marie, Millie, and all the boys are now Republican. The only person in our family that is still registered a Democrat is you. There is still time to register you as a Republican. I do not want to see some of the big city newspapers in the state report that *The Chairman of the Republican State Committee, Mr. Patrick Solano's grandmother is a Democrat!* Could you do that for me?" Mrs. Solano sat quiet for a few minutes moving her beads and seriously thinking. Finally she said "Patsy, I'm so proud and happy that you have such a big shot job in Harrisburg and you have such big shot friends in Pennsylvania *but I ain't going to be a Protestant for nobody!"* And just like my mother she died a Democrat.

Reader, there is a happy ending to this story. Both candidates for the chairmanship were very popular throughout the state that made it very difficult to select one. Pat made many friends the evening of the convention when he stood up when nominations were called and said, *"I nominate Cliff Jones as Pennsylvania Chairman of the Republican Party."* The delegates went wild. According to the *Harrisburg Patriot News* the applause lasted a full 5 1/2 minutes. From that day on Pat had a lot of "chips" to collect for many years. In fact, he is still collecting even in this year of 2002.

DATING

Until I reached the age of about 12, I thought that all girls were silly and I certainly would not call one my buddy. They had much better handwriting, better grades in school, they giggled all the time, and acted silly. I did not have much use for them. I changed my mind when I reached sixteen I definitely thought that they had potential. Before I proceed any further, I must explain how I selected whom I was to ask for a date. I agree with the saying that "beggars cannot be choosers," however, I felt that I was a special case. Well, not me exactly, but my 1931 Chevrolet sedan. In most respects this car served me well. I had serious problems with the starter. It looked good on the car but it was very temperamental. Most of the time it worked well but occasionally it did not work at all. Actually my biggest problem was with the battery. I always used "weak" batteries. I didn't know what it was to purchase a new battery from Sears Roebuck or other reliable store. All of my battery purchases were made at Moe's junkyard located on the outskirts of Shenandoah. Occasionally, I was fortunate to be visiting "Moe's Used Auto Parts Store and Junkyard" when a few wrecks were being towed into Moe's Junkyard. (Yet another victim of the infamous Telephone Pole # 39 located at the sharp right hand turn in Maizeville on the road to Shenandoah.) Pole #39 was the cause of thirty-six accidents from January 1937 to January 1942. Pole #39 was not moved until sometime in 1944. This Pole was a godsend to the local politicians in getting elected. They all promised to have it moved. Of course after they were elected, like all politicians they forgot about their promise. Well anyway, even before the car was unhooked from the wrecker, Moe sold me the battery for $2.50. We both took a risk, I felt that it may be an almost new battery and I suppose that Moe thought that there was a good possibility that the battery case was cracked because of the wreck. If I remember correctly, we were both wrong. The battery case was not cracked and the battery was not "almost like new."

To get back to the reason why I selected the girl I would ask for a date, I had to find out if there was a slight incline in front of, or near her home. Since my '31 Chevy had not only a very temperamental starter, it usually also contained a weak battery. If she lived on a hill and if she agreed to a date I knew I would not have any problem in starting the car since I could "Ketch" it in gear. First, the car must be parked on an inclined facing down. I would place the car in second gear, hold the clutch in and release the parking brake. After the car gains some momentum, release the clutch and the motor will start. You then drive around a bit until you find another hill where you could park.

Since a date usually meant going to the movies, I often selected the "Roxie Theater" in Girardville. Since Ogden Street was directly across the street from the Roxie and since the street was very narrow, I had to park parallel which of course allowed me to "Ketch" the car in gear after the show. I would have rather gone to the "Garden Theater" in Frackville so that all my friends could see that I had a date. The Garden Theater was located at the corner of Oak Street and Lehigh Avenue. Turning right on Lehigh Avenue, was a good-sized hill going down to Chestnut Street. The only problem was all the cars on Lehigh Avenue had to be parked "toe-in" to the curb, which meant that I would have to back the car out before drifting down the street. This meant that the Roxie Theater was my theater of choice.

I had my first real date when I was 17 years old. Her name was Arlene and she was sixteen and one half years old. I remember that it was a Sunday and we had a date to go to Lakewood Park. I polished and cleaned my 1931 Chevrolet sedan extra special for this very first date. The car had what we now call a bench seat. As soon as Arlene took her seat, I knew it was not going to be much fun since Arlene decided to sit real close to the door. I decided that we should use the roller coaster first; I thought that when we went around the curves she might bump into me. Once again she sat way over on the right and she held on tight. Lakewood Park had one hell of a ride called The Whip. This was one way that I could get her to bump into me even if I had to pay for three rides. Luck was with me because on the third ride, centrifugal force pushed her right into me. When the ride stopped, she said, "I'm sorry I didn't mean to bump into you." That's when I decided to take her home.

I had quite a few dates when I worked in Mt. Carmel since the factory where I worked was filled with young girls. I had a date with a girl called Olga. Her ethnic background was Ukrainian. This fact should have told me something, but I dated her anyhow. She wanted to see a movie that was being played in Shamokin. It was the worst film I ever saw. After the movie, we went back to her home in Mt. Carmel. Her mother was in bed; the floor lamp had a 15-watt bulb that pleased me very much. The large sofa had many white doilies on the armrests and across the back. We sat quietly for about a half-hour. We had a discussion about her sewing machine; she asked me if I could speed the machine up so that she could earn more money. After another half-hour of discussions about the factory, I decided to take things to my own hands, I put my arms around her waist, she didn't seem to mind but she continued talking about the damn factory. I decided that the only way that I could stop her from talking was to kiss her on the mouth. Which I immediately did while I had the nerve. She said, "You had your lips open." I said, "I know I did, isn't that way we are supposed to kiss?" She said. "No." I then asked her, "Well, just how are we supposed to kiss?" She said. "You must keep your lips closed." I said, "Ok let's try it your way." I'm here to tell you that it was not much fun. She said that it was not very sanitary since your lips were wet. I told her that my lips were always wet. If they dry out, I wet them with my tongue. I hate dry lips. All my friends told me that you couldn't educate a Ukrainian, especially a Ukrainian girl. So I decided to go home to Frackville and surprise my mother by coming home before 11:00 PM on a Saturday evening, a single guy, eighteen years old! I was ready to forgive her for suggesting that we see this stupid movie, but after two very dry kisses, I decided to forget about her and her stupid movie.

After the disaster with Olga, I decided to try to date a girl I'll call, Sylvia. (Not her real name) (Her real name was Jenny.) I was repairing a machine in the row next to where Sylvia sat. I saw that her lips were wet and when they got dry, she wet them with her tongue. She was not what one would call cute, but hell, I was not much to look at either

After four refusals and a veiled threat to slow down her machine, she decided to give me a date. I asked her if she would like to see a movie (a movie would cost substantially less than a dinner for two at the Silver Bell Tavern on Third street). I read in the *Shenandoah Evening Herald* that a movie that was shown in the Garden Theatre in Frackville a year ago was now showing at the Roxy Theater in Girardville. It was a very, very sad love story. It was so sad that she was crying so much that her lips were real wet. I couldn't wait to get back to Mt. Carmel so I could park in front of her house. When I arrived at her home, early in the evening, I noticed that the street light in front of her home was burned out, and the two maple trees directly in front of the house, were filled with very large leaves. I need not go into the details, but I left for home in Frackville at about 3:15 am Sunday morning.

A few days later, I was told by some friends in Mt. Carmel that "Jenny" had a boyfriend in the Navy who was on a 30 day leave and was due to arrive in Mt. Carmel in a few days. I was also told that he was a 220-pound former fullback for the Mt. Carmel Tornadoes. I also was told that after he had a few drinks he would go out looking for guys who were classified 4F in the draft. He had great fun beating them up. I asked the boss at the factory to give me a week off since our family was moving again and I had to help my mother move to a new house. After the crisis was over, I decided that "Jenny" was not for me. That's when I began dating Rosemary. Rosemary had a pretty face. She was short, a little plump and was of Italian descent. After a few dates I decided to take her home so that she could meet my mother. Mom didn't seem to be very pleased to meet Rosemary. I decided to take Rosemary to her home in

Atlas. It was a Sunday afternoon and I was back home in time for supper. I saw that mom was very quiet. So I told her that Rosemary was Catholic, this helped somewhat and Mom said, "She is all right, but couldn't you pick one that is just a little taller? During this period, I experienced my first strike. All the union employees of the Northumberland Dress Company Inc. decided to strike for an increase in wages. All they wanted was more money but the owners did not agree. The strike lasted three full weeks. I of course was a company man and not a member of the union so I was expected to work every day. The girls on the picket line (it really was not a line, it was one big crowd) did not mind that I was working. In fact, they greeted me every morning with a smile and occasionally some of the girls would ask me to oil and speed up their machines so that after the strike, they could earn even more money.

I must say that just about all of the employees (what the hell, **all** of the employees) really liked me. Some of the older women thought I was just too thin with the result that some of them would bring me cheese cake, heavy bread spread with honey, some kind of concoction of milk and other items that would put some weight on my bones. They told me a young man should weigh more than 127 pounds. My reason for telling you this story is that during this strike, the ladies continued to bring me all of these goodies. Morris, my boss would say to me "I can't understand this, I'm the owner, the person who pays them their wages, and they hate me, but you they love."

During the third week of the strike, other members of the union from other factories in the area came to assist the employees of our factory to receive a favorable reply to their demands. Things really began to get hot. A few of the union members that arrived with their cars began blowing their car horns and others brought whistles that they used with abandon.

Some pounded on the front doors and others were screaming. In their frustration, they did not act as ladies. The windows of the factory that faced the street were placed quite high. I remember, I stood on one of the machine tables and looked at the action in the street.

I was shocked and dismayed to see the person who seemed to be leading the charge was none other than "my girlfriend, Rosemary." Her face was red and she was very flustered. I could not stop looking at her. She certainly was using words that she was not taught by the good sisters at St. Peter & Paul's parochial school. I suddenly pictured myself coming home three hours late from work; the spaghetti on the kitchen table did not have the usual vapors rising from the pot. My two kids, one of whom was wearing a soiled diaper, his nose was running and his face covered in tears and screaming almost as loud as his mother. Rosemary had no tears but she sure was screaming. She did not give me the opportunity to tell her why I was so late for supper. I wanted to tell her that I stopped at a factory in Giardville to adjust a few machines for which I was paid the grand sum of $45.00. Just then, I heard Morris asking me "What the hell are you doing standing on that table?" I must say, that I was happy to be awakened from this daydream. Eventually the strike was over and so was my love for Rosemary.

In June 1946 I purchased a used Harley Davidson motorcycle. Before I had the Harley I had an Indian 74. In those days there were few motorcycles in the area. I really enjoyed having a bike. Early one evening I was returning home from visiting my sister Veronica who lived in Hazelton. It was dusk and I was approaching the railroad under pass entering Frackville from the North. As I entered under the bridge, in a split second I noticed a very large truck that is used in the coal stripping pits. This type of truck is not allowed on the highways. When these type of trucks need to be repaired by welding, a special permit was required to drive to the Frackville Shops for repairs. These trips were only allowed to be made during daylight hours.

The truck did not have any lights or reflectors, which resulted in my collision with the truck. I was unconscious and regained consciousness about one mile north of Ashland State Hospital. I was sitting up in the passenger side of a two-door coupe. The driver said "Don't worry kid, were almost at the hospital." I remember spitting out pieces of broken teeth. I tried to move my right leg. I placed my hand below my knee and felt the broken bone protruding through my pants. I found out later that both bones below my knee were broken. I remember I did not feel any pain. On the second day the doctors told me that they were going to operate and place a steel plate to hold the bones together. I later found out that the doctors were considering amputating my leg below the knee. Thank God I had a good surgeon. Dr. Scicchitano of Mount Carmel decided to save my leg. The operation was a success. My leg was placed in a wooden box that was filled with ice. The leg was extremely swollen and a cast could not be put on until the swelling went down. I was in the hospital for 2 ½ months. I was sent home and walked about on crutches.

During this time I did not have any income. My brother was in the Navy so I was the sole support of my mother and sister. I was sure that the coal company would pay for the loss of my salary. I felt that they were liable since there were no lights on the truck. I spoke to the operators of the coal company if they could compensate me for the accident that I felt they caused. I was very naive to think that they would settle with me since all I wanted was my normal salary that I received from my place of work.

I was finally advised to hire an attorney and to sue the company. I had a few meetings with the attorneys and to make a long story short, the case never went to court and I never received any compensation. I did receive a "bill for services rendered" from the attorney.

I called my boss, Morris Wapner and asked if I could come to work using crutches. I convinced him that I could do the work. I had no problem repairing the sewing machines, but I had great difficulty in driving my car with the heavy cast on my right leg and trying to shift gears using my left foot for the clutch and the gas pedal. I used the hand brake to stop the car.

After another month the cast was removed and I used a cane for about six weeks. I was practically as good as new.

In the spring of 1947, I began dating a girl named Dorothy; she was as we say, well built. While she wasn't very tall, she certainly was not short. She had a nice body. I know I am being very course and crude. She was what the guys in Frackville would say, "She is built like a brick shit house." Now this is never used in a derogatory way. In fact it was the highest complement a guy could say about a girl. Of course, the guys would never use this term in her presence. Dorothy really had a nice body. When I was in my 20s most of the girls had nice bodies. She had a small waist, full lips and long hair. But what really stood out (pun intended) was her breasts (actually we never used the term breasts, they were called tits.) were very large. Not too large, but large. We dated for about six months. Our dates consisted of going to the movies once a week, spending a few hours in the living room with some light petting after her mother went to bed, visits to amusement parks and also occasional visits to her married sister's home. I had two tickets for the Anthracite Concert Association. The concerts were held in the auditorium of the Pottsville High School. After attending one concert she told me that she did not care for that type of music.

We dated on a regular basis. There was no arrangement, it was just taken for granted that we would have a date every Wednesday, Saturday evening, and occasionally Sunday afternoon. She was really strange. On a few occasions when we had a date, she would meet me at the door wearing a flannel robe and her head wrapped in a great big white towel. I said, "I thought we had a date tonight." She told me that she decided to wash her hair. She did not invite me in, so once more I really surprised mom by coming home before 9 PM on a Saturday night. On a rare occasion we double dated. We were in a restaurant eating hamburgers and fries, and out of the blue she said, "I'm not going to marry Wally." The first thought that came to my mind was "Thank you, Jesus." That settled something that bothered me for quite a while. I thought "How can I break up with her without breaking her heart." George, a guy that we were with asked her "Why won't you marry him?" She said "My mother worked in the factory for thirty seven years, and I do not want to spend my life having babies and working on a sewing machine. I would only marry a man, who has a business or a position as a manager in a large company that would pay him a large salary." George asked, "What if you don't love him." She said, "The more money he would bring home the more I would love him."

During this time, my boss Mr. Wapner called me into his office to tell me that the factory was sold to a firm in Philadelphia and that they would take over in three weeks time. He swore me to secrecy and once again told me how much he appreciated my work. He also had a great surprise for me. He told me he was going to increase my salary by the great fantastic sum of $25 per week! He told me my new employer would continue paying my new salary. The plant employed about 350 workers. Seven girls worked in the office using an old "Royal" typewriter and a few hand-operated adding machines they did all the office work. This new firm made children's clothing by the brand name of "Mitzi Frocks." They, of course,

made many changes in the plant. One of the first changes was to upgrade the equipment in the office. The employees would no longer be paid in cash. A new machine was purchased that not only printed the checks but also kept a payroll journal. This of course meant that they would no longer need seven employees in the office. Mr. Jacobs was a fine man. He told the office employees that the last three girls hired would be offered a job on the factory floor if they wished.

Coffee Break at "Mitzi Frocks"

Two of the three girls decided to work on a sewing machine. One of the girls was a petite and pretty girl named Irene. With a great amount of pleasure I taught her how to operate a sewing machine. Within a few months I spent a lot of time telling her I had to check out her machine to make sure it was operating properly. In fact I spent most of my time taking care of Irene's machine. Dorothy and Irene worked the same type of machine. Their job was putting a 3-inch hem in little girl's pretty dresses. Dorothy didn't seem to mind that I spent so much time at Irene's machine. After all she was not going to marry me anyhow.

During one of my visits to see Irene's machine, Irene asked me if I would go on a double date with her and her boyfriend also named Walter. She told me one of her girlfriends who lived in Detroit and worked with her during the war years in Washington D.C. was visiting Mount Carmel and she did not have a date. This was my first blind date. I remember it very well. We went for dinner to "Danny's Hide Away" near Danville. Two years later I again met her friend Helen and did not recognize her, that's because I did not spend much time looking at her during my first blind date.

I had a date with Dorothy on Christmas Day. We spent part of the afternoon visiting her married sister. During our visit, Dorothy asked her sister if she was going out for New Year's Eve. Her sister said "I'd really love to go but we can't find a babysitter for the kids." Dorothy said, "I'm not doing anything, I'll sit with the kids." While we did not have specific plans, I was sure we would be going out on New Year's Eve.

During those times, the plant did not close for Christmas week. When we returned to work, as usual I decided to check Irene's machine. I saw that she looked very sad and unhappy. At first I thought that her boyfriend, Walter, gave her a very cheap Christmas present, but that was not the case. Irene then told me what happened. During Christmas midnight mass at Our Mother of Consolation Church in Mount Carmel, Irene who was a member of the church choir was in the choir loft looking down at all the people coming in for midnight mass. She could not believe what she saw. Her boyfriend Walter was accompanied by a girl that certainly did not look like his mother. She looked like she was going to cry.

I left her but within an hour, I was again checking out Irene's machine. I had a great idea. I told Irene that Dorothy decided to baby-sit for her sister on New Year's Eve and I was not invited to help her change diapers so that left me with nowhere to go. "Why don't we both go out to celebrate not only New Year's Eve but also our newfound freedom." She said she would think about it and would let me know later that afternoon. I did not receive many presents for Christmas, but later that afternoon I received a wonderful New Year's Eve present. Irene told me she would like to spend New Year's Eve with me.

I began trying to get a reservation at one of the clubs in the area without much success. I finally was able to get a reservation at Genetti's downtown Hazelton nightclub if we would be willing to sit at the bar. I would like to say that we spent the evening crying in our beers but that was not the case. We did a bit of crying, Irene in her whiskey sour and me in my dry Martini. (Just kidding, we were celebrating our new freedom and the New Year.)

We did not date again until a few weeks later. I had my mother worried. She asked me if I was sick or if I had a problem at work. She could not understand why I was home every day of the week including Saturday.

Irene and I began dating on a regular basis. It's not that we tried to hide the fact that we were going steady, but we thought it was not necessary to make some sort of announcement. Of course after a few weeks everyone knew that we were dating and Dorothy didn't seem to mind at all.

After a few months, I knew in my heart that I would not be a bachelor very long. It was time for me to begin to plan to build a new home in the best part of Frackville that had a toilet inside the house. I had purchased a lot a few months ago. We spent our Sunday afternoons visiting new homes and dreaming.

During Thanksgiving week Irene was going to Washington D.C. to have a reunion with the six girls she lived with during the war. The week before she was going to leave, I went to "Sol Leavitt's Jewelry Store" in Shenandoah. Mr. Levitt was born in Poland in the same county as my mother. They were friends. What little jewelry my mother bought, was purchased from Mr. Levitt. I had intended to buy a diamond for Irene. Since I always try to be different, I decided to buy a platinum ring instead of gold or silver. The day before Irene left for Washington D.C. I gave her the ring. Irene said it was perfect timing since she could tell her friends that she's engaged to be married.

The day that Irene came back to work with a platinum diamond ring on her finger, all hell broke loose! The production in the plant dropped 23 % on that day. Everybody was happy for us. That is all but my former girlfriend Dorothy. Dorothy was unbelievable. She came to my workshop that was located in the center of the floor (the workshop was actually a steel wire cage with a wire door) and asked me to take her back. She said she did not mean to say she would not marry me. She said she never loved anyone but me. I was extremely embarrassed because the hum caused by the sewing machines was practically nonexistent.

I felt that I was on a stage and everyone's eyes were upon me. Dorothy began to cry and in a loud voice said, "Do you want me to get down on my knees?" **And she did just that.** This was one time that I really did not know what to do. I told her that I was sorry but I wasn't going to change my mind.

A few weeks after the new owner, Mr. Herbert Jacobs purchased the company he called me into his office. By this time I was not only "Wally the mechanic" but I was also assistant manager of the plant. He told me that I was doing a good job and that he was increasing my salary by $25 a week! Within a three-month period I had an increase of $50 per week. I was earning $165 a week, a very large salary especially in 1948. I made myself useful and I gave myself some duties that were not asked of me. I began setting piece rates, hiring new employees and settling grievances with the union. When Mr. Jacobs first purchased the plant, he would come Monday afternoon and leave for Philadelphia Friday morning. After a few months he would arrive Wednesday afternoon and leave Thursday morning. He called me every day to ask production questions and gave me orders. When he first came to Mount Carmel he arranged for his head floor lady from Philadelphia to be the manager of the plant. Millie worked all her life for Herbert's father and he insisted that she move to Mount Carmel during the week and she went back to Philadelphia on weekends. She did not like the fact that I was moving into her territory. "Herbie" (he told me to call him Herbie) said, "I know that you are doing most of the work, don't let her brother you."

Meanwhile, our new house that would soon be our home was almost ready for us to set our wedding date.

In a future chapter I will write in detail on our wedding, our new home at 222 South Center Street, the birth of our children, the construction of our new home at 200 Butler Road, and other topics that I know you the reader cannot wait to read. However I decided to go "fast forward" and finish what I call "The Dorothy story."

We were married June 18, 1949. After returning from our honeymoon, we both returned to work in Mount Carmel. Two months after we returned Irene somehow became pregnant. I was very happy. I did not care if it was to be a boy or girl, as long as he was healthy. I had Irene quit work and that's when she became a full-time housewife.

About six months later, Dorothy married Patrick Smoke from Centralia. She kept working in the factory. Within a year, I decided to go into business in Frackville. I opened a very small garment plant with less than twelve workers. I named my plant, "Model Garment Co." It operated only in the evenings from 5:00 pm to 11:00 pm. During the day, I still worked in Mt. Carmel and after a quick supper, worked until midnight. There were many very good sewing machine operators in Frackville that could not work during the day because in those days, day care schools were nonexistent. They did not have anyone to baby-sit their children if they worked during the day. I had no problem getting employees since we only worked in the evenings when their husbands came home from work and were able to baby-sit. It worked out very well. Within a year my brother Pete joined the company and we moved to another building since we now had 60 employees. I left my job in Mount Carmel and both Pete and I worked full-time in our own plant.

Later on I will write in more detail how our business grew. Suffice to say we were quite successful and spent most of our earnings buying additional sewing machines.

Many years later, our son Tony was accepted as a student at

Georgetown Preparatory School in Washington D.C. During his
first year, he would come home by bus for a weekend occasionally.
We would then drive him back to school on Sunday afternoon. Since
Interstate 81 and Interstate 83 did not exist, we drove to Harrisburg
then to Gettysburg and finally to Washington DC.

Returning home Sunday evening on one of these trips, we
stopped at Zimmerman's Hotel and Restaurant near Harrisburg for
Sunday evening dinner. This was our first visit to this restaurant.
Zimmerman's also had a large antique automobile museum attached
to the hotel, which was another reason why we stopped there. I
had just purchased a new Jaguar Mark 10 Sedan and we really
enjoyed the drive.

The restaurant was very large, well decorated, and had a fine
reputation. The tables were covered with fine linen, good silver,
and linen napkins. The ambience was perfect. The lighting was
turned down low and a man was playing smooth music on an organ.
The hostess provided us with very large menus, took our order for
drinks, and told us that to our waitress would be with us shortly.
Irene ordered a Manhattan, I ordered a Chivis Regal on the rocks.
Our son Joseph ordered a large Coke.

We were more than shocked when the waitress brought our
drinks. The waitress happened to be, Yup, **"Dorothy."** A few years
ago we heard that Dorothy had five children and was getting a
divorce. We hadn't seen her for over 14 years. She still had long
hair and full lips but her finest attribute was missing. She was very
pleased to see us; in fact she spent a lot of time at our table at the
expense of the other diners. During our dinner, we saw Dorothy
speaking to the organist. She returned to our table, looked in my
eyes and said, "I asked him to play **"our"** song!" We couldn't
believe it, I knew she was strange but this was ridiculous.

THE WEDDING

W e selected the 18ᵗʰ of June 1949 as the date for our wedding. There were many reasons for selecting this

date. Our home in Frackville was finished and ready for us to begin our married life. Weddings in the Mother of Consolation Church in Mt. Carmel were u s u a l l y performed on Saturdays. The week of the Fourth of July was always vacation week so we did not have to miss a week of work. The 18ᵗʰ of June was also my birthday, which meant that I would never forget our wedding anniversary. Also I really never had a birthday party with so many people present. We had two cakes to celebrate the occasion.

The wedding party consisted of the bride and groom, my brother Leonard as the best man and Irene's girlfriend Helen Goerke of Detroit as the maid of honor. Irene wore a beautiful wedding gown and Leonard and I wore white tuxedo jackets.

The nuptial mass and wedding ceremony was held at 11 AM. By Father Andrew the assistant pastor of the Mother of Consolation Church in Mt. Carmel. Since Irene was a member of the choir; the entire choir came to sing the mass. There were quite a few friends and also some employees from the factory were we were employed in attendance. Since we arranged a very small  reception for our family members to be held at Irene's home, we could not invite our friends to attend.

I was very influenced by Polish and Eastern European customs. As an example, none of the fathers I knew as a child ever owned or wore a wedding ring. Of course I do not now agree with some of the customs but I did follow them at the time. So this was a single ring ceremony. Another custom was the seating arrangement in Church during Sunday mass. The men always sat on the right side while the wives sat on the left. As I remember it there were only two married couples that sat together in St Ann's Church in Frackville. They sat on the right side. I suppose the men thought that it was manlier that way. When children were born they were named after a saint's day that was in the week that the child was born. Our first son Anthony was born in the week that contained St. Anthony's day. Yet another East European custom. My brother

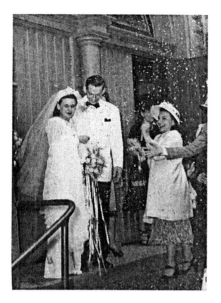

Pete was the photographer. This was not a custom that we followed; we chose it not only because he was a great photographer, but also he was working without any charge.

The wedding consisted of the two matriarchs of the families now joined as one, the mothers of the bride and groom. Irene's brothers and sisters and my brothers and sisters with some of their children composed the wedding party. We had about 19 people at the wedding reception.

The reception was held at Irene's mother's home in Mt. Carmel where yet another custom was performed. The mother of the bride would greet the wedding party at the door with a tray that contained a small loaf of bread, some salt and two glasses of wine. After partaking of the bread and salt and wine we were allowed to cross the threshold into the house.

When we returned to our home after our honeymoon, we decided to have a party for our friends who were not at our reception. Both Irene and I belonged to the choirs of our respective churches, Mother of Consolation of Mt. Carmel and St. Ann's of Frackville. The choir from Mt. Carmel had many members. They

charted a bus and arrived at our home at 222 South Centre Street in
Frackville.

There was a lot of room in our house because we had very
little furniture. The children's bedroom was completely empty with
the exception of a half barrel of beer in a galvanized tub and a few
chairs that we borrowed. We had a grand party; everyone at the
party had a good knowledge of the Polish language. The early part
of the evening was spent singing Polish songs that everyone seemed
to know.

We had a television in our
home in Frackville. It had a
seven-inch screen but I had
purchased a "plastic bubble" that
when placed in front of the screen
turned the seven-inch screen into
an 18-inch screen. The only
problem was that it had to be
viewed directly from the center.
Since it was a Saturday, the
programming began at 8 PM and
ended at 11 PM. In the early days
of television, in our area, we
were able to receive two
Philadelphia stations. Programs
were shown only on Friday and
Saturday evenings. During the week at certain hours, a pattern
was on the screen so that adjustments could be made to get the
best picture. Channel 10 of Philadelphia had a pattern with an Indian
chief head complete with feathers in the center and various width
lines radiated from the center to the top and sides. There were
three adjusting knobs on the front of the set and eight small adjusting
screws at the back. The antenna had to be placed as high as possible
and it looked like a huge letter "H" that was 12 feet long.

Most of the people at the party had never seen a TV in operation.
There is a Polish saying that it is very difficult for a group to stop
singing Polish melodies once they get started. Actually, they usually

stop when the barrel of beer goes dry. In our case, they stopped singing immediately after I turned on the television that began at 8 PM. (I was told that the Mt. Carmel group resumed their singing on the bus on their way home). Since our living room only contained a "parlor sweet" and one television set, everyone sat on the floor and watched the regularly scheduled program for Saturday evening which was "The Texaco Hour" starring Milton Berle.

HONEYMOON IN CUBA

We began our honeymoon trip on June 18, 1949. We drove to Florida and after a few wonderful days and fantastic nights we arrived in Miami. Again after a few wonderful and glorious nights, I read an ad in the newspaper of a package trip to Cuba. This was the beginning of our travels. A passport was not required; a driver's license, even though it did not have any photo for identification, sufficed. Irene did not have a driver's license, but she had something much better. She had our marriage certificate, which in those days was sometimes required to rent a motel room! My, how times have changed!

We arrived at the airport ready for our first trip out of the country. It was Irene's first trip by plane. As we walked to the plane parked at the edge of the Miami airport. Irene began having second thoughts when she saw the plane. It was an old Twin Engine DC 3 and some of the original US Army paint could be seen through the yellow color that it wore. When entering a DC 3 you have to walk uphill to your seat. I did not want my new bride to be frightened but I had noticed that while the pilot and his co-pilot were wearing parachutes, none of the passengers were assigned any.

The DC 3 makes a hell of a lot of noise and vibrates a lot. After it lands the oil leaks a lot from the engines, which is why they park it in an unused part of the airport. At first, I thought they were ashamed to have it parked next to the shiny Pan-Am, American Airlines and other real planes. After about an hour the plane landed at Havana's Marti Airport.

Again our plane was assigned to a parking place, way out, next to some planes that were being taken apart. After some time a bus came to take us to the terminal.

The terminal was really jumping. A few marimba groups playing great music; there were free rum drinks and hundreds of taxi drivers ready to take us into Havana. An employee of the tour company who spoke some English met us. Our group arrived at a very good modern hotel.

Included in the package was a dinner and show at the famous Copacabana Night club. The show was great. While the stage was under roof, the seating was all outdoors. A cast of what looked like over eighty members, including many long stemmed very scantily dressed beautiful girls. We had a great dinner and a great variety of rum drinks.

We were on our own for the rest of the tour. We had to make a decision about our finances since we did not own a credit card and we were 1344 miles from Frackville and gas cost 36.9 cents a gallon. We had a meeting on our finances and decided if we were going to make it home, we had to set aside enough money for gas first. After making sure that the car would be fed, we would spend the rest of our limited funds on cold cuts and day old bread and to visit attractions that were free, museums, parks, cemeteries etc.

We began using plan "A" while we were still in Havana. While sitting on a park bench one day in the merry month of June, we were approached by a middle-aged man who spoke English. He asked us how we liked Havana. I told him that we only saw a few areas where we walked and what we saw when we were on the bus to the nightclub. He then told us that for a few pesos, we could see all of Havana. He said if we would like, he would take us on the streetcar that covers the entire city and returns to the park. He looked OK so we paid our and his fare and began the tour. We rode about two hours.

The streetcar stopped at the end of the tracks near a very small village and the conductor told us the Spanish equivalent of "every body off the bus." We noticed some that got off, paid the fare and got back on the bus. By this time Irene began speaking Polish, especially when he suggested that we walk a few blocks

and go back to the
city by a ferryboat
that crossed the bay.
After I said a silent
prayer, I said to
Irene in Polish, "I'm
not worried a bit. He
looks like a good
honest guy and since
I am a lot younger
and stronger than he

Irene with Cuban guide

is, I can protect you." After all, I was now the head of our household and a few days ago I promised God and the Priest that I will be
with you in good times and bad and that as long as we have each
other, every thing will be all right." Sure enough, we got on the
ferry with a lot of local people carrying cheese wrapped in newspapers, chickens, ducks and one small goat. I said to Irene, "Irene
it must be market day. They are going to the city to get some pesos
so they can buy toys for the kids and some rum for dad." Irene
seemed relieved, and. after a wonderful but smelly trip of about an
hour with our guide explaining all about the buildings and parks, we
could see on the shore, with a complete history, including dates they
were built and who the dictator was at the time etc. The guide had
the attention of all the passengers, since he was speaking to us in
English. They hung on his every word even though they did not
understand what he was saying.

And sure enough, we landed about two blocks from where we
started our journey. I asked him if I could pay him for his service.
He said, "I would like to have just enough pesos for a bowl of
soup." I was very happy that we could give him the pesos even if
they came out of a lean purse.

Our trip back to Miami was without incident and we were happy
to start our journey back to our *new home* in Frackville. I calculated
on how many gallons of gas we needed to get back home. We put
that money in a special envelope. This way the car would be fed
even if we had to go without food. We did buy a few cans of beans

and we could sleep in the car if need be. For lunch I placed the can of Pork & Beans on the exhaust manifold of the engine. After a few miles we stopped at a roadside picnic table and had a warm lunch. We made it home in three days that was a record since we did not have any interstate highways. We arrived at our home on the fourth of July. The six County Firemen's convention was held in Frackville that year and their parade was going on. We had to wait until it passed to get to our home at 222 South Centre St.

What a wonderful surprise awaited us! Before we left we brought Irene's "Hollywood" bed and dresser from Mt. Carmel. The living room had a few pieces of overstuffed third generation furniture that we called "A Parlor Sweet." (Suite) a gift from my Mother. She gave us the set that was in her home on North Nice Street. The kitchen had a small table and three chairs that almost matched. When Irene went into the kitchen, she became very excited and called me. "Look what's in the kitchen!" There it stood, a wonderful brand new refrigerator! When Irene opened the door, another surprise! It was filled with food milk, cold cuts of meat, fresh vegetables, butter and even some fruit. We both sat down and cried. What a wonderful homecoming. My mother had all my brothers and sisters pitch in to buy us this wonderful gift. Not only did we have a brand new house that no one ever lived in, but also a brand new refrigerator full of food. Many years later when, Tony, married Sandy Best, they asked us to deliver some mattresses and bedding to their apartment in Allentown while they were on their honeymoon.

They had a big refrigerator in the kitchen that only held seven bottles of beer, period. We went shopping and filled the refrigerator with all the food they would need including some red beets that had large leaves which I put on the shelf so that when they opened the door they would fall out.

After we were home a few days, and I was back repairing sewing machines, we heard, from a friend, (?) a remark one of our new neighbors made after we moved in. "Well there goes our neighborhood." It took us about eight months to have these neighbors become our very good friends. I often use a quote that brother

Lenny wrote that worked for me all my life, "Let not praise alone thy ear unbend but sages those, and they are wise, who befriend the ones who criticize."

As we know, the United States had placed an embargo on Cuba after Castro and the Communists took over all the property and factories owned by Americans. For many years, citizens of the United States could not visit or do any business with Cuba. I read in the travel section of the *New York Times* that an arrangement was made with Pan AM Airlines and the US government to allow Americans to visit Cuba for a week.

It was a temporary lifting of the travel restrictions that were in effect. The arrangements were fly to Havana on a Saturday and the same plane would fly back to New York with the people that arrived the previous week. We were anxious to take this trip because we wanted to see the changes that were made since we were there on our honeymoon about twenty years ago. We asked our neighbors if they would like to go with us. "Great! We'll go."

When we arrived, soldiers carrying machine guns met the plane. An old bus was waiting to take us to the terminal for customs. There were no marimba bands or free rum when we arrived. The custom agents were very thorough in checking our luggage. They looked through each piece of clothing very carefully. After we finally cleared customs and Passport Control we again were bussed to our hotel. The hotel was the former Habana Hilton now called "Habana Libra." (Free Havana).

HOME

We changed our "house" into a "home" when we moved to, 222 South Centre Street, Frackville, on the Fourth of July, 1949. Irene and I were beginning a new life. God sure knew what he was doing when he put us together. The phrase, "We were made for each other" fit us to a "T." We really did not need a "Breaking in period." We were very fortunate that we were both first generation children born to Polish immigrants. We did not have to get accustomed to different foods. We shared the same faith. Both mothers-in-law were very pleased with the marriage. Irene quickly became friends with my sisters and brothers, and I was happy to call her brothers and sisters friends.

Our first home

I could honestly say that we got along well (well almost) from the day we were married. I spoke to a friend of mine who was married a few years and asked him if he could give me some tips and advice on how to live happily ever after. He told me I would have to change some of my habits "You'll have to be careful to replace the *cap* on the tube of toothpaste after you brush your teeth, and, oh yes, whatever you do, *Do not squeeze the tube of toothpaste in the middle!* They really hate that. One other thing,

Our second month anniversary

using the hand towel, wipe all the water from the bathroom sink." I asked him, "Is that all?" He said, "Yeah, the rest is easy."

A few days later we both returned to work at Mitzi Frocks. All the employees were pleased to see that we were back home. We both expected to be teased and of course we were. The girls wanted to know about our visit to Florida and Cuba, and the boys had a lot of questions on a different topic.

Since we both were now living in Frackville, I could no longer stay an hour or two after quitting time to take care of some unfinished work. Since I was on salary, it did not affect my paycheck. Irene said she did not mind waiting for me, but it was not fair since she would have to work when she got home-washing clothes, making dinner, pressing clothes and "cleaning" the house. I kept telling Irene, "It's a brand new house and it's not dirty. So take it easy."

One evening, after supper (I know it's supposed to be called dinner, but it was supper in Frackville) after Irene finished doing the dishes, she joined me on the sofa where I was watching TV. I could tell by the glow on her face that she had some news for me. She held my hand and said, **"We're going to have a baby!"** It was a very emotional moment. Throughout my writing of this book, I have been trying to write in a humorous vein (and sometimes it worked.) I am now sitting at my computer and I am having great difficulty in writing the words I would like to say. Having been raised without a father, I knew that I was going to be a caring and loving father to my child. I was very happy. I had it all. A beautiful wife, a new house, a job that paid very well, and now a baby!

In the next ten minutes I made my first important decision as a father to be. "Irene, I'll tell Mr. Jacobs that he now has to replace the "The very best blind stitch operator he ever had." I wanted Irene to become a full-time wife and mother. She wanted to work until Friday because she told me "I have a bundle at my machine that is half finished, I just can't leave it like that. I also will pick up my things that I keep in the machine drawer.

According to the doctor and Irene's calculations, the baby was to be born on June 18th. Our first wedding anniversary. My (our) *son* was born June 21st, three days after our anniversary. I was not prepared for what happened after I drove Irene to the Ashland State Hospital. The genealogist, Dr. Erlenbach, completely ignored me! *The Father!* I asked the nurse, "Where is the waiting room?" She said, "You are not going to wait. We will call you when the baby arrives." "But, I want to wait." The nurses in those days wore a tiny little starched cap on their heads. She had a stern look on her face. She looked like my seventh grade teacher at the Franklin School. Her eyes told me, "Do I have to call security?" I went home and I was very lonely since I was the only one in the house.

I called the factory early in the morning and told them that I would not be in since Irene was giving birth. I received a call from the hospital at about 11 AM and was told that the mother and the baby **Boy** were fine and that I could visit during the regular afternoon visiting hours beginning at 2 PM.

I arrived at the hospital at 1:30. I thought that I might be able to visit Irene. But it was not to be; a nurse told me that visiting hours begin at 2:00. I finally made my way to the maternity ward. There were no private or semiprivate rooms in the hospital that was built in 1882. All mothers and mothers-to-be shared the same ward.

Irene looked great. Irene did not see the baby. I rushed to the nursery to see my son. There was over fifteen babies most of which were crying. The little crib beds all had the family name on a small card. Looking left to right I finally saw the name "Baran." He seem to be bigger than most of the other babies. All the babies were wrapped tightly so that only their face was visible. I quickly ran back to Irene to tell her that he looked fine but all I saw was his face. I visited every day. On one of my visits to the nursery, someone said, "Look at the one marked, Baran. I don't think he is a newborn since he looks to be three months old."

I never met Dr. Erlenbach. He never bothered with the fathers of the babies he had delivered. I thought that the father's played a significant role in this whole procedure. He did not think so.

He made the following decisions without consulting the mother or father of the child.

> The mother was not allowed to help in the delivery of her child. She was given anesthesia. He made the statement that, "I do not want the mother to suffer any pain." Which meant the baby was delivered by using forceps.

> He did not believe that mothers should nurse the child. The baby was not brought to Irene every day since she was not nursing. I felt that the baby did not have the opportunity to be bonded with this mother.

He circumcised the baby without asking the parents. I felt that the parents of the child should make this decision.

Irene would have to remain in bed for a full ten days. She was not even allowed bathroom privileges.

The day before our son was born, on June 20th, my sister Helen Kiefer, gave birth to a boy at the Good Samaritan Hospital in Pottsville. I went to visit her and see the baby. I was surprised to see that the baby was very small. He was probably a normal sized baby, that's when I really knew that our baby was above normal in weight and size.

Irene's sister, Ann Heiser a registered nurse who lived in Reading, came to help Irene with the baby. Ann was a mother of a two-year old boy so she was a great help to Irene. Our son was christened with the name of Anthony but was called Tony by everyone in the family except my mother. She said, "Antoni is a beautiful name and he should be called by his full name."

Tony was a "colicky" baby. This meant that he did a lot of crying. Checking the dictionary I found that "colic" is not a disease or a birth injury, the cause is acute abdominal pain caused by various abnormal conditions in the bowels. His colic disappeared after he began eating baby food. I came to the conclusion that he had colic because his formula did not agree with him. He and his mother would not have suffered if his mother were allowed to nurse him.

After a few days, Irene called Dr. Thomas Hale our family doctor, to see if he could help her baby. Her sister, Ann, answered the door. "Well, hello, Miss Saukaitis. The last time I saw you was at the Frankford Hospital in Philadelphia where I was an intern and you were in training. How are you? Do you ever go back to see your friends at the nursing school? Do you remember when . . . . " "**Doctor, could you please look at my baby** (Tony as if on cue, began crying much louder) **I know that he is in pain and I don't know what to do.**" He told Irene "He has a little colic. He will get over it in a little while." The "little while" lasted five months!

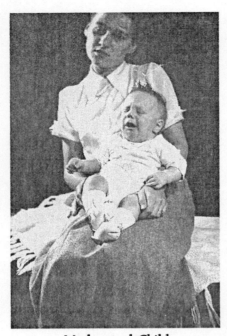

Mother and Child

Tony was a very light sleeper. One ring on the telephone would wake him. We could not pull the jack before going to bed because there was no jack to pull. All telephones were wired in. I took the telephone apart and wrapped the ringer with black friction tape. It then gave a dull sound. The telephone was near the kitchen. Irene often did not hear it. The only way she knew that we were receiving a telephone call was when Tony was awakened by the sound from his room at the other end of the house. She would pick up the phone and say "Hold the phone, I have to pick up the baby because he is crying." We received many telephone calls (especially late at night) from people who were looking for "Pete." I eventually found out that Pete was a bookie and we had his former telephone number. I believe that this early childhood memory is the reason why Tony rarely answers the phone on the first or even the fourth ring. "If it's important, they'll call back."

Before Tony owned his first means of transportation, he used to crawl on the floor all over the house. If Irene was in the bedroom making the beds, Tony would crawl into the kitchen, open the cabinet doors, and pull out all of the pots and pans that were stored there. After all of the pots and pans were removed, he removed the rest of the contents such as an open box that held the dishwater soap. I won't go into details, since you probably know what happened.

When Tony reached the age of nine months, he was a proud owner of his first four-wheeled vehicle. It was called a "Walker."

The walker did not have a steering wheel. It did have four wheels that swiveled. It took him *almost a full hour* to get the hang of it. He found out by using his feet he could go anywhere in the house. He would go into the small bathroom and come out without backing up. He could turn around on a dime! The entire first floor with exception of the kitchen had hardwood floors. They were perfect for speeding in his walker. Since he could not talk, he said to himself "Freedom at last! I could go anywhere I want."

One day, Irene went out to the trashcan and not realizing it, she locked herself out of the house. Tony was riding around in his "This." He only knew a few words and one of them was "This," He would point to the walker and say, "This." He spent most of his day driving his *this*. Irene looked through the door window and saw Tony driving all over the house. He went to the bathroom and unfortunately for Irene, there was a new full roll of toilet tissue in the holder. Tony took the end of the tissue in his chubby hand and drove from room to room until the entire role was spread throughout the house. She went to the neighbors for help. No one was home. She finally was able to get Mr. Knieb who lived across the alley from our home. He was able to break the lock on the basement door so she could rescue Tony.

When Tony was seventeen months old, our son Joseph was born. November 17, 1951. Same doctor, same hospital. The doctor made all decisions as when Tony was born. When Irene brought Joseph home, Tony was just starting his "Terrible Two's Period." Only in his case the "terrible two's" lasted almost three years. He loved his little brother. In fact he told Joseph, "You can use my car anytime you want." (By this time his *this* was now called his *car*.)

Joseph was a completely different baby. He was not colicky, he slept a lot, and did not care whether the telephone was ringing or not. As soon as I came home from work, I would hurry to his crib. I would call Irene and tell her, "He is not breathing." I could not see his little chest expand. I would put my ear close to his mouth and I could not hear him breathing. Irene said "Don't wake him, he is fast asleep." And of course he was. When he was in his crawling stage, he also managed to pull all the pots and pans out from the kitchen cabinets. With two very lively boys in the house, I had to put door latches high up on the basement door, our bedroom door, and even the bathroom door. If Irene was working in the kitchen, the boys would entertain themselves by pulling some of our clothes from the dresser drawers.

Tony sure loved sugar. When he was about three years old, he took the sugar bowl outside and sitting on the grass, began eating. I was able to find my camera and take a great shot of him with a handful of sugar in his hand; he had sugar on his lips and chin. Irene shouted at me, "Forget the camera Take the sugar bowl away from him. He's going to become ill." While looking through about 2000 old photographs for some pictures I wanted to use for this book, I found the photo. I also lost the photo. I'm hoping to find it before I finish this one-inch thick book. When Tony was about five years old, he saw children from the neighborhood ice skating at the end of the block in a low lying piece of ground that had a small stream. During the winter, the stream would overflow into this swampy area, ice would form between some of the small trees, and the small children would be able to ice skate. I took Tony down to this frozen swamp and he insisted right then and there that he wanted a pair of ice skates. I did not tell Irene but I went to Hack's Hardware Store and purchased a pair of shoe skates. If I told her what I was going to do, I knew she would say, "Are you crazy?" And I would have to agree with her. So I bought them before asking her. I told Tony that I would take him to skate on Saturday or Sunday afternoon. We could not go down after work since it became dark at about 4:30 PM. Tony could not wait to try out the skates. Since I bought them on Wednesday he would have to wait three days before he could skate. He drove Irene crazy. (Not really, it's just a figure of speech) He insisted to be allowed to skate that afternoon. She said, "You have to wait until Daddy has time on Saturday or Sunday. He carried on something awful! From her kitchen window, Irene could see the whole skating area. She finally dressed him in a snowsuit and put a jacket on top of his snowsuit. He wore a pair of warm mittens (they were attached with a cord that went through the sleeves so he could not lose or take them off.) He had to walk down our street with the skates on. She watched him fall a few times until he reached the skating pond. He was there alone; the kids were all in school. He kept falling on the ice. He would manage to get up skate about two feet, and fall again. Irene later told me, "I wanted to go down to help him but Joseph was taking his afternoon nap and I could not leave him." He was quite a sight. He had so many clothes on that he had difficulty wiping his runny nose on his sleeve because he could hardly bend his elbows. After about an hour, he began the journey home. He came in the house with the rosiest cheeks I ever saw on any child. "How was the skating?" "Mom, I had a real good time. I'm going to ask Daddy to bring Joseph with us so I can show Joseph how good I can skate."

Mrs. Chornack was our neighbor. She was a nurse and worked at the Ashland State Hospital. Tony was her first visitor of the day. She often worked night shift so this was a problem. He would appear at their patio glass doors, press his nose against the glass, and call, "Mrs. Chornack, Mrs. Chornack." She would appear at the door in her housecoat and let him in the house. Mr. and Mrs. Chornack did not have children and they were about ten years past middle age, so they loved Tony.

She had a special bench so that he could help her wash the dishes. Mr. Chornack was a hunter-small game and big game. Tony often had lunch at their home. He did not know it, but he often ate rabbit, squirrel, pheasant, deer, and even tasted bear meat!   Mrs

Pals

Chornack was a great help to Irene. Occasionally she would take Tony on the bus to Shenandoah just for the ride so that Irene could get some extra work done.

THE BABY

O n a beautiful Sunday afternoon, Irene, the boys and I decided to visit my sister, Verna, in Hazleton. We could tell when we entered her home, that Verna looked very worried. She told us that her daughter, Elsie, has been diagnosed with multiple sclerosis and she was in their fifth month of pregnancy with her seventh child. Verna said she did not know how she would be able to take care of her new baby since her children were all very young.

After we returned home, Irene and I made a decision. Since our boys were beginning school, we had been trying to have a baby join our family without success. We were concerned that a little sister or brother was not going to join our family. Irene and I both came from large families and we wanted another child.

We decided to talk to Verna and ask her if Elsie may allow us to take the baby and raise the child as our own. Verna thought that that would be a good solution. We then met with my niece, Elsie, and her husband, Stanley and told them that we would like to have the baby live in our home. We did not speak of adopting the baby. We told them (even though it would break our hearts) that if her health should improve we would bring the baby back to their home. We asked them to think about it and that we would call them in a weeks time. She called and agreed to let us have the baby under the conditions that we mentioned.

Irene began getting some baby things together. We have a crib and high chair and many baby clothes, and we were happy that once again we would have a baby in our house.

The baby was born four months later and we were very happy that it was a girl. When she returned home from the hospital, we visited with her and saw the baby. Elsie said that she would like to keep the baby for a few weeks. When a few weeks passed, she told us that she changed her mind. She said that her older children would be able to help her with the baby. At this time, she was still able to walk but her condition slowly worsened. We could see that Elsie loved all her children. We knew that she would not give up the baby. It was a sad time for us.

THUNDERBIRD

I was the proud owner of a 1955 Ford Thunderbird. On a sunny, Saturday afternoon, I decided to visit my sister Veronica in Hazleton. Joseph was taking his afternoon nap and I decided to take Tony (who was five years old) with me. Tony asked me to take the top off the Thunderbird. It had a fiberglass top with two portholes at the sides that had to be removed by lifting it off the car. "Make sure that he sits close to you and not near the door," Irene warned, and after listening to a few more instructions, we left for Hazleton by way of Shenandoah and Sheppton. My sister lived on a very small hill. While we were visiting, I noticed that Tony must have been bored and went outside. I came out the back door and looking at the street I noticed that my car was gone! I went to the street and looked down the hill and the Thunderbird was parked partly under a cement truck that was pouring a concrete sidewalk in front of a house down the street. I ran down to the car and saw that Tony was on the floor in on the passenger side of the car. "Daddy, I ruined your car." It seems he moved the gearshift lever out of "park." It must have gone down the street very slowly since only the hood and the front bumper was damaged. The windshield was not broken. I picked him up in my arms and tried to calm him. He was crying so loud he could not hear me asking him if he was hurt. He didn't even have a scratch on him. My boyhood friend, Joe Swingle, had a body and fender garage on Oak Street in Frackville. I called him and he came with his tow truck to take the car and us home. I kept telling Tony, "The car is not ruined. Mr. Swingle said he would fix it and no one would know that it was damaged." I had Joe drop us off on Chestnut Street so I could walk down to our home. After we came in the front door and Tony was running around, I told Irene what happened. "Oh my God, Oh my God." She picked Tony up and was examining him. "Irene, I checked him out real good. He is okay." I promised Irene that I would be much more careful in the future.

1955 Ford Thunderbird, the first car Tony drove

Many years later, Tony was in his first year at Lehigh University. Joseph was home from prep school. Since he was a senior he was allowed to have his little Fiat at school so he drove home for the Christmas holidays. By this time, Tony had a Porsche. It was parked overnight at the side of his fraternity house. He was loading his luggage (and laundry for mom to do) and he noticed that his car was leaning to one side. He looked at the passenger side and found that the two wheels were missing. A concrete block was under the front and back axles. He called home, gave us the news, and asked Joseph to pick him up. I told Joseph to take my Mercedes SL since it was heavier and had a little more room for the luggage. Even though the roads were clear of snow, there were some small patches of snow and ice on the road.

He left and while driving near the old "Red Church" near Orwigsburg, he hit a patch of ice on a curve and collided with a car in the left lane. A girl from Frackville who worked for Attorney Wilbur Rubright, Winnie Etherington, happened to drive by right after it happened. She recognized Joseph. After the ambulance took him to the hospital in Pottsville, she called me on the telephone to tell me what happened. Irene and I rushed to the hospital and found Joseph in the emergency room. He had a few cuts on his face when his eyeglasses broke. Other than that he did not have any broken bones. He looked at me and said, "I'm sorry Dad." "Joseph, the car is only metal and could easily be replaced, but you can't be replaced." He stayed in the hospital overnight so that they could take some x-rays and I brought him home the next day.

Mrs. Ann Lindenmuth, our neighbor on the north side of our house was a schoolteacher. She taught first grade at the Lincoln School. Tony was about four years old and he was yearning to be educated. It was very easy for Tony to get Mrs. Lindenmuth to agree with him, but getting Irene to let him go was another matter. As usual, Tony won the argument and Mrs. Lindenmuth took him to school for the morning as her guest.

Both boys were enrolled at the St. Joseph's Parochial School that was three blocks from our home on the same street. There were only four classrooms, first and second grade in room 1, third and fourth grade in room 2, etc. Because of their age difference, every other year they would occupy the same classroom. When Joseph was in the fifth grade, he and Tony as usual, came home for lunch. (They had a one-hour lunch period.) Joseph went to the bookcase and selected a copy of the World Book Encyclopedia marked "T", (like in telephone) with tears in his eyes. He was marking a page so he could quickly find it. Tony said, "Joe, forget about it. You'll only get in trouble with Sister. Leave the book at home." "No, she is teaching all the kids with information that is not correct. I'm going to show her the page with the correct information!" With that, with tears still in his eyes and a big heavy book under his arm, he left for the afternoon session at school. Irene, with tears in *her* eyes, watched them walk up the street. We really don't know what happened but Joseph was smiling all through supper!

One evening, Joseph handed me a letter and asked me to mail it for him on my way to work in the morning. The letter was addressed to the publishers of the World Book Encyclopedia. I asked him why he was writing to the publishers. He said, "There is a mistake in the section about the solar system and I'm going to ask them to correct it. "Joseph, could I see what you wrote?" "The letter is sealed and stamped." I said, "Joseph, I would really like to see what you wrote. We'll get a new envelope and stamp." He finally agreed. He went into his bedroom and continued reading the World Book; he was up to book "U." Irene and I sat at the kitchen table and read what he had written. I said to Irene, since he addressed the letter to the president of the Corporation, I doubt that it will get that far, but whoever does read it would probably say, "Both of his parents are college graduates and they dictated the letter which the boy then wrote in his own hand." Irene said, "This is a wonderful letter, he was letting them know in a very nice way that a mistake was made not only in the illustration, but the text as well.

In the year 2001, Irene was going through a box of old letters and she found the letter that Joseph wrote and a letter of response from the *Field Enterprises Educational Corporation*. The envelope also contained a copy of Joseph's letter that I asked him to make so that we would have a copy.

    The envelope:
    Field Enterprises Educational Corporation
    Merchandise Mart Plaza,
    Chicago 54, Illinois

    His letter:

200 Butler Rd.
Frackville, Pennsylvania

Dear Sirs,

In the 1960 edition of the World Book
encyclopedia, I have noticed an error. It
in the article about the planet Mercury. On
page 339 of the "M" volume, there appears the
following illustration:

INCORRECT

The Illustration should look like this:

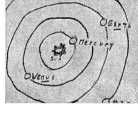

CORRECT

I hope you will notice from My drawings that Venus, and not the Earth, is second in order from the Sun. Therefore the planets are in this order: Sun, Mercury, Venus, Earth, Mars, ect.

I am notifying you of this mistake so that it will not be printed in a future edition of the World Book Encyclopedia.

Sincerely,

Joseph Baran

Age 10

Response letter:

Field Enterprises Educational Corporation/*Merchandise Mart
Plaza, Chicago 54, Illinois*

The World Book Encyclopedia/ChildCraft

Department of Research and Special Services

June 11, 1962

Joseph Baron (sic)
200 Butler Road
Frackville, Pennsylvania

Dear Joseph:

Thank you for your well-written letter regarding
THE WORLD BOOK Mercury article. Our research
department is always pleased to receive letters from
alert and interested students such as you, and we trust
that the following information would be of interest to
you.

While reviewing our 1960 Mercury article, our
Science Editor also noticed that the Art Department had
inadvertently reversed the positions of Venus and Earth
while preparing the drawing for publication. Subsequent
research confirmed the fact that the proper order of the
planets from the sun outward is Mercury, Venus, Earth,
etc. We of course took immediate steps to make the
necessary correction in the second printing of our 1960
addition of THE WORLD BOOK. We are enclosing a
copy of our 1962 Mercury article illustration for your
review.

You may be sure, Joseph, that our editorial staff
meticulously proofreads and reviews every article
scheduled for inclusion in THE WORLD BOOK. Despite

this careful pre-publication work, however, an occasional discrepancy may occur. Your thoughtful comments and clearly-drawn illustrations are certainly appreciated by our editorial staff, for such comments greatly assist our editors in their demanding tasks of maintaining THE WORLD BOOK's high standards of accuracy and reliability.

Thank you again for writing to us, and for so carefully explaining the discrepancy which you noticed. THE WORLD BOOK Editorial and Research Departments are always gratified to learn that our readers share our desire to produce and educational work which concludes only the most authoritative information. We wish you a pleasant summer vacation, and trust that you will continue to enjoy using THE WORLD BOOK ENCYCLOPEDIA in all of your research activities.

Sincerely yours,
FIELD ENTERPRISES
EDUCATIONAL CORPORATION
W. H. Nault
William H. Nault
Director of Research

WHN: C:
Enc

GOLF

During the summer, when they were about 8 and 9 years old, I decided that the boys should become acquainted with the gentleman's game of golf. Each Saturday morning the pro at the Schuylkill Country Club located in Orwigsburg, PA, taught about forty of the members children the fundamentals of golf. I made a big mistake, I should have *asked them* instead of *told them* that they would spend the next six Saturday mornings enjoying the fine game of golf. They each had a set of children's golf clubs and really great "Spike" golf shoes, Brown and white saddle style. They joined the other young kids at 8 AM. I would drive back to the office and work until about 11:30 AM then drive down and have lunch with them at the club. A tournament was held at the end of the program. When I came down to pick them up I really did not expect to see one of them carrying a trophy. Tony didn't seem to mind that I made him take these lessons. But Joseph, was mad as hell. He came in next to last. What made it worst, a girl was last. As a result, that was the last time he wore those beautiful small brown and white golf shoes and he never again touched a golf club.

The Georgetown Preparatory School sponsored a father and son golf tournament a few times during the year. The school has its own golf course on the grounds. I managed to play once with Tony. Joseph did not even show up to see me play.

Both boys were very interested in radio. I had many radios before I was married. I only saved one. It was a short-wave radio, in 1948 when I purchased it, (It was the only radio that I purchased new) It had the latest state-of-the-art technology. The boys found it in the basement of our home and began

experimenting with it. The radio required a long antenna. Their
bedroom window was about six feet away from our neighbor's
chain-link fence that was exactly 150 feet long. They ran a
copper wire from the antenna post on the radio and attached it
to Lindenmuth's wire fence. They were able to reach a few
short-wave stations and even a distant station in Pakistan! There
was only one small problem. If the radio was turned on, if Mrs.
Lindenmuth happened to be working in the garden with her
flowers, and if she touched the fence, she received an electric
shock. Yes it's true; she was shocked to be shocked! She told
Irene "Don't touch our fence, because you'll get a shock."
Eventually, the boys found out about the electric fence and they
solved the problem in short order. "Mom, tell Mrs. Lindenmuth that
we solved the problem and she would not get any more shocks
from the fence."

Early in June in 1960, my sister Helen called Irene and told her
about the 8th grade graduation ceremony that was being held during
the 9:00 mass in St. Joseph's Church. Joseph did not tell us that he
was graduating on Sunday. Since we were members of St. Ann's
church, we had no way of knowing that the graduation was taking
place. Joseph didn't seem to care about attending. He knew that he
had "Passed." During the graduation, Joseph received the highest-
grade average. He was first in his class. He received many firsts
that morning. If Helen had not called on Saturday we would have
missed his graduation.

It was tough for Joseph to be the "younger brother." He knew
he would be following his brother Tony for a long time. Tony was
accepted as a member of the First Form at Georgetown Preparatory
School in Washington D.C. When Tony received a car on his 16th
birthday, Joseph already knew at fifteen, that he would receive a car
when he turned 16 years old. Actually, Joseph had a better deal, I
selected Tony's car but Joseph was able to select the car he wanted.

I read a book many years ago titled *"My brother was an only
child."* I suppose that's how Joseph felt when he had to follow his
brother until he made his own choice of the college he wanted to
attend.

Thanksgiving, 1957, when Tony was seven years old and Joseph was six, we began a family tradition. We spent a long weekend attending the Macy's Thanksgiving Day parade in New York City. We had

MG Midget 1966

rooms in the Hotel Pennsylvania located at 401 7th. Ave and 34th Street. The hotel was across the street from Macy's Department Store. It was the perfect spot to view the parade. The day before the parade, we would visit Rockefeller Center to see the enormous Christmas tree but mainly to give the boys an opportunity to ice skate on the rink. We also took advantage to hire a Rockefeller guide and skating teacher to give the boys a skating lesson. Tony knew how to skate. Irene looked out the kitchen window when he taught himself how to skate on the swamp at the end of Center Street. (That's when Irene decided that he needed lessons) The teacher was from Hershey, PA. It was money well spent.

During one of these Thanksgiving weekend trips, we all attended a Broadway show-" The Music Man," starring Robert Preston. It was the boy's first Broadway show and it left them with a lasting impression. In fact, occasionally I hear Joseph singing (and occasionally humming) "**76 Trombone's**" la, la, la, La, la. When they were in their

Fiat 850 Spider 1967

middle teens, I was told, "Dad, I think we had enough of those parades."

NEW YORK CAR SHOW

Each spring, we would attend the New York International Car Show. The show was held during the last week in March or first week in April. It was a truly international show. If the boys were home for that weekend we drove to New York. One year, they took the Washington D.C. shuttle flight to New York City. They made their own arrangements to take a bus or taxi from the airport to our hotel. We stayed overnight and they flew back to Washington D.C.

Tony and Joe were very interested in radios. The spent a lot of time visiting Canal Street located near the Bowery at the lower tip of Manhattan. Many dealers that sold Army surplus were located on Canal Street. New York was safe in those days; the boys would make their own way to the surplus stores by using the bus or the subway. Irene was concerned for their safety. "After all, they are only fourteen and fifteen years old." They would come back to the hotel with boxes filled with tubes, resistors and occasionally, with an almost complete radio. Tony told me, "This radio cost the government over $1500. I bought it for $2.50." I said, "It looks like you made a great deal." "Dad put it down the basement on my table." Keeping the boxes together I added them to the growing pile of radio and radiophone parts. Irene said, "It's lucky that we moved to this much larger home. All this stuff would never have space at the first house we had."

During this time, we also opened a charge account for them at *Brooks Brothers Clothiers For Men and Boys.* Located on 54th Street and Fifth Avenue. Credit cards were very rare during those days. After they made their purchases, they simply said, "Charge this to Walter Baran's account." Brooks Brothers was a very fine store. Their Oxford button-down shirts were exceptional. While wearing their navy blue blazers with the shiny gold buttons and all wool trousers, no one would believe that they came from Frackville, PA

1957-FIRST TRIP TO POLAND

O ne of the most memorable trips we made was our first trip to Poland in 1957.
The travel section of the Sunday edition of the *New York Times* reported that for the first time the Communist government of Poland opened their borders to tourists from the West to visit Poland. The article also stated that arrangements could be made with the Polish travel agency "Orbis." The travel agency, like all other businesses (from restaurants, hotels and even shoeshine stands) in Poland, was in control of the government.

Orbis opened a travel office in New York City where I was able to get the necessary forms to apply for a visa, hotel rooms in Poland, and other information that was needed for travel in Poland. I applied to the Polish Embassy in Washington, D.C. for a visa to visit Poland in July of 1957. After a few weeks, I was informed that the visa would be granted after payment of the following fees: Visa-$55.00, $7.50 per person per day of stay. ($15.00 x 15 days $225.00) A total of $280.00. Orbis handled the entire trip, hotels, all meals, sightseeing with guide, and flight tickets with KLM Royal Dutch Airlines.

We left New York International Airport (now named JFK) on June 31st for Warsaw. It was a very long trip. A four-engine plane was used since Jet planes were not in-service by any airline. As far as we could tell, we were the only passengers for Poland. We made frequent stops for fuel. First stop was Gander, Newfoundland. We visited the terminal where we had a cup of coffee and a sweet gander (they did not have any Danish, only ganders). We also purchased two sets of earplugs. While the American Boeing Corp.

221

built the plane, it looked new, was very shiny and had all new seats, it was loud as hell, and even though we had perfect flying conditions, the plane shook a lot. After about two hours we were instructed to board the plane. The next stop was Ireland where some passengers left the plane and were replaced with passengers for Amsterdam. We landed in Amsterdam where we had to wait two hours for a small twin engine KLM plane to Warsaw. Again, we believed we were the only passengers from the United States on the plane. Most passengers were from Germany and other West European countries. We arrived in Warsaw 23 hours after we left New York. Many soldiers carrying rifles welcomed us. We were then escorted to customs. The Warsaw International terminal building was very drab. All of the immigration officials and custom officials were army officers. We had to declare all forms of foreign currency in our possession including traveler's checks. We also had to show them all of the vouchers for hotels and tours that came with the package. I actually had to open my wallet and count the dollars in front of the officer. He then looked at each traveler's check in our possession. Using a five-part form (complete with carbon paper) he listed all of the funds that we were carrying, the names of the hotels listed on the vouchers and other information. We were told that each time we changed dollars for Polish zlotys (zlotys mean goldens) the desk clerk at the hotel would deduct the cost in dollars on our pink form. This was done to prevent us from buying Polish Zlotys on the black market. The government bank rate of exchange was 24 zl for 1 dollar. At that time the black market rate was 100 zl for 1 dollar.

It took us about three hours to clear customs and have our baggage examined. We noticed that the other passengers only spent about one hour to be cleared. We finally entered the lobby area of the terminal. A young lady was holding an "Orbis" sign with the name Baran prominently displayed. We introduced ourselves to her and she arranged for our baggage to be carried to a taxi in front of the terminal. She spoke very good English. (We however, spoke very poor Polish).

We were shocked at all the destroyed buildings that we saw on the trip to the hotel. It was twelve years after the war, and yet many of the streets in the city were not paved. Many buildings and most of the churches did not have any roofs and only parts of the walls were standing. Later when we toured the city we saw quite a few churches that were rebuilt. In the vestibule of those churches, were "before and after pictures." The Cathedral of St. John was 95 percent destroyed. We were amazed that it was rebuilt exactly as it was before the war.

We arrived at our hotel, which was one of the few buildings that were not totally destroyed. It was the only hotel in Warsaw that was operating. The building held twelve floors. We were located on the 5th floor. Fortunately the elevator was operating.

Our guide informed us that a group of nine Polish-American tourists from Chicago were going to arrive within two days and that a tour of the country by bus was planned. That was fine by us since it would take a minimum of two days to get over the culture shock. Our room contained two beds, two chairs, a small table, and no telephone. We did not mind that since we had a full bathroom. The bed cover consisted of a blanket that was placed inside a white sort of gigantic, pillowcase and in the center of the bed, a diamond shaped opening about eighteen by eighteen inches was bordered in small lace so that one could see the beautiful blanket underneath. Since all of the meals were included in the tour, we ate in the hotel. Breakfast was always served "In the breakfast room" located on the second floor. (Most European hotels had a breakfast room). All other meals were located in the restaurant off the lobby. We were given a very large menu for dinner. Only the entrees that were available had the price penciled in. That did not mean that those items were available however. I selected a few that were not available. I then asked the waiter to point out those that were. The food that we received was well prepared and delicious. Every entree had the weight printed on the menu. "Turkey-125 grams, pork-144 grams," etc. Each table had a few bottles of mineral water and various soft drinks, none of which were cold. Ice was not available.

Since it was June, we opened the window that was facing the street. While lying on the bed looking out the window, a long wire made its way down from the window, above and stopped at our window. Since this was our first day in a communist country we thought that we were being "bugged," that is until we heard the radio in the room above us blasting away with "Big Beat" music. It sounded like it was a full band and drums were the featured instrument.

While walking down the street, we noticed a lot of new construction going on office buildings and apartments. Many were occupied. However, none of these buildings did not have a façade just raw concrete. Later, we did see a building that was being faced with limestone panels. We saw a few shops that were open selling kitchen utensils, a bookstore, a hardware store, etc. but we did not see any restaurants.

Finally the next day our "Fellow Travelers" arrived. The Polish Americans from Chicago. With the exception of one girl in her early 20s, the rest were in there 50s and a few were senior citizens. Three of the group were born in Poland and had immigrated to the United States before World War II.

The next day we began our tour. Eleven tourists, one guide/ interpreter and a friendly bus driver. For the next twelve days we traveled from city to city had all our meals together and got along reasonably well. When we reached the outskirts of the city, we passed small villages and well kept farms and it was a pleasure to leave the ruins of Warsaw. Here and there we saw some small villages that were destroyed by the war and some of the homes were being rebuilt. Driving through the small villages we saw large loudspeakers attached to the electric poles at every intersection in the town. Our guide told us that news and instructions from the "Party" were given to the people each evening. We did not see any of these loudspeakers installed in any of the cities. We also saw large displays when we entered and left the villages. The displayed consisted of about eight large red communist flags attached to a sign, which read "Long Live Socialism." These displays were set up at every crossroad between the villages. On entering a city the displays were extremely large and had about 25 large red flags. One guy from our group asked our guide "Who has the contract to make all those flags?" Our guide occasionally (and very carefully) made comments about the "Party." She had to be very careful so that someone should not report her to the authorities.

There were very few automobiles or trucks. The roads were used mostly by horse-drawn wagons. Some of the wagons were piled so high with hay that it was impossible to see the horse or the farmer. It was very dangerous since these wagons travel at about five miles per hour. We did not see a single tractor on the farms. On occasion we felt like we were in Lancaster County watching the Amish work their farms.

We left Warsaw early in the morning and arrived in the city of Torun located in the northwest section of Poland. We came to visit the city where the famous Polish astronomer, Nicholas Copernicus, the founder of modern astronomy, was born. In the year of 1530, Copernicus completed and gave to the world his great work *De Revolutionibus*, which asserted that the earth rotated on its axis once daily and traveled around the sun once yearly: a fantastic concept for the times. He made his celestial observations from a small portico situated on the protective wall around the Cathedral (as a Catholic priest he was assigned to serve in the Cathedral). His observations were made "bare eyeball," so to speak, and a hundred more years were to pass before the invention of the telescope. His theory was used to put man into space.

We toured the Copernicus Museum and the Copernicus University both located in the city of Torun. The next day our group left for the city of Poznan.

The city was only partially destroyed. It was a city of many hotels. For many years, Poznan was the center of commerce for all of East Europe. *The Poznan International Fair* (MTP in Polish) situated in the city center is the biggest center of international trade in Poland where trade fairs, exhibitions, and shows take place. The MTP calendar includes over 25 specialized events each year and attracts thousands of manufacturers, trading companies, scientific and research institutions from the entire world.

The next day we left for the city of Wroclaw formerly called Breslau when the Germans owned it, the fourth-largest city in Poland. We spent two days touring the churches, museums, the old square, and the many city parks. During our visits to the various cities, while walking in one of the many city parks, many people asked our guide, "Who are these people?" It seems strange to see eleven people following a young and pretty guide. When she told them that we were Americans, some senior citizens got up from the park benches, began to touch us, and occasionally kissed the ladies hands. "Conditions will get better in Poland now that the Americans have returned." We heard this comment wherever we went. We were told that many East Germans would visit the city so that they could take care of the graves of their families and to visit some of the homes where they lived. At the end of the war, the USSR carved up Poland. They moved the Russian border to the Bug River taking a large slice of Poland and attaching it to Russia. But they were very kind. They took a large slice of Germany and gave it to Poland. Many German families remained in what was once called Breslau.

Our next visit was to the small town of Czestochowa *Jasna Gora in Czestochowa* (Bright Mountain in Czestochowa.). The spiritual capital of Poland. Founded in 1632, the shrine withstood the attacks of the Swedish invasion of 1655. This great victory proved to be a tremendous boost to the morale of the entire Polish nation. It is a combination of Fatima, Lourdes, and other Catholic shrines in the world, containing a painting of the Blessed Mother supposedly painted by St. Paul. This holy painting enshrined at Czestochowa beamed as a lighthouse of hope during the painful years of national hardships and defeats.

We next visited Auschwitz (Polish Oswiecim) the town in southern Poland situated on the Vistula River about 32 miles southwest of Krakow, and site of the largest concentration camp and death camp run by Nazi Germany during World War II (1939-1945). The name Auschwitz is commonly applied to the complex of death and concentration camps near the Polish town of Oswiecim. The estimates of deaths range from 1.5 million to as many as 4 million. Jews comprised the largest number of victims, and Auschwitz had become the prime symbol that became known as the Holocaust of European Jewry; at least one-third of the estimated 5 million to 6 million Jews killed by the Nazis during World War II died there.

Large number of Poles, Soviet prisoners of war, Gypsies, Jehovah's Witnesses, and homosexuals also died at Auschwitz.

In 1946, Poland founded a Museum at the site of the Auschwitz concentration camp in remembrance of its victims. A guide told us that we were the first American tourists to visit the camp. Our small group purchased a huge floral wreath decorated with both the American and Polish flag. There is a small area named *Memory Wall*. This is a brick wall between two brick buildings. There was a four-inch thick mat covering the wall. The mat was used to stop some of the bullets that may ricochet from the wall. Many prisoners were shot here as an example to others who might disobey orders. There were many small wreaths attached to this mat and many candles placed on the ground. It was a very moving experience. We spent most of the day at Auschwitz and the adjoining camp Birkenau also known as Auschwitz II. We were all extremely depressed and two of our group became very ill. Most of you readers have seen photographs of an entire floor filled with shoes of the victims behind a wall of glass. There were also buildings filled with eyeglasses, prosthesis, luggage with the name of the owner, and one-half was filled with woman's hair and rolls of fabric made from woman's hair. While walking through the area I noticed a large mound of round clay tablets about three inches wide. Each one was marked with seven numbers. I asked a guide (he was once a prisoner at this camp) what they were used for. Each prisoner was given one of these tablets after he was completely undressed and told that he turn it in for a cake of soap and a towel. I asked him if I could take one home, he said "of course." Years later when I was working at the Department of General Services in Harrisburg, I was visited by a member of the staff of the proposed Holocaust Museum in Washington D.C. that was shortly to be built. Since I visited the Auschwitz camp on five different occasions and I occasionally spoke to various groups on Auschwitz in the Harrisburg area, they wanted me to share some of my experiences with them. I offered to give the Museum the clay tablet to be used in one of the exhibits. He told me that I would receive a letter explaining how this could be done. The letter instructed me to write a letter stating the date that I picked up the tablet, the names of witnesses, and other similar questions. I then had to swear before a Notary Public that these facts were true. I then sent the signed statement and the tablet by registered mail to the temporary office of the Museum. On my second visit to the Museum, I looked very carefully to see if I could see the tablet. Since I did not find it, I used the information telephone in the lobby. After giving my name I asked about the tablet. I was put on hold for about two minutes. The lady responding told me that I lived in Harrisburg and the tablet was the very first object they received that came from the German concentration Camp. She also told me that the exhibits are constantly changing and she was sure that the tablet was exhibited. I'm often asked why did I visit Auschwitz five times. On our many visits to Poland, friends asked me if they could accompany us to Poland to visit their relatives. If their destination was in the vicinity of Krakow, they also wanted to visit Auschwitz. A friend of many years, a member of the Antique Automobile Club of Poland, Stefan Arendarcyk who lives in Zabrze, only a few kilometers from the camp, was a part-time guide in Auschwitz. Even though we made quite a few visits to the camp, he suggested (almost insisted) that he give us a personal tour. During a normal tour, the guide did not have enough time to answer everyone's questions. This was a good opportunity to learn more of the tragedy of Auschwitz.

After spending three days in Krakow, we left the group since I had planned to visit my uncle Casimir Gibowicz who lived in Suwalki, a small town in the northeast section of Poland, bordered by Lithuania on the North and the USSR on the East. Since we had four days left on the tour we received train schedules and other information at the hotel about making this long trip. We sent a telegram to my uncle not knowing whether he would receive it. As it happens, he did not receive the telegram.

We arrived at the railroad station in Krakow with our luggage and headed for the ticket counter. Since this was our first trip abroad we soon realized that we had too much luggage. We were struggling with two large bags, one train case, and a small bag. Fortunately, a porter who asked if he could assist us approached us. He also asked *Czy masz Zielone?* (Do you have greens? That is, dollars).

In 1957, a one-dollar bill would buy enough food for a week. It was pure chaos at the ticket counter: A crowd of people trying to purchase tickets, and members of their families carrying flowers accompanied them. (There were about seven family members to each passenger). Our porter was a magician. He pushed and shoved his way to the first-class ticket window while carrying all the luggage. He had a stout rope that he tied to the handles of the large bags; put the rope over his shoulders that allowed him to carry the two small bags. I pleaded with him to allow me to carry the small bags. "Sir, I am here to serve you. A gentleman should not assist me in carrying part of his luggage." Since the express (I use this term loosely) train was scheduled to leave for Warsaw at 7:30 PM, I asked the porter if it would be possible to get tickets for a sleeping car cabin. We were both extremely tired and it looked like the trip would take many hours. He fought his way to the window and was told that all tickets were sold. He then said, "Follow me, and hurry." What happened later is hard to believe. It was a perfect plot for producing a Grade B movie! We left the station and followed him to the end of the platform. He began crossing the railroad tracks while he continued to look back to see if we were still behind him and kept shouting, "Hurry, hurry." The railroad yard was very dark. We crossed about five sets of tracks and we saw before us a single passenger car standing all alone. He approached the car still shouting, "Hurry, hurry." He found the lever that opened the door leading to the steps. He climbed aboard and invited us to go in. He opened the door to the first cabin, put down the luggage, and showed us how to operate the pair of door locks. It was very dark in the cabin. He then gave us his final instructions. "After you close both locks, pull down the two window shades. And do not unlock the doors no matter what happens." He informed us that this car would be attached to the express train leaving for Warsaw. I did not say anything to Irene since I did not want to interrupt her prayers, but I believe I was more frightened than she was. I found out later that she was not praying. She was telling God, "God, why are you allowing this to happened to me? I know I married him for better or worse, but this is ridiculous."

We sat very quietly for about a half-hour, when we heard a

steam engine going by and we felt a strong bump. I told Irene "It's not a train wreck, we're getting hooked to the engine." A short time later, another bump and within a few minutes the lights came on in our cabin. The room contained two bunk beds and a small sink in a corner. After about fifteen minutes, the stampede began. Loud voices, baggage being thrown about, and someone was trying to open our door. They began very quietly and later began pounding and kicking the door. They were calling for a conductor to assist them. I do not believe that they found him. There was a lot of shouting and cursing while we sat very quietly on the lower bunk bed. I said to Irene, "Irene, this is probably not the first time that this happened. I noticed that our porter knew exactly where the lever was to open the door to the car. Don't worry we will be fine." I was worried that if we ended up in Bulgaria, we would be in big trouble since I don't speak Bulgarian.

Finally the train started to move. After we left the station, I put up the window shades to try to figure out if we're going south or north. I wanted to go north real bad! The express train gained speed. Looking out the window I saw the names of the towns that we passed without stopping. I did not know where we were going but I told Irene "Irene, it's ok, all the names of the stations that we are passing so far, were written in Polish." I climbed into the upper bunk and could not fall asleep, even for 5 minutes. The tracks were not smooth and the train rumbled and swayed a lot.

Looking out the window, the sky was showing signs of morning. Within a half-hour we heard a conductor shouting "Warszawa" I immediately looked at Irene. She did not say anything but I could see what she was thinking. *"Oh God, what's going to happen now."* The train pulled to a stop and we heard people standing in the corridor next to our door. Again I knew it would be chaos. Many relatives were on the platform to greet the passengers. Everyone was excited. I heard the metal door open for the passengers to leave. I grabbed one large suitcase and the train case I told Irene "Irene, pick up your bags and follow me, fast! We had to fight our way to the metal stairs leading out of the car but no one approached us. There were no cousins on the platform to greet us with a bouquet of flowers. However someone who is even better than a cousin approached us. It was another porter who quickly picked up our bags. I asked him to assist us in getting tickets for Bialystok, which is a large city near Suwalki since I figured that the porter would not know of a small town called Suwalki. He was a big guy and he carried both large bags at his side spreading the people away for Wally and Irene to enter the ticket counter. He looked like a fullback for the Philadelphia Eagles.

Because of the lack of buses and trains, the stations that were operating were jammed with passengers but our porter informed us that the only train going north would be a local train and yes, the end of the line was Suwalki. We're fortunate to get tickets. We purchased some food and a few warm bottles of soda. Within about an hour we were seated with our entire luggage in a compartment that held three men and one-woman plus Wally and Irene.

The passengers in our cabin were very surprised that we were American. They wanted to know how we were able to visit Poland. They all had relatives in America. The woman was well educated and dressed rather well. She was the widow of a high-ranking Polish army officer who was killed in the Katyn Forest in Russia. I knew of the massacre since I read the book *Katyn, The Untold Story of Stalin's Massacre*. By Allen Paul. She was pleased to hear that a book on this tragedy was published in United States.

A few lines regarding the massacre in Katyn: In 1940, Stalin launched a deadly campaign of deportations from Soviet occupied Eastern Poland. When the deportations began, 15,400 Polish officers and noncoms, which had been captured by the Soviets the previous September, were waiting repatriation in three large camps. Among them were many of the nation's peacetime leaders. Within a few weeks, they disappeared. Then, early in 1943, the Wehrmacht stumbled upon the bodies of a third of the men in the Katyn Forest just west of Smolensk. Seizing the chance to split the Western alliance with the exposure of Stalin's immense brutality, Nazi propagandists cynically broadcast news of the massacre to the world. The Russians immediately announced that the Germans killed them. Facts proved otherwise and in 1999 the Russians finally admitted that they were killed on Stalin's order.

After discussing this massacre, the conversation turned to a lighter vein. The men started telling Polish jokes! These were the real ones. Most were political satire and quite a few of them were sort of blue. The train stopped in every village. At all these stops, a large display of red flags and a socialist message. It was not boring since we were traveling with some very good company. When we reached Bialystok all of our friends left the train. It was a short ride to Suwalki and we had the cabin to ourselves.

Suwalki was the end of the line. The railroad station looked like it was suffering from the effects of the First World War. It did not have any doors or windows. They were probably adorning a few of the houses in town. It did have a roof that did not leak. The waiting room did not have the usual benches. Approximately thirty-five left the train. We arrived about 10:30 AM. A few farmers waited for their families with their horse and cart. We set our luggage down on the curb of the cobblestone road and waited. We did not see any taxis about. However there was a one-horse cab exactly the kind to be seen in Central Park in New York. He came to pick up a woman who was obviously pregnant. I asked him would he please come back for us. I gave him the address of my uncle and he told me he knew him quite well and he promised that he would be right back. It was very quiet sitting on our luggage. There was no sign of life. We were in the middle of a forest and we didn't know how many kilometers the town was from the station. After what seemed like an hour, we heard the clip clop of the horse approaching. The town was about two kilometers away. He drove us directly to our uncle's home. The homes were on the street that closely resembled a town in the hard coal fields of Pennsylvania. Each home was on a lot about 50 by 100 feet. Most of the houses had four rooms and a path. I walked up to the front door and a small sign read, C. Gibowicz. I knocked on the front door and did not receive any response. We walked around the back where we saw a back porch that was turned into a pantry. The door was open so we walked in. I kept calling Wujek, Wujek (uncle, uncle). I was becoming very concerned. I knew that we had a flight leaving Poland in two days. I heard a noise coming from another room and in walked my uncle Charles. He was very very frightened. I kept telling him I am Walter your sister Antonina's son. I told him we sent a telegram from Krakow that we were going to arrive today. He did not receive the telegram. After a while I realized why I frightened him. Many young American men wore their hair "Crew cut style." My hair decided not to stand up. So I decided to use some hair pomade. I use the national brand *Brill Cream.* I used a lot more than a little dab. My hair was not only standing up but it was very greasy. I probably looked like a former German soldier. Since my uncle spent over two years in a German concentration camp, he had a reaction each time he saw someone who reminded him of a soldier. My uncle told me that the reason he was still alive was because he was a good tailor. He said, "The German officers wanted me to sew the seams of their trousers to make them skintight." He was very careful with his body language. He always stood ramrod straight. He tried very hard not to show any facial reaction in their presence. After the Russian soldiers liberated the camp, it took him many weeks to walk home. He told me he occasionally was given a ride by an army truck but mostly he walked. When he walked into his home, his wife did not recognize him. There is one story that he told me that needs to be told. After he was home, his wife bought a piglet that they kept in their backyard. There was so much confusion right after the war that various soldiers would walk through the town. One day a German soldier was walking back to Germany. He was disheveled, dirty, and his trousers were no longer skintight. My uncle was carrying a bucket of slop to feed the pig. The soldier took off his helmet, held it near the bucket and asked for some of the pig's supper. My uncle, the true Christian that he was, felt very sorry for the soldier and he poured some in his helmet. The soldier smiled and said, danka, danka. Thank you, thank you.

My Ciocia (Aunt), was across the street tending to their first grandson who was born two days before. My uncle was very emotional for us to be in their home and finally meeting members of my family. He was born after my mother left for America. They never saw or had a conversation with each other except by mail. My uncle excused himself and left the house. He went to the home of his son's in-laws where his son lived and asked if they would like me and Irene to be Godparents for this child. Within an hour he visited with the parish priest and also arranged to rent one of the two cars that were in the town. He then came in the house and asked us if we would be the Godparents. We had no intentions of staying overnight. In fact it was impossible since we had a return ticket to return to Warsaw on the train that left Suwalki at 7:15 PM. Usually a child is not baptized until it is at least two months old. I feel strange writing the word "old." When we went to see the baby lying at his mother's side, we asked, "How old is the baby." After the laughter subsided somewhat, they said, "He's not old, he was born two days ago." The proper way to ask the age of children would be: How many weeks, months or years does the child have? After the age of 50 it is proper to ask, "How old are you."

Within an hour the baby was placed on a large pillow. The christening dress was lying on top of the child and was held to the pillow with safety pins. The pillow was decorated with strands of dark green ivy vines. The ivy was placed on all four sides of this large pillow. We were driven to the church in a Russian Volga car. The owner and driver had very red hair. With exception of the new mother, the family and a few neighbors walked to the church for the baptism. I was told that since the child is a boy, the Godfather would hold the child for the entire baptism. I wanted to tell them that since I was born feet first and that my arms don't work too well that it was possible that I would drop the child. The godmother, Irene stood close to my side in case that happened. The child was christened and given the name "Christopher," the Saint of Travelers. Twenty-one years later we attended his wedding!

We spent about six hours in their home and after we were served dinner, it was time to leave for the railroad station. This time we arrived at the station by car. The train was only forty minutes late. My uncle was surprised that the train arrived almost on time. It took about five hours until we arrived in Warsaw. There were plenty of taxis available at the station. We arrived at the hotel and began packing since we were going to leave for an early morning flight back to New York.

The flight to New York was similar to the one that we arrived on. I will not go into details but if the reader would like, go back a few paragraphs and reread about the flight.

We arrived at the New York International Airport late afternoon. Tony and Joe spent the time we were away at their "Busia's" home in Mt. Carmel. Irene thought I was nuts, but I couldn't wait to be cleared by customs so I could get to a phone and talk to the boys. I knew that they missed us very much. Grandma answered the phone. I said, in Polish "Let me talk to my sons." It was only a minute or two but it felt like five minutes until Tony picked up the telephone and I said **"Tony, its dad!"** I'm going to now quote exactly what he said. "Dad, why are you calling me when I'm in the middle of my supper?" I just couldn't believe it. Irene asked me what he said. I repeated what he said and added, "I suppose he either missed his mother or Busia made one of her fabulous and delicious dinners.

POLKA MUSIC

I have a pet peeve that bothered me for many years. This may be the last opportunity I will have to reach thousands of my readers to inform them that the dance called "Polka" did not originate in Poland! As can be seen in the following paragraph, it began in "Bohemia" (The southern half of Germany and all of the Czech republic.) it was brought to America by immigrants from Germany and adopted by immigrants from Poland and other Slavic countries. I find no fault with those who enjoy this "Happy Music." In fact, as a youth I enjoyed dancing the Polka. I do however, object to the stupid, inane, idiotic and obtuse lyrics using very bad English and the Polish language.

Webster's New 20th Century Dictionary

Polka n [fr. and G.; Prob. from Czech *Pulka,* half step]

1. A fast dance for couples, developed in Bohemia in the early nineteenth century.
2. The basic step of this dance, a hop followed by three small steps.
3. Music for this dance, in fast duple time. (I checked three different dictionaries and each one spelled "double" as "duple" I wasn't about to argue with them.)

By this time I feel everyone reading this book should know by now that I am of Polish descent and that we traveled to Poland many times. I try to tell my friends that there are no "Polka" bands in Poland. They don't dance the Polka. There is a dance called the "Krakowiak" which is somewhat similar but is definitely not a Polka. We attended three weddings in Poland, one was in a small farm village, and another in a small city and one was held in the "Francuski Hotel" in Krakow, an elegant and expensive French hotel. The first two weddings we attended, the bride or groom were related to us. The third wedding was a college student. We became friends with him and his family and a few years later, we received a beautiful invitation to attend his wedding. We decided to attend.

Our son Joseph was spending the summer touring Europe, and since he had a new French Peugeot, we did not have to lease a car. We arranged for him to meet us in our hotel in Prague where we would visit with our friends and later drive to Krakow for the wedding.

Zbigniew Litwicki was a member of the "Szlachta" (Nobility.) We met Zbig in 1964. After visiting with him and his family, he told me that his forefathers were members of the Polish nobility. "I don't own a village or any peasants, I don't even own a small castle, but I do have the title." When I showed signs of disbelief, he went upstairs and brought down an old frame about twelve inches square. The frame held a parchment written in Latin dated 1642. The family surname, "Litwicki" was printed in large letters very prominently on the document. He told me that the parchment was handed down to the oldest son, through the centuries. His mother, who was a very honest woman, agreed with the story.

The wedding ceremony took place in the Chapel of the "Wawel" Castle in Krakow. He was allowed this honor because of his family history. Three cars were used to take the wedding party to the Chapel. A Mercedes was used for the couple, the second car was used for the witnesses and the third car was Joseph's. Peugeot. In the European custom, live flowers were tied to the roof and hood of the cars. Zbig arranged to have flowers put on Joseph's car and that gave us permission to enter the castle by using the moat bridge.

During the reception at the hotel, Irene, Joseph and I were

sitting with our backs to the double French doors to the dining room. Of course the French doors have French curtains, which were parted by a group of Polish American tourists. Later, they opened the door partway and asked me in Polish, "When is the orchestra going to play a Polka?" I told them, "This is a Polish wedding, and they don't play Polkas at Polish weddings in Poland." He wanted to prove me wrong, but was in a hurry to leave since his tour bus was leaving.

Polish Americans are convinced that Polkas originated in Poland. We occasionally had guests from Poland visit at our home and when they heard some of those stupid Polish lyrics, they were very embarrassed.

A friend sent me a copy of a "Letter to the Editor" written in one of the Polish-American newspapers from New York by a very angry Polish-American musician. He wrote . . . . Polkas are not Polish; you would not hear a single note of this kind of music if you visited Poland . . . . We have a rich cultural heritage and great Polish classical and folk music to enjoy and how the Polka is a big farce and that musicians like me just perpetuate it with our stupid songs about sausages . . . There is not a single "Polka" band in all of Poland. Etc.

The "Wall to Wall" type music stores in the large Super Malls in Warsaw and other large cities contain thousands of cassettes, compact discs, DVD's and music videos for all types of music including "Big Beat", Hard Rock, Country, Heavy-Metal, Classics and Jazz, (lots of Jazz) and South American music especially Tango's. The tangos are for the over 45 year old crowd.

Sadly, I feel that we Polish-Americans will have to endure these stupid lyrics until the next millennium!

GEORGETOWN PREP

W hile having dinner at the home of, Mr. John Walesky Esq. and his wife Albina, John asked me, "Did you make a decision on which prep school you are going to send the boys?" We had no idea to send our sons away for high school. We took it for granted that they would attend the local Catholic High School. "You have two very bright sons, while the local high schools are good, they would benefit greatly from a school with good teachers, very small classes and a school that would challenge them."

After returning home, Irene and I began discussing the good and bad points of sending the boys to a preparatory school. Irene had her mind made up, "We will not send them away, they will be going away to attend college soon enough." With later discussions with Mr. Walesky, I began to agree with him. His son was attending Wyoming Seminary located in Kingston. PA. He suggested Wyoming Seminary and a few others, The Potts School in Pottstown PA, Malvern Prep in Malvern PA and one or two others. Each year during the summer we visited with Irene's sister, Sister Pulcheria, a Felician nun, who was attending the Catholic University in Washington D.C. for credits for her Ph.D. in biology. I took the occasion to bring up the subject of a prep school for our sons. She thought that it was a great idea. I finally had an ally that would help me. Irene gave her view that she was opposed to the idea. "Irene, you're not thinking of the boys, you're thinking of yourself. Going to a prep school would be a great advantage to the boys if you can afford it. I strongly suggest that they attend a school where they will be better prepared for college." Since she lived in the Pittsburgh area, she mentioned a school near Pittsburgh and one in the

Johnstown/Altoona area. Later she mentioned the Georgetown Preparatory School on the outskirts of Washington D.C. Since we were visiting on a Sunday, I suggested that we drive to the school and possibly make some inquiries even though we knew that the office would be closed on Sunday.

Georgetown Preparatory School is an independent college preparatory school for young men in grades 9 through 12. Founded in 1789 by the Society of Jesus (the Jesuits) it is the oldest Catholic secondary school United States. It is situated on a 90-acre campus in Montgomery County, Maryland suburbs of Washington D.C.

Checking on the Internet, I found that presently 435 students are enrolled at Georgetown Prep. The student body represents 16 states and 18 foreign countries. Admission to Georgetown Prep is selective. 27% of the applicants for the classes of 2005 were accepted. The prospective student must submit an application, scores for the Secondary School Admission Test (SSAT) and three letters or recommendation.

After much discussion (and persuasion), a decision was made for our sons to attend Georgetown preparatory school. After contacting the school, we were mailed instructions, brochures and an application.

Tony did not have any problems being accepted. He made many friends during his four years at the school. He made very good (actually, excellent) grades in every reporting period. He was awarded the prestigious "Wills Roberts" gold medal at his graduation.

In the January, **1968** edition of the *"BLUE AND GRAY" The Student Publication Of Georgetown Preparatory School,* a three page article appeared,

HOW TO CONVERSE WITH A COMPUTER

An explanation of Prep's computer programming
by Joseph Baran

*. . . . the reason for these activities is Prep's new
"computer," installed at the beginning of January. The
students in room 306 are practicing "computer
programming," that modern-day phrase which, when
heard by most people, evokes a decision of little
bespeckled men in white gowns, sitting at huge panels
of buttons and blinking lights. The fact is, however,
there is nothing mysterious about computer
programming. It is simply the wording of problems
according to the rules of the grammar and vocabulary
of a language which the computer can "understand."*

*Father Murray has been teaching the basics of
programming to his math classes, and anyone else
interested, for over a year; but there was no practical
way for them actually to use a computer until now.*

*The machine they are using is not a computer itself,
but rather a Teletype machine, like those used in news
agencies for communication. It can be connected with
a central computer and a computer-renting company
in Washington by dialing the computers number on
the Teletype. There are at least 80 machines like it in
the D.C. area, all sharing time on the one computer.*

Even though the computer can work only one problem at a time, it operates so rapidly that each customer usually does not have to wait more than a fraction of a second for his turn. The user is charged for the actual number of minutes he uses the computer service. (Each month we received a statement from the school, 17 minutes computer time, 11 minutes computer time etc. I do not remember the cost.) . . . .

To have the computer work a program, one dials the computer's number on the Teletype. The computer answers by giving a tone, and asks for the user number. The operator types the number and the computer officially comes on, giving the time of day. It asks for the "language" to be used (in our case BASIC) and then asks "New or Old?" Which means, "is this a new program to be put in or is it one which had previously been stored in the computer's memory?" Programs must all be named for identification, so the next question asks for the program's name.

When it receives the name, the computer answers "Ready." The program may then be fed in on the Teletype. When the operator is finished giving the computer the program, he types the command "Run," which means "Go through the program and do what its says to do." If there are any mistakes in the program, the computer types out an "error code" which tells the operator what kind of mistake he has made and in which line of the program.

If there are no mistakes or if all the mistakes have been corrected, it types out whatever is in the "PRINT" statement in the program. In our previous example, it would print the sum of each pair of numbers. The

operator finishes by typing "Bye," after which the
computer shuts off, again giving the time.

You can request the complete article (which includes five photographs taken and processed by Anthony Baran) by sending me an SSAE (stamped self-addressed envelope) and I will send it out if I get the time.

During the graduation ceremonies, Joseph received the Gold Medal for, first in his class, and a Gold Medal for the highest average in mathematics. He also received other awards two numerous for me to mention here.

During discussions the boys, we told them that they could choose the University of their choice, as long as it was east of the Mississippi River.

Tony chose Lehigh University located at Bethlehem PA and Joseph chose Princeton University at Princeton NJ.

THE ROBBERY

I t happened on the Saturday before Christmas in 1967.
The *Thespian Guild* of the Fountain Springs Country
Club was scheduled to present the last of three productions of the
year by and for the members of the club. These "Shows" were
written and produced by members of *The Thespian Guild* to
enlighten, entertain, amuse, and to show the hidden talent of some
of the members. A member once told me, "It would be better for
the members if some of the talent would remain hidden!" Well
anyway, comedy was the theme of each show.

As a longtime member of the Guild and a former actor, director,
writer, and producer, it was my turn to write, produce, direct, and
have the starring role in this year's production.

Rehearsals were held each Wednesday in November promptly
at 7 PM in the basement of the clubhouse. It was my experience as
a producer/director to save the best act for last. I wanted the
audience to go home singing, or at least humming the musical theme
for the next four weeks after the show.

Since it was a Christmas show, it was decided for the last act,
we would do the "Dance of the Sugarplum Fairies" from
Tchaikovsky's Great Ballet, The Nutcracker Suite. Tom Goyne,
the assistant director suggested that men perform all the dances. I
thought, "What a Pregnant Idea." During the fall meeting of the
**"Thursday Evening—Five O'clock Golf Tournament
Committee"** to discuss the next year's schedule, the 19th hole
was filled with some very good prospects. I waited until the second
barrel of Heineken's imported beer was tapped, and asked for ten
volunteers to appear in the Christmas production of the *Thespian*

Guild Players. Many men volunteered. We selected the men by size. They had to be large! As an example, we had three former members (one a former fullback) of the Mt. Carmel "Tornadoes" football team. We also had a few alternates. Some of the men were experienced actors since they appeared in other productions at the club. I had their promise of faithful attendance at the Wednesday night rehearsals.

After the first rehearsal, I took measurements for the tutu that would be part of their costume. The designer who worked at the Model Garment Co. Inc., a manufacturer of high-quality woman's garments, would design and supervise the sewing of the "Tutu." The tutu would be made from a pink shade of organdy cloth; it would be heavily shirred and pleated. We were able to purchase woman's pink pantyhose size XXX-LARGE in the identical color of the tutu. The dancers were expected to bring a white T-shirt and a pair of "Jockey" shorts. That would complete their costume.

Irene and I decided to leave for the club at 5 PM. Even though we had many rehearsals, I arranged for one last rehearsal for the "prompter." I arranged to meet him at 5:30 in the rehearsal room located in the basement. I had a problem with the prompter. He had a copy of the script and was able to follow each act perfectly, but once again, I had to prompt the prompter. He was located near the stage so that he could prompt the actor when necessary. The prompter had a problem. He was not discrete; he actually shouted the next line. I told him over and over again, "You must whisper, which means that you should prompt in a very quiet manner."

We were ready to leave the house when the telephone rang. "When are you leaving for the club? Do you need any help with the stage props or sound system? If not, I'll see you at the club." Irene asked, "Who was that?" I responded, "I have no idea. I did not recognize the voice. It was a strange call."

We left for the club; it was a perfect winter evening. The air was crisp, the clear blue sky was filled with bright shining stars. The almost full moon was low on the horizon and was so bright that shadows were cast on the newly fallen white snow of the large, beautiful tall oaks that graced the large and beautiful lawn now covered with clean, soft, white snow in front of our home. As a reader of Joseph Conrad's novels, *Lord Jim, Typhoon, The Secret Agent, The Letters of Nostromo* etc. I became addicted to the descriptive style of his writing. And occasionally I lapse into what I call my "Conrad Phase"—I use five or six words when one would do. I ask you the reader, to be patient with me and to persevere reading to the end of my "Memoir."

Arriving at the club, my prompter was very prompt and was waiting for me with the script in his hand. Once again I tried prompting my prompter. "Whisper, whisper, whisper." I finally threatened him. "You must whisper, if not, I'll arrange that you will never work in show business again!"

At approximately 7:00 PM just as we were finishing our delicious, nourishing and well-prepared, and well-served dinner, a waitress came to our table to tell me that there was an important telephone call for me. My neighbor, David Smiley called to inform me that the local police came to use his telephone. The policeman called the Pennsylvania Sate Police to ask for assistance. He said, "There was an armed robbery at the home of Walter Baran at 200 Butler Road in Frackville. Their young son, Joseph, was alone at the home." I told David that I would be right there. I then called my brother-in-law, Bern Kiefer, told him about the robbery, and asked him to go to our home and that I would arrive shortly. I did not have any other information on what happened. I asked my friend, Nick Tatusko, to accompany me. I knew that Irene would be extremely nervous and upset so I told her that I had to run home because I forgot an item that I would need for the show. Arriving at our home I saw two state police vehicles and the local police car.

Rushing into the house, I saw Joseph being interviewed by the state police. My heart rate immediately began returning to almost normal. Meanwhile, one of the neighbors called the Country Club to inform us that the state police were at our home. Since I was not there, Irene took the telephone call. She tried calling our home but there was no response. It must have been extremely terrible for her. In retrospect, I should have taken her with me. I'm sorry to this day that I did not.

A few words of explanation: Our telephone system was "state-of-the-art." It had a built-in intercom, which operated on every phone in the house, the guesthouse, lower garage, bathhouse, and the patio at the pool. It was also used to answer the front door. It was easy to operate. It had a turn switch pointing to 'telephone' or 'intercom.' The last person to use the telephone did not switch from intercom to telephone. Therefore, the phone was inoperable. I immediately called the Country Club to tell Irene that Joseph was not harmed and that my brother-in-law, Bern Kiefer, was at our home and would remain with Joseph. Both of our boys were home from boarding school for the holidays. Tony was with his girlfriend, (later his wife) Sandy, at the movies in town and Joseph was in our basement recreation room watching television.

The state police gave me instructions, "Don't use your bedroom and don't touch anything in the room. Tomorrow the finger printing team of the state police will arrive to look for evidence."

It was amazing; Joseph was in better condition than I was. He said, "You have to go back to the club to put on the show." Bern said that he would stay with Joseph until we returned. I then drove to the club, changed into my tuxedo and appeared on the stage 18 minutes after curtain time. I know that the entire club knew what happened at our home. So I said, "Our son, Joseph told me that since I was an actor I must continue the tradition. "The show must go on." I told Irene, "This is one helluva way for you to get a new mink coat!"

I introduced the first act, a parody on "The night before Christmas" presented by a husband and wife team who were longtime members of *The Thespian Guild*, followed by Josie Farrell singing "Hello Dolly." Josie insisted on singing Hello Dolly at every show (no matter what the show theme was) ever since *The Thespian Guild* was formed in 1967! There were a total of twelve acts, each one better than the last one.

The stagehand working the tape recorder began, "The Dance of the Sugar Plum Fairies." The ten ballet dancers entered the stage in a straight line using the third position *Fouette en tourvant*. They quickly formed a circle and changed to a *Glissade*. The audience reacted with shouts, applause and whistling. They were so loud that the dancers could not hear the music which caused a few "faux pas" by the dancers. After the *Glissade,* they were to execute the *Pirouette sur le coup ve pied* using the fifth position. They performed the incredibly difficult, *arabesque penche* on point, instead. They finally finished with a *Grand jete,* a spectacular broad leap often used only by very experienced male dancers. It was a smashing success! After the show I heard, "Brilliant, Radiant, Dazzling, Luminous, Sparkling, Stunning, Resplendent" and other accolades that I cannot spell.

Immediately after the show, Irene and I drove home. Joseph and Bern were watching television. Joseph nonchalantly asked, "Was the show a success?" What a kid! Irene was standing with tears in her eyes and I said, "I told you he was okay." We then sat down and asked Joseph to tell us exactly what happened.

In Joseph's words: "I was watching television in the basement. At the end of the program, it was announced that the next program would be in color. (Programs in color were just being introduced and of course a color television set was required.) I shut off the black and white set, went upstairs, and turned on the television not realizing that I turned the volume up very high. (In those days) the TV set had to sort of "warm up" so I went to the refrigerator in the kitchen to get a Coke. When the TV came on it was extremely loud. I rushed in and turned the volume down. The show just began when I heard steps of someone coming down the stairs. I saw two young men using what I thought were handkerchiefs covering their face with exception of their eyes. The one in front was carrying a small nickel-plated pistol. He said, "Where did you come from kid?" "I was in the basement watching TV. I came to use the TV upstairs since it is a color set." He asked, "Where is the safe?" "I told him my dad has a large safe in his office at the factory." He then said, "Where is the money in the house?" "My mother keeps her wallet in the kitchen," He then walked into the kitchen opened the drawer and one of the men said, "Open the wallet and hand me the money." He then ordered me to go upstairs into your bedroom. The room was a mess. All the drawers from the dresser were pulled out and everything was on the floor. Some of the hanging clothes were on the floor. I asked them, "When did you do this?" But he then told me to lie on the floor on my stomach. He said "do you think I'm going to shoot you kid?" I did not respond. He then took a lot of your ties and tied my feet together at the ankles. He also tied my hands behind my back. I then heard them leave the house when they slammed the door shut. While they were tying my legs and hands I decided to tense my muscles so that when I relaxed my legs and arms were little loose. But there was no way that I could untie myself.

"I then rolled over to the nightstand and pulled down the princess phone to the floor. I could feel the metal ring on the dial phone. I dialed 0, and then I moved my head as fast as I could to the telephone. I told the operator that our home was robbed, my legs, and my arms are tied, and would she please call the police for me. The operator said, "I know that it is Saturday night and you kids always pull this trick on operators." I said, "Please, I really am tied up. Please call the police." She said, "I'll give you the number." I told her since I couldn't see the dial, I would not be able to dial. She then dialed the police. It rang a few times without being answered. Once again, I dialed the operator, and Thank God, it was the same operator, and I told her what happened. I asked her to please call Frackville Police Chief Petronko. I told her that he was the father of one of my schoolmates. By this time, I think she believed me. She dialed the number and Mrs. Petronko answered. I told her that we were robbed and I am tied up. I had a little problem because she did not believe me. I finally convinced her. She told me she would find her husband and he would come to our home as soon as possible. I heard a car stop. The police were trying to ring the doorbell and continued to knock on the door. I screamed as loud as I could, **"The back door is open. The back door is open."** I next heard the long narrow window glass directly beside the front door being smashed. **"I'm upstairs, I'm upstairs."** They came to the bedroom and they tried to untie me. The knots on the ties were so tight that they had to cut them to release me. The officer that was with Mr. Petronko then tried to use the telephone to call the state police. He told Mr.

Petronko that our phone line had probably been cut and he would use a neighbor's telephone. Chief Petronko was concerned that since our home was in Butler Township, he is not authorized to operate in another jurisdiction. He tried calling the Butler Township police without success, so he came to my aid."

On Monday, State Police came and asked us a few questions, but more importantly, they told us, "Your son, is a very bright young man. He told us the men wore clean, new khaki trousers, button-down shirts, had short hair and they spoke very good English. (I read the officers mind. He was thinking, "Well, that eliminates Shenandoah.") "He also told them that they were probably driving a modern car since it did not have a loud muffler and the doors had a "new car sound" when they were slammed shut as they drove away. He did not seem to be nervous or frightened though he probably was." The State Policemen said, "Your son would make a perfect witness, he acted perfectly under the circumstances. There might have been a tragedy here had he acted otherwise."

Meanwhile, upstairs in our bedroom, the detective and his aide were spreading a black powder on the furniture, the doorknobs, the stair railings etc. They spent about five hours in our home and that was the last we heard of them. We were not given any kind of report.

During World War II, Irene worked for the U.S. government in Washington D.C. but was never fingerprinted. I also have never been fingerprinted. I thought, surely a lot of our prints were in that room. Irene and I had expected that they would ask for our fingerprints. It did not happen.

When Joseph returned to Prep School, his friends did not believe that our house was robbed. We sent him a copy of the article that was printed in our local newspapers to show his friends.

OUR TRAVELS

I rene and I have had many travels out of the country beginning with our honeymoon travels to Cuba. I have decided to list some of these trips in a chronological order. I know it may be boring to the reader, but it's still better than watching slides of our various trips. You can't escape a slide show in someone's basement, but you can skip this chapter just by flipping a few pages. For those readers who are still with us, this is the story.

In June of 1949, passports were not required for travel to Cuba. We received our first passport on June 10, 1957. Between June 18, 1949 when we were married and June 10, 1957, we had two young babies at home. During these years, we did do some traveling but it was only to visit "Busia" in Mt. Carmel and a little closer to home, "Granny" in Frackville.

Our passports are dated, 1957, 1964, 1967, 1972, 1977, 1982, 1987, and 1997. A few of our passports had pages added to them by the State Department. They could not issue us a new passport just because all the pages were full of visa stamps, so they attached a foldout pages to the last page.

From 1957 to 2003, we made forty-four trips to Europe. In South America, we made nine trips to Columbia, Brazil, Argentina and Venezuela. In March of 1969, we visited Nairobi, Kenya, Africa. In the Middle East, we visited Egypt, Lebanon, Jordan and Israel. We also made a trip to Japan and Hong Kong. On another trip, we visited Australia and Tahiti. We had vacations on most of the islands in the Caribbean. In 1976 we decided to drive to California. We drove south to Florida, west to Texas, Mexico and California, north to Washington State, through both Dakotas, North to Québec Canada, and South through the New England states ending in Frackville, Pennsylvania. We eventually visited all 50 states.

One of the more interesting trips we made was our six-week trip in 1965 to Lebanon, Egypt, Jordan and Israel.

A student, Albert Nahas, from Beirut, Lebanon, attended Georgetown Preparatory School with our sons. We became friends with his parents, Gabriel and Vera. His father, Gabriel, was the "Onassis" of the Middle East. He controlled most of the shipping of the area. Albert, who spoke French, Arabic and English, had relatives living in Frackville—an amazing coincidence! He found out that the Baran brothers lived in the same small town in Pennsylvania as his relatives. Since he only went home to Beirut over the Christmas holidays, he spent a lot of time with our sons and visiting his relatives in Frackville. We met his parents when they occasionally visited Albert at school. We were invited to visit with them at their home in Lebanon. This was an opportunity to tour Egypt, Jordan and Israel.

Our travel agent informed us that we would have to take a circuitous route if we are to visit Israel. The Arab states bordering Israel would not allow anyone to enter if a visit for Israel appeared in his or her passport. Some tourists would remove the page in their passport containing the visa for Israel. The custom officials would count the pages and refuse anyone admission if a page was missing. Our route was set as follows: arrive in Beirut Lebanon, after two weeks take a flight to Cairo, Egypt (without flying over Israel airspace), after two weeks, fly to Amman, Jordan (once again flying over the Mediterranean sea).

Beirut a beautiful and exciting city called, "The Paris of the Mideast." Since Beirut was the financial center of the Middle East, each city block had at least three to six banks in every block of the city of many nations including the United States. Unfortunately, Gabriel and Vera had to leave unexpectedly for Athens, Greece, however, they made arrangements for our comfort while we were there. Reservations were made for us at the beautiful Phoenicia International Hotel. The hotel had two swimming pools of which one was built next to the bar/lounge. On the wall, there were large round circles of glass windows where you could see a group of beautiful girls, a few fat guys and a couple of children swimming underwater. Vera and Gabriel's chauffeur and a beautiful, very large Mercedes was made available to us. The chauffeur was given instructions to take care of all our requests. We wanted to see the ruins of the old Roman/Greek city called "Baalbek." This city was sort of like our "Williamsburg" except that it was built in 2300 B.C. It was 85 kilometers from the city. The Romans built the temple of Jupiter and Bacchus the Greeks the temple of Zeus. We spent the entire day there and it really was worth the drive. It also gave us an opportunity to see the small towns and villages along the way.

Reservations were made for us at a "five-star" restaurant in Beirut. Accompanied by our ever faithful guide and chauffeur, (I don't remember his name, but I knew that it was extremely difficult to pronounce.) He came not only to sign the check, but also to assist us with the menu since it was printed in French. The meal was superb but the Pulli fuisse was memorable.

Later in the evening we were treated to some Lebanese culture, Belly Dancing. This art form is much admired in Lebanon. The dancers wore a lot of clothing; the only skin they showed was their belly! They all had a large precious stone (?) placed in their belly button. Our table was placed next to the dance floor, and while they were dancing, one of the precious stone's popped out to the floor and skidded in my direction. Our guide told me, "Don't pick it up." I don't know the reason but he seemed to think that it was done purposely and aimed at an American.

We left Lebanon that was called by Lebanese "The Lebanon." When we reached Cairo the people we spoke to asked, "How did you like *The Lebanon?*" It's the only country that we visited that the prefix, "The" was always used. I should have begun this paragraph with, "We left *The Lebanon* on the morning flight to Cairo." If the reader has knowledge of why the country is called *The Lebanon* I would very much appreciate it if you would contact me by e-mail. My address is waltb@ptd.net

We had a morning arrival at Cairo. We decided to have lunch at the hotel and then arranged to take the CityTour that began at 3 PM. I forgot the name of the hotel but it was an Intercontinental five-star hotel. The lunch was a disaster. Very strange foods placed in little bowls and eaten with a piece of flat bread. No spoons, just tear off a piece of flat bread, dip it in one of the bowls, and place in your mouth. We had a choice of colors, brown, tan, yellow, black and purple. I did not try the purple. They were all sort of sauces but no bits of meat or vegetables.

We went on the tour that included a visit to the famous Cairo Museum. The museum was outstanding. It sort of made up for the lousy lunch we had. We decided not to leave the hotel at night so we had dinner in the main dining room. The menu was printed in Arabic that looked like the shorthand that I was taught by Mrs. Moyer in my freshman class at Frackville high school. It was also printed in French and English. I ordered fish, and Irene had some type of meat. We did not enjoy our food. After dinner, we went to the lounge for a few drinks. We were entertained by a group of three men playing various instruments that were strange to us such as a guitar with about eight or nine strings and a sort of xylophone and a three stringed, long, very narrow guitar. The music was very pleasant. They played very quietly; I think it was after dinner music. It was fascinating to watch them play. We were sitting on a long leather sofa. A young man spoke to us in English. He told us he was a student at Cairo University and he asked if we would mind his joining us since he wanted to practice his English. He was very well dressed and said that his family lived in Cairo. He offered to take us to see the Sphinx and the El Giza Pyramid's since they were quite near to his home. He told us that he had a car and he would be happy to show us the various monuments. He did say he did not want to be paid since we could pay him by teaching him English. Before Irene could tell me, "Here you go again." I accepted. He told us he would pick us up at about 9 AM. Later in our room, Irene said she was concerned. "This is a strange city and I am a little frightened since we don't know the young man." I said, "This will be another adventure."

He met us in front of the hotel driving a black Mercedes. We drove out of the city towards the Sphinx. At the edge of the city, he stopped in front of a large story home. He said that he lived there. "You're going get a good a view of the Sphinx from the roof of the building. It was a beautiful morning with a full sun and children were playing near the entrance door. I gave a nod to Irene that said, I'm sure that this is safe." We walked right through the building and entered a large courtyard. The home had about eight or more apartments. He introduced us to his mother who was sitting in a small chair shelling peas. She spoke to her son and told him that we were invited for lunch at their home. At the restaurant in the hotel, I did not mind leaving the uneaten food. But I could not do that in a private home, and besides she told him that we are going to have lamb for lunch. I said, "Please tell your mother, that we eat very little for lunch." She said something to her son who began laughing. "What did she say?" "She said, "We could kill a few pigeons." I said to him, "I hope we did not offend your mother." "He said, I told her that you do not have much time to spend in Cairo and that you and your wife are anxious to see the pyramid's"

We entered the building and went to the stairs up to the roof. It was like a giant patio. A few tables with chairs covered by huge umbrellas. Many children came up and were looking at these strangely dressed people. He told us that they were all his nephews and nieces. A wall about two feet high was at the edge of the roof. Standing at this short wall and looking East, we saw the huge Sphinx about four football fields away from the house. We realized then that this young man belonged to a very, very wealthy family. While we were on the roof, he explained the family structure in Egypt. His parents owned the home, and when a son married, he and his new wife would have an apartment in the husband's home. When we were in the courtyard, we saw three women and stitching a wedding dress. His sister was to be married. She would live in the house of her husband's family. There were six sons and they were all expected to live with their parents after they married. He explained the meals. The mother and all the women of the house would prepare the food. It was a large communal dining room and all the men ate first. The children would then be fed and the women would eat last. I asked, "How do five daughters-in-law get along with one mother-in-law? How are problems settled?" "It's very simple," he replied. "There just aren't any problems."

We then drove down near the Sphinx. After taking a few

photographs, I decided to accept an offer from one of the many camel drivers to ride a camel from the Sphinx to the pyramid's that looked like they were a mile away. Irene decided to join our driver in the car. It was very wise decision. I sat on that beast with my legs spread-eagled as far as they could go, and I swear that the pyramids were at least five miles away! After finally standing on the ground, I thought they selected the fattest, largest camel in Egypt for me to ride. I looked at the other camel's standing nearby. They all looked about the same size. I was able to walk afterwards, but with great difficulty. Our newly found friend suggested that I climb partway up one of the pyramids. Most of the square stones were two feet high; in one area, they were about 24 inches. With great difficulty, I climbed up two blocks so a photographic could be taken since I doubted that I would ever visit the pyramids again.

I spent the next day in bed trying to get my hipbones back in place. I asked Irene to go down to the street in front of the hotel and buy one of the pieces of bread that looked like a large Pennsylvania Dutch pretzel since I definitely did not want to eat one of their lunch meals. I noticed a Sheraton Hotel on the street so I suggested that we go there for dinner that night to get an American meal. Again with great difficulty (Don't you feel sorry for me?) we walked partway up the block to the Sheraton. The menu looked identical to the one at our hotel. We then went to the lounge to rest my hips and enjoy some of the great French wine that they offered. I also took advantage of the hot, salted almonds that were served on a hot linen napkin. We were very surprised since the very same item was served only in the very best hotel lounges in Poland!

We boarded an Egyptian Airline (none of the Arab countries had flights to Israel) to Jordan. We landed at the capital city of Amman, Jordan, that is about twenty miles to east of the Israel border. We spent two days in Jordan and we did not do any sightseeing. On the morning of the second day, we were told that we would be picked up at the hotel at 9 AM to drive to the border. We drove across the desert and were told by the driver that he could not go any closer but we would have to walk with our luggage about a quarter of a mile. We would enter through the "Mandelbaum

Gate" where we would be met with a car to take us to Jerusalem. Our travel agent in the United States made all of these arrangements. Irene and I were both 40 years old and it normally would have been no problem to carry luggage (luggage did not have wheels in those days.) However, I had a problem (which was self-induced) because my hipbones were not yet in place since the ride on the camel. We had two large bags and a train case. Irene offered to carry the heavier bag and I carried her bag and the train case. After along walk through the sand we approached the gate on a long high wall. There were soldiers with machine guns on top of the wall and as we approached, the large gates were swung open. We were very happy to see a car standing near the gate with the trunk lid open. "Mr. Baran?" We were pleased for that we did not have to wait, and it was really great to sit down in the car. We had reservations at the King David Hotel in Jerusalem. The driver told us, "You are going to stay in a very historical hotel. It was bombed in 1946 before the state of Israel was born and resulted in the deaths of 92 people. It was bombed as a protest against the British government, and the order was given by the future Prime Minister of Israel, Mr. Begin." I didn't know why he was giving us this information because he did not look like an Arab. I later made some inquiries and found that the British and the hotel management were warned that bombs had been planted in the hotel. They ignored the warning resulting in the deaths and injury to many people.

It was a wonderful old hotel and we finally were able to have a delicious dinner. In fact, in our two weeks stay in Israel, we did not have a single bad meal. I regained the weight that I lost in Egypt.

There was much to see in Israel, and we were very happy that we had this experience. We had a guide assigned to us for the entire time we were there. We spent about one week in Jerusalem a visiting the Christian churches, shrines, and the huge Moslem temple that we were allowed to enter after leaving our shoes outside. We also walked the Stations of the Cross to the site of the crucifixion of Jesus.

We spent one day at "Yad Vashem" which honors both Holocaust Martyrs and "the Righteous Among The Nations." There were many names of Gentiles who saved Jews during the occupation of all countries in Europe. Of all the countries listed, Poland had over 4000 names of Polish citizens that was far more than any other country.

In writing this story I decided to see what I could find on the Internet. I just typed in "Yad Vashem" and found over 100 sites that were available. I selected: www.holocausforgotten.com/yadvashem.htm the following is part of this site:

YAD VASHEM—THE RIGHTEOUS AMONG THE

NATION'S

Number of Holocaust Rescuers
by Country and Ethnic Origin
As of January 1, 2002

*T*he Yad Vashem Museum in Israel, founded in 1953, honors both Holocaust martyrs and "The Righteous among the Nation's," Gentile (non-Jewish) rescuers who have been recognized for their "compassion, courage and morality" because they "risked their lives to saved the lives of Jews." Poland ranks first among 40 nations with 5,632 men and women, almost one-third of the total, despite the fact that only in Poland were citizens (and their loved ones) were executed if caught trying to save Jews.*

There followed a list of countries and the number of "The Righteous among the Nation's." Poland lists 5,632; France is next with 2,171; Lithuania, 504; Slovakia, 375, etc.

And we were told that there are many others from many countries that were not listed. The Jews who were saved, gave the names of the Gentiles who saved them to be listed at the Yad Vashem Museum.

As an example, there is a woman living now in Frackville who immigrated to the United States to serve as a companion to her American-born Aunt, a widow, without children. Some years ago, an article appeared in the *Pottsville Republican.* It told of this woman as a child eight years old, and how her family saved the life of a Jewish man who came to their barn to escape the Germans. I say barn, because the Germans soldiers occupied their farmhouse and the family lived in the barn. On one of our trips to Poland, we visited this farmhouse and the barn. It was a very moving experience. I visited with her relatives and after returning home, I asked her to tell me the complete story. It went something like this: In the darkness of the night, they heard someone entering the barn. They did not have any source of light since candles, if they were available to them would be very dangerous to use because of the hay in the barn. They were asleep at the time and the man wanted to hide in the barn but was surprised that the entire family was lived there. His face and one hand were bleeding and he asked if he could stay a few days. Since the soldiers checked the barn every day, it was decided to hide him in the small shed that once was used for goats. They gave him some food and then taken to this shed. Each day, as a young girl she would carry a bucket of food for the pig. She also carried a small container of food for the man. She was chosen by the family to take care of the man since the Germans would not bother her. The Jewish man knew that the penalty for harboring a Jew would mean immediately death for the entire family along with the Jew. He told them that he would leave in a few days so as not to put them at risk. A few days later he was gone. They never heard from him again.

She told us there were many other families who helped hide the Jews. Their names will never be on the list at Yad Vashem. I also read in some of the sites I found information on the Internet, that to have a name included on the list, it would have to be verified by three or four eyewitnesses.

After a few days, and a few great meals, we left early in the morning to drive to our hotel in Tel Aviv. It was arranged that we would visit a kibbutz to have lunch. It was another wonderful experience for us to meet all these mostly very young people working very hard helping to build a new Israel. We ate with them in their common dining building. While the food did not compare with the restaurant at the Hotel King David in Jerusalem, it was plain but nourishing. After a brief tour of the farm, we continued our drive to Tel Aviv.

We arrived at our Hotel "Dan" that fortunate for us was located right off the beach. I found out that the word "Dan" was the name of a chain of hotels in Israel. During our stay, we met a couple from Canada and became good friends with them. I believe we were the only Gentiles in the hotel at that time. Since the meals came with the room, we had most of our meals in the restaurant or should I say restaurants. Each restaurant was split in half. One side said "Dairy" the other was "Meat" according to the Jewish dietary laws. One evening when eating in the Meat restaurant, we noticed a man sitting at a nearby table order a cup of coffee. Since the restaurant was not dairy, no dairy products could be served. After the waiter brought the coffee, he took out a small jar of "Cremora" and used a teaspoon to add it to his cup. Our waiter was very irritated. Since he was standing near our table he said, "Look at him. He knows better than to do that. We now have to break the cup and saucer and throwaway the teaspoon." When we first arrived in Israel, I always asked for cream for the coffee. I was told that I would have to eat "Dairy" if I wanted cream in my coffee. I had no problem with that, in fact I drank black coffee and found that it tasted much better without cream. To this day I drink only black coffee.

We had another wonderful experience while staying at this hotel. One evening we met our friends in the dining room and found that the entire room was set up for a banquet. There were many people already seated so I asked the waiter where could we have dinner. He told me, "Today is the Jewish New Year and you can sit at any table." This was Great! The dinner started with a rabbi explaining some of the traditions that were held by the Jewish people. The table was set with various kinds of food and fruit, each one with its own meaning. Eating honey with a slice of Apple had a special meaning (which I forgot.) Before the dessert was served, the singing began. We locked arms with our neighbors to the right and left, and began swaying left and right. Later on, a few men were dancing. While they did not wear any paper hats or blow any whistles, this was one of the best New Years Day that we ever spent.

Across the table from us an American asked me, "Where is home?" I began by saying, "We live in Pennsylvania and our friends are from Canada" "Just where in Pennsylvania?" I began by saying, "It is west of Philadelphia," he asked. "Just where in Pennsylvania?" He asked again. I thought of saying Scranton, or Allentown or even Harrisburg, but I said, "It's a very small town in central Pennsylvania." "Tell me the name of the town." He said. "We live in Frackville, Pennsylvania." To my surprise, he said, "That's next to Ashland. I spent a few years at the Ashland State Hospital as an intern. While there, I met Dr. Mulligan who was chief of radiology. He said that I would make a very good radiologist. I took his advice, and now I am the chief radiologist in a large hospital in Boston, Mass. I often think of him for guiding me to my life's work." Later during the conversation he told me, "When I married, my wife and I spent our honeymoon at the "Loeper Hotel in Ashland. My wife was not very pleased, but I was very happy to see Dr. Mulligan and other staff members since I left. I told my wife, in a few years after I pay my student loans and open my own office, we can go on a honeymoon wherever you choose."

I know that this has nothing to do with "Wally Baran's Memoir." But it is a very nice, heartwarming story.

After a wonderful stay in Israel, we flew Et-AL Israel Airlines to New York City and home. And, oh yes, the food on the plane was fabulous!

THE MODEL GARMENT COMPANY

Every Friday evening my brother Pete, his wife Amy, and
their six-year-old son George (Pat) came to our home at
222 South Centre Street to watch television. In 1948 we had an
eight-inch television in our home at 246 North Nice Street. Our
home was located on the highest elevation in Frackville that made it
possible to receive two television stations from Philadelphia. The
television reception depended a lot on the weather. On most evenings, we were able to receive a signal and, even though it was
summer, occasionally we had a lot of "snow" on the screen. During
the day, a pattern appeared on the screen with an image of an
Indian and many different width lines radiating from the center.
This was done to enable the television set to be tuned using the
eight adjusting screws on the back of the set. There were only two
hours of programs on Friday and about three hours on Saturday.
After our marriage on June the 18th, 1949, we purchased a new 10-
inch set that had new technology, and even though our home was
located on land that was about 300 feet lower than my mother's
home on Nice Street, the reception and the programming was much
improved. Friday evenings were very popular since "The Texaco
Hour" starring Milton Berle, a popular new comedian, was shown
at 8 PM.

Since our home was new and some homes were converting to
oil for heat, I wanted to support the anthracite coal companies that
gave employment to many men. I installed an anthracite stoker
furnace. A large bin that could hold about one-quarter ton of
buckwheat size coal was attached to the back of the furnace about
three feet from the floor. A shovel was used to pick up the coal

from the adjoining coal bin and fill the box attached to the furnace. In spring or fall weather, a bin full would last about a week, but during the winter it had to be filled almost every day. After six weeks of shoveling coal, I decided there might be a better way. (I know that this story carries the title "Model Garment Company" and you the reader are probably waiting to hear about this fabulous firm. Please be patient, I will get to the point in a few more paragraphs.) I was able to locate a three-inch diameter steel pipe that held a coal transporting screw. I decided to build an automatic coal bin filler upper. I attached a one-quarter horsepower electric motor with a gear-reducing pulley at the top. The bottom of the steel tube was located on the floor of the coal bin. The other end was attached to the steel bin at the top. When the motor was turned on, the screw would turn and the coal was transported to the top and into the bin. I no longer had to use a shovel! After a few weeks of turning the motor on and off, I decided to automate the system. After all, I was what Zuity Halaburda called "The Wild Inventor." I was the same guy who invented the tubeless radio. If Zuity saw my newest invention, even he would be proud of me. Well, back to the drawing board. I attached a hinged six-inch plate of stainless steel to the side of the coal box. I also installed a 12-volt micro switch on the steel plate. As long as there was coal on the steel plate, the motor would not run. Since the coal ran down to the furnace by gravity, when the coal moved off the plate, the micro switch would send a message to the motor, and coal was supplied to the coal box until it reached the top. The coal would then cover the steel plate and shut off the motor.

On a Friday while Pete and I were watching television, Pete heard a strange noise coming from the basement. He asked me "What's that noise?" I said, "Oh, I'm filling the coal bin." We then proceeded to the basement where he saw my "automatic coal bin filler" in operation. He was amazed at what he saw since it worked so well. When we were going up the stairwell, he noticed stored at the other end of the basement, 6 industrial sewing machines, a large 2 horsepower motor complete with a long shaft, an assortment of tables and work bins. He asked me, "What are you going to do with those sewing machines?" I said, "I'm going to open a garment factory." After we went into the living room, he actually turned off the television set and asked me to start from the beginning and tell him what the hell I was going to do.

The next few pages or paragraphs may be boring to the reader. I will not be offended if you decide to skip to the next chapter. That is one of the rights that have been given to you by the *Constitution of the United States. (Amendment No. 1, Bill of Rights)* "What a Country!" Of course you'll forever be denied the information that you will need if you decide to go into the "rag" business.

Pete arranged for me to get a job at the *Northumberland Dress Company* in Mt. Carmel. I began working June 9, 1942. My first job paid 25 cents per hour and I was a sorter/bundle boy. After two months, the job of "belt boy" was added to my duties. (To save me a lot of time, please re-read **"First Job."** *Thanks for your cooperation.*)

After spending only seven years in the garment business and many young men my age were serving in the armed forces during the war, there was a shortage of cutters, machine repairmen, and foremen, etc. That is the reason that I advanced *fast forward* from belt boy to assistant manager. One would think that I was a bona fide S.O.B. (son of the boss). In my case, my boss, Morris Wapner, only had three daughters. If you read **"First Job"** very carefully, you will recall that I not only repaired sewing machines, I also did some cutting, set piece rates, and scheduled production, and purchased all of the supplies such as thread, machine parts, paper cartons, and wire dress hangers. I said to myself, "Self, since you know so much about this business, why don't you start one of your own?"

When I was a child, my mother often told me, (pointing to my arms and shoulders), "You will not be able to work in the coal-mines like your brother's so you will have to (pointing to my head) work with this." Since I always listened to my mother, I decided to start on a small-scale and I was sure that eventually I would have the best state-of-the-art garment factory, at least in Frackville. Following my mother's instructions I began using my head and I came to these conclusions: There were many good sewing machine operators available that were unable to work during the day because there was no one to baby-sit for their children. Day care centers were not invented yet and many of their own mothers worked in a garment factory during the day but they were able to baby-sit in the evenings. If the husband was not in the service, he would be able to take care of the children after returning home from work.

I decided to open a factory with about ten operators. In my travels to other factories, I asked Mr. Cohen, owner of "Pottsville Manufacturing Co." if he would give me some work sewing ladies dresses as a subcontractor. I told him of my plans and he agreed to help me. We would sew the complete garment and he would press and finish it.

You will also recall in the same story how I traveled to a good part of Schuylkill County repairing sewing machines in other local factories. On these visits, I noticed that they had many older type sewing machines that were not being used. I began purchasing machines, motors, and other items that were used in a garment factory. You will also remember that I stored them in the basement in the new home we built on Centre Street in the center of Frackville (the one with a toilet inside the house.) I was able to lease a small former grocery store located on Lehigh Avenue to serve as my sewing factory.

I then spoke to my sister, Frances, and asked her if she would help me run this small factory. She was a good sewing machine operator but she was never a forelady. In all the factories that I visited or worked in, the foreladies seemed to be always angry, shouting at the girls, looking miserable, and didn't seem to have any friends except the boss. Frances was just the opposite, she would always help a new employee, and she was very patient with all the operators.

I was not sure if I had to fill out some government forms in order to open a new business. I knew that forms were needed to fill out for Workers Compensation Insurance and forms to withhold Federal I.R.S. taxes. (Pennsylvania did not have a state income tax at this time.) I acquired a few copies of these forms and I was

First plant. Model Garment Co.
Ten employees

ready to open for business. I also purchased a Workers Compensation Insurance policy from John Crane Insurance Company in Frackville.

The following week after I gave all this information to Pete, he suggested that we become partners. I agreed. It would be much easier to have help in setting up the machinery since Pete was an excellent mechanic and electrician. An electrician was very important since the motor to run the machines was 220 volts. Fortunately the former grocery store had a few meat grinders, etc. that required 220 volts. Later that evening while we were watching television, a program called "The Model Speaks" appeared on the TV. I said, "That will be the name of our company, Model Garment Co."

During this period, I received a call from my "Old Boss," Morris Wapner, who was the former owner of the Northumberland Dress Company in Mt. Carmel. This is the factory where I matriculated in "How to run and operate a garment factory 101." While I did not receive a diploma, I felt that I was ready to start my "Career." He asked me to stop by his new factory, "Miss Pennsylvania Inc." located in Pottsville. He was planning to order some new specialized sewing machines that just came on the market. He wanted to know my opinion if they would work in his operation. During my visit, I mentioned that I was going to open a small garment factory in Frackville. Answering his questions such as, how would you live until your business became profitable? You have a building? Do you have any machines? I gave him the full story that the factory would operate only in the evenings, that I had purchased some machines, and that the factory would be on a very small-scale. He then said to me "Wally, if you need any additional sewing machines, get a truck and you can borrow any extra sewing machines that I have here. "However, if you need to borrow money, you must give me at least two days notice." Needless to say, I was very pleased that he had so much faith in me. He actually encouraged me and offered his help if I had a problem. No, I did not have to borrow any of his sewing machines and I was very fortunate that I did not have to borrow any money.

Morris was a great friend for over fifty years. His daughter, Sandy, told me that I was the son he never had. I was very privileged that his daughters asked me to give the eulogy in the synagogue at his funeral. During the eulogy I said, "We often hear the phrase, "he was like a father to me." In my case, he **was** a father to me.

Within a few weeks, we began installing the sewing machines and Frances began calling her friends who might want to work for us. We did not have to advertise for help. After we hired a few operators, they suggested some others that would want to work in our new factory. While all the preparations for our start up were being made, I spoke to the owner of the Pottsville manufacturing Co. and asked him for a sample garment so that I could set the piece rates before we opened.

I also visited The First National Bank of Frackville and spoke to the cashier, Charlie Snyder. I filled out a loan application for $500. Pete and I had the money to cover the first payroll but I thought that we should have a "Cushion" in case some unforeseen problem occurred.

I had a checking, and saving account with the First National Bank of Frackville, I was sure that they would give me this loan. I knew that the bank board held their meetings every Friday morning. After lunch, I called Mr. Snyder. He informed me that the loan was denied. I could not believe it! He refused to tell me why the loan was denied. I kept bugging Charlie Snyder to tell me why it was denied. I finally threatened him that I would close all my accounts and transfer my mortgage to a bank in Pottsville. He finally told me that he would tell me but he warned me that his job was in jeopardy if I told anyone why the loan was denied. I was very shocked when he told me that the board decided, "Since we were not Jewish, we will never be successful in operating a garment factory. The bank would be doing us a favor by not giving us a bank loan and we would not waste our money in a venture that would surely fail."

Actually the bank did us a "favor" by not granting us the loan. It made me more determined than ever to succeed and show those directors what a determined young man could do. I believe that I was responsible for the new word "entrepreneur" that was added to "Webster's Seventh New Collegiate Dictionary" within two months of my being denied this loan by the First National Bank of Frackville. Swearing him to secrecy, I confided in my attorney, John Walesky, and informed him what had happened. The next day he asked me to come into his office. He handed me an envelope that held $500 in cash. "You can pay me 'without any interest' when you can. Do not tell anyone about our arrangement. I know you will be successful."

Fortunately, we did not need this additional money. I returned the $500 in cash to Attorney Walesky within a few weeks.

Your reading my "Memoir" this far tells me that you are a very patient person. I'm going to, once again, try your patience. I know that you are very anxious to read more about how "Model Garment Co." became a success. But I should tell you about my further relations with the bank.

I immediately opened two accounts, Model Garment Co. checking account and Model Garment Co. payroll account. I wanted The First National Bank of Frackville PA. to have access to all of our financial records so that they would have the opportunity to follow our growth and our success that was sure to come without the help of any of their money. Within a few short years, our firm grew as we moved to larger and better buildings. (All of the moving I did in my childhood had me well prepared for these moves.) They were very happy to have The Model Garment Co. as one of their better clients. They were happier still when I did not remind them that they turned us down for a lousy $500 loan. I always flashed a great smile each time I deposited a few large checks into the new savings account that we opened solely for the purpose of purchasing new equipment.

Many years later when we were well established, occasionally, especially during the Christmas season, our checks from the jobbers in New York would not arrive in time for the Friday payroll. I would simply call Charlie Snyder and asked him to "Please deposit $18,000 to our payroll account." This did not require us to transfer funds from our savings or other accounts nor to sign any kind of documents. It was just a service the First National Bank of Frackville PA gave to Model Garment Co.

A few years later when we purchased our first permanent building, I received a call from Judge G. Harold Watkins asking me to meet with him in his office. Since the bank was independent, the judge "sort of" ran the bank. He informed me that he was going to nominate me for a seat on the Board of Directors of the bank. This came as a complete surprise since I did not seek or have any desire to serve in that capacity. I thanked him but I told him that I did not own any stock in the bank. "That is not a problem. I can arrange for you to purchase the necessary 100 shares at a price of $30 a share."

The judge knew that I was on the Board of Directors of *The Broad Mountain Building and Loan Association*. After our first son was born, the BMB&L had a stock purchase plan that was available to anyone interested. The stocks were sold at $200 a share. The minimum deposit was $5 for the first month. $10 for the second month and an additional $5 until $50 a month was reached. It remained at $50 for the rest of the contract. As soon as our first son Anthony was born, I joined the plan so that I would have sufficient funds to put him through college. When Joseph was born, I created a plan for him. I really don't know why, but the chairman of the board, Mr. Hoppes asked me to become a director. Our business seemed to be growing each year, and the fact that I was an "all-around nice guy" I suppose helped.

The judge informed me that I would have to resign from the Building Loan Association when I became a director of the bank.

He then called Mr. Harry Strouse Esq. of Ashland to inform him that he should sell Wally Baran 100 shares of The First National Bank of Frackville stock.

During this same period, a prominent businessman of Frackville who held a few hundred shares of bank stock and was very anxious to be named a director of the bank began purchasing a few shares from small stockholders from the Frackville area. He was told that if he had enough shares he could not be refused to be a director of the bank He offered $50 per share and was able to purchase some additional shares to add to his holdings. I do not know the reason why the Board of Directors did not want him to serve on the board. I know that the board was not happy that he inflated the price of a share by $20. However within a year he was given a seat on the board.

And now, back to the Model Garment Co:

Our first "Plant" was located at 422 South Lehigh Avenue in a former grocery store. We had nine sewing machine operators and my sister Frances as the forelady. We were able to set up the machines in about a week and a half; after all, we were both experts nobody could tell us a thing! I visited the owner of the Pottsville Manufacturing Co. and told him that we are ready to start production. He gave me all the cut parts we needed to make one dozen ladies large size dresses. "Come back when you finish the dresses and I will make my decision to give you work." It only took Frances a day and a half to finish the garments. She could have been finished in about four hours but we had to make sure that every dress was sewn perfectly. After all these were "Samples" and they had to be perfect if Model Garment Co. was to grow into one of the largest employers in Frackville!

It is needless to say, but I will say it anyway, the garments were perfect! In fact they were made so well that they had to distribute them among the entire lot before shipping so that they would not be noticed with the rest of the dresses he made. The first lot that he gave me consisted of eighteen dozen. I really don't remember but I will cheat a little bit and say that it was Style #2580. I do remember (I will never forget) that they were very, very large size garments.

They began with size 52 and went up from there. The fabric was rayon and was printed with very large flowers (if they used small flowers, they would look ridiculous). The dresses were "Coat Style" that is, large buttons were used from the neck to the bottom hem. They had a small Peter Pan collar, two very large patch pockets, short sleeves, and a one-inch hem.

I had planned to eventually get a contract to sew children's dresses, Toddler to size Six Months and Size 4 to 6 x. The reason I wanted to work on children's dresses was very simple. The machines would not have to work as hard to produce dozens of small garments, but the main reason was that very little thread was required. Eventually we did get contracts for children's dresses and sportswear.

In the meantime, back at the plant we had to produce these enormous dresses. Everything went well but since the dresses had a lot of buttons that meant they had required a lot of buttonholes. We were able to purchase buttonhole and button sew machines. We also needed a blindstitch machine to sew the one-inch hem on the bottom.

We had a problem: There was no room in our "Plant" for these three sewing machines. Since our home at 222 South Centre Street had an unfinished attic, it was decided that we would open our second plant in our home. (Mr. Snyder and the people at the bank were very surprised that we were opening a second plant after only a few weeks of operation in Plant No. 1). Since these three machines could operate on 110 Volt motors, we soon had these machines in operation especially since we were able to procure three people to work without any salary. Pete's wife, Amy, was a button sewer for over twelve years' and my wife, Irene, operated a blindstitch machine at Mitzi Frocks Inc. in Mt. Carmel after she lost her office job when the new owner purchased "State-of-the-art" office equipment. She was the very best blindstitch machine operator in the factory. I really don't know but others told me that she was the best since "Wally the mechanic" taught her how to sew.

After the garments were completely sewn at Plant #1, they

were delivered by car to Plant #2 to be completed. A funny thing happened with these garments when they were on their way to J.C. Penney's. The buttonholes (there were 14 of them) were sewn first. The next operation was to mark their location so that the buttons could be set. Laying the garment on a long table and using a crayon pencil, a mark would be placed opposite the buttonhole. I know it was a while ago when I told you that the fabric was made of rayon, had big flowers, and was what we called "busy." Using a white crayon pencil Amy, had a difficult time in finding the mark so we selected a red color pencil to mark the location for the button. Amy did not have any difficulty in finding the mark. Everything went well until we shipped the garments to Pottsville. The manager wanted to know "why did you use red thread with white buttons?" I told him that we absolutely used white thread. He had some difficulty with the English language so I said that I would drive down to look at the garments. Sure enough, they were sewn with red thread. Actually they were sewn with white thread the thread became red when the needle and went through the red crayon mark. This was our first recall. We cut off the buttons and placed them 1 millimeter away from the red mark.

I know that you the reader would like to know more about Plant #1 and Plant #2 but actually I, the author, am getting very bored just writing about it. Perhaps when I write "feet first II," I could finish the story.

After only three months at the original site, our business increased to the point where the first expansion move became necessary. It was also decided to add more machines and that we would operate the normal day shift but also continue with a night shift because some of our loyal employees could not work during the day.

We were able to lease the basement of the old Natalie building located on Frack Street and Lehigh Avenue. It was located directly across the street from the First National Bank of Frackville. (The Bank that had refused us a $500 loan) During the Depression, President Roosevelt, with the consent of the Congress, began a program called Works Project Administration, W.P.A., to give work to the men who were unemployed. In Frackville, some streets in the center of town were paved with concrete. Most of the streets in the outlying areas of the town were not paved at all. I remember as a child watching these workers laying local stones carried from the nearby mountains to build good cobblestone streets. It was not much fun trying to ride a bicycle over these streets, but the streets were no longer covered with mud during the spring rains. These men did many other projects repairing and building stone bridges on the small creeks that ran through the town.

The women of the town also had work provided by the W.P.A. They worked in the basement of the Natalie building sewing items for the soldiers. My mother was one of those women. I believe that every home on our side of the railroad tracks contained a pedal operated Singer Sewing Machine. To get a job with the W. P.A. the ladies had to supply their own machine. The wages were very low but it helped to keep our family together. Later, during the Second World War, each Thursday the ladies from St. Ann's Church worked in the same room rolling bandages for the war effort. Other churches in town were assigned other days during the week. This was all volunteer work. No one received any compensation. Again, my mother was one of these ladies.

In 1951, Model Garment Company occupied this very room giving employment to 30 employees. Three restrooms were added, modern fluorescent lights were installed, and modern sewing machines operated by electric motors were in place. After contacting The Department Of Labor and Industry in Harrisburg, an inspector arrived who, lucky for us, did not look very smart and wore very thick eyeglasses. In anticipation of his "inspection" we turned every other fluorescent light off, showed him our brand-new shiny water cooler, and helped him walk down the four steps down to the floor where I congratulated him on his selection of the tie he was wearing. After a very short tour, he told me that we would receive the "Certificate of Occupancy" in the mail in a few weeks.

Even though this was a basement, the upper part was above ground and six large windows allowed natural light to fill the room.

When we reached a total of 30 employees, it was decided that either Pete or I would have to resign from our present job so that one of us could manage this growing company. I had a high salary since I was assistant manager of Mitzi Frocks Inc. and Pete was a sewing machine mechanic working at the "Janowitz Dress Co. Inc." in Mahanoy City. It was decided that Pete would be the manager. At this time, we were no longer making huge enormous dresses as a subcontractor for "Pottsville Manufacturing Co." Mr. Cohen wished us luck and offered his help in our operation. I obtained a contract from Mitzi Frocks Inc. in Mt. Carmel to produce children's dresses. Even though I continued to work there, they needed more production. It worked out fine.

When we had 30 employees, I contacted The International Ladies Garment Workers Union (ILGWU) and informed them that we would like our employees to be members of the union. Usually the union would allow a new firm to operate for about two years and they then held an organization drive to have the employee's petition the union as their representative. My friends in the business when told that we would become unionized immediately, thought we were nuts! It meant that we would have to begin paying the employees the union rate and other benefits immediately. I have witnessed many new garment firms that resisted being represented by the ILGWU until being forced to by the Pennsylvania Labor Relations Board. It was not a pretty sight. Some of the employees of these new factories resented the "bosses" and kept a grudge for many years. By signing a contract with the union immediately, we had very cooperative employees who worked hard and while they may not have "loved" us, they surely thought we were great guys!

For many years we had an independent contract with the union, which meant that we would negotiate our own contract. The owners of most garment factories sewing ladies wear belonged to an organization called "Atlantic Apparel Contractors Assn." located in Bangor, PA, who represented most of the owners of garment factories in Eastern Pennsylvania and New Jersey. The members belonging to this Association, "AACA," all had the same contract with the union. Every two or three years when a new contract was being negotiated, it invariably caused a strike by all members of the Association. Many years later, in about 1968, the jobbers we worked for forced us to join the AACA. The jobbers in New York signed an agreement with the ILGWU to pay a certain percentage of each invoice to a retirement fund, which was run and controlled by the union. The union would then issue the checks for vacation pay, set up a retirement fund for their members, etc.

While many members of the AACA had suffered strikes during the negotiations for a new contract, Model Garment Company did not have a strike since it began operations in 1950 until 1976 when an unauthorized, one day stoppage occurred when the union chairlady decided to call a strike without the authorization of the union. She was severely criticized by the ILGWU manager for calling this stoppage.

The fact that The Model Garment Company did not have a strike in 26 years of operation (in an industry that was prone to striking) was not because we were very liberal during the negotiations for a new contract, but it was because we were fair.

We no longer could be independent because the jobbers would not pay the percentage to an independent company. (A few years later I was appointed a member of the Board of Directors of the Atlantic Apparel Contractors Assn.)

Once again we outgrew the building at Frack Street and Lehigh Avenue. In 1952, we signed a lease with Studlick Brothers, the owners of a building that was formerly used as a roller-skating rink. It was located at North Lehigh Avenue and Catawissa Street. Part of Frackville's lore claimed that Catawissa Street was the shortest street in any town or city in Pennsylvania. The street was exactly as long as our building. I only mention this because I did not give up on my plan to produce a book that is one inch thick.

We now had 100 employees in our new location, which meant that I resigned my position at Mitzi Frocks Inc. in Mt. Carmel. Before I resigned a good job, I discussed it with my wife Irene that I would now bring home a check worth 50% less but I would be working for myself. She said "Wally, I still have a lot of recipes that use ground meat." Both Pete and I were now receiving a salary at Model Garment Company. I traveled a few times each month to the garment district in New York City and was able to get additional contracts at a very fair price. Within a year we decided to increase production by adding additional machines. The only problem was that the pressing and shipping department was taking up space where we planned to add the additional sewing machines. We had a lease that had eleven months to go, so we could not look for a larger building. We leased a former hardware store about one block away to be used as our pressing and shipping department. We added a truck to our equipment inventory. This truck would make a round-trip every 18 minutes to deliver finished garments to be pressed and shipped.

Once again, we needed more space. In October 1954, we purchased a large 50 x 100 foot building at 222 South Lehigh Avenue. It began life as a Studebaker Automobile Dealership. It was later purchased and used as a plumbing supplies store. We made an offer to the owner, John Sokena, to purchase the building. Mr. Sokena was ready to retire and we were successful in the purchase of the building.

The building had a large basement that was partly underground. After meeting labor and industry regulations, we moved the sewing operations on the first floor and pressing and shipping in the basement. Within a year Irene, stopped purchasing ground meat and we decided to build a two-story 50-foot extension on the back of the building. (I promise that I will shortly add a few paragraphs to make this story more interesting.) Moving from one house to another in my youth was paying great dividends. We decided to expand and build another building 50' X 150" on a vacant lot across the alley from our present building. The entire parcel of land was vacant from Arch Street to Chestnut Street with exception of two homes that were built near Chestnut Street. The Borough of Frackville owned this large piece of land. This was the site of the former "Wagner" ice dam. As a child, my friends and I would fish there. We were able to catch some Sunfish and if we were lucky, a large catfish. During the winter, it was our ice skating pond where we played ice hockey. We used "100" percent natural hockey sticks. We would select a small scrub oak tree pull it out of the ground and the root would become the club end of the hockey stick. Later when we decided to extend the building on Lehigh Avenue, I found one of these hockey sticks when the contractor was digging for the foundation. I still have this piece of sport equipment from my youth. It may be viewed at the "Wally Baran Antique and Classic Car Museum" located at Fountain Springs, PA.

The Frackville Borough Council refused to sell us the land. We desperately needed a building to be used as a cutting department. In our early years, we did not need a cutting room since all the garments were cut in New York. At this time we were offered a good contract providing we could cut our own work. A building in Frackville came on the market that was perfect for a cutting room. The former *Victoria Theatre* where I attended many Cowboy and Indian movies as a child was now for sale. The owner of the building leveled and installed a new floor and replaced the front entrance with a brick front that included a large window. The interior walls and the 35-foot ceiling were not changed. The walls contained the original cloth tapestries that were spaced 10 feet apart and were twelve feet wide and 25 feet high. The original projector booth was converted to a balcony to be used as an office. The building was 50 by 150 feet. In 1956, we made the decision to buy the building.

I asked Madge Kerrigan if she could do some research on the theaters in Frackville since the Kerrigan family operated two theaters in town.

She reports:

> *The first theater was built about 1870. It was called the "John Harris Theatre" it was built by the "Patriotic Sons of America." It was also known as the "J. Kehler Theater" and later the "Jim White Theater" The Kerrigan family bought the theater and it became "The Garden Theater."*

> *"The Victoria Theater" was built by Mr. Kerrigan in 1915. It usually played Western Movies and was a popular spot—when on Tuesdays in the summer, movies were 5 cents! The theater was sold to Wally Baran—*

who had the "Hampton House Art Gallery" until it became the Frackville Library.

Of interest to me is the fact that Stephan Kotch, my father was one of the original investors in the theater.

Madge

The building was built specifically as a movie theater. During the 1930's, the theater was opened only on weekends: Friday evening, a matinee on Saturday afternoon, and a Sunday evening show. Western films were featured. A typical Saturday matinee consisted of a cartoon, a full-length film starring Tom Mix, and a chapter of a serial movie. The serial ended with a beautiful blond girl, her hands and feet tied with a clean, new, white, stout rope lying across the railroad tracks, her long beautiful blond hair perfectly placed to both sides of her face, and a view of a steam locomotive exiting a tunnel through a mountain, running at full steam towards our heroine. Next, we see a view of our hero on a white horse running in full gallop towards our heroine. While sitting at the edge of my seat, a notice flashed on the screen **"Continued Next Week."** What a bummer!

We installed two long wooden cutting tables. After a year and a half, it was decided that we should install metal and fiber top cutting tables that could be used with modern spreading machines. Since the cutting room was 3 city blocks away from our main factory we knew that eventually we would need more than two cutting tables, and that the cutting room should be located in a building directly behind the building on land owned by the Borough of Frackville.

After many attempts to purchase the land without success, we approached Mr. Ted Bessasparis who owned one of the two houses located on this plot of land. It was a small building that housed his job printing operation. He lived in the small apartment above the print shop. He closed the print shop and was planning to move to Florida. We purchased the building and attached a concrete block building extending 150 feet to the alley in the rear. We used this space for a cutting room. Within two years, we desperately needed yet another building 50' x 150' to be used as a shipping room.

Again we tried to purchase the lot on the south end of our building. The Frackville Borough Council again refused to sell us the land. Meanwhile we received unexpected help from the Commonwealth of Pennsylvania. We did not ask for this help, but since we were both good living and honest people good things happen.

The Frackville Borough Council had been ordered by the Pennsylvania Department of Environmental Resources (DER) to replace the undersized sewer pump located on the west end of the town on the stream that flowed through Frackville.

In 1959, our honeymoon home on Centre Street was rather small. We decided to build a large home since we only had two children and were expecting a few more. I found a piece of land in the west end of Frackville where I tried to purchase three or four acres of land. Mrs. Richards of Frackville, a granddaughter of J.J. Kehler Jr., Was in charge of the estate that consisted of over 55 acres of beautiful land covered with large oak trees. She was a very fine woman and said that the only way she would sell this land was if I would buy the entire 55 acres. I discussed it with my attorney, John Walesky. I told him that I was prepared to purchase the land. He said "Wally, she's been trying to sell that white elephant for the last 25 years and you may not think so, but there are smarter people in this town than you and no one in town is interested in that land." I again thought of the advice my mother gave me years ago and began using my head. I decided to sell some stock and borrow the rest of the funds I needed. Meanwhile, I did find some time to play golf. I talked my friend, Nicholas Tatusko, into joining the Fountain Springs Country Club and we played golf two or three times a week. While we were both looking for Nick's ball in the deep rough on the fourth hole, I mentioned to him that I was going to buy 55 acres of land west of Frackville in Butler Township. I intended to build a new home and sell the rest off in building lots. He thought about what I said for a few days and later suggested that we become partners since he knew how to operate heavy equipment and I could arrange for a surveyor and do the basic bookwork that would be required. I obtained a plot plan from the Courthouse at Pottsville so that we could lay out the streets and provide for the water and sewer lines, that would be required. Now I know that I am supposed to be writing about the Model Garment Company. I didn't know it then but this land would be very important for the growth of the Model Garment Company. It may take a few more paragraphs, but I will eventually explain why.

Our new home in Walnick Manor

Nick and I made a decision to proceed. We paid a visit to Mrs. Richards to tell her that we agreed with her terms and wanted to purchase the entire plot. Before agreeing to sell us the land, she had a few questions. She already knew that I wanted to build a home and that we would divide the rest of the property in building lots. She said, "When I was a young girl my grandfather, told me that he would love to see beautiful homes set among all the oak trees." She was also concerned that certain businesses would be located on the site such as a coal preparation plant or a grocery store.

I told her that we would include restrictions in each deed stating that only residential homes would be built on the site. She said, "I will meet you tomorrow after lunch on the road under the high tension electric lines. Make sure you wear heavy shoes. I will show

you where all the surveyor's steel rods are." I told her that there
was no need to visit the site since we had a plot plan from the
courthouse, but she insisted. The next day we met at the site. She
was wearing men's boots that came up to her knees. As we walked
along through the heavy forest, she asked, "Do you see those piles
of stones that are scattered through this whole area?" I did wonder
about those piles of stones on the many trips I made trying to
visualize how a new housing development would look on this plot of
ground. She then told us this story. "During the long coal strike in
1902, the miners had no income to pay for food. They did have
some help from the Salvation Army who supplied them with food
packages occasionally. My grandfather and my daddy (Webster
Kehler) (she was about 88 years old but she still called her father
daddy) saw many men who were idle standing in groups in town.
He selected about forty men each day and he paid them $1.00
dollar per day to pick stones that were on his land. Each day he
selected different men. They began this work early morning and he
would arrive with his horse and wagon at lunchtime giving them a
sandwich and coffee. She said he did this for a few months. $1
went a long way in those days." That pile of stones that you see is
the work that these miners did."

A little history: Her grandfather, J. J. Kehler Sr., was the owner
of the Kehler Hotel. He was also the owner of the "The Citizens
Water Co." previously called "The Mountain City Water Co." built
in 1882 by Frances S. and John Haupt and sold in 1903 to her
grandfather J. J. Kehler. Her father, Mr. Webster Kehler was the
owner of a large hotel about one block away from the passenger
railroad station. He also owned various tracts of land in the Frackville
area.

We were successful in purchasing this plot of ground from the
Kehler estate. We now finally come to the point on how this
purchase of land would be of great help to continue the growth of
the Model garment Company.

As was mentioned previously, the Frackville Borough Council
was ordered by the Pennsylvania Department of Environmental
Resources (DER) to replace the undersized sewer pump located

on the west end of the town on the stream that flowed through Frackville. The good news was that Walter Baran and Nicholas Tatusko now owned all the land adjacent to the existing sewer pump. They formed a development company called "WallNick Manor." The Frackville Borough Council had been cited a few times by DER to replace this undersized pump. They were finally given 90 days to comply.

While the Frackville Council members did not contact me directly, it came to my attention that they wanted to buy three acres of land at the present site of their undersized pump. I know that they could have claimed "Eminent Domain," they then would take the land for a reasonable price. This however would have taken six months to go through the courts even though we had an agreement with them. They only had 90 days to comply. I wrote a letter to the Frackville Borough Council advising them that I would trade three acres of land for a lot 50 feet by 150 feet that adjoined our factory building on Balliet Street. They readily agreed to make the trade. DER knew that they could not build the edition for the new pump on time, but since they now owned the land they were given additional time to comply with their ruling. Since all sewer systems work by gravity, all of the sewage on the west end of Frackville was diverted to this pump. Since Frackville did not have a sewage preparation plant, this pump was used to send the sewerage to a higher point in Frackville and then the sewerage ran by gravity into an abandoned coalmine. This went on for years. Since the entire old coalmine filled with water, eventually the water mixed with sewerage ran into the local streams. DER finally made all of the communities in our area install a treatment plant.

With the completion of the new building to be used as a cutting room using the newest state-of-the-art cutting tables and automatic spreading machines, we had no further use for the former *Victoria Movie Theater*. The old-style wooden cutting tables were still in the building. Using my mother's advice I once again began using my brain to see how I could put this building to use and earn some additional income. I remember that on a Saturday afternoon I entered the building, sat on the cutting table, and thought, "Mom, give me an idea." After about fifteen minutes I decided what I was going to do.

I decided to open a "Factory To You store." In 1957, there were no "Outlet stores" in our area. From Wilkes-Barre in the north to Hamburg in the south and Sunbury in the East to Allentown in the west, no outlet stores existed. Malls did not exist.

During the late '40s when I was in my third year at the "Northumberland Dress Inc. University." I traveled to other factories repairing sewing machines and became friends with all of the owners. I also knew that every factory had extra garments, broken sizes, and odd lots that I could probably purchase. I began by calling my friends asking them to sell me their surplus garments. I insisted that I would not buy any seconds. Every garment had to be first quality. I began with our own factory "Model Garment Company Inc." where we had ladies jackets, pants and blouses. I was able to get a very good assortment of various garments for men, women and children. One of my best resources was John E. Morgan of Tamaqua. Mr. Morgan was the inventor of Thermal fabric used in underwear. He also made wonderful men's T-shirts. They were full-sized extra long, and sanforised.

I made a few racks for the garments that were on hangers and placed them along the wall. Most of the items were in boxes that I set on the cutting tables. I arranged a small counter near the door, purchased brown bags in various sizes from the Pennsylvania Paper Supply Co. in Pottsville, placed an empty cigar box on the counter, and I was ready to sell. A large piece of white cardboard was placed in the window with the name "Model Factory Outlet" first quality garments at factory prices. Opened every Friday evening 6 PM to 9 PM. Saturday 9 AM to 5 PM

I decided that I was going to "bunch the customers." When I was in New York on business, I would visit Macy's department store to check on prices and I noticed that they had a "bargain table." The garments were in a mess from people crowding around, and shoving each other to get at the bargains. They "bunch" the customers so I decided to do the same. The first Friday evening that the "Outlet" was open, I had about 10 customers. I decided not to have a "Grand Opening." On Saturday, things were looking up I had 12 customers. And so it went for about a month and a half. Sales did not improve much for the first few months. Since I was a "przeciwny" guy, I would not give up. Some Friday evenings I was alone in the store. Occasionally my golfing buddy Nick Tatusko would keep me company. Later on I decided to advertise. I advertised only in the *Shenandoah Evening Herald.* And the sales went up tremendously. I had a few "leaders" such as John Morgan's 100% cotton sanforised T-shirts that I sold for 50 cents. I paid Mr. Morgan $5.50 per dozen. My cost, 46 cents each. Some customers bought two shirts. After they washed them a few times, they came in and bought them by the dozens. They also made a lot of other purchases. Since it's much too late to make a long story short, I will try to speed it up.

I began advertising in three County newspapers. *We are open only on Friday evenings and Saturday to 5:00. On Mondays, Tuesdays, Wednesdays, Thursdays, Friday, we are busy in our factory making more bargains.*

I purchased a used cash register. I hired a salesperson. I hired a second salesperson. I hired a cashier. I began taking a large bag to the night depository at the First National Bank of Frackville on Friday evening and late Saturday afternoon.

I began traveling to New York to buy, well, "Everything" men's shirts, socks, ladies bras, (some men bought them but they told us it was for their wives), heavy winter coats for men, children's outerwear and, well, I guess you get the idea. We added Thursdays to our open schedule. Nick Tatusko stopped visiting me at the store. He said, "I just can't stand crowds."

My brother and partner Pete, was not interested in the store. When I first opened, he called it "Wally's folly." When I purchased merchandise in New York, I arranged to have it shipped to our factory. He would check the packages that came in looking for a shipment of thread. When he saw that it was boxes of sweaters, he would say "more junk for the store." After I purchased a brand new cash register, and a new large sign made by a professional sign maker that read, **MODEL FACTORY OUTLET** he told me that he would be able to help me on Thursday evenings. He then also worked in the outlet on Saturdays. In fact we both spent most of our time in the outlet. Our sister Frances was running the factory. Pete was a good partner and we got along fine for many years. He wanted to change things at the store. "We should be opened every day of the week." We should buy chrome plated racks to hold the garments." Etc. I tried to tell him about Macy's bargain table but he would not listen.

The Outlet was very successful. Everything was going well, and it was a very profitable business. At this time we were advertising in five newspapers. We ran many humorous ads. One advertisement had pictures of a bus, passenger train, a small airplane, a station wagon, and a small rowboat. And the following statement: **We do not know how you arrive at our store; if you are coming from Sunbury or Williamsport take Route 122 South. From the Bethlehem and Allentown area, take Route number 309. From Harrisburg and Pine Grove, take Route Number 22 then 183 to 122. If you get lost, please follow the car in front of you since he is probably coming to our store.**

On a very sunny Saturday in July, a forest fire on the mountain south of Frackville caused a serious problem. The entire town was without electric power. While the advertisement quoted above was "Tongue in cheek," we did have people driving a long distance to shop at our outlet. Fortunately, Pete suggested that we use the portable gas powered generator that we had at the factory. Since the power panel was located on the balcony at the front of the store, we placed the generator on the sidewalk, ran the wires through the window, and connected them to the fuse box. It worked! It supplied enough electricity to light two rows of lights and more importantly, the electrically operated cash registers. We were the only merchant on the street that had power. My good friend Harry Lehman from "Harry Lehman the Workman's Store" (we competed but we sold mostly lady and children's clothes) walked down, looked at the gas generator operating and said, "You guys just can't be stopped." Frackville did not have any power until the following Monday morning.

Steve Zenimer, CPA, our accountant, asked to have a meeting with us. He had two monthly statements, the factory and the store. He said, "You guys have to make a decision. Close the factory or close the store. The factory is going down the tubes." During this time, we both spent some time at the factory, but not enough. There were many problems. We were doing work for about five different jobbers from New York. Two of them no longer gave us work. The unpaid bills were piling up. We could not agree what to do. I suggested that it might be time for us to dissolve the partnership. I said, "I will give you a choice; you can take the factory or the store, your choice. Mr. Zenimer will give us the value of each." After thinking about it on the weekend, Pete said," I know it's not fair, but if you mean what you said, I will take the store." I was now on my own at the Model Garment Co. Inc.

I rolled up my sleeves and went to work. After six months time, the factory began to show signs of life. I was able to find a new jobber who supplied us with good work. The operators were earning more because we've worked on the same style for months at a time. It looked like Model Garment Co. was going to survive and even expand.

In the meantime Pete decided to make changes at the store. He purchased chrome clothing racks; he bought men's T-shirts from some guy that sold them for 3 dollars a dozen and he continued selling them for 50 cents. The label was marked "sanforised" and by George, the label was sanforised but the rest of the shirt shrunk after just one washing. He then did an amazing thing. He announced that the outlet will be closed for one month for remodeling. He put in a second floor, installed new lighting, and tile for the floor. He now had a modern store that was open all week including Saturdays. The customers were no longer "bunched." There was now a lot more room in the aisles and the customers now had space for leisurely shopping.

After two years the Model Outlet Store began having serious problems. I was still supplying Pete with garments that we made at the factory. Pete was a very proud man. When I asked how things were going he said, "It's slow now, but it will pick up in the spring." Spring arrived but sales got worse at the store. He announced in the newspapers that he was going to have a "Going out of business sale." The sale lasted about two months. Since I was sitting on the board of the First National Bank, his mortgage was discussed during a meeting. The bank was ready to foreclose. After the meeting, the bank cashier, Mr. Ben Stone, suggested that I take over the mortgage. I approached Pete (it was extremely difficult for me to do this) and told him what I heard at the board meeting. He readily agreed since he would not have to declare bankruptcy.

The building was vacant for over a year. In our travels, we purchased many oil paintings and other works of art for our home. I decided to open an art gallery in the building. We did some remodeling: New wall paneling, a small vestibule divided the space into two rooms, new front doors, a beautiful blue awning, and some authentic copies of French furniture. The room at the rear was used for art lessons. We purchased seventy-five wooden folding chairs that were used when a slide show was held for children from the local schools. We had slide shows of famous paintings for various groups, senior citizens, elementary and high schools, woman's clubs, etc. Mrs. Willard Long (Steffi) was the curator and manager. She was a very knowledgeable and capable art connoisseur. She ran all of the art lectures and set up the schedules for the various schools. The Schuylkill County Council of the Arts held its annual weeklong exhibit at the Hampton House Art Gallery. It was well received. We knew when we began that this would not be a profitable operation. I hoped that we could sell a few paintings that would help pay for the upkeep of the building.

The Frackville Free Public Library was located on the second floor of Alexander's 5 and 10-cent store located on Lehigh Avenue. The library board was notified that to continue to receive state grants, the library would have to be accessible to the handicapped, which meant that an elevator or escalator would have to be installed. Since this would be a very expensive solution for the problem, it was decided to look for space on the first floor of the building located in the center of town. I was approached by a member of the Library Board and asked if the art gallery would be available for their use. At this time, the gallery was in existence for over two years. The building was remodeled with beautiful paneling, a new ceiling with excellent lighting and a large storage room located at the rear of the building. The library would not have any expense in occupying the building. Knowing the importance of the library to the town of Frackville it was with a heavy heart that I decided that Frackville had greater need for a library rather than an art gallery. The building was leased and later sold To the Frackville Free Public Library.

I then purchased the former Acme Market in Ashland and established a new firm, "Ashland Sportswear Co. Inc." I installed about 60 new sewing machines and after a slow start, the company became profitable. After about six months of operation, I called my brother Pete to see if he would be willing to manage the business and later to become a partner. He accepted and after about six months he became a 50 percent owner. About a year later I sold him my shares of stock. His son George later joined him in operating the plant.

Our son Tony was always interested in the garment industry. During the summer's vacations from Prep School, 1965, 66, and 67 he worked full-time at the factory.

He entered Lehigh University in 1968. He soon found out that the University had a radio station and since he was interested in radios his entire life, he decided to take the examination as a certified radio operator. The examinations were given at the U.S. Customs Office in Philadelphia. The test contained four elements.

No appointments were necessary to take these examinations. He appeared at the customs office and informed the man in charge that he wanted to take the radio operators examinations. The man looked at Tony with a jaundiced eye. He first noticed Tony's very long hair. He also noticed that he did not wear socks, and on his bare feet he wore a scruffy dirty pair of tennis shoes. I really should describe the shirt he was wearing but I cannot since it was indescribable. But I could tell you that the trousers he was wearing was worse than his shirt.

The examiner picked up a sheet marked "Radio-First element." And I would really like to say that he handed the sheet to Tony but that would not be honest. He flipped it on the counter and it almost fell to the floor. Tony, always the gentleman, said, "Thank you."

Element No. 1 was only three pages long. Within fifteen minutes,

Tony was finished, approached the counter, and asked for the next part of the test. The examiner was required to check the answers before issuing the next element. By using the form designed for that purpose, he could see that all of the answers were correct. He then gave him the next test. This one took Tony about 45 minutes. The examiner once again checked and saw that Tony had responded correctly to all the questions. Most of the applicants taking this examination would take one the first day, and come back in a few days and take the third test and within another week take the final test. Tony was now working on the third element of the examination. The tests became much more difficult as he went along. It took Tony about an hour and a half to finish. He approached the desk and asked for the fourth and final test. The examiner no longer looked at Tony's uncombed hair, in his eyes Tony was wearing the latest preppy clothes purchased at *Brooks Brothers* in New York City. The examiner said, "Sonny, you have been working very hard, go have some lunch, take a little rest, and if you care to, come back in an hour and finish the test. Tony said "I have to get back to the University to study for a test I'm taking tomorrow morning." I don't think I have to write the following line, but I will anyway. Surprise! He passed the test! In one day, he received his First Class Radio Operators License. He was now qualified to work as an engineer in any radio or television station in the entire United States of America.

He worked at Lehigh's radio station "pro bono." He also managed to work for three radio stations in the Allentown, Bethlehem, and Easton area for which he was handsomely paid. He mainly had to check if the stations were tuned to their assigned frequency. He also had to occasionally climb the radio tower antennas to make the necessary adjustments. He often worked on two stations the same day since it only took an hour or two to make the adjustments.

On occasion, the station disc jockey would be detained at "Harry's Tavern" so Tony was asked to play a few records, give the weather and traffic report. His friends at his fraternity found out that he was filling in for *"Polka Joe's Polka Hour."* They began calling the station with requests for their favorite polka! It wasn't funny.

In the spring of 1960, I decided to hire a manager. I approached a friend of mine, Willard Long. Willard was a department manager for the Philip Van Heusen plant located in Pottsville, Pennsylvania. I asked him if he would consider the position of manager of Model Garment Co. I suggested that he meet me at our main plant on a Saturday morning so he could see the type of garments we were producing. He could also see the equipment we had and I would respond to any questions he might have.

I asked him to think about joining our firm and suggested that we meet again the following Saturday at which time I would make him an offer. I said, "I do not know the salary you are presently receiving, nor do I want to know."

After discussing the offer with his wife, he decided to accept the position. He intended to give 2 weeks notice to his employer at Philip Van Heusen. They were not very pleased that he intended to leave their employ. The Philip Van Heusen Corp. had a long history and was listed on the stock exchange. Willard was a member of their employee stock plan where certain employees were able to purchase stock at a special rate. Willard told me that they listed the advantages of remaining with the company and what they perceived as disadvantages of working for Model Garment Co. "The Model Garment Co. is only 10 years old. They rose fast and it's possible that they would fall even faster. They could be out of business in six months or a year." I told Willard, "They are absolutely right. It is very possible, but not very probable."

Willard Long made the decision and worked for Model Garment for over 30 years! While his style of operating was different than mine, we were very compatible and we got along fine. As the years went by, Model kept expanding and the business was getting more complex each year. I suggested that we create another position, that of assistant manager so that Willard could pay more attention to the quality of our products. At this time, we had a high school student who worked part-time on Saturdays and evenings. We had a small group of sewing machine operators that worked evenings only. He would supervise these employees, close the building at the end of their shift, leave a written report listing the work done, etc. I suggested to Willard that we hire him after he graduated from high school, full-time to be the assistant manager. Willard did not think that was a good idea. He did some checking such as, his rank in the graduating class, his family history, etc. He felt that he would not be capable to do the job.

I said to Willard, "Using your criteria, you would never hire me, a dropout from the 10th grade who had mediocre grades in school and lived in a home without a father." That settled it and Wayne also worked at Model for over 30 years. Willard worked very well with Wayne and he became a great help in managing the factory.

Tony graduated from Lehigh University in January 1972. He received his four-year degree in three and one-half years. And was very anxious to show his dad how to run the business. He began to insist that we buy a computer. He told me that it would save money in the office. I asked him, "How many employees do we have in the office?" He said "Three." I asked him to follow me and I asked him, "How many employees do you see on this floor?" He said, "About ninety." I asked, "How many would we need if we had a computer?" He then gave up. Or so I thought. I found out later that a computer has to be ordered six months in advance. After five months had passed, a couple of huge cartons arrived containing a B700 Burroughs computer! I asked, "What's going on?"

"You told me not to *buy* a computer, so I leased one." I found out later that it would cost $50,000 to purchase and only $650 a month for a lease. Well, I was wrong! Not only did it do the payroll, make the bundle tickets, could trace every garment back to the operator who worked on each operation, and we were able to ship the garments in less time than previously. After a year, we purchased an IBM 36 computer. We were the only garment factory in eastern Pennsylvania and part of New Jersey that operated with the help of a computer.

Tony worked in every department from the cutting room to the shipping room. Though as a child he did not have the pleasure of moving to from one house to another as I did, (he only lived in two houses until he was married.) He surely made up for it by constantly suggesting locations for new factories. I suppose it was in his genes! After a sewing machine salesman told him of a rather large factory located on Allen Street in West Hazleton that was for sale, within two months we purchased and renamed the new factory "Penn Allen Inc." It was a difficult job retraining the 130 employees to our methods of operation. It took them approximately three months to realize that our way was really the "best" way. Their grouchy faces turned to smiles when they received their weekly check.

Penn Allen Inc. was purchased a year after we purchased a factory located on Spruce Street in Sunbury. It was named Penn Spruce Inc. It took over six months to turn a profit since all of the equipment was antiquated. (I'm trying to be fair about this but some of the operators were in the same condition.) However being "przeciwny," we persevered and succeeded in "Making a Pearl from a Sow's ear." We now had over 400 employees in three plants.

Tony wasn't finished yet. He convinced me that cutting in one building and sewing in another was not being very practical or financially wise. Land was available in Frackville's new Industrial Park that would allow us to build a 40,000 square foot air-conditioned state-of-the-art garment factory. Room was available for an adjoining 40,000 square foot building to be used as a receiving department and cutting room. The building had three truck docks. The docks were very important since we received a few very large trailers each day delivering the rolls of fabric directly to the factory from the mills in North and South Carolina.

One of our largest resources was Glamour Sportswear of New York City. We now had 80,000 square feet of space and were producing about 650 dozen (yep, that's 7,800 pair from our Frackville plant) of lady slacks per day. All of our production was shipped to a warehouse in Bangor, PA, owned by Glamour Sportswear. Since Model Garment Co. owned 10 acres of land in the Industrial Park, an arrangement was made with Glamour Sportswear to purchase 3.5 acres of land adjacent to our building to build a receiving and shipping center. This would save thousands of dollars in shipping costs and would enable Glamour to process and ship the garments immediately after we manufactured them. They built a 60,000 square foot building that was connected by a tunnel directly from our pressing department.

An "Eton Unit Production System" a high-tech delivery system was installed in the sewing and pressing departments. All parts of one pair of pants including the waistband, the size ticket, union label etc. was hung by hand to the trolley by one operator. This was the last time that the garments were handled by hand. The garments were hung on the overhead trolley that rode its way to each individual sewing operator, there was no need to handle bundles, no need to list the amount of garments for each operator.

Each operator had an employee number, and as every garment left her station, she was credited by computer for garments sewed. The system was very efficient. Model Garment was the only firm in Eastern Pennsylvania to install this system. Walking into the sewing room one would see garments in various stages of completion constantly running from one area to another. After being completely sewn and still on the trolley system, the garments would be sent to the pressing department that operated in the same way as the sewing department. Here the pressing operator removed the garment from the trolley and after pressing it, would place the garment on a garment hanger. It would be sent by trolley to the plastic bagging area where a machine would automatically place a plastic bag and deliver it back on the trolley that then transported it through the eight-foot long tunnel that joined our building to the Glamour shipping building. Using this system a garment would make the journey from cut parts to completed garment in 45 minutes!

Special notice

In all the preceding paragraphs, I reported only the "Good News" about the rapid growth of the Model Garment Co. I probably have misled you. If this report had been printed in about 1960, anyone with $1000 would immediately go into the garment manufacturing business and make loads of money! It did not happen that way. For the first 10 years, my work schedule was as follows:

Breakfast at 6 AM

Arrive at the factory at 6:20 AM (During the winter
months, arrived at the factory 5 AM to coax the coal
furnace to produce some heat for the arrival of the
employees at 6:50 AM)
Lunch at home at 12:05 PM
Back to the factory at 12:30 PM
Arrive home at 5:30 PM for dinner
Back to the factory at 6 PM
Arrive home about 10:45 PM
Most Saturday's we worked until noon.

The hours we spent at work were very productive, and I did
not mind the long hours. But we had many problems too numerous
to mention here. Suffice to say that on a good day we had only five
problems. When I came home in the evening, Irene (who knew me
like a book) could immediately tell if I had a "good" five-problem
day, or one of those horrible twelve problem days. In fact, just
sitting here writing these words about all the problems makes me
want to cry, but Irene cleans and rearranges my desk and my
computer room each Friday morning like clockwork. I do not mind
that I have to occasionally spend some time rearranging the various
papers on my desk so that I could find what I want, but she did not
replace my "crying towel" that I keep near to my computer.
However, after about eleven years, as I mentioned previously, Irene
no longer purchased ground meat and I began buying antique cars.

And to the "entrepreneurs" who may be reading this, I have some
advice. *"The load is heavy, but the rewards are heavenly."* I did
not read this quote anywhere, I just made it up. Feel free to quote me.

During the '90s, the garment industry was hit with a serious
"Virus," a double whammy." The garment companies were no longer
just leaving for South Carolina, Georgia, etc. They were now moving
offshore to Jamaica, Haiti, Dominican Republic, and other islands
in the Caribbean that were not unionized and paid extremely low
wages. Even though Model Garment Co. had the most modern and
efficient plant in Pennsylvania, it was getting very difficult to
compete with the cheap imports of clothing coming from Taiwan,

Hong Kong, and other Asian countries plus the American firms moving to the Caribbean.

As could be imagined, all of the owners who held contracts with the "International Ladies Garment Union" began through the Atlantic Apparel Association to ask for some small changes that would assist those plants that still remained in Pennsylvania. As an example, the factories under the ILGWU had a 35-hour contract, while the Amalgamated Union who represented all the factories making men's wear had a 40-hour per week contract. While most of the employees were willing to work 40 hours, the union would not negotiate.

In January of 1979, I left to accept a Thornburgh administration appointment as Secretary of General Services for Pennsylvania, a position that I held for eight years. During this time I was not involved in any way with Model Garment Company. Early 1980, my son Tony finally convinced his brother Joseph to join him in managing our various operations. I retired in January of 1986 and was no longer involved in the family business.

By 1989, the apparel contracting business had become unprofitable, and the future outlook for unionized operations such as Model Garment was bleak. Joe and Tony had recognized the inevitability of this for some time, and had begun to plan a new business. They incorporated a new firm, "EXTOL International Inc." in October of that year, and in 1990 closed Model Garment Company and devoted their full attention to the new business. EXTOL is a product software company that develops and markets sophisticated data transformation software used by corporations to exchange business documents with their trading partners. The first customer installation of the software occurred during 1991, and at the current time there are over 600 installations. The first employee was hired in 1993, and employment has grown to 60 employees. In 1994 they opened a sales and marketing office in Franklin Lakes, NJ, a NYC suburb, and in 1997 the corporate headquarters, product development and customer support operations moved from Frackville to their current location in Pottsville.

THE CONCORDE

During the first week of April 1978, I received a telephone call from my friend Phil Taylor of Birmingham, England. During one of our visits to his home, I told him that I would like to own a "20/25 Bromley Town Saloon" Rolls Royce from the early '30s. He called to tell me that he found an original 1935 20/25 Bromley Town Saloon owned by one of his neighbors and was available for sale. It was not restored and owned by the same man for many years. More importantly, he told me that the price was very reasonable. The owner was R.A. Bonham-Christie, an elderly gentleman that had to sell the car because of his health. It was his intention to move into an elder care facility.

I read in the travel section of the Sunday edition of the *New York Times* that the Concorde had scheduled flights from London to New York / Washington D.C. Since I was going alone and only expected to stay in England for one or two days, I thought this would be a great opportunity to fly on the Concorde. I asked my son, Tony, if he could fly me to the airport at Philadelphia in his single-engine four seat Cessna 182, and on my return, pick me up in New York. On April 10th, 1978, Tony flew me to the airport at Philadelphia. I did not have reservations on any flight. When I arrived, I went to the British Airways counter and saw that there were three flights to London that day. I noticed quite a few college students waiting for standby seats that in 1978 were sold at a discount. When the first flight was called, an announcement was made that there were standby seats available. All the students ran to the gate. I decided to wait for the second or third flight. I flew standby on the third flight that had an arrival time in London at 13:35 (1:30 PM). The cost for the flight was about $100.

When I arrived at the Heathrow Airport in London, I called Phil Taylor to tell him that a flight to Birmingham was available and it was leaving at 15:35 (3:35 PM). He told me to buy a one-way ticket since he would drive me back to London in his newly acquired Rolls Royce "Phantom Four." I purchased a ticket from London to Birmingham on British Midland Airways. £17.50 about $28.00. I then went to the Concorde counter at British Airways and inquired about a flight to New York leaving April 13th. I was told that I had a choice, I could fly direct to JFK in New York or a direct flight to Dulles Airport in Washington D.C. I said I would call my son and ask which airport would be more convenient for him. I was directed by the clerk to the Concorde lounge where I could make a call to United States without charge. Tony told me to select the Dulles Airport since it was not as busy as JFK. The flight was scheduled to leave London/ Heathrow at 13:00 hours (1:00 PM.) The ticket for the one-way flight cost £ 479.50 approximately $800.00. I usually do not keep any old tickets from various flights that we have made but British Airways gave me a beautiful carrying case with a lot of goodies enclosed such as, Concorde writing paper with envelopes, postcards, writing pen, earphones, booties, bumper sticker etc. It was very convenient to put all my tickets and receipts so I have a good record of this trip.

I will digress to tell you about Phil Taylor's RR Phantom Four. First off, it is gold in color, had a very light blue leather interior, a bar with six Waterford Crystal glasses, and two beautiful crystal decanters that held English sherry and the best Scotch that could be produced in Wales, an Intercom system, curtains on all rear windows, a three band radio, and a sound system that was the best available for the year 1975. The Taylor family, Phil, (his wife Bess did not own a car) his sons Andrew, Nicholas, and daughter, Sue, own eleven Rolls-Royce automobiles. All but two were antique. I'll write more about how I met this interesting family later in this story since I don't want to miss my flight to Birmingham.

The flight to Birmingham was less than one hour so upon my

arrival at the Birmingham Airport, Phil and his son Nicholas decided to drive me immediately to see the 20/25 Bromley Town Saloon. I did not mind since I only had a mild case of jet lag. The Wraith was only about one half mile from their home. While I don't really know, I believe that Phil called Mr. Bonham-Christie and told him to expect us at his home to see his car. We arrived and I was very pleased with the condition of the car. The engine ran very smoothly and extremely quiet. Mr. Bonham-Christie said "I feel that you should take it for a drive on the M-5 Dual Carriageway. You will find that it operates well on the country roads as well as the Dual Carriageway." We drove the car on a few of the streets but it was beginning to get a bit dark and I suggested we go back without motoring on the Dual Carriageway. Being a very smart businessman, I told him that I would have to sleep on it before I make a decision. Of course I was lying. I wanted that car real bad!

Since the Taylor home had only four bedrooms and there were 5 adults in the family, Phil made arrangements for me to stay at an old inn a few miles from Birmingham. This was not a bed and breakfast. It was over 200 years old and it was a lovely small hotel. I arrived late in the evening. The gentleman at the reception wore very proper English attire and was super efficient. After I signed the quaint registration book he asked me, "What do you read?" I thought of telling him that I am partial to reading the biographies of early Americans such as John Adams, Thomas Jefferson, John Quincy Adams, The Life and Times of Frederick Douglass, Benjamin Franklin's autobiography, and a few novels by Joseph Conrad and Dostoyevsky's Crime and Punishment etc. I hesitated a bit and he suggested that he could arrange to get a copy of the European edition of the *New York Times Herald*. I guess he recognized me as an American. Probably because of the clothes I was wearing. I asked for the London Times. My room was on the second floor or I should say rooms, a large bedroom, a drawing room, and a bathroom that was as large as a non-smoking room at the Holiday Inn in Gettysburg, Pennsylvania. I only packed a small bag containing a fresh change of linens, two pairs of socks, and a clean shirt. I later realized that I did not pack my silk drawing robe so that I could have my morning tea properly attired. He also asked me how do I take my tea. Again I hesitated a bít and he asked "With warm milk or cream?" I asked him. "Could I have a cube of sugar." I took a bath in the huge tub; I didn't have to use the bidet since I was taking a bath. The bed was enormous. It did not have a little step to get on the bed; it had a two-step affair that made easy for me to get in bed. All the furniture was very old. The beautiful but old I guess you would call them all English antiques.

Since I had jet lag I was out of bed early. I heard a knock on the door and a tiny voice called. "Your tea Mr. Baran" This is where I could have used my silk drawing robe I also forgot my evening slippers. Here I was standing in my underwear so I said, "Leave the tray at the door please" She walked so silently I did not hear her leave. I should have heard her leave since there were no carpets in the room or in the hallway, just shiny wide boards. There I stood wearing my clean linens and I decided to open the door a bit to see if all was clear. It was. So I opened the door and I found the tray on a little shelf beside the door that was turned down so that the tray could be placed on it. It was a huge Silver tray. On the tray were one single rosebud, the London Times, and a day-old copy of the European edition of the *New York Times Herald.* A Silver pot of tea (the pot was covered with a beautiful cloth embroidered with small pink and blue flowers. This cover kept the tea warm) a charming teacup and saucer, 4 slices of toast inserted into a four-place Silver toast holder, the toast was held vertically. I suppose it was to make sure that the toast would be cold. Another very small container that matched the teacup and saucer contained the most delicious orange marmalade I ever had on cold toast. There was another small plate that matched the cup and saucer and the small container with the great orange marmalade. It held an apple and a wedge of cheese. Before I had this great breakfast repast, I put on my trousers and the clean pair of socks. When I was half thru with breakfast, (I found out that this was not breakfast.) I went down to the lobby where I was invited to the "breakfast room" and delivered a real English breakfast. Two soft-boiled eggs. One egg was in an eggcup that matched my cup and saucer from my tea service. A

Silver scissors that was made to place on top of the egg to cut the top off. The other egg was on a small plate that of course matched everything. A very thick wedge of smoked ham, two small pork sausages, fried potatoes and 4 slices of meat that I did not recognize or eat. When I started on the second egg, I heard the sound of horse's hoofs. They seem to be going round and round the inn. I hurriedly finished most of my "Real English Breakfast" so I could go out to see the horses. It was a sight to behold. A few young ladies and young men properly attired, riding down the lane besides the inn. I stood there and a young girl said, "Good Morning," in a most beautiful voice. It was spring in England. The birds were singing and for the first time I saw the absolutely beautiful English garden that surrounded the inn.

Phil Taylor arrived in a new car. He asked if I had breakfast. I informed him that I had two breakfasts and I was quite ready to make arrangements to purchase my first Rolls Royce.

I informed Mr. Bonham-Chiristie that I would wire him the necessary funds and that I had given Mr. Phil Taylor power of attorney to act on my behalf. It took three weeks until the necessary documents were ready and the funds were transferred by wire to his bank.

I had at last, purchased as the British would say, "A Proper Automobile." The Rolls-Royce Company uses ethereal names for the different models, such as "Silver Ghost", "Silver Wraith", "Silver Dawn", "Silver Cloud", "Phantom", and "Silver Shadow." I was now the owner of a 1935 Rolls Royce 20/25 Bromley Town Saloon. All English cars registered in England received a license registration number that stays with the car from owner to owner. My 20/25 Bromley Town Saloon has a registration number of CYL 25 and is affectionately known as "Chloe."

Phil and his wife Bess decided to visit the "Colonies" and to escort "Chloe" to the United States. They came over on the QE2. The trip took five days. "Chloe" did not mind the trip, but she was very upset when she found out she had to share a motor house with American Fords and Buick's, to say nothing of those horrid, dreadful French cars!

Phil and Bess spent one day in New York City so that they could get an early start to see if they could find Frackville. I suggested that I meet them in New York in case they may have trouble with the Wraith. Phil was highly insulted! After all it was a Rolls Royce and only 50 years old. They drove up our driveway in Frackville just in time for lunch.

Before we boarded the plane, we spent some time in the Concorde lounge. I have been in a few first-class lounges, but this was by far the most elegant room staffed by a permanent steward and stewardess to wait on the passengers and satisfy their every need. All of the liqueurs were top shelf. Chivas Regal Scotch, Harvey's Bristol Cream Sherry, French champagne, and German beer. Small canapés were being served with Russian caviar and exotic looking meats. Many phones were available to make free international telephone calls. Hell, I could have stayed in that lounge for a few hours.

MY IMPRESSIONS ON FLYING TWICE THE SPEED

OF SOUND

All you can hear is whoosh, whoosh. Compared to most Trans-Atlantic planes, the Concorde is a small plane. It carries 100 passengers. There are four seats across the cabin two on each side of the center isle. My seat was halfway down the aisle. I had the aisle seat. My flying partner was Dan Rather of TV fame. (He did not spend any time in the lounge) Besides me, he was the only other celebrity on board. He looked up at me and said" hi." I responded also with a "hi." He immediately went back to reading a copy of Esquire Magazine. When the plane took off, it seemed as though it was going straight up. My body was pressed into the seat. It soon leveled off and the captain began with the first of his many comments. "As you can see on the instrument on the bulkhead, we are only going at the speed of sound. We have to fly slowly over Ireland since our boom sound blew out many windows on the first flights of the Concorde in the towns that we passed over. We were told that our insurance company would not pay for any more windows in Ireland." Within a half-hour the gauge showed that we were going twice the speed of sound. 1350 miles per hour. I no longer felt the pressure as we did when we took off. The captain also said "Do you see that jumbo jet below us on the right side of the plane? He took off an hour before we did and will arrive in United States possibly three hours after we land." The windows in the plane were very small about the size of a small luncheon plate. We were told that the windows were 4 1/2 inches thick. Every seat was first-class. Large wide leather seats. It was very quiet in the cabin since I suppose we were flying twice the speed of sound the sound must have been about five miles behind us. And no, the restrooms (called by the British "The Necessary") did not have gold plated faucets.

When we were into the flight for about two hours, Dan did not say a word. He kept reading every page including the advertisements. Finally he turned to me and said sort of, "What's your line." I told him that I spent the last 42 years in lady's pants. I quickly added that we were also into lady skirts and jackets. He told me that was a helluva line and he gave a good laugh. He told me that he normally takes the flight to New York twice each week. "Today I have a meeting in Washington that I must attend." I believe that he thought that I did not recognize him when I sat down. He told me that he could not have a quiet flight no matter who was sitting next to him they kept giving him advice "You should have an entire program on the Chinese problem." Why do you, why can't you, ad nauseam." He spent the rest of the flight telling me about the hectic life he was leading and how difficult it was to please the producers etc. When we were picking up our luggage he said, "Wally, keep your sense of humor."

That plane was so damn fast that we arrived in Washington before we left London. We left at 1 PM and arrived in Washington at about 11 AM of the same day.

Tony told me that his plane would be parked in the area called "General Aviation" I asked a few questions and found my way to general aviation. Now, I had a few flights in Tony's Cessna, it was a large plane for a single engine. But when I approached it felt like I was sitting in a kite, a real big kite. But just like the Concorde, Tony's Cessna was very comfortable and got me home safe.

THE TAYLOR FAMILY

W hile attending an antique car rally held at the foothills of the Tatra Mountains in Czechoslovakia, I met Andrew Taylor. It was an international rally with participants from Europe and England. Rallies are usually held for three days. This one lasted a full week. I attended with a few friends from Prague. Since I did not care to ride in a 1921 car for about 900 kilometers on roads that really were worse than those we have in Pennsylvania. Irene, Franciszek Vocka and I flew from Prague to a small town in what is now Slovakia, near the Russian border. The rally headquarters was a large campground of log cabins and a few rather large buildings. Franciszek loved beer so we did not see much of him. Among the cars from England was a Rolls Royce owned by a former officer of the British Armed Forces. He was the driver and Andrew was the pilot. They did not have any difficulty following the route but they didn't speak a word of Czech. They asked me and Irene to ride with them so we could translate for them. I almost understand the Czechs and they can sort of understand my Polish.

We have been friends with the entire Taylor family for over 45 years. They all have made numerous trips to Frackville and we have also crossed the pond to visit them.

The Taylor's live in the city of Birmingham. They also have a beautiful cottage in the very small village of "Little Inkboro." Not to be confused with the small village of Inkboro. Their cottage "Yonda" has a thatched roof, two rather small bedrooms on the second floor, (Mind your head, you are directly under the roof.) There is a stair leading up to the bedrooms. Each step is different. The risers are various heights, and the steps are of various widths. Phil Taylor tells me they were designed to foil robbers and highwaymen if they should break into the cottage they would stumble on the steps which would awaken the "Lord of the Manor." Who would then have an advantage over the intruders since he would be higher on the stairs and would be able to use his sword more effectively.

The cottage has a large fireplace that is used to heat the building. Phil installed a few panels of electric heat. He did not care to get up at 2:30 AM to replenish the wood in the fireplace. There is a small modern bathroom upstairs and a modern cooking stove in the kitchen. Since energy is very expensive in England, most homes have two electric meters. One is used for measuring the energy during the day (expensive.) The other is used from midnight to 6 AM (cheap.) The stove is made in Sweden and it has state-of-the-art technology. At midnight, the stove automatically turns on the power. The oven and the area under the four heating surfaces are stored with special stones that become very hot. The heating surfaces are covered with a special lid that does not allow the heat to escape. During the day, the stove could be used without turning on the power.

About a half a mile from the cottage is the village of Little Inkboro where fresh bread could be purchased from the bakery and cold milk in bottles! Further down the lane could be found the butcher shop. To purchase groceries, you have to walk another half-mile to the village of Inkboro.

Each time we visit "Yonda" Phil tells me the same story. "This cottage was built 480 years before your Harvard was founded." Since I have no way of checking these facts, I have to accept them as true. The lane leading into the village is very narrow, in fact it is only one lane wide. Their son Andrew tells me "the hedges on both sides of the lane are so wide, that they rub both sides of the car." We usually spend a week at Yonda visiting the local sites, such as, bridges that were built during the Roman occupation. Of course the only way to tour in England is in a vintage Rolls Royce that they provide for our use.

ALLIANCE COLLEGE

A lliance College was founded in 1912 by the *Polish National Alliance*, Chicago. The largest Polish fraternal organizations in the United States. *The Polish National Alliance* was and still is a very successful life insurance company.

The college was founded to educate the sons of Polish immigrants. It began as an engineering school for sons of ironworkers and coal miners located in Cambridge Springs, PA a small town in the northwest corner of Pennsylvania. Cambridge Springs was suggested as the site for the school because of its location halfway between Chicago and Philadelphia/and New York.

The President of the United States, Theodore Roosevelt, gave the first address in 1912 during the dedication of the college.

In its early years, all instruction was given in the Polish language. In 1925, both the Polish and English language were used. Beginning in the late 30's, all instructions were given in English.

The College library had the largest collection of Polish books in the United States. Approximately 35,000 cataloged and 15,000 uncataloged volumes. The material is primarily in Polish, and is particularly strong in Polish language and literature, history, and the Polish experience in United States. Also included are such additional subject areas as Polish music, art, folklore, science, economics, sociology, government, and foreign relations. During the 68th Commencement of Alliance College on May 16th 1982, I was conferred with the degree of *Doctor of Humane Letters* (Honoris Causa.) by Mr. Hillary S. Czaplicki, Chairman, Board of Trustees of Alliance College.

Alliance College

By the authority of the Board of Trustees and upon the recommendation of the faculty hereby confers upon

Walter Baran

the degree of

Doctor of Humane Letters

with all the rights, privileges and honors thereunto appertaining.
In witness whereof we have hereunto affixed our signatures and the seal of the College in Cambridge Springs, Pennsylvania, this 16th day of May, 1982

Seal

President of the College

Chairman of the Board of Trustees
Dean of the College

The Honorable Walter Baran

Distinguished public servant, businessmen, humanitarian, and scholar, he is the personification of the American dream. Born of Polish immigrant parents in Frackville, Pennsylvania, he utilized his talent and energy to establish and manage three of the most modern garment manufacturing facilities in Pennsylvania, namely: Model Garment Co., Inc., Penn-Spruce Inc., and Penn-Allen, Inc. in 1979, he was appointed to his cabinet post of Secretary of General Services for the Commonwealth of Pennsylvania by

Governor Richard Thornburgh. In his capacity, he administers a staff of 1500 and a $35 million annual operating budget. His department oversees the leasing, purchasing, transportation, construction, and maintenance service for all agencies of the Commonwealth. He assisted the Governor in establishing the Pennsylvania Heritage Affairs Commission. He has been cited numerous times for his active roles in Polish-American civic and charitable organizations such as the Kosciuszko Foundation of New York, the Polish-American Activities Council of Philadelphia, And the Polish Beneficial Association in which he serves as a fraternal lodge President. He is an author of articles on antique cars, a collector rare books and documents, and a scholar of local history. Alliance College takes great pride in saluting him for his achievements and services to his fellow Americans and Poles oversees.

Note

I am including a copy of the Commencement Address that I gave during the 68th Commencement of Alliance College.

My Address was very well received. During this time, Poland was still under Communist domination this gave me the opportunity to compare the American and Eastern European education system at the university level. This was sort of an "Ethnic" commencement address.

COMMENCEMENT ADDRESS

Walter Baran
Alliance College
May 16, 1982

I consider this a great opportunity to be here today as an honorary member of the Class of '82. I want to express my sincere thanks to the trustees, faculty, and students of Alliance College. As I have had an opportunity to meet a few members of the graduating class, I feel that I am in distinguished company, and as an honorary alumnus, hope to return in 2007 for our 25th reunion.

Graduation represents the culmination of four years of struggle, sacrifice, and achievement and success. There is one group here today that probably struggled and sacrificed just a little bit harder and longer than four years of anticipation of this event, and are often overlooked in commencement programs. And, of course, I'm speaking about the wonderful parents and your family who are proudly sitting in the audience. I would like to ask the graduates once more to face the audience, and now you applaud your parents and friends. Can we do that please?

The faculty and administration who have completed another successful year of educational service might pause for a moment to think about what they represent. They represent everything that is good about the fine educational system we're so fortunate to have in this country. In my travels to Poland and other Soviet Block countries, I have seen how different it is. You never realize how important words like freedom, opportunity, and truth are until you visit places where these things just do not exist.

We often hear that education in the Communist regimes is free and that everyone has the same right to get the best education and that everything depends on only individual talent and effort. It's nice to hear but it's not exactly the truth. The so-called "classless society" is more stratified than one would expect. This is a major factor in a person's chance on entering college. While there are entrance exams similar to our college boards, test scores account for only a portion of the points required for admission. Position in the party hierarchy accounts for so many points as does the parent's position in society. For example, the son or daughter of a local party secretary has an automatic advantage of one-third of the necessary points for admission. How different it is in our country where no qualified student is denied entry to college. Once enrolled, students in Soviet Block countries do not have nearly the same academic freedom that we do.

As you can imagine, the word 'elective' just doesn't exist. Marxist philosophy or as they call it, "Scientific Communism" and Russian language are compulsory. Western philosophy and social sciences are presented in lectures called "The Critique of Western Science". There is no access to original sources. I asked a friend of mine who recently defected to this county from Czechoslovakia to comment on this. He said, "Such a strict arrangement leads to the total moral and physical corruption not only in political circles but in the whole society which calls itself the most just society of the future." This friend is one whom I got to know during various visits to Czechoslovakia. He had been a broadcast journalism student and he's one of the most brilliant individuals I've ever met. Had he grown up in America, he would undoubtedly become another Dan Rather. But his brilliant mind and his quest for the truth got him in great trouble. In his country, a broadcaster is simply told what to produce, like documentaries about agricultural output. But he persisted in presenting things as he saw them. Eventually, he was forbidden to practice his profession and he and his family were continually harassed by the authorities. In a somewhat risky and daring escape, this man came to America last year with my help. And he was very fortunate to bring his wife and son a few months later. And it is a thrill for me to see this boy enrolled in third grade in our elementary school where he can look forward to the same educational opportunities and freedoms that all Americans enjoy. Even though their stay in this country is somewhat uncertain, they proudly refer to American as "our country", and they have become the most patriotic Americans I've met.

When my son graduated from college ten years ago in '72, it was not exactly a time when patriotism was in vogue. I wasn't afraid to say it then, and I certainly don't expect any kind of protest today when I talk about my belief in the principals of democracy and free enterprise. Democracy as a system of government and free enterprise as an economic system are responsible more than anything else for the most remarkable achievements of our civilization. Equally important is the concept of freedom—freedom of speech, freedom of assembly, and religious freedom. These are the very things for which the Polish people are fighting for today. Unlike most of the conflicts elsewhere in this world, the Polish struggle is the purest and the most noble quest for freedom and democracy since our own American Revolution two centuries ago. Freedom and democracy and free enterprise are so difficult to attain, yet they're so easy to lose. We Americans who have had it so good for so long must never take these principals for granted. With these freedoms that we enjoy, also comes a tremendous responsibility on all of us to preserve and perpetuate them. It's not easy. In fact, it becomes more challenging everyday. Our way of life is threatened all the time by economic, political and social upheaval. We are threatened daily by our own technology. Our civilization is as wonderful as it is complex. Our problems and challenges are so vast that we must have a tremendous capability and a tremendous commitment to deal with them and hopefully to solve them.

You people who are receiving diplomas today have spent the last four years not merely passing courses and earning credits toward that diploma. That diploma represents more than a partial ticket to graduate school or to the business world. That diploma attests to the fact that you have a tremendous capability and a tremendous commitment. But a capability and commitment for what?

In this country, you are free to pursue just about anything you want. No matter what course in life you chose to pursue, you will find opportunities to serve society, to be part of the solution rather than part of the problem. To see those opportunities, you need only to have a proper outlook, a concern for the condition of the world, and faith in the ability to improve those conditions. An important ingredient in your outlook is that you must be a humanitarian. Think of some of the great humanitarians of recent history: Dr. Albert Schweitzer, Dr. Tom Dooley, and Mother Theresa. If all of us had only a portion of their zeal, most of the world's problems today would be far less threatening. A humanitarian is anyone who has love, respect, and compassion for all of humanity. A great humanitarian is one who combines those feelings with their own capability and commitment. You need not spend the rest of your life feeding the starving children of Asia or Africa to be a great humanitarian. There are opportunities everyday which are much closer to home. Since most of you will probably spend the majority of your life here in America, perhaps even in this state and perhaps in one specific community, you should be looking for those humanitarian opportunities which are closer to home. Raise your family to be good citizens, love your neighbor, serve your community. These are very realistic humanitarian objectives.

I speak often to Polish-American organizations about ethnic heritage and ethnic pride. This is a great trend which has emerged in our country in recent years. It preserves our tradition and it enriches our culture. But I always warm against allowing the pride of one group to express itself as the hatred or resentment of another. Ethnic tensions and discriminations are probably the cause of more strife in America than any other factor. It is fine to be proud of one's own group but think about what pride really is. It is the quest for acceptance, admiration, and respect. To seek these things while denying someone else our acceptance, admiration and respect is nothing short of hypocrisy. The history of this nation is one of immigration from all the shores of the world. The melting-pot syndrome is what made our country great. At the same time, it manifested itself in many ugly forms of ethnic persecution along the way. Each arriving group, poor and different, desperate to work for low wages was perceived as a threat and scorned by earlier arrivals.

In a generation or two, that group got established and protective of what they had struggled to acquire. They exhibited the same suspicions and scorn of subsequent arrivals. This has become even more complicated in recent years as Chinese, Puerto Rican, Vietnamese, and others have arrived in this country with the same hopes and dreams of a better live that our own forefathers once had. For them, racial discrimination and barriers are even stronger than ethnic barriers. To be true Americans, we must be true humanitarians. We must understand and defend the principal of equality for all human beings. The principal which was William Penn's seed of a nation three centuries ago when he established the world's first truly equal and democratic society right here in Pennsylvania. Be a humanitarian first and make your imprint on society by focusing that capability and commitment represented in your diploma on some worthwhile pursuit of your own choosing. Our complex society and our threatened way of life are depending on the capability and commitment of your generation.

Today as you embark on those pursuits in life, you are leaving behind this great college campus and a four-year period which many of you will look back upon as the greatest period in your life. I can tell you that even more exciting chapters in your life lie ahead, and don't think that because you've received a diploma your education is complete. Education is a lifelong experience and there will always be new things to learn to absorb and appreciate no matter where you are and what you are doing. The world has been my classroom for the past forty years, and I view everyday as an opportunity to improve my grade point average. Your opportunities are even greater and so are your challenges. Your parents, your teachers, and I have great confidence in you, and sitting there with that cap and gown on, I'm sure you can't help but have confidence in yourself.

I wish you all the good fortune, success, and happiness that this world has to offer. And I hope that contributions you make in this life are meaningful and rewarding to you and to humanity. Good luck, and thank you so very much for allowing me to share this wonderful day with you.

I have received many congratulations upon attaining this honor, but none that moved me more than the one I received from Dr. Bob Wilburn. I would like to share it with you.

COMMONWEALTH OF PENNSYLVANIA
GOVERNOR'S OFFICE
HARRISBURG

Robert C. Wilburn
Secretary of Budget and Administration

May 17th, 1982

Dr. Walter Baran
Secretary of General Services
515 North Office Building
Harrisburg, PA 17120

Carus Gualterus:

Gradu honorio doctoris tibi a Collegio Alliance tributo, gratulari Meris. Aliquem monstrae qui meilus de hoc honore meretur non possum (ne Eduardum Muskie quidem).

Propter multas res gestas Dux Operarum Generalium tributo gratulari Meris. Quomodo has auctoritates conficere et eodm tempore operam familiae, Civitati et heritati dare possis me obstupefacit.

Interim tibi gratulor!

Sine cera,
Robert C. Wilburm

My son Tony, who had four years of Latin at Georgetown Preparatory School, liked it so much that he took it as an elective when he attended Lehigh University. He was able to translated it for me.

Dr. Wilburn also gave me an English translation.

Dear Walter:

You deserve to be congratulated upon having an honorary doctor's degree conferred to you by Alliance College. No one else who has received this honor deserved it more than you (not even Edward Muskie).

You also deserve to be honored because of the many good things you have done as Secretary of General Services. Just as it is stated in your degree, I too am astounded that you can find the time to give to your family, the state and your heritage.

Again, congratulations to you!

Sincerely (without wax (seal))
Robert C. Wilburn

PHILADELPHIA COLLEGE

A year after I left State Government, I received a letter at my home advising me that I had been selected to receive a *"Doctor of Laws"* degree (Honoris Causa) on Friday, December 18th, 1987.

The Philadelphia Textile School was founded in 1884 and began a formal educational program for America's textile workers and managers. The college applied for and was granted university status by the Commonwealth of Pennsylvania in 1999. And, in a historic move, the Board of Trustees voted to change the College's name to *"Philadelphia University,"* the first private university to be named exclusively after the city of Philadelphia. Today, Philadelphia University attracts students from 46 states and 48 countries, offering graduate and undergraduate degrees in more than 40 areas of study. The university has grown from one school to five schools including:

- School of Architecture and Design
- School of Business Administration
- School of General Studies
- School Science and Health
- School of Textiles and Materials Technology

The Philadelphia University is located adjacent to Fairmount Park, the largest urban park system in the nation on a beautiful, park-like campus.

The news release is as follows: Philadelphia—Frackville native Walter Baran, former Secretary of General Services for the Commonwealth of Pennsylvania, was Selected by Philadelphia

College of Textiles And Science's trustees to receive the honorary Doctor of Laws Degree at the college's December commencement. The commencement speaker was Jacqueline G. Wexler, president of the National Conference of Christians and Jews.

In presenting Baran with the degree, college trustees Natalie Saxe sided his national reputation as a leader in the textile industry, his outstanding performance in public service, and his extensive involvement in community development projects in Schuylkill County. College president James P. Gallagher, Ph.D. added that Baran's career and personal life "exemplify the American commitment to hard work, free enterprise and community involvement" that serves as a strong role model for today's graduates.

Baran, the recipient of many other honors and awards statewide is a former President of Model Garment Co., which he founded in 1950. He also organized two affiliate garment firms, Penn Spruce Inc. of Sunbury and Penn Allen, Inc. of Hazleton. In 1979, he transferred the management of these major manufacturing facilities to his two sons, Anthony and Joseph. He and his wife, Irene, have long been leaders in Polish-American cultural and philanthropic activities.

AUTOMOBILES

I have been fascinated with automobiles all my life. Well, not exactly all my life; I began getting involved at the age of eleven. My fascination grew and reached its peak on the 14th day of June 1950. That is the day when I purchased my first antique car, a 1930 Ford Model A. Within a few months, I purchased a 1909 Maxwell Roadster. This was the beginning of my stable of thirty-two antique cars.

1907 Buick model 10	1934 Studebaker sedan	1954 Citroen limousine
1909 Maxwell Roadster	1935 Buick 4 door	1955 Packard 4 door
1915 Oakland Touring	1935 Chrysler 4 door	1957 Rolls Royce limousine
1920 Ford Model T. touring	1936 Chrysler sedan	1959 Bentley 4 door
1923 Studebaker truck	1936 Rolls Royce sedan	1963 Trivan truck
1924 Dodge 4 door	1936 Packard convertible	1963 Citroen 4 door
1926 Ford T. 2 door	1938 Bugatti Coupe	1966 Daimler limousine
1927 Packard Hearse	1939 Tatra 4 door	1967 Chrysler 300
1927 Packard sedan	1950 Daimler limousine	1973 Citroen SM 2 door
1930 Ford Model A.	1951 MG TD roadster	1977 Daimler limousine
1930 Chrysler Coupe	1951 Jaguar roadster	

A list of passenger cars. I do not have an accurate list, but I will try to list them in the order that they were purchased.

1931 Chevrolet sedan-used	1964 Chrysler LeBaron	1976 Mercedes
1935 Packard sedan-used	1966 Volkswagen	1977 Volkswagen Van
1941 Packard sedan-used	1966 Jaguar Mark III	1978 Mercedes sedan
1947 Oldsmobile sedan-used	1967 Mercedes 230 SL	1980 Mercedes SL 350
1949 Studebaker sedan	1968 Warszawa sedan	1983 Mercedes SL 450
1952 Packard sedan	1968 Maserati Mistral-used	1985 Mercedes sedan
1953 Packard sedan	1970 Ferrari 365 2+2	1993 Mercedes sedan
1955 Ford Thunderbird	1970 Mercedes sedan	1996 Infiniti sedan
1955 Packard 400	1974 Mercedes 250 SL	2000 Jaguar type S.
1961 Chrysler sedan	1975 Rolls-Royce Shadow	

TATRA

We had many interesting experiences in purchasing some of our antique cars. As an example, the purchase of a 1947 "Tatra" in Czechoslovakia:

On our many trips to Poland, we would pickup our car at the Mercedes factory in Sindelfingen/Stuttgart Germany, drive through East Germany, a communist country, and eventually drive across the border into Poland. We had no problems driving through West Germany. When we arrived at the border to East Germany, we had to do the following: purchase gas coupons for more gas than we could possibly use and remove our West German license plates and install East German plates. We had to exchange $50 dollars into East German deutsche marks for the purchase of food. The gas coupons and rental of their license plates had to be paid in western currency. We were informed that we could not change our route until we reached the Polish border. We had to use the autobahn that was built before the Second World War. After leaving the modern autobahn in West Germany, it seemed as though the one we were on then was built before the First World War. The autobahn had four concrete lanes. All of the overhead bridges were bombed and not replaced. The local roads that used these bridges merged onto the highway by going down a steep hill and crossed the autobahn. It was no longer a "limited access highway." From Berlin to the Polish border, there were over 40 of these bridges that were not rebuilt. On the concrete autobahn, sections of the highway immediately before and after passing a destroyed bridge could be seen large circles of the highway that was repaired with cobblestones. The Russian bombers were not very accurate in just bombing the bridge.

A few of the bombs landed on the autobahn just before and after the bridge.

We were able to stop for gas and some food only at the few gas stations and restaurants that were on the autobahn. The contrast between West and East was indescribable. This is one area where the phrase "You have to see it to believe it" is the only way to describe it. We tried to spend as much of the worthless East German deutsche marks before we entered Poland. There was not too much to be had. No candy bars, cookies, or 35 mg film, Just some bread, salami, and warm bottles of soda.

When we arrived at the border, we had to spend a few hours while they studied our passports, the documents for the car and especially the invoice since the car was recently purchased. We had to remove and return the East German license plates. We were not allowed to replace them with the West German plates until we crossed into Poland. The custom inspectors went through our luggage very carefully. Both the front and rear seats were removed and checked. The hood was open for inspection a square mirror attached to two small wheels and a handle that looks like it was removed from a umbrella was used This device was put under the car while the soldier examined the underside of the car. We then waited an additional hour to receive our passports and only then were we allowed to proceed.

We crossed the a small river and entered communist Poland. The Polish custom officers took our passports and asked to examine our luggage. They were looking for cigarettes, liquor, candy bars, etc. It's not that these items were illegal; they just love to smoke American cigarettes and occasionally drink English Scotch. They did not seem to care what else we carried. We had to fill out a form listing the amount and kind of western currency we were carrying. After we gave them a few packs of cigarettes, we were told to proceed. We spent about one hour on the border. We put on the West German license plates and continued for about 1 km to a combination gas station and restaurant and more importantly the currency exchange office. After exchanging some dollars into Polish Zlotys, we continued on our trip. We went through this torture about seven or eight times. I then looked at a map and decided that on our next trip, we would enter Poland by going through Czechoslovakia. West Germany bordered on Czechoslovakia. The following year, we drove to Nuremberg, located near the Czechoslovakian border. We would spend one day in Nuremberg. Since we did not know the language, we were fortunate in getting tickets for a concert or opera being held in the Symphony Hall.

Going through the Czech customs, took about one hour. The Czech's were firm but nothing like the East Germans. Each following year we used this route.

By now dear reader, you're wondering what the hell this has to do with collecting antique automobiles. One fall day early in the month of September 1970 while driving north towards the Polish border, Irene said, "Look at all the antique cars up ahead." Sure enough, a rally was being held. I followed them for about three km and they all stopped at a restaurant named "Biala Roza" (White Rose.) Even though we had lunch about 45 minutes before, I developed severe hunger pains and I suggested to Irene that we also stop for lunch.

There were about thirty-five antique cars in the group. Many Czech models, German, French, and a few American cars, A beautiful Packard from the '30s, a Marmon Roosevelt, a great looking Cord, and a 1915 Buick touring car. As is usual, a lot of local people and others who were driving by stopped to look at the cars. I approached one of the drivers and tried speaking Polish. He sort of ignored me until I showed him some photographs of my cars that I just happened to have with me. He tried speaking to me in German, then Czech. I responded in English, then Polish. We somehow managed to understand each other, mostly by pointing and using a sort of sign language. He took me around and pointed out some of the fine points on some of the cars. We then exchanged business cards. He told me to write to him in English since he had a friend who could translate for him. Because of this short encounter, we have been friends for over 30 years. I could now speak some Czech and he could speak quite a bit of Polish. He visited with us in the United States four times. He arranged to come to the United States during the second week of October so that we could attend the Hershey Antique Automobile Show. We also visited with him each time we are in Czechoslovakia. I met many of his friends who are members of the "Prague Veteran Car Club"

1947 Tatra T 87

The Czechs have been building and designing automobiles since 1889, Tatra, Walter, Skoda, Lauren Klement, Areo, and a few others. I was particularly interested in the Tatra. While production on this car began in the early 20s, I was interested in a Tatra that was built during the '40s. I asked my friends if one was available for me to buy. After a couple years (time moves very slowly in Czechoslovakia) they sent me a photograph of a 1947 Tatra. It was the exact car that I wanted. I began negotiations to acquire the Tatra in 1975. I negotiated for four years with the various governmental departments in Czechoslovakia, both by letter and on numerous trips to the country specifically to make arrangements. During this period, my friends were restoring the car. We then had to have an appraisal made by in their Bureau of Motor Transport. Permission had to be granted by the Bureau of Museums and Antiquity. Friends from the Prague Museum of Automobiles and Transport aided me in this effort. Finally, I was notified by letter that the car would be ready to remove from the country in October of 1979.

When I purchased the car in 1975, I paid at that time for its shipment to E.H. Harms & Company in Hamburg, Germany. I first attempted to have the car shipped by rail to the Czech border and then to Bremerhaven, the German seaport. The Czechoslovakian authorities informed me that this would be impossible and I would have to drive it out of the country personally. I therefore arranged to fly to Prague early in October of 1979. I made the final arrangements with the Czech authorities and received documentation to remove the car. I had the necessary papers for the border but I did not have the title to the car. I was only provided with the bill of sale.

I then drove the car from Prague to the Czech/Austrian border. My friends from the antique auto club followed me on the 120-mile trip to the border. I had made arrangements to deliver the car to Schwertberg in Austria. I chose a crossing point near this town. We drove through a heavy forest on the narrow two-lane road. The border crossing was one that looked exactly like you would see in a grade B movie. A young man of about 17 years old stopped us wearing a soldier's uniform, complete with all equipment including a rifle on his shoulder, approximately one-half mile from the border. After showing him our documents, he entered the small 3x3 foot guard station, (this station is manned for 24 hours. It gives a soldier some protection during a rain or snowstorm. I found out that the soldier was on 12-hour duty. There is no heat. He turned the crank on the telephone, spoke a few words after which he allowed us to proceed. My friends were not allowed to follow me to the border. I asked them to wait a period of one hour. If I did not return in that time, they could surmise that I had successfully completed arrangements and crossed into Austria.

There are not many of this type of automobile left on the Czechoslovakian roads. The border guards were very courteous and showed a great interest in the car, which meant I waited on the border for over two hours. The only vehicles we saw during the two hours were very large Austrian trucks that were hauling sand from Czechoslovakia to Austria. The truck box was about eight foot deep and carried about twenty tons of sand. Empty trucks entering Czechoslovakia were allowed to proceed within about fifteen minutes time. However, the trucks full of sand took a minimum of one-half hour before allowed to proceed. We noticed a few large ladders standing against the building. We found out what they were used for when the first trucks full of sand arrived. The custom officers stopped looking at my Tatra told me to wait and placed four ladders-two on each side of the truck. Carrying a 10 foot steel rod about a half-inch thick, they began poking the stick through the sand. I thought this very strange and later I asked one of the custom officers what the purpose was for this exercise. I was told that when the Austrians first began purchasing sand, a wooden box large enough to hold one or two persons was placed in the truck before being loaded with sand. There were air holes at one end of the box that were placed near air holes on the truck. After the Austrian truck drivers were paid a bribe, they smuggled some Czech citizens to freedom. The steel rods put a stop to this enterprise. I was anxious to get to Schwartzberg, Austria, to drop off the car before the office closed for the weekend at 6 PM. I had no way of notifying them that I was on my way. After crossing into Austria, the border guards in Austria would not allow me to enter the country because I did not have a title to the car nor did I have a green card showing that I was insured. Green cards are usually purchased at the border. However, you must prove ownership. Naturally all this was complicated by our difficulty in communicating. For me, German is a third language, slightly better than my French, but not good enough for such a detailed discussion.

In anticipation of such problems with the various authorities, I brought a Pennsylvania antique auto license plate from my 1927 Hudson. I felt it might assist me to use this plate while in transit. It worked in Czechoslovakia in fact; everyone who passed me waved and gave me the thumbs up sign. The efficient Austrians were not as impressed. The Austrian border guards called their supervisor and, as luck would have it, he not only spoke some English but he was an antique car buff. So I knew I had it made. He turned to his subordinate and said the German equivalent of "just do it."

Since the Tatra did not have modern turn signals, (it uses the semaphore system in the doorposts) my Czech friends attached a hand-written cardboard sign on the back of the car stating, "Ohne Blinken" (no turn signals.) After driving an additional 16 miles through very picturesque towns in Austria on a very narrow two-lane highway, we arrived at our destination just fifteen minutes before the office was to be closed for the weekend. Schwertberg seemed to me to have a population of about 800 people. It is a major center for transport of new automobiles throughout Europe. The lot held over 5000 automobiles ready for shipment.

Once again the clerks at Schwartzberg would not accept the shipment because I did not have a title although I did have a paid invoice for the car. We again had the language problem, but once again lady luck was with me. The supervisor for the transport firm came along and asked what the problem was. Since he did not speak English, I pointed to the parking lot were my Tatra was standing. He called his son from his office to interpret for us. He told me that in 1945 he owned a Tatra of the same type. He was also a collector of antique cars. He then instructed the clerks to take care of the matter. With a wave of his hand, he accomplished what the clerk had said was impossible. After taking me to view his own antique cars, he made reservations for us at a local hotel and had one of his employees drive us to the hotel. When we departed by train for Frankfurt on our homeward journey, I could only hope and assume that my arrangements for the Tatra's shipment to the United States would be carried out as planned. Exactly sixteen days later, I received a telephone call that my Tatra was finally in Baltimore, Maryland.

On November 27th I drove with my friend David Morrison to the docks of Baltimore, picked up the Tatra, put a few gallons of gas in the tank, and began the drive to Harrisburg. While driving on the Baltimore beltway, I was in the center lane when the wind opened the hood and it slammed up to the roof and totally blocked my view of the highway. Since I did not have any turn signals, I tried to get into the right lane to somehow park on the shoulder of the road. All the cars ignored me. I could see through the right passenger window that the traffic did not slow down, and I was concerned that I would have a collision from the rear. I knew that David, driving my Mercedes was directly behind me, and had his turn signal on to turn right but it was ignored. Since I could not see through the windshield, I took a chance and kept edging to the right side. The cars passing me on my right kept blowing their horn trying to tell me to stay in the lane. I took the risk and slowly forced my way into the right lane and parked on the berm of the highway.

When the custom people at the Baltimore docks were checking the car they failed to lock the handle on the hood. We pulled the hood down and tried to straighten it out so that I could see through the windshield. We found a piece of rope and tied the hood to the front bumper. During this episode the following happened: I lost 4 1/2 pounds, no one stopped to assist me, and the State Highway Patrolmen were nowhere to be seen. I spoke to the Tatra and said, "Welcome to America." With David following close behind me, we were able to drive to my home in Harrisburg, and the next evening continued to Frackville without any further incident.

The Tatra was admitted to the car body hospital where the hood was repaired and the entire car was repainted. We also replaced the upholstery on the seats, the doors, and ceiling. The Tatra was finally ready to tour the United States.

The type 87 Tatra with an air-cooled V-8 engine is very rare in the United States. In 1975, there were only three type 87 Tatras in the U.S. There were also nine smaller 6-cylinder cars called Tatraplan in the U.S.

In March of 1995, I received a letter inviting the Tatra to be exhibited at the Montreal Museum of Fine Arts in Montreal, Canada. The exhibit would consist of 50 automobiles with a rare exotic design. The exhibit was opened May 11th to October the 15th, 1995.

Many very valuable and rare cars were sent by airfreight including the original first Mercedes-Benz, and other French, Italian, English, and a few American cars. The museum arranged to pick up my car at my Ashland garage. All of the owners of the 47 cars that were exhibited were invited to the grand opening. Among the guests were designer Ralph Lauren and Wally and Irene Baran from Ashland. Pennsylvania. The exhibit was a smash hit. As an exhibitor, I received all of the articles written about this exhibit from all over the world. Over $12 million was raised for the museum.

In May of 2000, I received another letter from The National Czech & Slovak Museum Library located in Cedar Rapids, Iowa. The dedication of the museum occurred on October 1995 and was attended by three presidents: U.S. President Bill Clinton, Czech Republic President, Vaclav Havel, and Slovak Republic President,

Michael Kovac. The exhibit called *Czech Technology in Motion* was held from April 29th to October first 2000. There were six Czech cars and four Czech motorcycles on exhibit. The museum is housed in a very large new and impressive building. We were also invited to the grand opening. People from Czechoslovakia settled Cedar Rapids and all the surrounding towns many years ago. Many still speak and use the Czech language even into the fourth generation. Even though it did not rival the exhibit in Montreal, it was considered a great success.

September 1970, I read an advertisement for a 1965 Maserati-Mistral in the classical car section of the New York Times. I saw many articles on this fine car in various automobile publications and was familiar with the body style and great 6-cylinder engine. The price was quite reasonable and when I found out that it was a great red color, I was convinced that I *must* have this car. After many phone calls and reviewing many photographs of the car, I made arrangements to purchase the car.

A well-known dealer of exotic cars who was located in St. Louis, Missouri, was selling the car. The dealer told me that his mechanics were tuning the engine, changing all filters etc. to make sure that the car was in first-class condition. I was also given a date when I could pick up the car. Irene and I flew to St. Louis were we were going to sign the necessary documents, stay overnight, and leave early in the morning to drive 846 miles to Frackville, PA. When we arrived, I was told that the Maserati was not quite ready. I asked to go into the shop to see the car. It was a large shop with Ferraris, Lamborghini's, Bugatti's, and one bright red Maserati Mistral with the engine head removed and valves and pistons and an assortment of nuts and bolts spread out very carefully on a sheet of cardboard next to the car. The salesman told me that it would be ready in two days! It was decision time. The leather seats and the entire interior were in perfect shape. The clutch and break pedals did not have any signs of wear, it was a low mileage car. I had no idea if the odometer was rolled back. Since all other areas of the car where in such good shape, I accepted the reading on the odometer.

We had two days of unexpected sightseeing in St. Louis. We had a few good dinners, took the elevator to the top of the famous St. Louis Arch, and had a great view of the Mississippi River. The work on the engine was completed, and on the second day, I took it on a test run on one of the interstate highways. The salesman did not care for the way I drove the car. We were about 25 miles west of St. Louis when he took the wheel and showed me how this car should be driven. *Fast. Very fast.* I was pleased that Irene was waiting at the showroom (it had only two seats made of extra soft, red leather.) If she was along, I was sure that she would surely faint and would not allow me to buy the car.

Since the tank was filled with high-octane gas, we pointed it towards Frackville and began to drive home. It sure was a "Good looker." The police on four different locations in various states stopped us. I certainly was not speeding, but I have to admit that I could not wait to get back to Schuylkill County and while Irene was preparing dinner, I would have a great opportunity to see if I could drive as good as the salesman who sold me the car. The highway patrolmen all asked the same question "What kind of car is it and could I see the engine." After their curiosity was satisfied, they said one word, "Thanks."

After two days of driving, we arrived safely at our home without any problem. After one month, I noticed some noise in the engine. I was sure that the timing chain was loose. The only dealer that I knew who handled these high performance cars was Algar Ferrari of Rosemont, PA. While he sold Maserati, he specialized in Ferraris. I made an appointment to have his mechanics not only look at the timing chain but to also adjust the three carburetors and also "tune" the engine. They made some adjustments with the timing chain and it seemed quiet on the way home.

FERRARI

O n my fourth service trip to Algar, a Ferrari salesman who wanted me to test drive a 1970 Ferrari approached me. Twelve cylinders, black leather interior, and was burgundy in color. After driving the Maserati with a loud engine, this was damn, quiet Ferrari! Since it was last year's model, he told me he would give me a great deal. He quoted a good trade in price on the Maserati. I never said, "I'll have to ask my wife." Because I never had to. "Wally if you think it's a good deal and you want it, that's fine with me." I did tell the salesman to give me a week to think about it. He called me in five days and I told him that I was not interested. He increased the value of the Maserati by a few hundred dollars. In the two weeks that followed, he kept increasing the value of the Maserati. I thought to myself, "Wally, you're probably going to be the first guy in Frackville to own a brand new Ferrari." On October the 12th, 1971, I became the owner of a new 1970 twelve cylinder Ferrari.

In early September of 1973, after picking up our 1974 Mercedes 350 SL in Stuttgart, Germany, we began our long trip to Modena, Italy, to visit the Ferrari factory located about fifteen miles south of Modena to a small town called Maranello a distance of 528 miles. We drove through Germany, crossed the Alps through Switzerland then drove to the great city of Milano. Milano was not directly on the route to Modena, but we wanted to visit the most famous opera house in the world, LaScala. We were fortunate to get hotel reservations in the LaScala hotel next to the opera house. We knew that all performances were sold out for the entire year! We managed to get tickets for a tour of the opera house. We were fortunate that during the tour, rehearsals were in progress so we were able to hear at least part of an opera.

The next day we drove to Modena. After an overnight stay at a hotel, we left for the small town of Maranello. A new "Autopista" was under construction and we had to take a small two-lane road. Marinello was about 14 miles from Modena. We decided to stop along the road for some lunch. We stopped at a tavern where we saw men and some women drinking wine and eating cheese. We sat down and asked for a menu. In my best Italian I asked for a "listino." He didn't understand me, so I pointed to my mouth and said "mangia." (Eat) He could not understand my coal region accent, but he knew what I wanted when I pointed to my mouth. He pointed to a staircase. When we approached the stairs we heard many loud voices. I told Irene I believe they are having a Rotary/Lions Club dinner meeting. We were surprised when we entered the dining room. There were only six men sitting at a table. We sat down at one of the five tables that were unoccupied and I noticed the waiter carrying food to the men at the table. I got up, pointed to two of the plates, and motioned one for me, and pointing to my wife, motioned one for her also. While waiting for our food, I called the waiter and asked him for "Wino Blanco" Using hand signals I asked for a small bottle. He arrived with a green bottle without labels that held a minimum of one liter of wine. "Piccolo bottiglia di vino." (A small bottle of wine.) He kept saying the word "piccolo, piccolo" which meant this is the smallest size they have. The food and the wine were both delicious. I had wide green noodles with a creamy sauce and Irene had some small dumplings in a marinara sauce. Irene wanted to use the restroom before we continued on our journey. I sure as hell was not going to ask the waiter (using hand signals) where the restroom was. I looked around and I saw a door with a large circle 'O' with a 'V' over the '0'. I told Irene this is it. She went in while I stood guard. She came out laughing so much that there were tears in her eyes. She described the "restroom." It had a round hole in the floor and two shoes outlined beside the hole. Many years later we found the same type of "restroom" when we toured Egypt. When we arrived at the entrance to Maranello, it was a large three-story home with a wide-open porch on the side and front with a small sign that read "Ferrari." The porch was filled with tourists. Most of them were Americans with a sprinkling of English and German. I proceeded to the window where a clerk sat looking at a pile of papers. I approached and said that I would like to take a tour of the factory. She asked my name and told me to wait. I overheard some of the people complaining that they had been waiting over an hour. We decided to wait. We could hear the unmistakable sound of Ferraris driving behind this home where we could see some factory buildings. Within fifteen minutes of our arrival, the girl in the window said, "Mr. Barone, Mr. Barone." I approached and was told that a guide would be out to take us on the tour. Everyone in line, especially the Americans, were not very happy to see us get this preferential treatment. We later found out that when she looked in the records she found that we purchased a new Ferrari from Algar Motors in the United States.

The tour took 45 minutes. It was the cleanest manufacturing plant that I have ever seen in my life. All the employees wore very clean white coats. A computer screen stood beside each machine. The machines were completely automated. We watched while the engine block was turned on its side and eight drills drilled holes. The drills went up the block automatically, were turned to its other side, and the process was repeated. The block was then turned upright and additional machining was automatically done. It was fascinating. The drillings (chips of metal) were pulled into a container so they would not fall on the floor. I told Irene that the box contained an electromagnet.

We saw Ferraris in every stage of completion. We had to be careful when moving from one building to another since Ferraris, some were complete cars and others were just chassis driving as fast as they could go between the buildings. Our guide would exit first then put his arms out until it was safe for us to cross the narrow entryway. On our tour, Irene saw a door marked "Dames." She wanted to check out the restroom. She told me the restroom was completely automated. The most modern plumbing was used. Pure white porcelain commode, lavatory, and a supply of clean white linen towels were on a small table. Marble floor and two upholstered chairs completed the furnishings. When our tour was completed, our tour guide gave me a card reading, "Dinner for two including wine at the "Cavallione" restaurant, (owned by the Ferrari Co.) directly across the street from the Ferrari office. It was the most elegant restaurant we were in while in Italy.

Speaking to our tour guide, we mentioned that we drove from Germany over the Swiss Alps. He told me that the pass over the Alps closes at the first snowfall. "If it is not too late you may still make it. If not, you will have to take the tunnel under the mountain which is not only expensive, but you may have to wait in a long line to enter." After spending a night in the hotel, we left immediately and were very fortunate that the road was not closed.

We left our hotel in Modena at 7 AM to begin what would be a 1,676-mile trip to the Port at Hamburg, Germany. Our intention was drive to Nuremberg to have our Mercedes serviced. For the warranty to be effective, the car had to be checked after the first 1,000 miles. After spending two days to Nuremberg, we

1970 Ferrari 365 2+2

would drive to Prague where we expected to spend about three days visiting with friends. Our next stop would be Krakow where we would spend five days again visiting with friends. Then onto Warsaw, Poznan, Berlin, and finally Hamburg. Since we drove from Stuttgart in Germany to Modena, Italy, a distance of 537 miles, on our trip of thirty-three days, we traveled approximately 2213 miles. Yes, the trip was worth it since we had the pleasure of visiting the home of "Ferrari."

1907 BUICK

I n September of 1988, we had visitors from Czechoslovakia at our home. Frantisek Vocka and Miroslav Kratochvil from Zlonin, a suburb of Prague, were in the United States to attend the Fall meet of the Antique Automobile Club at Hershey. While in this country, they had the opportunity of visiting all the antique auto museums within a 150-mile radius of Frackville, PA. We also visited my friends who had antique cars. One of these friends had a collection of fine restored automobiles: Packard's, Buick, Ford, Chrysler, and many cars of the 1930s. When we entered the building, I began explaining the fine points of a beautiful 1926 Packard that was located at the entrance. I noticed that my friends were not listening to me, their eyes were directed to the back of the garage where they saw a rather strange car. It looked like it was from the early 1900s. Although I had seen the car many times, I had really never paid much attention to it.

My Czech friends, who have restored many very early cars (1905 Darracq, 1909 R.A.F., 1925 Tatra, 1930 Marmon Roosevelt), were very excited about this car. It looked complete. It had a Buick Medallion on the front and we were told that it was a 1912 model. My friends said, "Mr. Baran, you must buy this car and restore it." Easier said than done! But I was recently retired and was looking for a challenge. While I have always done some of the restoration work on each of my cars, this Buick would be my first real challenge. After negotiating with the owner, I was able to purchase the car.

The title was not clear as to the model and year of manufacture. I began my research to identify the car. This problem was solved when I later removed the leather from the seat. A tag attached to the woodwork stated "1907 MODEL 10 FRONT SEAT—PUT IN BOTTOMS—BUICK MOTOR CO."

After towing the car to my workshop, I began to carefully look over the entire car. It was then I discovered that the oil pan was missing! After I recovered from the shock, and after a fitful night of attempted sleep, I returned the next morning and calmly asked the young man who worked for my friend, "Could I please have the oil pan for the car I purchased yesterday?" After he looked around the garage for a few minutes, he returned and told me that it wasn't there. Another employee told me that a few months earlier a large truckload of car parts, tires, and assorted "junk" was put in storage in another building twelve miles away. This was happy news! I was told that someone would go to the building in a few days and while there, would try to find the oil pan. But it was not to be. A few days later I received a call that the pan was not there!

I then requested permission to go to the warehouse with one of the employees. Armed with flashlights, my friend Dick Flail and I began our search. While Dick was working through one pile, I noticed an odd part on the floor a few feet from the pile of parts. It was a steel shaft about four inches long, square on one end, and with a spring attached about three inches long. I have no idea why, but I thought that this might be an important part. Meanwhile, Dick announced, "**I FOUND IT!**" We now had our oil pan. After further study, a brass oil pump was found attached to the pan. Looking at the pump I saw a square hole the exact size of the square end of the shaft I had found earlier. I knew there and then that the restoration would be a snap!

I was certain that the engine would be seized tight, and it was. A full month was spent trying to remove the pistons. It was very discouraging work. When I was really down, all I needed to bring me back up was to remember the "miracle" of the oil pan. Finally, with a lot of patience, one cylinder was freed and the other three soon followed. The rest of the engine work was easy and in less than one year the motor was ready to be placed in the car.

The entire car was completely dismantled. The woodwork

needed some replacement and a new radiator core was made. The rest of the restoration was time-consuming but went rather well.

After the car was complete and running, I attended the Fall Meet at Hershey. I was prepared with photos, and I was sure that I would find an early Buick on the grounds. I met an AACA member with his 1907 Buick. After some conversation, I showed him my pictures and he told me that he recalled seeing a framed photo of a car event in which my car was distinctly visible. What's more, he said the picture was hanging on a wall at the AACA Headquarters at Hershey! On my trip to Hershey, which occurred a few weeks later, Bill Smith and his staff warmly greeted me. Bill took me to the picture, which was hanging in the corridor. It was indeed my car. On the photo was written:

Sixth Annual Antique
Automobile Derby
Rayburn Plaza, Philadelphia
November 12, 1936

With this information in hand, I then paid a visit to the State Library in Harrisburg, P.A. The people there were very helpful in assisting me. I asked for the microfilm of *"The Philadelphia Bulletin"* and the *"Philadelphia Inquirer"* for November of 1936. I was pleased to find an article about this very same event, also with a photo of my car. The *"Philadelphia Evening Bulletin"* of Thursday, November 12, 1936, listed the owner as Mr. Bert Muskin of Scranton, PA. and the caption under the photo stated, "It's a toss-up as to which did the most shivering here, the car or the driver. Bert Muskin rolled in onboard his 1907 Buick from Scranton in five hours and 23 minutes, and reported that the all-draft ventilation worked perfectly coming down to town over the mountains."

The article on the Derby stated, "Bert Muskin and Walter Schell made the 140 mile trip from Scranton without a miss, knocking off 35 to 40 miles most of the way."

Since the owner's name and city were listed, I was able to

begin my search. I called the Scranton Chamber of Commerce and other sources with no results. It seems that the Muskin family had disappeared. I did find out that the family was in the steel and scrap iron business. I had a friend who was in the same business and was living in Florida. I called my friend Al and asked, "Do you know a Mr. Muskin once owned a steel company in Scranton?" He replied, "Not only do I know him but we have dinner together about once a month. Do you want his phone number?"

I spoke to Mr. Muskin and he informed me that he was a second owner of the Buick. The car was originally purchased in February of 1907 from the firm Warfel and Arbuckle, Peach and 16th streets, Erie, PA. The price was $900. An Erie Railroad Vice President, who was the person in charge of the repair shops for the railroad, purchased it. The new car was taken directly to the railroad workshop with instructions to convert the car so that it had the look of a locomotive. Now this was quite an undertaking. First the wooden floorboards and fenders and the radiator were removed. Wooden patterns were made for these items and then they were cast in heavy aluminum. A completely new brass radiator shell was made. It received a cast, round aluminum piece, which was fashioned for the front of the radiator to give the appearance of a locomotive boiler.

Casting objects in metal is a laborious and expensive process. To make a casting, a full-size wooden model of the part to be cast must be made. The pattern maker would then carve out of wood an exact copy of the part. This wooden pattern is then placed in the container of special sand. The sand is then heated at a very high temperature. After cooling, the wooden pattern is removed and the form is filled with molten aluminum. This is a very time-consuming process and when many parts are to be made, it is cost-effective. But to go through this for one car is amazing!

The car has many special items made from brass: a brass ring on the radiator shell similar to the ring on a locomotive, brass foot rests and, brass handrails so that one might easily enter the car. The car also has a special two-impeller water pump, one that can be controlled with a dash mounted controlled lever. Other extras are a dash mounted intake control for the carburetor, a rearview mirror, oil pressure gauge, and oil level gauge, and an oil flow gauge. A brass fire extinguisher is located under the floor and is accessible from the top by a fitted lid. All of these items were fabricated just for this one car!

A propane lamp, which is to be used for night driving, is located in the center and just below the two seats. The propane headlamps as well as the interior lamp are controlled by shut off valves that are also located below the seat. While many cars of this era had carbide lamps, this car has a nickel-plated propane tank, complete with a gauge, located to the rear of the chassis. Brass side lamps and tail lamps used kerosene. The rear of the car also had special treatment. A fine wooden cabinet with two drawers and a storage bin over the gas tank was installed. The gas gauge attached to this cabinet is a brass boiler gauge of the type normally seen on high-pressure boilers.

In the early 1930s, the auto was sold to Bert Muskin, the second owner mentioned above. He enjoyed the car, maintained it, and eventually entered the "Sixth Annual Antique Automobile Derby" in Philadelphia (it must have been a long trip on 1936 roads from Scranton to Philadelphia.)

Sometime in the year 1941, the Buick was placed inside a boxcar that stood on the railroad siding on the grounds of Mr. Muskin's business. It waited there for 28 years until it was purchased by my friend from whom I purchased the car. He had the car for about 20 years. I became the owner in 1990.

This is a "One only" car in the world!

1907 Buick

BUGATTI

I have written a few articles on some of my cars for *"Antique Automobile"* the official publication of the *Antique Automobile Club Of America, Inc.* and other magazines such as *Auto Week, Car And Driver,* and a few others.

I also wrote an article in October of 1984, for the magazine *Pur Sang* (Pure Blood,) a publication of the *American Bugatti Club.*

Since I am writing this book without an editor or ghostwriter, I will write anything I damn please as long as it helps me to reach my goal to write a book at least one inch thick.

Restoring a Type 57 Ventoux
by Walter Baran

In the year 1980, I realized my ultimate dream of owning and restoring a Bugatti. I have been fortunate enough to acquire a stable of 32 antique cars in the intervening years, and I would characterize myself as a jealous collector since I have never traded or sold a car that I acquired. Even with some very fine cars in my collection, including a number of "proper" English cars, it soon became apparent that my acquisitive urge was not be satisfied until I obtained a Bugatti. My wife tried in vain through many Christmases and birthdays to appease my long-standing wish, but no quantity of Bugatti books, models, cufflinks, or highball glasses could suffice for the real thing.

I have always been interested in learning how a particular car was found, purchased, and restored. Likewise, I always enjoy relating the drama of my own stories. In 1979, the citizens of Pennsylvania elected a new governor who asked me to serve in his cabinet as the Secretary of General Services. Among my duties in this office, I was frequently required to meet with architects and engineers. During one of these dinner meetings, an architect knowing of my interest in cars asked me if I had purchased a new old car lately. Another man at the dinner casually remarked, "A friend of mine owns a Bugatti, but he has not run it for about 25 years." After I regained my composure, I asked if I might have an opportunity to see it. For the remainder of the dinner, I was unable to concentrate on architecture or my Beef Wellington. I repeatedly returned to our conversation to the subject of Bugattis and my desire to see this one. The gentleman responded that it surely was not for sale and even a glimpse of it was unlikely. Finally exasperated by my persistence, (I was also the official who selected architects and engineers for Pennsylvania building projects) *he agreed to see what he could do. Luck was with me, and an appointment was made.*

A few very long weeks later, I stood in front of a large doorless and dilapidated garage containing the project of my dreams—a type 57 Ventoux Bugatti produced in 1938. The owner was a fine retired doctor who immediately informed me that it was not for sale. I told him that I could understand his feelings, because if I owned it, I also would not sell it. However, I would dearly love to own and restore it, I explained, as I persisted in pleading the worthiness of my intrusion upon the good doctor's privacy. After about an hour, I was invited into his home. We exchanged cards. He looked at photographs of my cars and heard tales of my sincerity as a collector. At last, his wife said, "Dear, you won't ever restore that car." And God bless her, because the doctor relented and told me I looked like the person who should own his Bugatti.

Arrangements were made for me to return with a trailer to pick up the Bugatti. A short time later, I established probably the most brilliant contract arrangement in my automotive *restoration career. I had recently helped a Czechoslovakian gentleman, **Dusan Nuemann**, to come to this country. A talented photojournalist and an antique automobile enthusiast I had known for a number of years, he had been denied work at home as a result of a documentary he had produced about a 1976 Trans-American tour of two vintage Tatras.* (That is a story in itself: in fact, it is published in the September-October 1977 and May-June 1980 issues of Antique Automobile Magazine). *Now residing in Frackville, Dusan had agreed to undertake a full-time job of restoring the Bugatti. His precision, skill, and artistry in automotive restoration is matched only in his documentation of this process. All of the following text are his.*

RESTORATION BEGINS

AS RECOUNTED

BY DUSAN NUEMANN

The garage door opened and light penetrated the inside space. There stood a car, alone, rusted, and neglected. The ghostly witness of better days. A Bugatti 57 Coupe Ventoux— the car that symbolizes the end of golden era of motoring in Europe. The end of times when creativity, fantasy and imagination still governed the minds and hands of automotive manufacturers.

I can't say how my passion for Bugatti's developed. Perhaps, because I was born near the site of the hill-climb race Zbraslav-Jiloviste, one of the oldest European races. There in the mid-twenties roared supercharged engines of racing Mercedes, Alfas, Delages and Bugatti's. There such drivers as Lautenshlager, Carracciola, Stuck and Divo won their golden wreaths. But it was the unforgettable Eliska Junek (more about her later) who brought the famous Bugatti to my attention. Perhaps it was the apparent disparity between this fragile and tiny looking lady and a deadly powerful racing thoroughbred, Bugatti T 35, which appealed to my imagination most. Perhaps it was the personality of Ettore Bugatti, which generated my admiration for his cars more than sole technology and racing results.

I have seen tens of Bugatti's, I have touched a couple of them, I drove one—but here, in the small garage in Frackville, PA., I stood in front at a great challenge. Actually we were three that garage: I, a former Czechoslovakian journalist, the silent car and it's happy, proud discoverer, Walter Baran, willing to start a new adventure—to let me restore that abused jewel. I hesitated for just a fraction of a minute. Man has to prove to himself at least a couple of times in life that he can accomplish a "real" thing, I agreed to go ahead with full restoration.

I take my diary and opened to the first page dated June 23, 1981 . . . ."Today I organize a working place, clean the garage and made an inventory of tools. First touch to the car—I removed a hood and radiator holder."

The next few days were dedicated to cleaning. Pounds of old dirt covered every exposed part of the car. Aluminum parts were covered with mold-like oxide; steel and cast-iron parts sported flowers of peeling rust. In the broken headpipe was a mouse nest. The rear lights were without lenses. Interior leather panels were covered with mildew and mushrooms. But the car was complete. When I started to take the body apart I discovered more unpleasant features missing bolts had been replaced with SAE stock regardless of metric threads in counterpart. The car had apparently been wrecked and repaired already in the states. The right front fender was slightly different from the left one. It is impossible to say when and how it happened. Either the wrecked one was replaced with a Colmar modification or was hammered after the accident to that simpler shape. A broken doorpost and the front body-shell brackets were strengthened with a piece of flatiron stock and carriage bolts. Because of that, new holes were drilled through the firewall. Nor had a trunk escaped "professional" repair. The lower part had been cut-off and replaced with a steel metal sheet directly riveted to the aluminum casing. The result: total corrosion in the joint areas.

Note

Since I believe that I reached my goal of a one inch book, I decided not to print Dusan's complete report as was printed in two issues of *Pur Sang*. It is very technical and would take twelve pages of this already one inch thick book. If you are a Bugatti person, you can find the complete story in *Pur Sang,* a publication of the American Bugatti Club. **"Restoring a T-57 Ventoux"** (page 11) **Vol. 24 Spring 1984. Part I and** (page 19) **Vol. 24 Winter 1984 Part II.** Or contact the author of this book and I will send a photo-copy of this interesting story written by Dusan Neumann.

1938 Bugatti

DONALD O'CONNOR

A dear friend, Ione Geier, a Features Correspondent for the *Pottsville Republican* writes only "Happy stories." She writes nothing but "Good news." Memories from her childhood, etc.

On August 30th, 1985 the *Pottsville Republican* ran a full-page story on a visit that actor Donald O'Connor made to Schuylkill County. Without her permission, (I know she would not mind) I will reprint part of her article.

Star is car buff

"This is the story of how entertainment celebrity Donald O'Connor happened to be in Schuylkill County Saturday.

O'Connor is starring in "How to Succeed in Business without Really Trying" at the Claridge Hotel in Atlantic City. (This is before casinos came to Atlantic City) On his free days, he and his wife, Gloria, spend a great deal of time with an Ambler couple, Peggy and David Stern (it was Stern who wrote "Frances," the book that was the basis of six highly successful movies starring O'Connor).

At a dinner party in the Philadelphia area several weeks ago, Stern and O'Connor were talking about the latter's interest in antique automobiles when one of the guests mentioned that "in upstate Pennsylvania, in a little town called Frackville, there's a man who has a fantastic collection of old cars."

Stern has friends in Frackville, Paul and Madge Kerrigan. When the Ambler author called Mrs. Kerrigan to find out if she knew the car collector, she immediately identified him: Walter Baran, State

Secretary of General Services. She also arranged for the Sterns and O'Connors to see Baran's collection and to have lunch with him At the Pottsville Club as her guests.

Saturday's trip to Schuylkill County wasn't the first for O'Connor. In 1940, he played at the Hippodrome Theater in Pottsville as a member of his family's vaudeville act."

End

Donald O'Connor at one time owned a Bugatti Ventoux identical to the one I own. It was a Type 57 made in 1938 and had a body designed by Jean Bugatti. He told me that he was anxious to once again see and drive a Bugatti. After a wonderful luncheon hosted by Madge Kerrigan, we left for my garage located at Fountain Springs. Mr. O'Connor was very pleased to ride to Fountain Springs in my Bugatti. His wife Gloria, and his friends followed us in his car. While he did show some interest in the other cars, he asked many questions about how I was able to purchase and restore a Bugatti. I certainly did not go into detail as it appears in the story above since he only had about five hours to spend at the garage.

During the same Saturday afternoon, a wedding shower was being held for my niece Patti Kiefer on the grounds of our home in Frackville. Irene knew that I was having lunch with Mr. O'Connor but she did not tell all the ladies at the shower that I was meeting with him. Later at the garage, I asked him, "Would you like to make a lot of young and not so young ladies happy by appearing at a wedding shower for my niece, Patti Kiefer that is being held on the grounds at our home." He said, "No problem, I will be happy to greet the young future bride." I then called Irene and asked her to tell the ladies that I am bringing a guest.

One of the girls (dare I say middle-aged girl) who fell in love with Donald O'Connor when she was sixteen years old and claims that she is still in love with him refused to believe that her idol was going to pay a visit to our home in Frackville. The eyes of all of the guests at the shower had their eyes on Barbara Herwick when I introduced her to her idol. I'm not sure, but everyone expected her to faint. She didn't faint, but she decided to do a scene from one of his movies! She got down on one knee, and with all the proper gestures sang a song from one of his movies. Donald (by now, he called me Wally and I called him Donald) was very happy and pleased that someone remembered a scene that he did long ago. He then knelt down on one knee and repeated the song. He told me later that he was very moved by what she did. He also said, "She really has a good voice." I told him that she is a semi-professional. She sings for many weddings and other occasions.

He invited Irene, me, and another couple to Atlantic City to see the play. He said, "I will arrange for you and your party to have rooms at the Claridge Hotel, four tickets for the show, all at no cost. Just give me a call and I will arrange it." Irene, my sister Helen, and her husband Bernard Kiefer and I checked into the hotel. His wife, Gloria, saw us in the lobby when we were checking in. She was very pleased and surprised to see us and said, "You should have called us." She then invited us to go back-stage to see Donald after the show. During the show, the owner of the "Widget" fac-tory played by D o n a l d O'Connor, was speaking to all his employees (I will paraphrase)

Left to right: Gloria & Donald O'Connor, Irene Baran, Helen & Bern Kiefer & niece Patti

"You all know that sales of our widgets has been falling lately." "I have hired, at great expense, a super salesman. He is quite eccen-tric and strange in his ways. I know it will be difficult, but please give him your full cooperation, your job depends on it." In the next scene, the super salesman entered. He was dressed to the nines from his straw hat to his brown and white wingtip shoes. He was tonsorialy correct. He made a great impression before he said a word. "I'm very pleased to introduce to you our new head of sales, Mr. Walter Baran. Please give him your full cooperation." Hell, I nearly died. Throughout the rest of the show all the actors called him, Mr. Baran. There were only four people in the theater that knew that the real Mr. Baran was sitting in the seat watching the play.

After the play, we went backstage. I told the doorman that we are friends of Mr. O'Connor. He didn't believe me until I showed him Mr. O'Connor's visiting card. We entered, and I felt like we were in a scene of one of his movies. Donald was seated in a wingback chair dressed in a beautifully flowered silk robe with black lapels, holding a glass of champagne in his hand. "Gloria told me that you were in the audience." We were each given a glass of champagne and offered a tray full of miniature sandwiches. I said, "Donald, that was a five-star performance!" I knew that he had to do another performance that evening, so I thanked him and made an effort to leave. "I have plenty of time. I know that Gloria would like me to take a nap but I rather hear a bit more about how you found the Bugatti. I briefly related the story about having a lunch with a group of architects and . . . . (I don't have to repeated it here, go back a few pages and you can reread about this marvelous lunch that led me to be a proud owner of a Bugatti.)

Fact:

A person has ***much better*** odds of winning the multimillion-dollar "Powerball Lottery" then finding a restorable Bugatti.

After about half an hour we thanked him again and left for home. It was a marvelous afternoon.

Just another day in the life of Wally Baran.

CARL BRANDT MD.

Much has been written about my Bugatti, but to me, more can always be written.

I became friends with Dr. Carl Brandt, the man who sold me the car. We had many visits to his home in Johnstown PA. while the Bugatti was undergoing a complete restoration. I offered to drive him from his home in Johnstown so that he could see the progress that we were making on the Bugatti. One day, he and his brother drove to Frackville. He called me from the motel asking for driving instructions to our home. He was very pleased to see the quality of work that was being done. We drove to the woodworking shop where all the interior wood was being replaced. We visited the machine shop where a genius, Mr. Brill, was machining new parts using a part of a gear as a pattern to make a complete gear. Our last visit was to the body shop where the fenders were receiving the 12th coat of black paint. The engine and the frame were in my shop where another genius, Dusan Neumann, was completing the complete overhaul of the engine. We had dinner that evening and he insisted on picking up the check. I had arranged with my friend who owned the motel to pay for the room. Again I was not successful. After failing to take care of these small expenses, I thought I was losing my power of persuasion. But then I thought "Wally, you may not have powers of persuasion on small items, but you did persuade Dr. Brandt to allow you to not only restore a Bugatti, but at long last to actually own one!"

After three full years of restoration, the Bugatti was an excellent working condition. I called Dr. Brandt to tell him that Irene and I will drive to his home in Johnstown with the Bugatti so I can fulfill my promise to take he and his wife in for dinner in the Bugatti at a fancy restaurant. On the day we were to leave for Johnstown, the weather report called for possible rain. It did not rain until we entered the Pennsylvania Turnpike at Carlisle. The rain stopped just as we took the exit for Johnstown. Mrs. Brandt and Irene sat in the back on the beautiful soft and elegant English leather seats. Irene told me "I know what you're thinking, don't you dare ask Dr. Brandt to drive." I must admit it did cross my mind. After a wonderful dinner we spent an hour at their home. I thanked Mrs. Brandt for allowing him to sell the car to me. She told me "I just knew that you would be the best person to own the car." We left the motel right after breakfast and drove home to Frackville on a beautiful sunshiny day.

MADAME JUNEK

A few years after I began collecting antique cars, I read an article in a magazine about the fabulous Bugatti car. Being young and foolish, I began reading the ads in *Hemmings* (a monthly listing of antique cars and parts for sale). I wanted to own a Bugatti! I began reading books on the Bugatti, lots of books!

On my yearly trips to visit my friends in Czechoslovakia, I found that Bugatti sold many cars in this small country. I also found out that one of the first women to race Bugatti's in the '20s lived in Prague. I asked my friends to assist me in finding one that was for sale. They knew the location of every Bugatti in the vicinity of Prague. I was able to see three Bugattis that needed a complete restoration. They were for sale but they could not be exported out of Czechoslovakia.

I mentioned to my friends that I read about the young lady by the name of Junek who won many races using the Bugatti. "Would you like to meet her?" Wow! I did not realize that she was still alive. Arrangements were quickly made for Irene and me to meet her the following afternoon.

Eliska (Elizabeth) Junek lived on the third floor of the Swedish Embassy. She was 85 years old. She was the most fascinating, intriguing and interesting person I ever met in my life. My vocabulary does not have enough words to describe her. Many people make the statement, "The most interesting person I ever met in my life," however in my case, I could truly say that in the 78 years of my life, I never met a person who impressed me as much as Madame Junek.

When we entered her apartment and were introduced, she said,

"First, you must see my city from this great vantage point that I enjoy." The left bank of the city is on a hill and all the very important landmarks such as the Castle and many of the fine large churches including the famous St. Vitas Cathedral are located there. The third floor of her apartment was probably a large attic in this very imposing old house. She led us to a window facing the city that had a very tiny balcony. "Here you can see my Golden city of Prague." She then pointed out the various landmarks. It was a beautiful day filled with sunshine and indeed the domes and steeples did look like they were made of gold. She then invited us to join her for afternoon tea.

She spoke perfect English. She was fluent in Czech, French, German and Italian. We made three visits to her home in the next few years.

As a member of the *American Bugatti Club,* we attended many functions; one of which was the annual spring *Chanteclair Luncheon Revival.* A quote from *"Pur Sang"* the quarterly magazine of the American Bugatti Club:

> At precisely 1:30 PM on Saturday the 25th March, (1985) an overseas operator in Manhattan was struggling to connect her party with a number in Prague, Czechoslovakia. The caller was Wally Baran, the calling place, Harvey's Chelsea Restaurant in New York City, and the party being called—none other than Madame Elizabeth Junek!

> The event was the annual Chanteclair Luncheon party in New York where some 45 of the faithful had gathered to restore their faith in the Marque with the help of some good wine, food and the best of fellowship.

> But to get back to the telephone call, Wally had met Madame Junek during a recent visit to Prague and thought it would be a nice idea to give her a ring from the luncheon so that some of her old friends could wish

her well. Rene and Maurice were of course ready to oblige, as did her countryman Dusan Neumann. Madame Junek took this opportunity to congratulate the American Club on its 25th anniversary and to express her best wishes for the International Rallies held this coming summer.

The Rene mentioned above is Rene Dreyfus of France, the most famous racecar driver in the world during the 1920's and 30s. Maurice is his brother. In 1935, Rene won the "Prix du Million." He beat the Germans at Pau, and became a hero to the Jewish schoolboys.

In 1940, Rene Dreyfus came to the United States to compete at Indianapolis. Then Paris fell to the Germans; he was stranded here. When the U.S. entered the war, Rene joined the Army. He received a battlefield promotion to Master Sergeant for exemplary performance while under fire.

Returning to the United States after the war, he and his brother Maurice opened a gourmet Restaurant in New York City called "Le Chanteclair" a gathering place for racecar drivers from all over the world. The Restaurant closed in 1980.

The reason for this long explanation is that in the early 20's, Madame Junek defeated the great Rene Dreyfus a few times. (She stopped racing after her husband Cenek, was killed in Nurburgring on July 15th, 1928.) I then suggested that Madame Junek be invited to attend the 25th anniversary of the club to be held at Rockport, Maine, August 7/11/85. This met with approval by everyone present. Since it might be difficult for her to get a visa, I suggested that the president of the club issue the invitation and I offered that I would make all the arrangements for her flight and that she would be a guest at our home in Frackville.

Everything went very well and Irene and I met her August 1, at the JFK Airport in New York. We made arrangements to drive to Rockport leaving Frackville August 5. Dusan and I drove in our 1938 Bugatti Ventoux, and Irene and Madame Junek followed in our Mercedes. The Bugatti suffered three flat tires. We used regular rubber tire tubes. The wheels were covered with a heavy felt liner to prevent the heads of the wire wheels from puncturing the tube. Since the tires were very narrow, the felt padding would move from the center to the side resulting in a puncture. We later found special Dunlop tubes made in England that was used for wire wheels. The center of the tube was made from very heavy black rubber while the rest of the tube used normal red rubber.

Each time we had a flat tire, Irene and Mrs. Junek sat at the side of the road in the Bugatti while we went into the nearest town to find a motorcycle dealer. We used motorcycle tubes, because nobody on the road carried narrow antique car tubes. The wheels had a very small hub similar to a motorcycle wheel. After two long days, we arrived at the headquarters hotel. Five miles before we were to enter the hotel, Madame Junek took the passenger seat in the Bugatti so that she could arrive in style.

The Great American Rally
25th Anniversary American Bugatti Club
Samoset Hotel, Rockport, Maine
August 7th to August 11th 1985

Guest of Honor	Elizabeth Junek, Prague, Czechoslovakia
Honorary	Marshals Rene Dreyfus, Forest Hills, New York
	Henry A. Clark Jr., Glen Cove, New York
	Hugh Conway, London, England
	Alexander Ulman, Sagaponack, New York
Rally participants without Bugatti	
	Jurg Brigel, Fechy, Switzerland
	Maurice Dreyfus, forest Hills, New York
	Roger Howard, Stockport, Cheshire, England
	John Venableac Lewelyn, Newbridge on Wye, England
	Hamish Moffatt, Bosbury, Herefordshire, England

Jerome Morici, Clifton, New Jersey
Arthur Eldredge, Peterborough, New
Hampshire
John Ould, Melbourne, Australia
John Fitzpatrick, Sydney, Australia

As reported by Hugh Conway, autumn 1985 edition of Bugantics
(Bugatti Club of England)

. . . . *Wednesday August 7. The evening was completed by a Club reception that was supposed to involve a cash bar, but everyone seemed to be drinking without paying! Here we met some of the car-less guests: Elizabeth Junek as guest of honor, brought over from Prague by courtesy of Walter Baran and well looked after by him—she as cheerful and energetic as ever; Rene and Maurice Dreyfus, J. Brigel from Switzerland, and of course Howard, Llewelyn and Moffatt from England! . . . .*

. . . . *Friday August 9 . . . . If the sight of 90 lobsters waiting to be broiled in a portable steamer was not enough the unforgettable moment of the evening was watching Elizabeth Junek tackling the consumption of a whole lobster with great aplomb, with the two distinguished restaurateurs Rene and Maurice Dreyfus on either side of her gazing with astonishment at her technique! In New York, London or Paris, you would expect a lobster to be split in half and parts of the stomach removed! Elizabeth's Czech technique was to grab a whole lobster in her two still-strong hands, twist the tail and body so that the tail flesh comes out in one piece, eat that and then dig out what you want of the body. You do get a bit wet in the process! We learned afterwards that the locals in New England use the same technique and we are looking forward to try it out at Bentley's-if we can afford a whole lobster.*

Saturday August 10 . . . . Elizabeth Junek and Rene Dreyfus were taken up by Jim Rockefeller in an old Waco biplane to have a look at the coastline . . . .

Sunday August 11 . . . . the programme listed a "Bald Mountain speed trial", which turned out to be a grass-covered airstrip up the Mountain and across its top. A course was marked out up the hill, round the top and down again and the winner was to be he or she who closely matched the time on two circuits—Elizabeth Junek and Rene Dreyfus were the starters . . . . That evening saw the final dinner at the Youngstown Inn nearby and excellent food and ambience. Elizabeth Junek made a short speech and Andy Rheault announce the prizewinners . . . .

Elizabeth Junek and her husband had a remarkable collection of Bugatti racing (and a few touring) cars in the period 1922-1929. They purchased 11 Bugattis. Madame Junek gave me photocopies of many letters from Ettore Bugatti, all written in French.

After returning home to Frackville from the Rally, Madame Junek spent two weeks with us at our home. She returned safely to Prague where we visited with her the following year.

She died in 1994 at the age of 93. Her funeral cortege included many Bugattis.

GOVERNMENT SERVICE

In the spring of 1978, I received a call at my office. "My name is Dick Thornburgh, and I would like to meet you. I am a candidate in the Republican primary election for governor." I asked him, "Are you sure you want to talk to me? While I am a Republican, and I support Republican candidates, I am not actively involved in politics." He told me he would be in Schuylkill County later in the week and would like to meet me. He also asked if I could arrange a meeting with former Superior Court Judge, G. Harold Watkins. I called Judge Watkins and a meeting was arranged to meet with Dick Thornburgh for the following Wednesday at 2 PM. We were to meet in Judge Watkin's office in the Law Building in Frackville. Dick Thornburgh arrived at my office at about 1 PM, and I accompanied him to Watkins' office and introduced him to the Judge. Judge Watkins as usual, was very courteous and listened when Dick Thornburgh asked for his support in the upcoming primary. After the half-hour interview, the Judge informed him that he was backing Mr. Bob Buteria even though he really wanted to back Sen. Henry Hager of Williamsport. He also told Thornburgh that he would never win the primary. The Judge never minced his words. We left, and I noticed that Dick Thornburgh was not a bit worried.

In April 1978, I had a visit from a friend, Mayor Bob Allen of Pottsville. He asked me to serve as the treasurer for the newly formed "Thornburgh For Governor Committee Of Schuylkill County." ("You won't have to do anything; we just want to use your name.") Yeh, ha! Since I never do anything halfway, I decided to help as best I could. At this time, this new committee consisted of about four members.

The Schuylkill County Republican Committee endorsed Mr. Bob Butera of Philadelphia.

The President of the Pennsylvania Superior Court, Judge G. Harold Watkins of Frackville, was the *unofficial* head of the Schuylkill County Republican Committee. To say that he was a bit upset about the Mayor of Pottsville, Bob Allen and businessman, Walter Baran of Frackville, forming a committee to elect Dick Thornburgh Governor would be putting it mildly. He was furious and mad as hell!

His threats notwithstanding, we began making plans on ways to carry Schuylkill County for Dick Thornburgh during the primary election. I suggested to Bob Allen that we contact 1000 people residing in Schuylkill County and ask their permission to have their names listed in an advertisement promoting Dick Thornburgh in both of the newspapers in the County. We created a form stating, "We the undersigned Schuylkill Countians, support Dick Thornburgh etc.," which I distributed among my employees. Most of them signed and a few asked for copies of the form so that they could have their neighbors and friends also sign. Bob Allen had also collected many names from the Pottsville area. In less than a week, we had sufficient names to run the ad. Shenandoah (the only western town in the East) always had difficulty in counting paper ballots. They were always a few hundred votes more or less in their count. It all depended on who the candidates were. Even though both newspapers were given the same list, Shenandoah Evening Herald listed 875 names while the Pottsville Republican listed 909.

Tuesday May 9th, 1978, a full-page advertisement was printed in the *Pottsville Republican* and *the Shenandoah Evening Herald*. In the center of the page a small block three columns wide and four inches deep, was surrounded by names of citizens of Schuylkill County (which I am sure held quite a few registered Democrats) placed haphazardly throughout the page. This was our sole advertising effort. Dick Thornburgh did visit the County a few times where we arranged meetings with the local radio stations, small group of citizens, and the local newspapers.

Our efforts produced the following results:

FEET FIRST

Dick Thornburgh carried Schuylkill County in the primary by over 1200 votes! Bob Allen was defeated (payback time) in the next election and the city of Pottsville had a Democrat as mayor for the first time in many years. Bob Allen joined the ranks of the unemployed. He was later hired by The Department of Environmental Resources (DER.)

Prior to the general election in November, Dick Thornburgh made quite a few visits to Schuylkill County. A good friend of mine, Stanley Miller, the owner of the "Miller Auto Stores" drove Thornburgh to Schuylkill County and would meet us at the Tremont exit of Interstate 81. Bob Allen would arrange for him to meet with various groups. One of these meetings was held in a small restaurant in Tremont at the ungodly hour of 6:30 AM. Dick was surprised at the large amount of Tremont citizens who came out to meet him.

During Thornburgh's visits to the County, I mentioned to him that I was not interested in an appointment of any kind in his administration. I told him that I was happy with my job and my business. All I wanted from his administration was good conservative government. He told me he was pleased to hear that. I have always supported Republican candidates, but this was the first time that I was really active in supporting a candidate. After his election in November, the *Shenandoah Evening Herald* began writing editorials and news stories suggesting that I should be appointed to a high position in the Thornburgh Administration. This proved very embarrassing for me. I decided to write a letter to Mayor Allen in Pottsville to help stop some of these rumors.

Walter Baran
200 Butler Road
Frackville, PA.
17931

13 November 1978

Mayor Robert Allen

Pottsville City Hall
401 North Centre Street
Pottsville, P.A. 17901

Dear Bob:

I certainly enjoyed working with you this year on the campaign for Governor of Pennsylvania. I, like you, had a lot of faith in Dick Thornburgh from the early days of the Primary campaign. At that time I told you that should he be successful, I would not be interested in a job or appointment within his administration.

A few days ago, an editor of a local paper with much too fertile a mind, wrote that I should be appointed to a high position within the new administration. Since I have neither the talent nor the training for such a position, this editorial has caused me much embarrassment. I might as well have applied for the position of Chief Brain Surgeon at the Ashland State Hospital!

During his campaign, Dick Thornburgh promised to appoint only those with the highest qualifications to serve the people of Pennsylvania and I expect him to do just that. My sole purpose in supporting him is my belief that he is best qualified to bring good, honest and effective government back to Pennsylvania. I would appreciate your help in squelching rumors of my appointment to a position as a result of my efforts on behalf of Dick Thornburgh.

If you could arrange it, however, I would not be adverse to accepting an invitation to one of the inaugural parties that will be held in Harrisburg next January.

Best regards,
Wally

Walter Baran

I sent the letter to Bob hoping that he could get in touch with Governor-elect Thornburgh to once again inform him that I was not interested in serving in any position in any area of state government. The Governor-elect was extremely busy preparing to take over the reins of the Pennsylvania government in January. I'm sure that he was not even informed of a small town newspaper in the coal regions writing articles and editorials promoting one of their subscribers to be placed in a very high position in his administration. Hell, they were not only promoting me, they were practically insisting that I should have a cabinet position! A new rumor began stating that many of the girls from the factory were planning to visit the State Capitol building to petition Governor-elect Thornburgh to give "Our boss, Wally Baran, a job." As the days went by, things really became ridiculous. I told Irene, "I thought that they liked me, but now I see they only want to be rid of me." I was approached by one of the ringleaders, Jenny, if I could advise them where and what day would be best. I advised her not to picket in front of the main Capitol building since he would not be there. I suggested that she find out which Holiday Inn he was using in the Harrisburg area as his temporary headquarters before she began to picket. This rumor is so stupid that I will not spend any additional words on it.

A few weeks after he was elected governor, I received a telephone call on a Sunday morning as I was dressing to attend church. He said, "Wally, I want to appoint you to be the Secretary of General Services." At first I thought it was one of my friends doing a great job imitating Dick Thornburgh's voice. I finally said, "Who is this? This is no time to joke." He then put his wife Ginny on the phone and I knew then that it indeed was Dick Thornburgh. I reminded him that I did not want any kind of an appointment and you know that I meant it. I reminded him that I did not have the political experience or the expertise to be a member of his cabinet. In fact, I had no idea what "General Services does." He told me that he would call me in a few days. On Wednesday morning, I received a copy of *The Pennsylvania Manual* with a paper clip marking the page titled "General Services." At the end of the week he called again and asked if I carefully read the duties of The Secretary of General

Services. I told him that I did and after reading the duties, I was now very sure that I could not do the job. He asked me to think about it since in the short time that he knew me he was sure that I would be a success in this department. I thanked him for considering me but I was now even more convinced that I did not have the experience, so I respectfully declined his very kind offer.

I suppose I misjudged Dick Thornburgh. I began receiving telephone calls from friends and strangers to change my mind and accept the appointment. I received telephone calls from the Polish American community informing me that a Polish American never served in a cabinet position in Pennsylvania. "We have been petitioning for over 100 years to have a Polish American serve in the office of a Governor." Polish priests from Erie to Philadelphia called me to accept. I had a few calls from Superior Court Judge G. Harold Watkins stating that it would be a great thing for Schuylkill County. A federal Judge from the Scranton area also called me to accept. It was extremely embarrassing for me since I knew this was a very high office and there was many outstanding citizens who would be honored to serve as the Secretary Of General Services.

During this period my son Tony, having graduated from Lehigh University began to work full-time for Model Garment Co. It was upsetting to me that whenever he took a business call from New York for Mr. Baran, after telling them that he was Mr. Baran, he heard "We mean your dad." The business was growing by leaps and bounds. Tony began computerizing the operation. We just built a huge 40,000 square foot air-conditioned building and were planning an additional 40,000 square foot. He was actually running the operation even if some people in New York still said, "I want to talk to your dad."

During a discussion with Irene she said, "Tony will never run the operation as long as you go to your office every day." I agreed with her. I did not have a single doubt in my mind that Tony would be able to run the company better than I could. It was a large operation. We now had the main plant in Frackville, and we opened a plant "Penn Allen," in Hazleton with 125 employees, also a plant,

"Penn Spruce," in Sunbury with 100 employees. They were all established and working well. I began reading *The Pennsylvania Manual* again. This time much more carefully. I asked my friend and attorney, Wilbur Rubright, for some advice. He told me that I would do great in that position. After all, the "Department of General Services" has 2000 employees. Surely you will be able to find a few smart employees in the department that would be able to assist you." I told Irene "I'm going to accept. Even if I only last six months it will look good on the obituary column in the newspaper that I was once a member of the Governor's Cabinet."

After I made the decision, I met with my friend Wilbur Rubright Esq. and asked him for some guidance. He told me, "The first thing you must do is to find someone to be your executive assistant. It should be someone who does not have any connection with the political scene in Harrisburg. He must be *your man.* To act as your "alter ego." He should have a good personality, experience in writing speeches and letters, be available to attend functions during the evenings and weekends and if possible, someone who does not as yet have a family." "Where in the world will I be able to find a person that could fill these requirements." "Well, you can ask one of your sons if they know of a fraternity brother who is looking for a demanding but exciting position." I then asked my son Tony if he knew anyone who could at least fill some of the requirements for this position. "I know just the guy—David Morrison. His home is in suburban Philadelphia. It's been a few years since I saw him (actually he attended Tony and Sandy's wedding a few years before) I do not know if he would be available to take the position. What I do know, is that he would be perfectly suited to the job. He has a great personality, writes very well and is an "all-around nice guy." I will try to contact him and if he is available I'll have him send a resume and you can interview him." Tony was able to contact him and made arrangements for him to meet me at my home in Frackville. He was working as a representative for his fraternity, Phi Delta Theta and he was willing to make a change. I was very pleased that he would join me in Harrisburg.

INAUGURATION

A fter the inauguration of Governor Thornburgh, a formal introduction of the governor and his newly formed cabinet was held in "Founders Hall" in Hershey PA. The Governor, Lieut. Governor and the entire cabinet accompanied by their spouses were located on the second floor balcony. "Ladies and gentlemen" "Gov. Dick Thornburgh and his wife Ginny." They received thunderous applause when they walked slowly down the elegant marble staircase. "Lieutenant Bill Scranton and his wife Coral" more applause. The members of the cabinet with their spouses were then introduced to the enthusiastic gathering. It truly was an elegant black-tie affair, an evening to remember.

Other activities followed for the next few days. A performance by the Harrisburg Symphony Orchestra was held in the Forum auditorium with Governor Dick Thornburgh reciting Sandburg's **"Portrait of Lincoln."**

Since the Department of General Services served all of the departments and agencies, I began serving as the acting Secretary of General Services on January 20th 1979 before being confirmed by the Senate.

One month later, I appeared before the Confirmation Committee of the Senate to be questioned on my ability to serve in the capacity of Secretary of General Services. Before appearing before this committee, I was coached by the Governor's staff as to the questions I would probably be asked. I was provided with facts and figures on the department and I was told that rule No. 1 was "Respond to any questions using as few words as possible, do not expand on your comments to any question, when a simple yes or no would suffice." I was not concerned about appearing before this committee and a few members of the staff that I inherited were surprised by my calm appearance. I made up my mind to answer all questions truthfully thinking to myself, "What you see is what you're going to get."

The confirmation hearing went very well. After reading my prepared statement that hopefully would answer some of the questions about me personally, and how best I could serve the Commonwealth. Each member welcomed me to state government and the "quiz" part of the program began.

"What is the total amount of funds and other services that you provided for the election of Governor Thornburgh?"

"What experience do you have in the construction of large buildings?"

"I read in the press about a statement that you made that you would only approve leases on their merits and not on the recommendation of a third party. What do you mean by that?"

I said, "If my action did not benefit all the citizens of the Commonwealth, I would not sign the lease."

"Are you telling me that if a legislator called you favoring a lease by one of his constituents, you would not take that into consideration?"

"If my action did not benefit all the citizens of the Commonwealth, I would not sign the lease."

"I do not feel that I have to inform you that you are not as yet confirmed before responding to my next question. What if I called you to favor a certain lease?"

"If my action did not benefit all the citizens of the Commonwealth, I would not sign the lease."

"Be very careful in responding to my next question, what if Governor Thornburgh called you about a lease. How would you respond?"

"If my action did not benefit all the citizens of the Commonwealth, I would not sign the lease. *However, if Ginny called . . . .*"

I know that he was "Pulling my chain" since he was smiling

when he finished his examination. There were other questions that treated me very kindly from my republican friends and my newly found democrat friends.

Toward the end of the hearing I was asked, "Do you know what your name means?" Keeping in mind rule #1, I responded "Yes." After a few seconds that seemed like minutes, I said, "I know that I am here to only respond to your questions. But against the advice of my staff I am going to risk asking you a question. "Do you know what it means?"

"Yes, it means, a sheep." "Well not exactly, it indeed is a sheep but it's the one with the big horns on his head, called a RAM."

Everyone smiled. The chairman of the committee thanked me for my comments and I went up to the dais and shook every members hand.

A week or so later, I decided to visit the East Mall for some small items that I needed, and while there a member of the confirmation committee approached me and said "I have attended many confirmation hearings in my years here in Harrisburg, and I want to tell you, I actually enjoyed your comments and especially your candor in responding to the various questions. I wish you the best, and you will do fine, if you do not lose your sense of humor.

I was confirmed unanimously and was sworn in by the Secretary of State in the Governor's reception room of the Capitol. I received a tremendous reception by my friends from Schuylkill County who arrived in three buses. The room was filled to capacity and spilled out to the hall to the two large doors in the reception room. I overheard John Scotzin, a reporter from the *Harrisburg Patriot News,* say to another reporter "Let's get the hell out of here, I did not know it was going to be a coronation!"

Immediately after I was sworn in, a reception was held in one of the large hearing rooms on the first floor of the Capitol. There was plenty of good food, accordion music, and a great crowd of well wishers to greet me. The reception was sponsored and paid for by Senator Joseph E. Gruzenda D-29 the Senator from my district. I did not know him very well since we belonged to different parties. He was very kind to me. He introduced me to the Senate

Confirmation Committee before my hearing. He was very proud to have a Member of the Cabinet in his district.   *Regan-Bush*
Senator Gruzenda and many other legislators, members of the AACA and friends, attended a reception held in my honor at the Host Inn, Harrisburg on March 20, 1979. The Atlantic Apparel Contractors Association hosted it.

I was told that John Scotzin began representing the *Patriot News* during the Governor Pennypacker administration. I later found out that he arrived during the Gifford Pinchot administration toward the end of his first term 1923-1927. Gov. Pinchot also served as Governor for 1931-1935. He also reported on both of the terms of Governor Thornburgh 1979-1986.

He was a nice old guy and treated me fairly. Scotzin was known for reading the entire 829 pages of the *Pennsylvania Manual.* The manual is published every two years and contains more information that anyone could possibly use. The Pennsylvania Constitution, biographies of the state officials, the general assembly and the judiciary. It is a great reference book containing information on all 67 counties, the election results by district, a listing of all Governors of the 50 states etc.

All the readers of *the Harrisburg Patriot & Harrisburg Evening News* anxiously wait for John Scotzin's review of the current edition of the *Pennsylvania Manual* to appear. He gets his "jollies" by reporting an error, a misspelled name etc.

The Pennsylvania manual is published by the Department of General Services, Walter Baran Secretary. It is very difficult for the editor to have the members of the General Assembly, cabinet members, various boards and commissions respond to the editor's request for information regarding their biographies or other facts that have to be updated. When the editor, Gail Ackley began to prepare volume, 106 1982-83, she asked me if I would like to add to my biography. I said, "Add that I am' An all-around nice guy.'" She said, "Do you really mean it?" I said "Yes, no one will read it with the exception of some members of my family." She sent the information to the typesetter who immediately called her and asked, "Is someone playing a trick on the Secretary?" She responded,

"He told me so himself. I suggest you call him and he will verify it." I completely forgot about John Scotzin and his semiannual review of the Manual.

One of the main reasons I decided to accept the position of "Secretary of General Services," was that it would be a way to give back to this great country and great Commonwealth, all of the opportunities that were given to me that could only happen in America.

What I am now about to write, may sound "corny" and a bit of flag-waving but like all the rest of the stories in this book, they are true.

During World War II, all of my friends volunteered or were drafted into the Service. Friends from school, my neighborhood, and from my church, were in the various armed services with the exception of Bill Borowsky and me. Bill had his right leg amputated when he was a child. After failing the physical examination, I asked and was given an appointment with the draft board. I wanted to know if I could serve as an ambulance driver or some other non-combat role. I was given a telephone number for the Special Services Department of the Red Cross in Philadelphia. During the meeting, I was told that it was possible to be assigned to an army unit in Africa. I would receive food, shelter, and the Red Cross uniform without charge. I was then told that I would have to personally pay for an ambulance. Of course this was impossible. Some of the men from the Frackville area suggested that I take a job as a welder at the shipyards at Marcus Hook near Philadelphia. I was told that the wages were very high and that I would be helping the war effort. Since there was no shortage of applicants for the job, I decided to stay at my job in the garment industry.

After being confirmed by the Senate, I began my duties as the Secretary of General Services. Keeping in mind my effort to contribute to the Commonwealth in lieu of serving in the army during the war, I decided not to take any "perks" that came with the position. For the eight years that I served, I used my own car and car telephone and did not contribute to the pension plan. I have never submitted an expense voucher for the use of the car or other expenses in my travels throughout the state. My department did pay for my trips using commercial airlines when I had business in Pittsburgh or Erie. As a member of the "National Conference of General Services Officers" (in 1983, I was elected to serve as Chairman) I attended the annual meetings held in various states (no, we never met in Alaska or Hawaii) I flew at the governments (taxpayers) expense.

Contrary to some local "experts." I do not receive any pension nor do I have a prescription or health plan or any other compensation for serving in the Commonwealth of Pennsylvania for eight years.

I find it very difficult to write a chapter on the time I spent with The Department of General Services. I have decided to use an update article written by my Executive Secretary, David J. Morrison, in 1985 explaining the duties and some of the accomplishments made during my tenure. I will, however, write some short anecdotes that may be of interest to the reader.

THORNBURGH CAMPAIGN

I n the years 1977/1978, Dick Thornburgh campaigned throughout the state of Pennsylvania during the primary election and more importantly the general election for the office of governor of Pennsylvania.

During his travels throughout the state whether it was in a large city a small town or hamlet, after giving his speech, invariably a prospective voter would approach him and ask, "My church, St. Basil's in Duquesne is undergoing a complete remodeling in anticipation of celebrating its 100 year anniversary in 1981. If we give you two months notice, will you join with our congregation at the rededication of our church and speak at the banquet that will follow?" Dick Thornburgh would turn to one of his aide's and say, "Take all the information about the rededication of St. Basil's church in Duquesne "Mr. Tobias here will give you all the information you need." Thornburgh would receive at least one or more requests every day when he was campaigning. While speaking to The Philadelphia Horticultural Society, he was later approached by Mrs. Cynthia Foxworthy the esteemed President of *The Philadelphia Horticultural Society* and informed him that the Society would celebrate the anniversary of its founding. She did not ask him to attend the gala occasion, she more or less ordered him to appear at this momentous anniversary. Dick, to his aide: "Please get all of the information from Mrs. Foxworthy."

Since the Governor could not possibly attend all of these very important functions, he enlisted the cabinet members to represent him and occasionally to present a framed document of congratulations, etc.

SENATOR HALL

I received a call from a staff member of the governor's office asking me if I would attend a political meeting in Montgomery County, "And, oh yes, say something ethnic." It was scheduled for a Sunday afternoon and was to be held in Norristown. Our son Joseph had a home in nearby Audubon so this would be an occasion to visit with him and his family. I drove Irene to his home then left for Norristown to attend the meeting. Whenever I attend a function to speak or to represent the Governor to present a handsomely framed letter of "Greetings" or proclamation, I usually call the Senator and Representative about a week before the event (providing of course there is a "R" after his name) to advise him/her the date and time of my appearance. As was my custom, I called Senator Hall to inform him that I would be speaking at the meeting to be held in Norristown. Senator Hall was a good republican but he was a little strange. He loved you one day, and hated you the following day. It all depended how he felt when he got up that morning. I placed a telephone call to his office in Harrisburg and was told that he was attending a meeting but would call me at his first opportunity. "This is Senator Hall, what do you want?" "Senator, I'm going to be in your district next week to address the meeting of the Republican Club of Montgomery County and I would like to know if you would like me to mention someone in particular or any other item that would be of interest to your constituents." He said, "This is a very important meeting that I never miss. I have another appointment and will not be able to attend. Get a paper and pencil. Write down the name of, John Doe, he is in the roofing business and has been a good supporter of mine." He then gave me three more additional names and he also mentioned a local construction project in his district by The Department of General Services. "Did you get all that? Read it back to me. I want you to know that this is very important for me and since it is impossible for me to be in attendance, I want to make sure that you mention all that I told you."

I arrived at the meeting a half-hour before time. I was surprised at the large crowd that was assembling. Standing in front of the dais, was the county chairman, Bob Asher, the county commissioners, some of the row officers from the county courthouse and other important Republicans, a group of about 12 men. They were discussing the printed program with me. Meanwhile, an exit door at the rear of the hall opened and Senator Hall walked in! When they saw him, Bob Asher and the group in unison, said, "Aw shit."

"I'm going to introduce the Secretary." "But Senator, we have the programs printed since you told us you could not possibly attend and we have someone else to introduce Secretary Baran." After the opening remarks and some introduction of guests, the Senator approached the microphone and began. "When Gov. Thornburgh wanted to have someone to run the business end of Pennsylvania government, he wanted someone with business experience. A person who met payrolls, a person who dealt with unions. A person who had experience in constructing large buildings. A person who was not active in politics. So he named a businessman, Walter Baran, as the Secretary of General Services. I'm very pleased to introduce to you Secretary Walter Baran."

After he was seated and I was standing at the microphone an idea came into my head.

"Thank you Senator Hall. I'm sorry to tell you this, but I do not believe that it happened that way. (Senator Hall's face turned red and then blue and he was ready to explode.) 'As I understand it, Gov. Thornburgh and his staff were meeting in a suite of rooms at the Holiday Inn. They were in the process of selecting cabinet members for the various departments. One of the staff members proposed Dr. Larson for the Secretary of Pennsylvania

Department of Transportation. Everyone agreed. Secretary of Banking, we need someone from the Northwestern part of the state. Ben McEnteer, a banker from Titusville was suggested. Great! They then asked for suggestions for the Department of General Services. Someone from Delaware County was mentioned, then Allentown, Pittsburgh and Philadelphia. After 20 minutes of suggestions without getting anywhere, a staff member said, "Let's take a Pole." The next thing I knew, I was standing in the Governor's reception room, my left hand on the Bible and my right hand raised and I was taking the oath of office.' I could hear Bob Asher and his friends breathing a sigh of relief. I quickly looked at Senator Hall and he actually smiled. I did not even begin my speech, and I was loudly applauded. I also thought to myself, well I said something ethnic.

I then began reading my remarks (I used speech No. 5: "The Governor has many programs that he wants to introduce and he needs your help. He needs more Republicans in the Senate and the House to get his programs passed etc. etc." I had my executive assistant, David Morrison write six generic speeches:

#1   for service clubs.
#2   for interdenominational churches.
#3   for Catholic churches.
#4   for Polish/Lithuanian/Ukrainian/German/Irish groups.
#5   political meetings.
#6   for school graduations (high schools and colleges.)

After giving a few of these speeches a few times, I did not need to refer to my notes.

PLUM BOROUGH

O n another occasion I was asked to appear at a republican rally held in Plum Borough, near Pittsburgh. It was held on a Sunday afternoon at 2 PM. There was a lot of traffic on the turnpike but I finally arrived at 2:15. I was there to support the Republican candidate for the House of Representatives. The information card I received before leaving Harrisburg listed his qualifications, the names of his wife and children and gave his occupation as a bookkeeper. I'm sorry to say that he did not look like a strong candidate. In fact I visualized him sitting at a desk with garters on his shirtsleeves and wearing a green plastic eye shield. When it was my turn to present my candidate I gave a very short version of speech #5. "The Governor has very important legislation that he needs to be passed in the next session He needs Joe in Harrisburg to help the Governor etc."

There were many state and local candidates some of which were present or had presenters speaking on their behalf. After some of them were presented, the chairman asked, "Is there anyone here to speak on behalf of our candidate for Attorney General, Leroy Zimmerman?" No one responded. I then asked the chairman if I could respond. "Having spent a few years in Harrisburg I had many occasions to speak to Mr. Zimmerman on matters pertaining to my department. He has a very good reputation, (I noticed that most of the people in attendance were of Italian descent.) He will make an excellent Attorney General and more importantly, *his Italian mother* would love if you would vote for her son. Wow! I wasn't exactly mobbed but many people came to me and asked, "Why weren't we told that he is

Italian?" "Is he really Italian?" I said, "No, he is half Italian." I was then told that there are many Italians that are registered Democrat but that they will vote for him. Right then and there I heard some of these Republicans putting a phone chain together. Not only for Plum Borough but also for the entire region including all their relatives that live in Pittsburgh. I gave my card to a committeewoman and asked if she would send me the local newspapers after the election so I could see how well Zimmerman did in that area. She gave me her husband's business card that I still have in my files. The family had a garbage disposal business. Mr. Zimmerman did very well in Pittsburgh and especially Plum Borough.

STATE EMPLOYEES

Before the Commonwealth of Pennsylvania employed me, I, like many other misguided citizens, did not think much of state employees. "They could not make it in the private sector. They are all political appointees. And other such comments that I am ashamed to have said." After only a few months in Harrisburg, I realized that most state employees are very capable, talented, honest and hard working. For the next seven years, while making speeches to various groups, I always include a few lines in praise of our state workers. Of course, like any very large corporation, there are a few state employees that do not deserve any praise. As an example.

BLOOMSBURG UNIVERSITY

Columbus Day, was a paid holiday for state employees. There were certain state employees that have to work on holidays. Inspectors on all construction projects in DGS had to work since it was not a paid holiday for the construction companies. I spent the weekend at my home in Frackville and I decided to take Irene out for lunch at the McGee Hotel in Bloomsburg. They served a fantastic buffet lunch! Their own baked bread, an amazing array of dishes, desserts you would die for, and food to live for. It was a cold wet October day but Irene and I were in very good spirits after enjoying a great meal. I asked Irene if she would mind waiting in the car while I checked out one of our DGS projects while we are in town.

"The James H. McCormick Center For Humane Services" was under construction. It was a large three-story building housing the school of nursing, a TV studio on the first floor and at the time of my visit it was 90 percent finished. I parked my car as close to the building as I could since it was raining in the morning and the area around the building was a quagmire of mud. A few boards were laying on the mud from the parking area to one of the entrance doors. I entered the first floor and found a few employees of the contractor installing HVAC (heating, ventilating and air-conditioning) vents. I asked them, "I'm looking for the DGS inspectors." "Haven't seen them all day, probably because it's a holiday today." I then took the stairs to the second floor were the electricians were running conduit for the lighting system. "Could we help you?" "I'm looking for the DGS inspectors." "I don't believe they are in today." I then decided to drive to the DGS construction trailers to check on the inspectors. I walked into the office and found five DGS inspectors. Two of them were looking at a shotgun catalog. (It was hunting season) Another was eating a banana and reading a newspaper. There were many engineering drawings opened on the drawing boards. I asked, "Is the boss in" "He went to visit another job in Sunbury." "When will he be back?" "Tomorrow morning." "Are you looking for a job? We have all the good jobs here and there are no vacancies." I was dressed in an old pair of trousers and I was wearing a heavy sweater. I then gave him my business card. The one with the Pennsylvania Gold Seal at the top. It read:

Commonwealth of Pennsylvania
Departmental all of General Services
Room 515 North Office Building
Harrisburg

Walter Baran
717 787-1992   Secretary

"Would you please have him call me at my office in Harrisburg tomorrow morning." One of the inspectors said, "We were in the building this morning but we had a late lunch." I asked them, "Why is it that I'm the only in here with mud on my shoes?" I received a call the next day from the superintendent. He said, "Mr. Secretary, you can be sure that I will reprimand my men. It will never happen again." I thought, well, at least he did not deny it.

SOMEBODY

While walking through the rotunda of Pennsylvania's Magnificent State Capitol Building, I noticed a group of children with their second grade teacher preparing to leave the building after their tour of the Capitol. A pretty little girl left the group and approached me. Her head was turned looking up to someone who appeared to be a giant and said, "Are you somebody?" I looked down at this pretty and sincere young lady waiting for my answer. I said, "Honey, everyone is somebody. Your teacher is somebody, I'm somebody and you are somebody." After spending about an hour touring this beautiful building and while she didn't say so, she was not successful in meeting a "somebody," like the Governor, a Senator or even a member of the House of Representatives. I just knew that she would like to go home and tell her parents that she met "Somebody." I told her that I was privileged to work in this building every day. You can tell your parents, "I met a State Employee."

COLORING BOOK

This little story allows me to cleverly lead into one of my more successful small projects. The Department of General Services is multifaceted I like to compare it to a beautiful diamond. Each cut of the diamond when joined with others, becomes a perfect stone. DGS seems to be in charge of "Everything." It is the central maintenance, purchasing, publishing and building construction agency for departments and other agencies of the Commonwealth. The Department is responsible for the Capitol police, architects and engineers, the leasing of space for agencies, the purchase of ballpoint pens, helicopters for the state police and about 27 other "jobs."

In this article, I want to discuss two areas: The Bureau Of Publications and Paperwork Management and the Bureau of Buildings and Grounds which includes the maintenance, operation, repair and housekeeping functions, facilities and grounds in the Capitol complex.

Each schoolchild from K to 12 is given a beautiful and expensive four-color brochure as they are leaving the building. The brochure gives a detailed description of the Senate and House chambers and other important areas of the Capitol.

The yellow school buses are parked near the entrance to the William Penn Memorial Museum. As the children leave the Capitol and walk to their buses, many of the children (of course, excluding the little girl who asked me if I was a somebody) dropped these beautiful and expensive four-color brochures that they just received on the ground on their way to the bus. Some of the students who are members of the "Keep Pennsylvania Clean" Club discarded their brochures in the waste receptacles that were placed near the entrance to the museum. Since DGS is responsible for the maintenance people that take care of the Capitol grounds, it was their duly to pick up the brochures. Since these beautiful and expensive four-color brochures were written for adults, many of the younger children discarded them.

I decided to create a brochure for the young that they would want to take home. After sleeping on this idea, I decided that a small coloring book might be the way to go. I discussed this with members of my staff and I was told that an art student from Kutztown University was a summer intern at our print shop located on 17th Street. I made an appointment to meet with her. I saw some of the samples of her work and I was very impressed. I told her that we wanted to create a coloring book to give to the younger school children when they came to tour the Capitol Building. I made the following suggestions: Newsprint paper should be used. The booklet should be 8 1/2 by 11 inches. Using this measurement there would not be any waste of paper. I felt that all the state symbols and that the state bird, state dog, state flower, and state tree should be included along with a few puzzles and follow-the-dots puzzle. Since I could see that she was a very talented and creative person, I told her to use her creative ideas in designing the rest of the book.

After a few days, she called and asked if I wanted to see the work she had done so far. I was very pleased. On the cover, she had the Capitol dome and large block letters "LET'S DISCOVER PENNSYLVANIA." There were tiny figures of children sitting or hanging from some of the letters. The inside cover consisted of the following message:

> The Commonwealth of Pennsylvania welcomes its young citizens to Harrisburg!

> Presented in this coloring book are some facts about Pennsylvania history and State government which children visiting the Capitol are able to take-home with them.

All Pennsylvanians are invited to visit the Capitol. The
Department of General Services Conducts guided tours
year-round, Monday through Friday.

Advance reservations should be made for groups with
more than ten members.

Call: 717-787-6810

Published by the Department of General Services
Illustrations by Lou Ann Donnelly

The second page contained an outline of the map of
Pennsylvania. Various cities and towns were placed on the map
each with an illustration such as Philadelphia, Independence Hall
and Liberty Bell; Gettysburg, a union soldiers cap Harrisburg, the
Capitol building; Pittsburgh, a steel mill; Erie, a trout leaping from
the lake; and Scranton, a railroad car filled with coal. I told her I
wanted to make in addition to this map. I asked her to put the name
of my hometown, Frackville, located halfway between Harrisburg
and Scranton. It did not have an illustration.

The rest of the pages had a figure of William Penn, the founder
of Pennsylvania, the four branches of government beginning with
the executive branch with a sketch of Governor Thornburgh. Proper
illustrations of the legislative & the judicial branches waiting for the
children to use their crayons to complete the book.

The bottom of each page had a very simple message such as
under the map, the words "You live in Pennsylvania."

"William Penn called Pennsylvania a Commonwealth, which
means "for the public good."

"Philadelphia was the first Capitol of our state and of our nation."
"Did you know that Pennsylvania is 300 years old?"
"The State Coat of Arms"
"The State Dog-Great Dane, etc.
We printed a trial run of 25,000 copies. The children were very

happy. The teachers were very happy. But the grounds maintenance crew was actually thrilled!

It was a huge success. But not everyone was pleased. I received many letters from some of the bureaucrats in the Department of Education. "Why did you not clear the wording that appears on the bottom of each page? We have the expertise and qualifications to use proper words that young children would understand." I responded to one of the letters by stating "Because, I wanted to have these coloring booklets available to the children before Governor Thornburgh left office." They responded with a letter that contained some words that I had difficulty understanding. I gave an order to our print shop to print another 50,000 copies before the education department would find a directive that gives them the right to in fact "censor" our coloring book.

I also received some correspondence from one of the directors of the William Penn Museum suggesting that a page be included promoting the museum since the children always visit there after the tour the Capitol building. I thought it reasonable so I instructed that one page be used to promote the museum. I even allowed them to approve the page and to write the caption at the bottom. It read:

> You can learn more about Pennsylvania by visiting the William Penn Memorial Museum located near the Capitol. I did not ask them if they had approval from the Department of Education. The bottom line is, everyone with the exception of the Department of Education was very happy and the taxpayers did not really know it but this coloring book saved the taxpayers a big bunch of money!

After a few weeks a reporter on his way to the press room (supplied free to press by the citizens of the Commonwealth), picked up a copy of the coloring book from the tour guides' table and discovered that Frackville was on the map. He tried calling the Frackville Chamber of Commerce (there was none.)

He was eventually connected to the President of the Frackville Businessman's Association, Edwin (Doc) Herwick at his hardware store. He asked Doc, "What historical significance does Frackville have?" "Doc replied, "The only historical building in town was the town clock school building but that was torn down about fifteen years ago." He then called my executive assistant David Morrison, who also served as my press officer, and asked him, "What historical significance does Frackville have since it is listed on the map in the State coloring book." He suggested that he call me directly. He called and asked me the same question. I told him, "It does not have any historical significance. When I was leaving Frackville to take the position of Secretary of the Department of General Services, a few of my friends said, "Wally put Frackville on the map. This was the first opportunity that I had to put Frackville on the map."

Governor Thornburgh did not seem to mind since occasionally he would introduce me as, "Wally Baran, the guy who put Frackville on the map!

STEELE SCHOOL

During my stay in Harrisburg, The Department of General
Services, participated in a new program called, "Partners
in Education." We were assigned an inner city school located about
five blocks from my office in the Capitol Building. It was the
beginning of a wonderful experience. Steele School is an elementary
school for classes four, five, and six. 350 students, 97% were African-
Americans.

On the first visit I made with my staff, we toured the school,
spoke with the teachers, and asked them about their needs and
how the Department of General Services could be of assistance to
the students, teachers and the school.

Here was a public school supported by the taxpayers and yet it
was obvious that they did not receive the funds or attention that
public schools in the Harrisburg suburbs received. They had a few
old computers that were standing on wooden crates for lack of
computer tables. The teacher's lounge had a few folding chairs
and a small table. Since DGS is responsible for the State and Federal
surplus program, we soon rectified some of their problems. The
computer department now had twelve almost new computers and
tables. The teachers lounge received a shipment of "like new"
furniture. We supplied reams of paper pads, art supplies, TV sets
complete with VCR's and many other items, all free of charge.
State surplus was sold to the public but there was no charge for
schools or other non-profit organizations.

My staff, God bless them, helped the school in many ways. We
attended their special programs, plays, and every special program
that the school presented. The department held a career day. Since

DGS had many professions and trades under their jurisdiction, we had one of the best career days in any school in Pennsylvania! Which included Architects, Engineers, Printers, Attorneys, Capitol Police, Computer Technicians, Nurses, Secretaries, etc. (I knew that many of their parents worked as custodians for the State but I purposely did not have them represented in our career day program)

I spoke before the entire assembly on how very important it was for them to work hard, especially Math and English, listen to their teachers and attend school every day. The students then reported to their various homerooms and the various professions moved from room to room. "How much do you get paid?" "How long did you have to go to school" "Could girls be Lawyers?" It was a great day. We made it an annual event.

I became very involved with the school. We had suggestions from the students, teachers and members of my staff on how we could improve Steele School to make it the finest intercity school in the entire Dauphin County. I must say that we succeeded beyond all expectations. Some of the new projects we introduced to the school:

> The annual yearbook. We arranged for a few older students to take photographs throughout the year that would be included in the 48-page yearbook. The cover included a new logo **"SES" Steele Elementary School— Where Kids Really Learn.** The first edition included a photograph of the principal of Steele school Mr. Musmanno and Secretary of General Services Walter Baran, signing the official documents creating a partnership. Looking on were the four deputies of the Department. Dr. John Lawless, Merle H. Ryan, Thomas J. Topolski and Donald E. Smith. All the deputies were to contribute to the success of the venture

The yearbook was a fine publication and it was published (illegally) without any costs to the school, by the State Printing

Department, which was under the jurisdiction of the Department of General Services, Walter Baran Secretary.

The office of the Governor had a program called "Governor for a Day" for local schools from the area. Steele School was never invited to participate. This was changed the very first year of our "Partnership." The teachers selected about 50 students to visit with the Governor. The yearbook contained many photographs of Governor Thornburgh greeting and answering the student's questions. During the visit each student had an opportunity to sit in the governor's chair. It was a day the students will never forget.

The Department of General Services was in charge of the Annual Christmas Tree Lighting Ceremony held in the Rotunda of the Capitol Building. I requested the teachers to select 15 students who had not missed a day of attendance during the month of December, to attend and pass out the printed programs for the occasion.

Since "Hanukkah the Jewish Festival of Lights," occurred within the Christmas season, I suggested to the Governor that a Hanukkah program should be held for the children of the local Jewish schools. He enthusiastically agreed. I then contacted the teachers of the Jewish schools to prepare a program. The First Annual "Hanukkah" was held in the Governor's reception room. Again I asked six students from Steele School to give out the printed programs.

During Hanukkah, the children were given a small gift for the eight days of Hanukkah. They were given a "dreidel" (a four-sided top,) but the most common present is "gelt," or gold coins. These are chocolate candies, covered in gold foil. These "gold" coins were usually placed in a small yellow net bag. I purchased a carton of these gold coins and I gave them to all the children who participated. While these gifts are usually given only to the "good" children, I decided to give one to my good friend, Murray Dickman, who was on the governor's staff. He sort of gave me a promise that he would be good (at least to me) from that day on!

Many of the students were interested in music. I decided to introduce them to classical music. The Harrisburg Symphony

Orchestra performs a program for two days. The opening night at the Forum is filled to capacity. The second performance on the following day has many seats available. After discussing a "A night at the Forum" with my staff, it was suggested that we print a small booklet with illustrations of various instruments, a few small stories on famous composers and other items that would be helpful to introduce the students to classical music. We also included a chapter on "The proper conduct that is required when attending a performance in a concert hall."

There were approximately 100 students that were chosen to attend. I was very pleased to welcome these children dressed in their Sunday best accompanied by a few teachers, parents and chaperones. We made arrangements for a school bus to transport them to the "Forum auditorium" one hour before the performance so that they could meet a few of the musicians. This meeting was held in the "Green Room" directly behind the auditorium. This was a very elegant room used by the guest soloist of the evening's performance. After the performance, invited guests have an opportunity to meet the soloist and conductor where they occasionally enjoy hors d'oeuvres and champagne. In our case, all the children sat on the floor while a few musicians explained their instruments. The one I remember most was the harpist. The kids really enjoyed her explanation of the humble beginnings of a harp. "A few thousand years ago, a soldier listened to the sound made by the string from the bow after he shot an arrow. The tighter the string the higher the sound. He then put a few additional strings on the bow, one tighter than the other. When he strummed them with his fingers, he was able to play music. That's why the harp was the first musical instrument ever invented." She then gave a demonstration and asked a student to assist her. There followed other demonstrations with a trumpet, a cello and a drum.

After the demonstration, the students all entered the concert hall and were seated together in one section. It's difficult for me to describe their enthusiasm. They saw over 80 musicians on the stage and as they were taught, they applauded when the conductor stood on the podium. I was sitting in the center of all my young friends. I particularly paid attention to a beautiful child wearing white gloves, sitting at the edge of her seat. I could not see her face, but I was sure that her eyes were wide open. Everyone paid attention and were well behaved. I know that it was a success. After the intermission, when most of them were back in their seats, a gentleman whom I did not know, walked up to the area where we were seated and said to me, "Mr. Baran, *your* children behaved as well in the restroom as they did during the performance." It was one of the finest complements I ever received.

My executive assistant, David Morrison, and Ozzie Dukas from my staff were very helpful and accompanied me to the school when we attended various functions. One of these was to have lunch about once every three weeks with the students. Since they did not have a cafeteria, they picked up their lunch in the hall and returned to their homeroom. I was asked by one young man, "Why do you always have lunch in room 203? I'm in room 108. If you would have lunch with us, you will see that we are much better eaters!" From then on I would pickup my half pint of milk and sandwich and visit each room in turn.

In the spring, I brought one of my antique cars to the playground during recess. The teachers had a difficult time getting the students back in the building after recess bell. They formed a ring around the car and I had difficulty leaving the yard.

The teachers had the children write thank-you notes to me after one of our activities. I received many wonderful thank-you notes. One that moved me very much and I will never forget it. It said, "I wish you were my dad."

THE ADMINISTRATIVE

CODE OF 1929

ARCHITECTS AND ENGINEERS

Don't let the title of this article frighten you. Please keep in mind that I was only a temporary "Bureaucrat." For those of you who never had the pleasure of working for government, I will try to write this article in "Layman's terms."

The Administrative Code of 1929 has been amended and some sections have been repealed every year (on occasion, every few months) since it was written in 1929. Somehow, many parts of the original code are still included.

The "Code" was my "Bible" when I served in the Department of General Services. The Code is a wonderful instrument and, by following its instructions, it kept me on the straight and narrow path. I did not have to "check with legal" before I made decisions.

During my tenure, 1979 to 1986, I was bound by:

Article XXIV. Powers and Duties of the Department Of General Services. Act 45 of 1975. § 905 Procurement of design professional services, paragraph (19) (There were 64 sections in the Department of General Services. I am going to address only section 905.)

The selection of architects and engineers was an awesome task. I was determined to be fair and honest in selecting professionals for projects costing hundreds of thousands and even millions of dollars. During the first few months that I was in office,

I received many telephone calls from legislators, Presidents of Universities, heads of large corporations and businessmen asking me to favor an architectural firm. I have never received a call from the governor's office on behalf of an architectural firm, not even a hint.

I took the following steps:

I instructed my secretary not to make any appointments with architects and engineers unless they had already been selected for a project. It's not that I didn't like architects and engineers, (my son Joseph has a degree in architecture from Princeton University) but I had to be extremely careful and fair in my dealings with them.

I know that I promised to be writing only in layman's terms, but as a former bureaucrat, I will have to break that promise.

In Section (19) states: "The governor, in order to assist the Department in the selection and the appointment of architects and engineers on the basis of merit, shall appoint a Selections Committee consisting of five members, none of whom shall be employees of the Commonwealth or hold any elective office or office in any political party or body, and shall be composed of architects, engineers or other persons knowledgeable in the field of building construction. Each appointed member shall be reimbursed for reasonable travel and other expenses incurred incident to such attendance and to such a sign duty and also a per diem allowance as determined by the Executive Board. The Selections Committee shall have the obligation of giving public notice of projects requiring the services of architects and engineers, and of publicly recommending to the Department three qualified architects and/or engineers in order of its preference for each project. The Department shall have the duty to select or appoint one of the persons or firms which have been recommended by the Selections Committee. In exercising its responsibility, the Department shall consider the following factors:

> *(i)   An equitable distribution of contracts to architects and engineers.*

(ii) Particular capability to perform the designer construction services for the contract being considered.

(iii) Geographic proximity of the architect or engineer to the proposed facility.

(iv) That the architect or engineer selected as a necessary available manpower to perform the services required by the project.

(v) Any other relevant circumstances peculiar to the proposed contract.

I took these five factors very seriously. By my using them, it gave me a lot of problems with the Selection Committee. Since the Selection Committee submitted three firms in their preferential order, No. 1, 2, 3. My predecessors, because of political or other reasons, always solved their problem by choosing their first selection. By using this system, they put the onus on the committee so that they could respond to the legislators and others who were favoring a certain firm "Since the Selections Committee are the experts, I chose their No. 1 selection." In my reading of the code, the Secretary of General Services had different criteria than the Selections Committee. The Selections Committee usually met once a month. I remember that during the first month of my tenure, I received five projects for my consideration. Out of the five projects I only selected their No. 1 choice once. On the other four, I selected their second or third choice. That's when the stuff hit the fan! "How **dare** you not follow our recommendations?" (None of their complaints were given to me in writing.) I began to receive complaints from legislators and others asking me to justify my action. As soon as the three firms were selected, it was printed in the *Pennsylvania Bulletin,* the Commonwealth's official gazette for information and rulemaking. The firm chosen No. 1 by the Selections Committee, immediately called their legislator or other friends in high places to see what the hell does Baran think he's doing! I responded with a very polite letter including a paragraph from the code, listing the five factors that I **have** to follow. I reasoned that if I always selected their first choice—there was no need for the Selections Committee to send them to me for my approval.

I took this part of my job very seriously. In fact, for the entire eight years that I was in office, I only worked on the selections after 5 PM so I would not be disturbed. Word soon got around that I was in the office after hours; especially on the day I was given the projects from the Selections Committee. I began getting telephone calls since they knew I would answer the telephone. I solved this problem very easily, I **lied**. *"I'm a custodial worker, please call tomorrow morning."*

I devised my own grading system. 1 to 5. Five, as the highest grade. My staff at public works included a complete history of the firm, and their proposed contract that allowed me to comply with the five factors listed above. That is (i) to (v).

> (ii) I began by giving 5 points to all the applicants. Since the Selections Committee chose their three recommendations as capable.
>
> (i) Equitable distribution. If a firm never had any work with the state, I gave 5 points.
>
> (iii) geographic proximity. If it was a very large project, I gave 4 points to a large firm regardless where their office was located. On smaller projects I selected small firms that were near the project, etc.

The firm with the highest grade would be selected regardless of their preferential standing. I continued to receive calls from legislators and others asking me to favor one firm over another but there was a 26% drop in calls. I was very courteous in responding to these calls informing them that I would carefully follow the Pennsylvania code in making my decision.

Sometime in September of 1982, I received word that I was to receive *The Pennsylvania Award* by the Pennsylvania Society of Architects. I was somewhat concerned whether I should accept this award because of my policy not to meet or socialize with architects and engineers that may seek contracts with the State. I called my friend in the governor's office, Jim Seif, and asked his opinion whether I should accept the award. He strongly advised me to accept.

The award ceremony took place at *Fallingwater* the famous home designed by Frank Lloyd Wright. This was my first opportunity to actually see this architectural masterpiece. It was a black-tie affair. A chamber group played baroque music in the home and a small jazz ensemble played on the patio. The libations, hors d'oeuvres, and the dinner that followed were first rate! I knew immediately that the party was designed by some of the greatest architects of Pennsylvania and engineered by the best engineers that Pennsylvania had to offer.

During the libations, and after the hors d'oeuvres, Irene and I were sitting on a beautiful designed carved wooden loveseat when I was approached by an architect who asked to have a few words with me. He said "I have a small firm of four employees and I have been bidding on projects for many years. I only bid small projects, since it was not costly to prepare plans for small projects. I made the "preference list" of the Selections Committee a few times, second or third-place but I never received a contract." He also stated that, "I never supported any party whether Republican or Democrat" I told him, "*Since I make the final selection, that is not one of the five factors that I consider.*" He told me that he was shocked when he received Information from the Bureau of Public Works that he was selected for a project. "I thank you and congratulate you. You are worthy of receiving the award today."

Later, driving to the motel I spent a lot of time explaining to Irene about the workings of the architects and engineers Selections Committee and my involvement in the process.

THE PENNSYLVANIA AWARD

The Pennsylvania Society of Architects of the

American Institute Of Architects

Is Honored To Convey This Award to

The Honorable

WALTER BARAN

IN RECOGNITION AND APPRECIATION OF HIS
DEDICATION AND FAIR TREATMENT OF THE
ARCHITECTURAL PROFESSION IN HIS DUTIES AS
SECRETARY OF THE DEPARTMENT OF
GENERAL SERVICES

October 4, 1982   Louis D. Astorino, ADA,
                                   President

This award is rarely given. I was the *first* person to receive this award. 17 years later, February 23rd, 1999, the Honorable Matthew J. Ryan, Speaker of the Pennsylvania House Of Representatives, was the second person to receive this award.

THE PENNSYLVANIA AWARD
The Pennsylvania Society of Architects of the
American Institute of Architects is Honored To
Convey This award to

The Honorable

Matthew J. Ryan

Speaker of the Pennsylvania House of
Representatives

IN RECOGNITION OF HIS VISIONARY
LEADERSHIP IN INITIATING IN GUIDING
THE RESTORATION AND PRESERVATION
OF THE PENNSYLVANIA CAPITAL

PRESENTED ON THE OCCASION OF THE 90TH

ANNIVERSARY OF THE FOUNDING OF THE PENNSYLVANIA SOCIETY OF THE AMERICAN INSTITUTE OF ARCHITECTS

February 23, 1999   William J. Helsley, AIA,
President.

GOVERNORS AWARD

I have received many awards in the eight years I spent in Harrisburg. One that I value most was "The National Governor's Association" award given to me on August 9, 1982 in Afton, Oklahoma.

We were having dinner at the home of our son Tony, when I received a call from governor Thornburgh who was attending the annual meeting of the National Governors Association. He said, "Pack your tuxedo and get on a flight to Oklahoma as fast as you can." I knew the governor was away but receiving the call especially in our son's home on a Saturday night surprised me. The governor said, "We won, we won."

I completely forgot about a call I received a few weeks ago from Gorham Black, the Secretary of Aging. He told me he received a call from the Governor of Vermont who was an old army friend asking Gorham, "How well do you know Walter Baran? Governor Thornburgh had nominated him to receive the Governor's award for distinguished service to state government. Is he as good as Thornburgh said he is?" Secretary Black told me that I was on the short list to receive this award so I was not too surprised when the governor called.

Irene and I arrived in Oklahoma on the last day of their meeting. During the dinner I was shocked to see over nine hundred people at the dinner. Since there are fifty Governors, I expected about 200 attendees; I suppose most of the people attending were staff.

Irene and I were ushered to an adjoining room where only the governors and their wives/husbands were waiting to make the grand entrance into the ballroom. They were enjoying some small hors d'oeuvres and libations. The Governor "worked" the room introducing us to some of the other governors.

The program began after the dinner when various governors made remarks. When my name was called to approach the dais, the band began to play, "The Pennsylvania Polka" A thought came into my head, "When will Pennsylvania have a state song that all Pennsylvanians could be proud of?"

I was very pleased and proud to accept the plaque that read:

The National Governors Association

Award for Distinguished Service

Is presented to

Walter Baran

August 9, 1982

Afton, Oklahoma

Sunday Patriot News, August 1, 1982

Governors' Group Lauds State's Baran

State Secretary of General Services Walter A. Baran has been named to receive the "Award For Distinguished Service to State Government" from the National Governors' Association, Gov. Dick Thornburgh Announced.

Thornburgh, who nominated Baran for the award, said the Secretary "was recognized for his outstanding contribution to State Government and his commitment to applying modern management and efficiency techniques not only in his own department, but throughout State Government."

Baran was one of ten State Government award winners selected by a nine-member panel appointed by the NGA's executive committee . . . .

CAPITOL ROTUNDA

W elfare protesters from Philadelphia occupied the Capitol rotunda area for a few weeks during the summer of 1983. They moved in with their sleeping bags, mattresses, cooking equipment and other personal items. The group included a few old men, young mothers with children and a few young men who came only on weekends.

Article XXIV. Powers and Duties of the Department of General Services.

§ 2416. Capitol Police Commonwealth Property Police.

Section 2416 (a) To enforce good order in State buildings and on State grounds in Dauphin County, in the Pittsburgh State Office Building and the grounds, in the Philadelphia State office Building and grounds; . . . . amended September, 1978, P.L. 775 No.149)

> *(a) To enforce good order in State buildings and on State grounds in Dauphin County, In the Pittsburgh State Office Building and grounds, in the Pittsburgh State office Building and grounds . . . .*
>
> *(c) To exclude all disorderly persons from the premises of the State Capitol and . . . .*
>
> *(g) To order off said grounds and out of said buildings all the vagrants, loafers, trespassers, and persons under the influence of liquor, and, if necessary, remove them by force, and, in case of resistance, carry such offenders before an alderman, Justice of the peace or magistrate and to arrest such offenders . . . .*

My first action was to order the Capitol Police to inform them that while they have the right to express their views during normal office hours they would be trespassing if they stayed in the building overnight. They informed us that they have no intention of leaving and were prepared to stay as long as it takes to have the Governor and the Legislature respond favorably to their demands.

After a meeting with the Capitol Police, it was decided not to take any action on the first day because we did not want to create a racial problem. I asked a few legislators for their assistance in solving this problem. They were not successful. After the first few days, I received many complaints from legislators and state employees. Our custodial workers could not do their work in the rotunda area and the restrooms. We placed large trash containers in the restrooms. We canceled all the scheduled tours for the school children. On one of my visits to the area, Sandy Starebin, a reporter for radio station KY W in Philadelphia, approached me. "Baran, I advise you not to use force to remove these people. You would be risking bloodshed." I asked him "What suggestion can you give me to solve this problem?" He said that negotiations would eventually be successful.

The young men who came from Philadelphia on weekends usually left the building on Saturday morning about 10 AM to purchase food and other items for the coming week.

With the assistance of our Bureau of Central Services and the Capitol Police, a plan was made to clear the building in their absence. A large conference room located in a building occupied by the Public Works Department at 18th and Herr Streets was made available to move the welfare people from the Capitol rotunda. School buses were parked on the driveway in front of the main entrance to the Capitol building to drive the people to the Public Works Department. A detail of State Police entered from the back entrance to the basement of the building. They were to be used only as a backup.

Lieut. Leonard Lemell, an African-American, was in charge of the Capitol Police, spoke to the occupiers and told them that plans are made to move them to a larger facility complete with soda and food coin machines, large restrooms and better living conditions.

They were told to take their personal property and enter the bus in front of the building. Secretary Baran will personally pay the fare for those who would want to return to Philadelphia, the school bus would take them to the railroad station. The others would be taken to the building at 18th and Herr Streets.

The Capitol Police assisted them in leaving the building. No one entered the buses. A light rain was falling and the older men and women with children sat on the steps using a blanket as a cover. The news reporters and TV photographers were present taking photographs and interviewing some of the people. All the doors on the Capitol were secured and after about an hour all the welfare people eventually left.

I was very pleased that the Capitol Police did a wonderful job and no one was hurt. I was also very pleased that there was no leak to our plan. The reporters arrived late, after all of the welfare people were out.

Usually some of the employees in the governor's office worked on Saturday morning and occasionally the whole day. I tried to call to inform them that everything went well and that the crisis was over. I received no answer. For the first time during the Thornburgh administration the office was not occupied on a Saturday. A few people from Central Services and Secretary Wally Baran carrying their "walkie-talkies" left at about 7 PM.

Just another day in the life of Secretary Walter Baran.

THE WHITE HOUSE

In the spring of 1984, I received a call from the Polish American Congress in Washington D.C. informing me that I would receive a call from the White House inviting me to attend a meeting with President Reagan to discuss martial law that was imposed in Poland by President Wojciech Jaruzelski.

A few days later, I received a call from the scheduling office in the White House. After responding to their many questions and giving them my social security number, they informed me that I would receive another call advising me of the time, date, and the gate I was to enter.

I selected my one and only conservative suit. I had difficulty finding a conservative tie since I did not own any. I hurried to Martin's Menswear, the only men's store in Harrisburg that catered to the Legislators. I was never in the store, they specialized in polyester suits. I asked the clerk for a conservative tie. At first he thought I was a new member of the House of Representatives. But after looking at my 100% all Virgin Wool suit, he knew I was not in the Legislature. He selected a tie that I would never be caught dead in. In fact I have instructed Irene not to get any ideas about saving it for the absolute last time that I would be dressed, wearing a suit and tie!

He asked me if he could help me with something else. I felt sorry for the salesman so I asked him to show me some shirts. He showed me some white shirts but I didn't care for them. The last time I saw similar shirts with the very wide collars was on some pictures of Herbert Hoover I saw in some old National Geographic Magazines. I did want to buy something so I asked if he had some plain black socks. He went to the stock room and came back with some anklet socks. I told him that I'm not a legislator and that I wear my hose high, in fact almost to my kneecap. He told me that he had some boxes marked, "Knee Garters" in the stockroom but he did not have the "socks" to go with them. To keep the conversation going, I asked him why there weren't any customers in the store. He said, "Because it's Thursday." "So?" "The Legislators always leave early every Thursday." It was quite some time since I had had such an interesting conversation, so I then asked, 'Do you occasionally have some sportswriters come in here with a healthy looking specimen that resembles a fullback at Harrisburg High School, or possibly from Bishop Hafey High school?' As soon as I asked the question, I said to myself, "Self, look at the suits on the rack. Why did you think any member of the Harrisburg Tigers or the Bishop Hafey Angels would be found wearing one of these suits regardless of what color he may be?" He finally wrapped the tie box, but he did have a bit of trouble finding the string and then the scissors to cut the string. Well I think that the reader has had more than enough of how I was able to find a very conservative tie.-So back to the "White House Episode."

A half hour before the appointed time wearing my conservative suit and conservative tie, I stood before 1600 Pennsylvania Avenue looking at the White House and the two Marines in their resplendent non-conservative colorful uniforms waiting to open the big front doors of the White House for Wally Baran, the kid from across the railroad in Frackville, PA. I had a difficult decision to make: should I carry my copy of *The American Spectator* with me? I did not want the President to think that I was a super right wing conservative. I decided to leave the magazine in the car.

I presented myself at the gate and after some preliminaries and a phone call, they told me to proceed.

When I approached the front entrance, the Marines, without any questions opened the doors for me (it took the two of them). I entered the vestibule. A staff person greeted me. He opened a door off the hall to a small room where I met the other eleven men who were there for the meeting.

I had no idea who or how many were asked to attend. I recognized Mr. Aloysius Mazewski, President of the Polish American Congress from Chicago. The only other person I knew was Mr. Edward Musial, President of the Polish National Alliance, also from Chicago. I found out later that some of the others came from Florida, Connecticut, Massachusetts, and other parts of the country. I felt like one of the twelve Apostles. We were ushered into the President's Cabinet Room! The room held a conference table and very high-backed leather chairs. Each chair had a brass plaque listing the name of the cabinet officer to whom it belonged. I sat in the chair of Jeane J. Kirkpatrick, U.S. Representative to the United Nations. We were told to sit on one side of the room. I found the reason for this later. A few staff members and Vice President Bush entered and sat across from us. The Vice President gave us a briefing. President Reagan came in, greeted us, and thanked us for attending. I almost committed a fox pause. I was going to thank him for including me to attend this very important meeting. He asked for our opinions on various proposals that the State Department was suggesting. He said he did not want to hurt the Polish people, but he had to make a strong protest against Prime Minister Jaruzelski.

We were all given a legal pad and a pencil. Since I did not pay too much attention when I was a student in Miss Guy's eighth grade civic class at Franklin Elementary School, I decided to let the other guys do all the talking. Meanwhile, I kept the pencil in my hand and was making notes. I wasn't taking notes, I was making notes, and 'like what kind of tie Reagan was wearing.' I noticed that all the staff and the Vice President were wearing similar conservative ties and suits. After a while, the Vice President and most of the staff left. One of the questions the President asked was, (Scouts Honor, this is true!) Should the United States continue to supply chicken feed for the Polish chickens! It seemed that the United States was shipping a lot of corn and wheat and whatever else chickens eat to Poland to feed the chickens. He was told if the shipments were discontinued many millions of Polish chickens would die. This is the only time I offered a statement. I said, "I'm for that." Every one agreed and I saw a staff member taking notes. There were, of course, many questions asked and suggestions made in the half hour meeting. Later the President spoke about how he was shot and that his injury was not as serious as when the Pope was shot. He spoke very highly of the Holy Father and predicted that he will do great things to change the history of the world! He also said that a lot of buildings and monuments are named after Presidents. "The only thing named after me is a saloon in the village of Ballyporeen, County Tipperary, Ireland, called, "The Ronald Reagan Pub." In fact he said the paint on the sign was still wet when he arrived since it was changed right before his arrival.

At the end of the meeting, he walked around the room, shook everyone's hand, and spoke to everyone present. He asked me, "How many Cabinet meetings does Governor Thornburgh call?" I told him that in the beginning of his administration, we had a meeting every three weeks, and after six months, we had one every six weeks. In the sixth year, we usually met at his call. He said, "I thought so." He then asked me to give the Governor his regards. He then presented each of us with a glass jar full of jellybeans. He was into jellybeans at the time. I brought mine home. While I was deciding on how many I was going to bronze, I found the jar empty!!! I asked Irene what had happened to the jellybeans. Irene said, "The kids ate them." What a bummer!

After the meeting was over, the press was invited into the conference room. There were four doors on both sides of the room. When the doors across the room were open, a mass of reporters and TV cameramen complete with powerful lights came in and set up in what seemed to me a very few seconds! The room temperature rose at least 15 degrees.

They were given about 12 minutes and they were out of there. The meeting was over and we made plans to leave. Mr. Mazewski informed me that we would meet for lunch across the street at the Washington Hotel to discuss the meeting. When I looked out the window, the press was interviewing Mr. Mazewski and some of the attendees. Each reporter had his own TV cameraman. I did not want to be interviewed since my notes were not about the meeting, and I sure as hell did not want to talk about chicken feed. My first thought was, "I'll ask the marines if I could go out the back door." I decided against that. I then thought that if I hold my legal pad and put my pencil on my ear they might take me for a reporter for the *Shenandoah Evening Herald.* I knew that would not work since all reporters had a very large tag attached to a small chain around their neck. I had another problem: I was carrying a glass jar of very colorful jellybeans. I was going to ask someone on the staff for a brown paper bag but I thought better of it. Besides I did not want anyone to think that I was taking the remnants of my Danish in a doggie bag! I thought of hiding the jelly jar inside my coat, but I saw a few guys that were wearing an identical pin on their lapel and they all had an identical bulge under the right side of their coats. I then decided to use plan 8-JJ (I work for the government, so we don't use a simple Plan A, Plan B etc.) 8-JJ was for me to plant the Jelly Jar in the nearest shrub. By the time I decided to just walk out, looking out the window I noticed that the only people left on the lawn, were the gardeners. Another successful mission completed!

Some time later I was again summoned to the White House by President Ronald Reagan's office. This time I was one of about 45-five "Super Polacks" that were invited. We entered the old Executive Building through a side entrance because of the large group. Before the luncheon meeting, we were ushered into a very small auditorium where we were told what to expect now that Poland had gained her freedom from the Communists. Before the meeting began, Ms. Kay Troynosky of Frackville came to see me. She worked for many years in the White House and knew that I was present and came into the auditorium to chat. It was a pleasant surprise. The President spoke briefly and then we were invited to lunch.

We left the building and entered the White House for lunch with the President. Lunch was served in the Roosevelt Room. It was oval shaped and the tables were set for six people each. A cabinet officer was assigned to each table. Deputy Secretary for National Security Affairs, Robert C. McFarlane, was at my table. Actually, I was at his table. He asked me if I had ever visited Poland. Boy did I tell him! He was, or appeared to be, very interested and asked many questions. Some of the attendees at this meeting were Mrs. Johnson of Johnson & Johnson, Blanka Rosensteil of the Seagrams Liquor family, Bobby Vinton of "Moja Droga Ja Cie Kocham" fame, a few of the attendees from the first meeting, and Wally Baran of Frackville, PA.

The luncheon was held to discuss the future of Poland and how the Reagan Administration was going to assist Poland in the future. It does not take a Rocket Scientist or a Computer Programmer to realize that the election for President was to take place in a few months and he would need all the votes he could get. The only really exciting thing that happened was that Bobby Vinton walked out before the dessert was served. The President introduced some of the celebrities present, Mr. Al Mazewski, Blanka Rosenstiel, and a few others but Bobby Vinton was not mentioned. When a friend of Vinton was asked why he suddenly left, the friend said that he had an early engagement to perform at the "Sobieski Club" in Wilkes Barre, PA.

I also met President Reagan in Philadelphia. A rally was held at St. Hedwig's Parochial School hall for the Reagan/Bush ticket. St. Hedwig's is located in the center of the Polish section of Philadelphia. Governor Thornburgh and many prominent Polish Americans were present including Wally Baran. I was asked to sit on the stage with the other dignitaries. That great democrat better known as "Mr.

Polish American, Michael Blichasz" was introducing the people on the dais. He introduced everyone on the dais. He introduced me as "Secretary of General Services," Our own Walter Baran, a member of Governor Thornburgh's Cabinet. Secretary Baran is also the "Pennsylvania Chairman of the Reagan/Bush Nationalities Committee." When he mentioned Nationalities Chairman for Reagan/Bush, the President left his seat, crossed the stage to where I was sitting, and shook my hand and thanked me for my help. All this while Polish Mike was speaking.

How did I become the Nationalities Chairman for Reagan/Bush? I received a call from an official of the Pennsylvania Republican State Committee in Harrisburg with a request. He asked me if I could get a list of names and addresses of Polish Americans who reside in Pennsylvania. I made a few calls to some people who called or wrote (about 1000 letters) congratulating me when I was appointed by Governor Thornburgh to serve in his cabinet. They all were very proud that after 200, years a Polish American was finally appointed to a high position in Pennsylvania. I saved the letters since I thought they might be of use some day. Most of the calls and letters mentioned, "If we could help you in any way, please call and let us know." So I let them know. I asked, "Could you send me a computer list of your members of the Polish Beneficial Association who reside in Pennsylvania?" I also contacted the Polish National Alliance in Chicago for a list of their members residing in Pennsylvania.

Both are Fraternal Insurance Company's and have thousands of members. When I told the Republican Committee that I had these lists, they thanked me and asked if I could get such a list for Italian Americans.

They told me they had tried but were unsuccessful. I called my good friend, Mario Meli, who often told me during the many dinners we shared (and he paid for) in Harrisburg and Philadelphia, that he had friends in very high places and could help me in many ways. Mario was a member of the Pennsylvania Liquor Commission and indeed had many friends throughout the State. He provided me with a list of members of the "Sons of Italy." When I called the

Republican Committee, they were ecstatic; they asked me if I would be willing to serve as Pennsylvania Chairman for the "Reagan & Bush Nationalities Committee." They would provide me with all the supplies I would need, envelopes, postage meters, and some volunteers to address and mail the letters.

In other words they would do all the work, all I had to do was stuff all the pre-folded letters with a message signed by Walter Baran, prominent Polish American Citizen, seal, apply the postage, and mail them. I immediately went to work. I asked my immediate staff if they would help me, it did not matter to me whether they were Republican or Democrats, especially those who owned a non-government typewriter, preferably at home! We worked at my home in Shipoke. We had typewriters on the kitchen and dining room tables, and on the coffee table in the living room. (Notice how I cleverly used quite a bit of words to describe where we had set up the typewriters? if I keep doing this I could use regular paper and still have a one inch thick book.) Since there was limited space for me to prepare and eat my "Lean Cuisine." I called Mario to see if he was in town so that I could thank him personally for providing me with the list of the Pennsylvania members of the "The Sons of Italy." I also knew that he dined only in the best restaurants in town. Hell I'm no dummy!

I appointed my executive assistant, David Jenkins Morrison as the official scheduler to set the times and days as workdays, (which were actually nights), to do the work. After a week of typing and hand addressing the envelopes, I could see that we could never finish the mailing in time. I then put in plan "4-HU" into effect. I told everyone to select only the **short** Polish and Italian names, that way we would be able to address more envelopes and also cover all parts of the State. They thought this was very funny. I told them that I never fool around when high efficiency is at stake! In fact, I should of thought of this plan ("4-HU" hurry up) sooner. Since we started with the "A's" and worked down the alphabet, I knew that every family from the first half of the alphabet would receive my letter. However at the rate we were going, all those with long Polish names for the rest of the alphabet would not receive the letter.

Since I was working for the Government at the time, I was very, very careful not to discriminate. I knew that seventeen duplicate forms, eleven of which required a Notary Seal, would have to be filled out since my Department set all the regulations for acts of discrimination no matter how small the offense was. We sent out 36,436 letters. We knew the exact number since the Pitney Bowes Postage machines had a very accurate meter. It's much too late to make a short story of this, but that is why the Reagan/Bush ticket was successful in winning Pennsylvania.

You see, the Polish Americans and the Italian Americans were mostly registered as Democrats, but after they received my Polish letter (the salutation and the thank you at the end were written in Polish) and the Italian letter signed by the Co-Captains Walter Baran and Nicholas DeBenedictus, Secretary of DER, most, if not all, voted for the Republican ticket for the very first time!

Regan- Bush

CIA

In June 1984, a meeting was held in Washington D.C. chaired by, Ronald C. Kaufman the Northeast regional political director for the "**Reagan&Bush Nationalities Division**" Mr. William Casey the director of the CIA was the main speaker. I attended as the Pennsylvania Chairman Of the Nationalities Division.

Polish American delegation

Left to right, Walter A. Baran, Pennsylvania. Edward L. Rowny, Former Ambassador and Retired Lieutenant General, US Army, Washington D.C., CIA Director Robert "Bob" Casey, John E. Barkiewicz, Connecticut, Stanley A. Glod, Massachusetts.

Another visit to the White House

President Bush signed a bill passed by Congress, to create a fund to assist Polish entrepreneurs to start-up businesses in Poland. A Board of fifteen members was to be nominated to select the recipients who would participate. The amount that was funded initially was $500,000.00 with possibly additional funds if the program was successful. (I told you that this was a Government project). Yes, I, Wally Baran, former H.G.O. (High Government Official) not only was nominated for this position, but also was on the Short list! This meant that I had to appear for an interview at the White House, the one located at 1600 Pennsylvania Avenue in Washington, DC. Since I was not required to send a Curis Vitae, I knew that I could not possibly be appointed to this board because of my lack of credentials. I knew I could do it but they required someone with a few college degrees There were eight men and one young lady. My interview lasted about eight minutes. A staff member interviewed me. After the interviews were completed, President Bush came in to thank us for taking time to come to Washington. He then shook hands, which meant, you could leave now. No Jelly Beans, not even six lousy golf balls, nothing!

GENERAL SERVICES 1979/1985

I went to Harrisburg with a two-page résumé, and, in each successive year among Pennsylvania's politicians and power-brokers, my official bio got a little more grandiose. The version as follows was the last, produced about a year before the end of the Thornburgh Administration; it ran nine pages, typed double-spaced.

In those days, each time we changed a statistic or added some minor triumph, the whole thing had to be typed from scratch. We sent it out when groups requested information about me. It was lengthy because we wanted them to realize that a lot was being accomplished by the Thornburgh Administration.

Since I was giving talks to a wide array of business groups, from telecommunications to architectural to office furniture people, not to mention ethnic groups and antique car enthusiasts, my staff felt it was important that some phrase in my bio pertained to each group. So it got longer and longer.

The humor in all this occurred more than once when I was invited to speak somewhere and the person responsible for introducing me felt obligated to read the entire biography to the audience. What an embarrassment! This was a problem long before it grew to nine pages in length. To solve it, I requested that a very short two-paragraph version be sent for all speaking engagements.

In any event, my official government bio sums up a good bit of my eight-year career in State Government, so I'm reprinting it as-is:

Walter Baran
Secretary of General Services

Commonwealth of Pennsylvania
515 North office building
Harrisburg, PA 17125

Walter Baran, 61, was appointed Secretary General Services for the Commonwealth of Pennsylvania by Gov. Dick Thornburgh on January 16th, 1979, continuing in the cabinet position following the governor's reelection in 1982. A self-made industrialist from Frackville, Schuylkill County, PA, Mr. Baran has earned national acclaim for his success in bringing business expertise and efficiency to state government, and achievement that has been a cornerstone of the Thornburgh Administration Record.

At Mr. Baran swearing-in, Governor Thornburgh noted that the Department OF General Services "does business in the best sense of the word because it has charge of all the far-flung responsibilities and contractual undertakings. When you have an operation that does business, you want a businessman in charge of it . . . Wally Baran has a spotless reputation for integrity and business acumen."

Mr. Baran has a staff of 1400 as diverse as architects, locksmiths and capital police officers, and he is responsible for business transactions and contracts totaling nearly $1 billion annually, including:

*more than $600 million in purchases of supplies, office equipment, vehicles and other commodities.

*the design and construction of state-owned facilities amounting to $120 million in annual expenditures.

*leasing of some 2000 privately owned offices in buildings for which the annual rental is $45 million.

*provisions for telecommunications, computers, printing, insurance and other operating requirements of state government.

Responding to Governor Thornburgh's mandate that government "do more with less," Secretary Baran has brought about broad changes in state business operations, saving millions of dollars through greater efficiency, office automation, energy conservation and spending controls. Since 1979, he has served as chairman of the Governor's Cabinet-level Cost Reduction Study Team, an effort which became the prototype for similar initiatives throughout the country including the well-known Grace Commission established at the Federal level by President Reagan. As a result, many Pennsylvania accomplishments have been examined and adopted by other governmental bodies.

The sharing of better ideas with other states accelerated during the administration's second term when Governor Thornburgh, Lieutenant Governor Scranton, Secretary Baran and other Pennsylvania officials assume prominent roles in their respective national counterpart organizations. In 1983, the same year that Bill Scranton was elected chairman of the National Conference of Lieutenant Governor's, Wally Baran became chairman of the National Conference of State General Service Officers, hosting the groups annual meeting that summer in Harrisburg.

That gathering provided an opportunity for state officials from as far away as Hawaii to examine first-hand such current Pennsylvania achievements as:

> *The new 65,000-square foot State Records Center, built by General Services as a highly efficient headquarters for state publishing and print related activities, a $26 million per year operation which Secretary Baran reorganized into a single, professionally managed, self-supporting entity;

> *The newly renovated Forum Auditorium, a 2000-seat Art Deco performance hall within the Capitol Complex, which under professional management, recruited by Mr. Baran, likewise has become self-supporting and a primary cultural asset in Harrisburg; and

*The $117 million addition to the state capital building, currently under construction, a long dormant project to complete the Pennsylvania Capitol initiated by Thornburgh and Baran in 1980. Adding nearly one million square feet of office space, public areas, landscape plazas and underground parking, it combines state-of-the-art technology with classical architecture which complements and connects the surrounding edifices. Upon completion in late 1986 the facility will effectively resolve long-standing operational and space deficiencies, and its innovative engineering system will reduce the Capitol's energy costs by more than $1 million per year.

Although he is quick to point out that he had no government experience prior to 1979, Mr. Baran's business background has included extensive involvement in construction of large manufacturing, medical and recreational facilities, each project receiving the detailed attention of a practitioner who hand crafted his first home in Frackville as a post-war newlywed. Since then he has built factory and warehouse buildings for Model garment Co., the ladies' sportswear manufacturing business he established in 1950, and a modern 128 bed nursing home, Broad Mountain Manor in Frackville, of which he was also a founder. In addition, as a board member of both the Ashland State General Hospital and the Fountain Springs Country Club, he was appointed to personally oversee the construction of new quarters for each when the need arose. He has played a leading role in such real estate projects as the development of Frackville Industrial Park and Walnick Manor, a suburban residential area where he and his wife, Irene, now reside.

Mr. Baran's interest in construction is surpassed only by a lifetime passion for automobiles, of which he is a noted restorer and collector. That interest led, when he took command of the State's 10,000 vehicle automotive fleet as Secretary of General Services, to his first governmental cost reduction project in early 1979. That was the selective recall and elimination of 1300 vehicles from the fleet which Mr. Baran determined had grown too large and inefficient. Since then he has tinkered with virtually every nook and cranny of the sprawling Commonwealth Garage in Harrisburg, from the grease pits to the gas pumps (which he converted to self-service), reorganizing, modernizing, computerizing and downsizing the fleet to efficient subcompact models. The result has been a savings of more than $3 million and a fleet management program which no private company has been able to match, despite many invitations to do so.

Long an advocate of free enterprise, Mr. Baran's ultimatum to in-house government services has been to operate better than the private sector or see the function turned over to a "tax producing" firm. In one such instance, he closed the state's costly airline ticket office and offered the business, employees at all, to a travel agency a block from the Capitol building, continuing the same service at no cost. Noting that success, in 1984 he called for greater savings, seeking the travel agency which could provide the greatest rebate to the state on tickets sold. Additionally providing reduce rates for hotel rooms and other travel arrangements, the current contract saves about $300,000 per year and is being quickly copied by other states and a unit of the Federal General Services Administration.

Competition for state business has been significantly heightened during Secretary Baran's tenure. Telephone systems previously leased from the phone company are now competitively bid, as are computer systems previously deemed available only from the industry giant. Bell of Pennsylvania, long the provider of the Commonwealth's long distance network, nearly lost the business to an aggressive competitor until Baran, poised over the competitor's contract, challenged, "You're the experts. Give us a better proposal and you'll get your business back." They did. In the later encounter, Bell of Pennsylvania agreed to an offer from Baran to buy some 50,000 existing phones at the Capitol Complex and elsewhere at a price that is saving $32 million over five years.

Secretary Baran's policy of aggressive than competitive business negotiation, while benefiting the taxpayers, has earned their respective Pennsylvania businesses, who readily prefer market rules over political rules. Various business and professional organizations have honored him and his staff. In 1981, the Pennsylvania Society of Architects presented him with the "Pennsylvania Award" in recognition of his fair treatment in selecting architectural firms to design state construction projects.

In 1982, Baran Was a Recipient of an honorary doctorate degree from Alliance College, Cambridge Springs, PA. In the same year, the National Governors Association selected him to receive the associations seventh annual Award for Distinguished Service to State Government. Other awards indicative of his wide-ranging activities have ranged from Frackville B.P.O.E.'s "Elk of the Year" award in 1979 to the University of Pennsylvania School of Veterinary Medicine's Centennial Award of Merit in 1984. In 1985, Steele Elementary School in Harrisburg, which was "adopted" by the Department of General Services as part of Governor Thornburgh's "Partners in Education" program, dedicated its first school yearbook, whose production was one of many collaborative projects between the school and the department, in Secretary Baran's honor.

Mr. Baran has been an enthusiastic booster of Harrisburg's role as Pennsylvania's Capitol City. A homeowner in the city's historic Shipoke section, he has been a patron of the Harrisburg Symphony Association, the Wednesday Club Concert Association and other cultural groups, regularly attending concerts and programs in the restored Forum Auditorium. As Secretary General Services he has presided over some $150 million in State Construction Projects in the Harrisburg area, and he initiated the leasing of numerous historically restored downtown office buildings for government use.

Until his appointment to the Cabinet, Mr. Baran was active in virtually every aspect of the economic, civic and cultural affairs of his hometown of Frackville. During his presidency of both the Broad Mountain Nursing Home and the Fountain Springs Country Club, he assumed a daily involvement in both organizations, revising menus, hanging artworks, inspecting boilers and enjoying the challenge of maintaining maximum efficiency and service. At a time when similar organizations struggled with the burdens of rising costs and modernization, the entities under Mr. Baran's watchful eye continue to flourish. During his presidency of the Frackville Merchants Association, a time of increasing suburban retail competition, he initiated downtown Christmas decorations, an anti-litter program and other shopper amenities. He was a founding member of the Frackville Lions Club, and as Grand Knight of the Frackville Knights of Columbus he presided over the acquisition and equipping of a permanent headquarters. Likewise, he was a member of a group that built Frackville's municipal swimming pool, and the local library and volunteer fire company count him among their most dedicated supporters.

Long interested in music and art, Mr. Baran has been a member of the Anthracite Concert Association since childhood and he has sung for years in the choir of St. Ann's Roman Catholic Church. Numerous formal recitals featuring emerging performers have been presented in the Baran home. An avid collector of art, for several years Mr. Baran operated "Hampton House Art Gallery" in Frackville, personally selecting or commissioning works by European artists and frequently opening the Gallery to school groups to whom he lectured.

In addition to his presidency of Model Garment Co., established with 10 employees in 1950, Mr. Baran organized two affiliate Garment firms, Penn-Spruce Inc. of Sunbury and Penn-Allen Inc. of West Hazleton. Today, with a total employment of 600, these enterprises constitute the most modern Garment manufacturing facilities in Pennsylvania. In 1979 these interests were transferred to his sons, Anthony and Joseph.

Mr. Baran is a former director of the Atlantic Apparel Contractors Assn., the Greater Pottsville Industrial Development Corp. the American Bank and Trust Company of Pennsylvania advisory board and its forerunner unit, the First National Bank of Frackville, and the Broad Mountain Building and Loan Association. Most of these directorships he resigned in 1979 to devote full time to his governmental duties and to avoid any possibility of conflicting a collector and restorer of antique automobiles, the most noted of which is an exceedingly rare 1938 Bugatti, Mr. Baran maintains a private museum near Frackville and he has written numerous articles for the magazines of various American and European antique automobile organizations with which he is affiliated.

End

THE COMPLETION OF THE CAPITOL BUILDING

Additions to Main Capitol Building

Commonwealth of Pennsylvania
Governor's Office
Harrisburg

The governor

April 7, 1980

Hon. Walter Baran
Secretary of General Services
515 North Office Building
Harrisburg, Pennsylvania 17120

Dear Secretary Baran:

With the attached documents, I'm approving a project to make some significant renovations to the Main Capitol Building. My only concern in approving these renovations is that the historical significance of the building not be compromised in completing the project.

Please take whatever actions are necessary, including the use of appropriate architects and advisers, to ensure that the historical significance and beauty of the Capitol Building is preserved.

Sincerely,
Dick Thornburgh
Governor

With this short two-paragraph letter, Governor Thornburgh sent me on a journey that would last over 10 years, seven years and three months as Secretary of General Services and three years as a private citizen.

Commonwealth of Pennsylvania
Department of General Services
Harrisburg
Walter Baran
Secretary

April 9, 1980

The Honorable Dick Thornburgh
Governor of Pennsylvania
To 2 5 Capitol Building
Harrisburg, Pennsylvania 17120

Dear Governor Thornburgh:

I am in receipt of your letter of April 7, 1980 with the attached approvals to proceed with the renovations to the main Capitol building.

I share your feelings that the historical significance and beauty of the building should be preserved. You can be assured that in the orientation procedure that lends itself to the planning, design and construction of this project, special provisions will be made to guarantee the preservation of its historical value.

Sincerely,
Walter Baran

ADDITIONS TO MAIN

CAPITOL BUILDING

W hen I first became Secretary of General Services in January of 1979, I was asked by the General Assembly to add space to the existing Capitol complex to alleviate severe crowding. A plan developed by my experts in space and facilities management recommended construction of two levels of underground parking and 120,000 square feet of office space. A "Request for Project Action" was sent to the Governor through The Budget Office, Office of Administration April 7, 1980, I received a letter of approval signed by Gov. Dick Thornburgh. I also received a document signed by, Robert Wilburn Secretary of Budget and Administration and Gov. Dick Thornburgh. It included a description of construction required: construction of Plaza and three levels of Office, Service and Parking. The level immediately below the Plaza was to be approximately 120,000 square feet office and service level . . . . The remaining two levels were to provide underground parking for approximately 800-1000 cars.

A request was made by the General Assembly originally in 1965 for additional space for the Legislature. Preliminary plans were made including a model of the proposed structure. At a meeting with the professionals at the Public Works Department at 18th and Herr Streets, I was shown the model. It was a rectangular building of five stories, and would take up one-third of the parking lot that existed directly behind the main Capitol and between the North and

South office buildings. It would also completely obscure the view of the Capitol looking south on State Street. It was ugly!

Since it would take a book of over 500 pages to describe **"Addition to the main Capitol Building"** project, I will list only a few highlights.

FOREIGN STEEL?

I received a call from a member of the House of Representatives, a Democrat from the Reading area to inform me that the "House Select Committee" was to investigate if DGS was in compliance with the Steel Products Procurement Act that prohibits use of foreign-made steel in state projects. He told me he "thinks" it had something to do with the steel drainpipes that were being installed in the new addition to the Capitol Building. I was somewhat surprised that a Democrat was warning me about a potential problem. I asked him, "Why are you helping me?" He said, "While I don't know you, I was told that you were fair in dealing with all the Senators and members of the House. I thanked him and called the Deputy Public Works for an immediate meeting. Members of the engineering department also heard a rumor that the stainless steel drainpipes have possibly been made in a foreign country. After a thorough investigation that lasted an **entire day**, it was found that the all documents showed that they were manufactured in the USA. A physical examination of the pipes and fittings showed that all part numbers were not painted on, the numbers were stamped directly on the metal. I later found out that a "committee" of House members did a physical examination and found that there was no truth to the rumor.

A few weeks later, a few "I" beams that were used by a subcontractor were indeed made in Japan. Even though the beams would not be a permanent part of the building, I ordered them to be removed as soon as the concrete hardened. Since it was illegal for DGS to deal with any of the 50 subcontractors that were on the site, we contacted Dick Corp. of Pittsburgh, the prime contractor for the project, to inform his subcontractor to remove all foreign steel from the site. I also asked Dick Corp. for a statement listing the total costs that were paid to the subcontractor for the use of this steel.

An article in *The Patriot*, Harrisburg P.A. Thursday, October the 11th, 1984 the headline screamed,

"REMOVE STEEL OR QUIT POST, Baran Urged.

By Jerry Dubbs
Staff Writer

A state House committee yesterday called for the resignation of Walter Baran, Secretary of The Department of General Services, if Baran fails to order the immediate removal of foreign steel from the Capitol addition project.

Representative Fred Taylor, D—Fayette, said if "Baran does not order the steel removed, and refuses to resign, then the Governor should fire him" . . . .

The following week another article appeared in *the Patriot News*.

Removal of beams not enough—state panel

By Rod Snyder

Harrisburg, P.A. (UPI)-Temporary foreign steel beams are being removed from the Capitol expansion project, but that's not satisfying a special legislative committee that wants state officials to recover any money spent on the steel.

As the panel approved a motion Wednesday asking General Services Secretary Walter Baran to not only ensure the foreign steel beams were removed from the construction site, but to also see that state funds used for the steel are recovered.

Under the motion, officials would have to determine the worth of the foreign steel to determine the worth of the foreign steel to the $117 million project—and not simply it's dollar value—which

Reizdan Moore, a lawyer for the committee, said could run into "the millions of dollars." *(I'm going to write this again,* **"the millions of dollars"** . . . .)

A few days after this article appeared, I received an anonymous letter at my office. The letter was not complementary. In fact, it stated that I would be killed if I did not remove the foreign steel immediately! It was a rambling letter about the steel workers that worked so hard making this country great, etc. There was an entire paragraph consisting of curses and filthy language.

It was signed by "A Proud American"

I was ready to throw it in the wastebasket when one of my deputies came into my office. He immediately took it up to "Legal." The next thing I knew, it was sent to the Attorney General. I began receiving threatening telephone calls at my home in Shipoke.

An anonymous caller said, "My great-grandfather, grandfather and now I worked in the steel mills in Steelton. You're not getting away with this. We know where you park your car." Etc. I was not concerned since I heard someone in the background throwing darts and ordering another Budweiser. After the third call, I told "Legal." The state police put a "tap" on my phone line. After four weeks the tap was removed.

Within a week, I received a report from the Dick Corp. regarding the total amount that this foreign steel cost the state.

My department immediately issued a press release to *The Patriot* and other newspapers so that they could report to their readers the facts of the case. The press release was dated October 30, 1984. Our press release never made the newspapers (or so I thought.) After many inquiries to the Patriot for a copy of the news story, none was forthcoming. Early in December of 1985, I contacted Mr. Carmen Brutto, a staff reporter for the *Patriot News.* Mr. Brutto was formerly a reporter for my hometown newspaper, *The Shenandoah Evening Herald.* I asked him if he would please send me a copy of the article that appeared in the *Patriot News.* Sure enough, it was reported but somehow we missed it. I'm very pleased to be able to share this article with the readers of this book.

The Patriot, Harrisburg, PA, Tuesday, December **(25**

Christmas day!), 1984 page, A19

$ 730 OF FOREIGN STEEL USED IN CAPITOL

Foreign steel used in the Capitol addition was worth about $730.00 according to General Service Secretary Walter Baran.

The steel, about 5000 linear feet of I—beams used as a temporary supports while concrete was poured, was leased by a subcontractor for 18 months, but was removed as soon as it was discovered. Baran said all of the beams were gone within 53 days.

The cost of the foreign steel was charged to the subcontractor and not to the state, Baran said.

Initial accounts set the value of the steel in the millions of dollars and a special House Committee launched an investigation. Baran said yesterday however, that 5000 of 90,000 linear feet of the steel supports were not made in the U.S.

But even a small amount made him "very angry," Baran said, "Within twenty minutes, I had a promise from the prime contractor [the Dick Corp. of Pittsburgh] to remove it immediately."

End

What a Christmas present I received! The Pennsylvania taxpayers also received a gift on Christmas Day December 25th, 1984. I was never good to math. Perhaps some reader could calculate the following math problem: Deduct $730 from millions of dollars. While I don't know the answer I'm sure that it's a helluva lot of money!

This same committee, chaired by Rep. Nicholas Colafella D-Beaver, then began investigating the granite that was used on the building. This episode was called "Granitegate" by the *Patriot News.*

It was not my intention to bore you with all the publicity (most of it bad) I received during the last six years I served in Harrisburg. Since I already have achieved my goal of writing a book that is one inch thick a few chapters back, I'm going to finish by including a few news articles that tell the story.

ANOTHER STEEL STORY

During the steel "crisis" in October of 1984 A.D, I issued a directive to the Deputy of Public Works to appoint a member of the project inspection team for all 645 projects that were proposed or underway, to act as the inspector responsible to see that only American products will be used in the construction of the building. This inspector's name will be posted on the bulletin board of each project's office. All inspectors are to report to him if they find any product not made in the United States of America. However, he is the main person responsible to follow this directive.

I received an anonymous call informing me that foreign steel was being installed in one of the five prisons (now called Correctional Institutions) at the former Retreat Hospital site that was being converted to a prison. I was told the exact location where I could find foreign steel already installed. I found in my eight years as a government employee, that there are many so-called "whistleblowers" that send anonymous letters or calls to heads of departments to inform them of some infraction of the laws.

If it is a Republican administration, the Democrat employees do it. And of course in a Democratic administration, it's the Republican employees that do the calling.

Since I live in Frackville, I decided to visit the site on Monday morning because I would be halfway to Wilkes Barre, and then continue to Harrisburg.

I entered the DGS office to look for the directive on foreign-made products on the bulletin board for the inspector who was in charge. I then proceeded to the site and asked that a ladder be placed against the scaffolding. I climbed the ladder to the

449

top and sure enough, a twelve-inch "I" beam was plainly marked, "Made in Japan." I asked the inspector, "How did that get there?" He did not seem to know. I asked him, "Don't you inspect the steel when it's unloaded on the ground?" I informed the contractor to remove the steel and send in a change order for the costs. Since the state is responsible for this cost, the contractor will be compensated in full. When I returned to my office in Harrisburg, our people at the Public Works Department already had all the information. I instructed that the employee be immediately discharged.

I later found out that this inspector was a brother of the Democratic legislator for the district. I was also informed that two years later he was reinstated with full back pay.

I gave a report to the Legislature about my findings. No action was taken. No newspaper articles appeared.

What a Country! What a state!

YET ANOTHER STEEL STORY

During the steel "crisis," I was asked to speak at a Society of Engineers that were meeting at the Hershey Lodge. I do not remember the exact name of the group but I know that my topic was: "The Architects and Engineers Selection Committee." I was very surprised to find that over five hundred engineers/wife/husbands were in attendance. It was a group of engineers from Northeast, Pennsylvania, New Jersey, New York and Maryland.

After dinner before I began my speech, I informed them that I know that the Commonwealth of Pennsylvania does not own or operate the Hershey Lodge and was very concerned about my dinner. It looked great but I noticed that both of my spoons were made in Taiwan and the knife, fork and dessert spoons were made in Japan! Since I come from a cultured background, I hesitated eating with my fingers.

I do not know how many in the audience knew about the "Pennsylvania Steel Crisis." They probably do not read the *Patriot News* when they are attending a conference.

It was amazing; I never saw or heard anything like this in my life. Everyone began turning his or her "silverware" to see where it was made. It made a strange noise sort of sound, like distant thunder. I noticed that the Pennsylvanians were informing the engineers from New York etc. what the hell I was talking about.

My speech went very well, it was double-spaced using a 16 font. I did not stumble on a single word. It was not reported in the local press.

Admiration
Baran lauded at budget hearing

By Harry Stoffer
Post-Gazette Harrisburg

HARRISBURG—A Thornburgh cabinet member, under fire from a special House committee investigating the Capitol expansion project, was showered with praise yesterday by both Democrats and Republicans on the Senate Appropriations Committee.

General Services Secretary Walter Baran appeared before the Senate panel to explain governor Thornburgh's 1986-87 budget of $62.9 million for his department and to respond to questions.

At the start of the hearing Senate Appropriations Chairman Richard Tilghman, R-Montgomery County, ruled out of order any questions about the $117 million dollar Capitol expansion project or charges that questionable business practices and possibly illegal activities inflated the $30 million cost of granite for the project.

Tilghman said his ruling was based on the fact that at least three investigative agencies, including a federal grand jury, are already looking into the charges.

Not only did no one challenge the ruling, but many of the senators used their time to praise Baran and his management of the department that handles state purchasing and oversees its properties and equipment, including 645 current construction and improvement projects.

Among several Democrats lauding Baran, Sen. James Romanelli Of Squirrel Hill, Pittsburgh, called him the best appointment Republican Thornburgh ever made.

Outside the hearing, Romanelli told reporters he is not "privy" to the information gathered by the house committee about the expansion project but nonetheless doesn't believe Baran "has a dishonest bone in his body."

Baran should stay in office beyond the end of the Thornburgh administration in January, even if a Democrat becomes governor, he said.

Sen. Edward Early, D-Ross, told Baran he has never encountered anyone in the bureaucracy as cooperative in responding to legislators questions and concerns.

Rep. Nick Colafella, D-Aliquippa, chairman of the House of Representatives' committee investigating the expansion project, said he was surprised that Tillman wouldn't want questions raised about the cost overruns and other criticisms of Capitol project management.

Colafella, his aides and other house committee members have questioned whether Baran acted legally in authorizing quarrying for the project prior to approval of a no-bid contract for the granite.

The committee is also looking into whether Baran misspoke or lied when he testified he discussed with no one outside his department the details of the general contractor before it was awarded.

It has since been disclosed that Baran met with Thornburgh and other administration officials about the general contract between the bid opening in May 1984 and the contract award in June 1984.

A Thornburgh spokesman, who previously said only generalities were discussed at the meeting, indicated an answer is likely this week.

Baran's written statement to the Senate committee did address the expansion project and pointed out that the cost only doubled while its size tripled.

End

The Patriot-News, Harrisburg, PA

0h, Manual, Who's ' Nice Guy' to You?

Now it's official.

State Secretary of General Services Walter Baran really is an all-around nice Guy.

Who says so?

The state's official publication, the Pennsylvania Manual, the repository for facts, figures and biographies about the Commonwealth and its officials says so.

The latest issue of the manual, now being distributed, contains capsule biographies of elected and appointed officials in the executive, legislative and judicial branches of government, among more than 800 pages of other facts.

For Frackville native Baran, however, there is a deviation from the cold listing of background. Baran, the biographies says, is "an all-around nice guy." Not even Gov. Dick Thornburgh got that kind of plug.

And who and what else is Baran?

Baran is the boss of the people who edit the manual.

End

1 suit dismissed in Capitol granite-cost case

The Patriot-News, Harrisburg, PA,

A federal judge has dismissed a lawsuit filed by the state against several companies accused of overcharging for granite used in the Capitol addition.

The order by U.S. District William W. Caldwell allows the state to pursue a similar lawsuit filed in September in Dauphin County Court.

In April 1987, the state filed an antitrust lawsuit against the companies, alleging a conspiracy on charges for the now-completed $122 million addition. The State says it was overcharged by more than $2 dollars a cubic foot for 147,000 cubic feet of granite, for a total of $323,000.

In it's county court complaint, the state asked that the federal antitrust charges be dismissed against defendants Carl H. Lunderstadt of Pittsburgh, Bradford C. Bernardo of Wakefield, R.I., and Providence Granite Co. of South Kingstown, R.I.

The defendant's moved for summary judgment on the federal suit, and argued that the county suit was simply an attempt to circumvent the legal system and to harass the defendants.

They said the state has learned that it was not defrauded. The defendants argued that they saved the state thousands of dollars.

End

Patriot News, Harrisburg May 27, 1989

Granite suppliers cleared of misrepresenting costs

By Tom Dochat
Patriot-News

After three weeks of testimony, a Dauphin County jury yesterday ruled in favor of the suppliers of granite for the Capitol addition, saying the two men and a company did not mislead the state about the cost of granite for the project.

The state Attorney General's office had contended that it was defrauded of some $323,000 by the suppliers, who provided about 147,000 cubic feet of granite for the addition.

Judge Sebastian D. Natale, (a Democrat) who presided over the trial, threw out the fraud accusations earlier this week, leaving the jury to simply decide whether the suppliers have been negligent in their representations to the state. The removal of fraud allegation of intentional misrepresentation precluded the state from seeking any punitive damages.

The suppliers-Bradford C. Bernardo and his company, Providence Granite Co. of R.I., and Carl H. Lunderstadt, former President of North American Industries of McKeesport-had argued that the state received a good deal in the granite purchase and they were able to save Pennsylvania millions of dollars in the project.

But the state contended that it was misled by the suppliers because they said they would be purchasing the Woodberry granite at $9 dollars a cubic foot, plus additional cost for winter quarrying and inflation. The state maintained the suppliers knew all along that they would be purchasing the granite $8 dollars a cubic foot, with no inflation or winter quarrying markups.

Based on the higher figures, the state said it agreed to purchase the granite through the suppliers at $11 a cubic foot.

But the supplier's attorney, Charles F. Scarlata of Pittsburgh, had argued that the state never quibbled with the $11 cost. In fact, he said, the state never asked for a breakdown of the suppliers' costs, but was satisfied with the $11 price because it was happy to receive granite from the same quarry used to supply materials for the main Capitol building, completed in 1906.

Scarlata also argued that Lunderstadt and Bernardo saved the state millions of dollars because they suggested that the quarrying activities begin early so that the materials will be available when construction started on the addition.

The state agreed to a sole-source contract to purchase the granite in May 1983. The general construction contract was awarded in 1984.

End

Judge scolds state's conduct in long Capitol granite fight

By Matthew P. Smith
The Pittsburgh press

In a scathing opinion, a Dolphin County judge sharply criticized the state Attorney general's office for its conduct in a case against two men who supplied granite for an addition to the state Capitol.

Common Pleas Judge Sebastian D. Natale made his comments in **(ordering the state to pay $309,513)** in legal fees for the men, Carl H. Lunderstadt, former president of North American industries of McKeesport, and Bradford C. Bernardo, president of Providence Granite Co. of Rhode Island.

A civil jury in May 1989 ruled in favor of Lunderstadt and Bernardo, saying the two and a company did not mislead the state about the cost of granite for the Capitol project.

The men had been accused of fraud, but Natale, who presided over their trial, dismissed those charges before the case went to the jury.

It his order issued Tuesday, Natale criticized the attorney general's office for pursuing the case against the two defendants when it knew it lacked evidence to support the charges.

"If ever a legal proceeding was brought and conducted in an arbitrary, obdurate and vexatious matter, this entire action is that case," the judge wrote.

Pittsburgh attorney Charles Scarlata, who represented Lunderstadt and Bernardo, said he was delighted with the decision and said that Natale's strong comments were justified.

"I hope it sends a message to attorneys in general, and particularly to Commonwealth lawyers, that they are not immune from acting without regard to the rights of human beings," Scarlata said.

Robert Gentzel, spokesman for Attorney General Ernie Preate Jr., said the opinion is under review and no decision has been made on a possible appeal.

The case was brought by Preate's successor Leroy Zimmerman, Gentzel said.

Of the three assistant state attorneys who handled the case, Eugene Waye, David Cole and Carl Hisiro, only Hisiro is still with the attorney general's office. Waye has retired and Cole is in private practice, Gentzel said.

None could be reached for comment.

In it's case against the two businessmen, the state contended it was defrauded of $323,400 by the suppliers, who provided about 147,000 cubic feet of granite for the Capitol addition.

Much of Natale's 18-page order granting the legal fees centered on the actions of the assistant attorneys general in pressuring Emery Thurston, described by Natale as a "low-level employee" of the Department of General Services, to testify against the defendants.

The attorneys' actions were documented in internal memorandum introduced into evidence during two hearings on the request for the legal counsel fees.

End

The New York Times, Sunday, October 6, 1989
Architecture View/Paul Goldberger

A bit of old Athens on the Susquehanna

This is an exceptionally long article. I will include only a few excerpts. A copy of the entire article is available by writing to the author of this over one inch thick book.

Harrisburg Pennsylvania

. . . . For sometime the government of Pennsylvania handled its expansion problems by erecting stylistically compatible buildings on adjacent sites, doing this so well in the 1920s and 1930s that it managed to assemble around the Capitol one of the finest groupings of Classical buildings in United States, a cluster that brings to mind such better known places as the Federal Triangle in Washington and the Civic Center in San Francisco.

. . . . But by 1965 the state legislature was insisting that it needed more space under the Capitol's own roof, and a series of expansion plans came forth. The first, for a five-story rectangular box, was rightly dismissed as an architectural mistake before it ever got started. But somehow by the 1980's the odd combination of politics and architectural luck that has characterized capitol-building in Harrisburg in this century came into play once again—which is how the Commonwealth of Pennsylvania came eventually to build the remarkable $127 million, million square foot complex of fountains, pediments, columns, plazas and balustrades now known as the Capitols East Wing.

The East Wing, or Capitol extension as some call it, was finished not long ago, and it is perhaps the most ambitious work in the Classical mode in the United States in a generation: a low, strong structure that attempts, as earnestly as any public building of our time, to carry the Classical tradition forward. It's difficult to talk about the revival of Classicism in this country without thinking about this project.

The architects were the firm of Celli-Flynn of Pittsburgh, working with the engineering firm of H. F. Lenz Co., also of Pittsburgh, and they have produced a design that manages at once to enrich the original Capitol building and to defer to it. The addition, roughly 640 feet long by 320 feet wide, is almost, but not quite, an underground building. It is best described as a series of terraces, hugging the ground and filling up a site of about five acres that is enclosed by the Capitol on the West and two distinguished, Classically inspired state office buildings on the north and south.

. . . . These three buildings join to form the walls of an outdoor room of truly noble proportions, which the state planned in the 1920s to make into a formal plaza, to be called the Court of Honor. Unfortunately, certain practical needs got in the way of the Court of Honor and it was never built, and this space just beside the Capitol spent most of the last quarter-century as a parking lot instead.

. . . . The grandeur of the site is enhanced still more by the fact that is stands at the end of one of the most spectacular formal axes in any American city, State Street, which extends beyond the new building's site through yet another formal plaza, this one a kind of miniature version of the Mall in Washington, past a pair of monumental Art Deco pylons, across a bridge and through the city. Harrisburg is no Paris, but this sequence is as good as they come.

. . . . As it turned out, Mr. Celli did not tinker significantly with anything that Houston designed—at its highest point this new extension's central dome barely creeps above the lowest level of the old Capitol. The addition nuzzles at the base of the Capitol if anything this big can be said to nuzzle, it's essential architectural idea is the combination of monumental outdoor public space and deferential architectural form. Mr. Celli has not designed a building so much as a huge, Classically inspired terraced Piazza, with offices and atriums tucked underneath.

At its low-level, below ground, the building contains parking for 840 cars and loading docks to serve the entire Capitol complex.

. . . . It is a splendid plan, for it manages at the same time to enrich the urban texture, provide truly sumptuous public space and support the Capitol as a work of architecture.

. . . . But isn't a fancy, Classically inspired Mall still progress, given the level of most public architecture of the last generation? I think it is, and to be fair, this complex looked vibrant one day late last month as it was flooded with crowds who had come to Harrisburg for a political rally; its sprawling public space seem to make it, if not a temple democracy, at least the Mall of democracy. The Commonwealth of Pennsylvania began the century by doing the right thing when it built Joseph Houston's capital in 1906; this project shows that it is approaching the end of the century with it's architectural values intact.

.... This new East Wing of Pennsylvania's Capitol is perhaps the most ambitious classical work in the United States in a generation.

Note-All items in parentheses and bold type are mine.

INVITATION

During the second week of November 1987, nine months after I left office, I began receiving invitations from the leaders of the House and Senate, inviting me to take part in the dedication of the new addition to the Main Capitol Building. The ceremony was to take place on Thursday, December 3rd, 1987 at 11 AM. I was told that I would be listed on the program and that I should prepare some remarks for the occasion. They did not suggest a subject nor how much time I would be allotted.

Folding chairs were set up the members of the Senate and House in what some people began to call "The little rotunda." The rotunda and the balcony were filled with staff members, state employees, citizens and many reporters. Minority leader, Matthew Ryan, House speaker, K. LeRoy Irvis, House Majority Leader, James Mannarino, and Senate President Pro Tempore, Robert C. Jubelirer, made remarks.

A news article reported "In his address, Baran ignored the controversy that plagued the project when he served under former Gov. Dick Thornburgh." When I began my speech, I was greeted with mild applause. The legislators did not know what this "Loose Cannon" was about to say. I must say that I spoke and acted like a gentleman and after the speech I was greeted with very enthusiastic applause. They didn't exactly stomp their feet, but it sounded like they did. Susan Taylor our houseguest from Birmingham England was on the balcony armed with a video camera. The photography was dark but my voice and the thunderous applause was perfectly clear.

I was "flabbergasted" to read these words:

"The ceremony centered around two men, one who died more than 250 years ago, and another who oversaw the expansion project during it's darkest hours—William Penn, and former General Services Secretary Walter Baran."

Could you imagine, a son of Polish immigrants being aligned with the founder of Pennsylvania, William Penn! My God, how I wished that Helen Guy, my eighth grade teacher at the Franklin School was in the audience to hear this.

After all the speeches, a man I greatly admire, House Speaker, K. LeRoy Irvis, came to my seat and asked me to join him in unveiling the plaque bearing the names of all 253 members of the general assembly. This small act on his part told everyone else, "He is an all-around nice guy!"

A great day for Walter Baran from Frackville.

Expansion project gets Capitol dedication
by Eric Conrad Patriot News

December 3rd, 1987

Yesterday was one of ceremonious reprieve for the Capitol expansion.

Former state officials, the buildings architects and engineers—the men behind the East Wings $124 million price tag—were lauded as heroes.

Legislators who once spoke cautiously about a 20-month investigation into the buildings construction, said the final product is something Pennsylvanians would use for centuries. They proudly unveiled plaques bearing the names of all 253 members of the General Assembly.

Even in the East Wing's escalator, which hasn't been used since the building opened two months ago, ran without a hitch.

With hundreds of Capitol workers looking on, legislators dedicated the building during a brief lunchtime ceremony. They said it completes the Capitol Complex between Foster and Walnut Street's.

"It was a courageous act to move ahead with his building in face of some criticism, "said House Minority Leader Matthew Ryan. "This is a worthy addition to the Capitol Complex. It is a worthy addition for the people of Pennsylvania to be proud of."

The ceremony centered around two men, one who died more than 250 years ago, and another who oversaw the expansion project during its darkest hours—William Penn, and former General Services Secretary Walter Baran.

House Speaker K. Leroy Irvis said Penn dreamed of founding a land in which all men could live together in peace regardless of religion, race or creed.

"It's a dream that's not quite done today," he said. "But we are blessed in many ways, and it's not a blessing of fine buildings. It's a blessing of fine men and fine women."

Senate President Pro Tempore described the expansion as "The house that Wally Baran built." Baran, he said, is the only state official ever described in the Pennsylvania Manual as an "all-around nice guy."

In his address, Baran ignored the controversy that plagued the project when he served under former Gov. Dick Thornburgh. He said he was proud of the extension's "innards."

Fire detection equipment installed in the East wing will eliminate fire-code violations that for years has plagued the overcrowded Main Capitol building, the same site where lawmakers past fire-safety laws, said Baran.

An electrical system was built into the expansion to handle the computerized demands of modern government, he said. An underground parking garage and beautiful building replaced what Jubelirer described as "a less than grand parking lot" on which the wing was built.

The expansion opens as the General Assembly, for whom the building was erected, celebrates its 305th birthday, said Baran. The Legislature is the "oldest democracy in the world," he said.

House Majority Leader James Manderino said the expansion was needed because serving in the Legislature grew into "a full-time, indeed job more than full-time, job." He said the building should solve the General Assembly's space problems for decades.

Neither Jubelirer nor Irvis mentioned absences of Thornburgh or Gov. Robert P. Casey.

Jubelirer, noting the dedication of the main Capitol drew President Teddy Roosevelt, said: "The speaker and I have made every effort to have Teddy Roosevelt once again, but you're stuck with us."

Note: Bold print is mine.

LETTER TO THE EDITOR

I decided to send a letter to the editor of the *Harrisburg Patriot News/Harrisburg Evening News*, published on June 29th, 1984 titled **"Baran Challenges Capital Completion Critics."**

My decision to have the letter published caused me great pain and later some joy when I received many letters (I am including one of these letters at the end of the article) and many telephone calls at my home in Shipoke, my home in Frackville and many calls to my office that agreed with my decision.

On the evening before the letter was to be printed, I attended a fundraiser at one of the large restaurants on the West Shore of Harrisburg. During the evening, the Governor spoke to me about the letter I had sent to the *Patriot News*. He was extremely angry with me and he let me know in no uncertain terms that he was very upset that I would do such a thing. It was suggested that I call the newspaper to stop the printing of the letter. It was impossible to stop since it was being printed as we spoke. I spent a few sleepless nights and seriously considered resigning my position as Secretary of General Services. I did not tell anyone about my conversation with the Governor. I did discuss my conversation with the Governor and my thoughts of submitting my resignation only with my wife Irene.

In the next few days, after receiving encouragement from Republican and *Democrat* legislators and state employees that I met during the day, I decided to continue to work hard and somehow regain the confidence of the Governor that he once had for me.

And of course I was pleased that within a period of time, I was again in good graces with the Governor's office.

Since I was a businessman first, and later a very naive politician, I should have known that the Governor's office should have been notified before submitting my letter to the editor.

There were many demands that I resign because the department purchased granite "sole source" and foreign steel was found on the site (it was part of the steel scaffolding used by a subcontractor), the purchase of "foreign" trees that were grown and imported from New Jersey etc. All this during the time when my department had over 300 construction projects under way that received little or no mention in the press.

All the newspapers in Pennsylvania and a few from New Jersey and Maryland carried many articles about the "Scandal." At the end of my term, the staff at the bureau of Public Works gave me a very large three-ring five-inch thick binder that contained newspaper clippings all dealing only with the capitol extension project. Those articles did not keep me from the job I had to do. A special house committee chaired by Nick Colafella, D. Beaver, did cause my staff and me many lost hours of production. My staff had to produce volumes of records while I had to spend endless hours testifying before this committee. During this entire period, I did not receive any help or encouragement from the Governor's office or from the Republican legislators. I really did not expect any since I know that they could not help me, with such a large project, there may have been a member of my staff, a contractor (or even me) who may have broken the law.

I felt that the taxpayers had to be informed about many of the erroneous statements that were made in the press and during the hearings of the Select House Committee. While I know that a person should never argue with someone who purchased ink by the barrel, nevertheless, I decided to write "My side of the story."

Since I went to my home in Frackville only on weekends, I had evenings free during the week. I began composing the letter. I spent a few weeks writing in longhand on a yellow legal pad. Each morning I would find my Executive Assistant, David Morrison and hand him my evening's "homework." I would give him an outline of a speech or letter and he produced a good finished product. He not only corrected my grammar and my spelling but after two years he was able to decipher my handwriting. The final letter was concise, well written and I knew the readers of the *Patriot News* would now have "The other side of the story."

I hand delivered it to the editorial department of the *Patriot News* and was informed that it was too long and would not be accepted. I then asked if they could print it as an Op-ed article. This was also refused. I then decided to print it as a paid advertisement. They told me they could not accept it since it is not their policy to print this type of "Advertisement" on the Op-ed page. I returned later in the day armed with a few recent copies of the *Patriot News* that contained an article from a local bank that listed in detail a new policy that the bank was installing. The advertisement was about the same size as my article and was printed on the Op-ed page. My "advertisement" was then accepted. I insisted that my photograph and a border be used. I then wrote a check to the *Patriot News* for the sum of $1125.00 dollars.

The rest is history.

Baran Challenges Capitol Completion Critics

by Walter Baran
Secretary of General Services

A message to the readers of the Patriot News:

I feel it is important that a balanced discussion be presented to you regarding the Capital Completion Project. The following letter was not accepted for publication because of its length, so it is being printed instead at my personal expense.

"Capital Project Probe Widening." When that headlined topped all six columns on page one of Sunday's Patriot News—a banner I normally associate with major assassinations, declarations of war or approval of UDAG grants—I suppose a few scandal-seekers, starved for another season of Dynasty and Dallas, were disappointed by the paragraphs that followed. Some may have been satisfactorily shocked, but I can only suppose.

On the other hand, I do know of a few dozen people whose reaction was more painful: those on our staff in General Services whose responsibility for managing this project has been further burdened in recent weeks through the supplying of hundreds of pages of documents to the stories two authors. Not one of them has done anything illegal. Not one of them has even committed errors above the significance of a misspelled word. In fact, by burning the midnight oil and sensing the historic importance of their assignment, they have done and are doing no less than an outstanding job. On Sundays, they sit home and read of "allegations."

"All we've got so far are allegations and traces of evidence," said a "source close to the probe," who declined to identify either himself or the traces of evidence. Allegations, except to their targets, are no big deal; they're easy to produce an easier still to market; they sweeten revenge and they grease the machinery of election campaigns. You expect them, and you live with them, because no amount of honesty or brilliance can guarantee immunity. It's merely sad that the inevitability of allegations drives so many good people from entering or staying in public service.

I don't intend to be driven from public service, but I frankly, have difficulty in living with allegations. We've now seen in print allegations of "wrongdoing," "kickbacks," "favoritism," and "corner-cutting," cranked out with all the ease and delectability of a Big Mac hamburger. People don't ask for them, but they buy and swallow them before they're cold. But, Hey! Where's the evidence?

Sole-source purchases are something that seems to have aroused unusual suspicion. I've probably processed 5000 sole source purchases in five years, and there were thousands before that, right back to the day the Dutch bought Manhattan from the Indians: presumably somebody could have sold them a better island at a cheaper price. It's a matter of judgment. Judgment, which factored in nearly every accomplishment of human history, alas has become something that is so suspect and feared in administrative government that it has been all but replaced by a cumbersome overlay of standard procedures, legal precedents and decisionless envelope-opening. Government workers have become so terrified of the consequences of making decisions and exercising judgment, best-selling tensions notwithstanding, that we've reached the point were deciding nothing and initiating nothing has become the ideal state of affairs. Emptying the in-basket according to procedure is the safest route to promotion and pension.

By those standards, we have been wise to leave the long-dormant Capitol Completion proposal for some future generation to pursue, and spend our time issuing studies. But my staff are probably mavericks by those standards. When the project engineer recommended half a dozen items of equipment as specifically essential to the success, longevity and efficiency of the building, it meant that random substitutes from other sources were either unacceptable or impossible to utilize. In doing so, he was exercising the ability of professional judgment for which he was hired. The same intellectual talents are required of our staff, for it is their job to review such proposals and either reject or endorse them.

In the case of the various items of electronic and mechanical equipment, the recommended items were found to be uniquely and supremely suited to the demanding requirements of the building: it's long lifespan, the intolerability of equipment failure and a common-sense desire to minimize scheduled maintenance costs. The approval of the selections was intelligent and based on thorough research. That approval was seconded throughout the chain of command, on up to the Board of Public Grounds and Buildings, chaired by the State Treasurer. No sole-source purchases approved by the Board without the toughest security. The Board routinely receives sole-source recommendations ten days in advance, and frequently more time is requested before a decision is rendered.

This was nothing more than a decision-making process, prescribed by law and safeguarded by extensive review and approval. Were they the right decisions or the best decisions? I think so, and certainly everyone including the Board of Public Grounds and Buildings concluded that they were preferable to no decision or random selection by low bid. This is far more assurance that is expected in private business, although obviously there is no such thing as a one-hundred-percent assurance. Just as obviously, there is no such thing as something that cannot be done a better way next time.

This may sound as if I were opposed to the low-bid purchasing system. Quite the contrary. Competitive bidding is an ideal method of impartially obtaining the best price among equivalent alternatives. It is even used with enthusiasm in private business. In General Services, where we conduct the vast majority of all state purchasing by competitive bidding, we have vigorously expanded its use into new areas during the past five years. Where IBM, Xerox and Bell Telephone-AT&T are still viewed by many governments as a sole source of their prospective office products, **Pennsylvania has led the nation** in moving to the competitive purchase of such equipment. This has saved the taxpayers millions of dollars annually. The day, the week, the month before we begin buying phone systems by low bid, do we conclude that those final sole-source purchases were illegal? No, they were based on the best judgment available at the time.

Judgmental decisions will always be open to second-guessing, and I have no doubt that there will be a great deal of second, guessing regarding the Capitol Completion project. It is one thing to be a Monday-morning quarterback and quite another to make real decisions in a time frame necessary to complete an important building. But second-guessing a decision is nothing compared to making allegations of deliberate wrongdoing, especially when there is no evidence whatsoever to support such allegations—certainly none that I'm aware of.

Meanwhile, the positive and significant aspects of the Capitol Completion Project seem to be entirely obscured by the border-induced scandalmania. In 1978, Pennsylvania's Capitol Building was cited by its own Labor and Industry Department for 52 major violations of fire and safety laws—laws enacted in the very rooms being cited. This was primarily due to acute overcrowding that had gone unresolved for years. Overpopulation resulted in violations of exit requirements. Overloading of electrical systems with more and more office machinery had created severe fire hazards. And laws aside, the lack of suitable working space was an obvious hindrance to the efficiency of the Legislature and its staff.

Agreement was reached in 1979 that there could be no further procrastination of the expansion project that had been proposed and substantially designed in 1965. The designs were updated, yielding a considerable improvement over the contemporary-style structure favored in the Sixties. While replacing the crude asphalt parking lot with attractive exterior plaza that had been envisioned since 1922, the new facility will also provide 160,000 square feet of additional space. This will accommodate more than 100 legislators as well as committee rooms and staff support areas.

Fronting Commonwealth Avenue, the new facility will enjoin the North and South Office Buildings and the Executive Building as well as the Main Capitol, creating a single, interconnected office complex blending modern operating efficiency with the architectural heritage of the Capitol.

While parking is an issue on which there are all opinions, it is nevertheless a critical and long ignored issue. The 500 surface spaces are replaced with underground parking for 850 cars, which will substantially ease the congestion and return sections of curbside parking to taxpayers and visitors, whom we first accommodated, albeit temporarily, in 1980. An underground truck delivery network will service all five adjoining buildings, eliminating the congestion, noise and double-parking which has prevailed in the immediate area for years.

It should be noted that the Capitol Completion also will bring about energy cost savings of $1 million per year by enabling link-up of the Capitol and other nearby buildings to the vast underground heating and cooling plant completed for this purpose in 1969. The central plant was designed for tremendous efficiency when used to full capacity, but it has been under-utilized for 15 years, which was most unfortunate, especially during the energy crisis period of the

Seventies. The white elephant of 1969 will become the working elephant of 1989, 2089 and beyond. I would call this a rather basic, common-sense-decision.

The exterior of the facility will be characterized by a small dome and other features that visually extend the style of the Capitol. Exterior walls, which comprise relatively little area in the concourse-line structure, will be faced in granite from the same quarry that supplied the granite for the Main Capitol in 1906. (Indeed, that quarry by consequence of geology is a sole source, but the approved granite purchase's nevertheless being questioned. This tries one's patience.) Elsewhere, original balusters and paving blocks removed from the adjoining North and South office terraces will be relocated to further enhance architectural continuity while making use of existing craftsmanship.

In addition to the practical and functional aspects of this project, which in themselves are important, we cannot underestimate the historic importance of appropriately completing Pennsylvania's number-one building, which is both a National Landmark and acknowledge as the finest Capitol building in the United States.

Anytime you undertake a project such as this, in full view of a captive audience of professional critics, you're going to get a certain amount of probing, second-guessing and allegations. We knew this when we started. But we knew also that long after the criticism fades, we will have created, or at least preserved, an international monument whose usefulness and dignity will long be a source of appreciation and pride to current and future generations of Pennsylvania employees, citizens and visitors.

Gratitude should never be the inspiration of worthy accomplishments. The architects of European castles usually had their eyes plucked out; my staff and I are perhaps fortunate by comparison.

Walter Baran
Secretary of General Services
PAID ANNOUNCEMENT

Note: *The Patriot News* highlighted the first few words of each paragraph of my letter.

Sample response letter

H & J Realty Corporation
Francis. Ford's Inc.
H & J Gross Inc.

GROSS INVESTMENTS POST OFFICE BOX 3626
HARRISBURG, PENNSYLVANIA 17105

June 29, 1984

Walter Baran, Secretary
Department of General Services
North Office Building
Harrisburg, Pennsylvania 17125

Dear Mr. Baran:

I read your letter in today's Patriot. Twice. With even more satisfaction the second time.

I must say you did approach the problems of sophomoric criticism and the media drool with considerable tact. Nevertheless, the barbs seep through in good measure along with your point by point tutoring of the unwashed. Better yet, there was no apology.

That must have been rather irritating to a small number of lesser legislators.

All in all, it wasn't a bad morning for Patriot readers. They needed some honest and thorough investigative reporting, missing far too long. They should have paid you.

Sincerely,
Jack Gross

Finis

EPILOGUE

As I entered my "Golden years," I had time to reflect on my long life. From my childhood to my old age, I had a great ride. And, I ain't done yet! Perhaps my childhood would have been better had my father not deserted me, but I don't think so. I had a terrific childhood. I never did hate my father. I really did not know him. I do know he never changed my diaper, or gave me my first haircut or ever held me on his lap. What I do know is that he left me with real good "genes." The three Baranowski kids, Leonard, Walter and Helen were fortunate to have inherited good genes. I certainly knew that my mother had good genes, but it was much later in life that I realized that my father also had good genes

Because I was a breech birth, my teenage years created some problems. I was not able to participate in sports. I suppose that's what turned me into a "nerd," I was not called a nerd since I believe that word only came into use during the early '70s. I was fascinated by radios, anything that ran on two or four wheels and anything mechanical. I was very fortunate to have two older half brothers (I really hate that word "half" but that is the word my friends used when talking about my brothers) that really looked after me during my teen years. They always had big open cars, took me and other kids from the neighborhood to swim in a real swimming pool, taught me how to shoot a 22 rifle and even instructed me how to "roll" a cigarette

When I was sixteen years old, I left home and joined the Civilian Conservation Corps (CCC.) It was a marvelous experience. I learned how to live with others with different cultural and ethnic backgrounds. I advanced very quickly through the ranks and became a "Leader." This is the first of many times in my life where I did nothing to advance myself. I never asked or sought a new position and I never asked for an increase in my salary.

When I entered the labor market and began working in a garment factory at the minimum rate of 25 cents per hour, I again, advanced very quickly without any effort on my part. Of course, if you call getting to work ahead of time, working hard and not complaining, never getting sick, respecting my boss and all my fellow workers, promoting myself to get ahead, then I suppose I am guilty. In seven short years, I became the assistant manager of the garment factory that employed over 300 workers.

When I reached the age of 25, I decided to go into business for myself. I was going to say that "Lady Luck" was with me. That would not be a true statement since luck had nothing to do with it. Perseverance, hard work and believing in myself was the answer to what little success I had.

At age 35, I began to branch out into other fields, retail sales, real estate, and home construction. I had it all. A good marriage, two very bright sons, and good health.

In my middle age years, I was asked to serve as the Secretary of the Department of General Services for the Commonwealth of Pennsylvania. It was the greatest challenge of my life. With over 1500 employees, a yearly budget of $65 million, with a lot of perseverance, hard work, and the help of a great staff, I was able to do the work and to complete two terms in the administration of a truly great Governor of Pennsylvania, Dick Thornburgh. I was amazed by the high quality of people selected by Governor Thornburgh to serve in his cabinet, many who left higher-paying positions in order to serve the people of Pennsylvania. I was amazed and somewhat frightened to be included in this group of talented people. In my position as the Secretary of General Services, I was in contact with every member of the cabinet since DGS supplied them with space for staff, automobiles, parking space, procurement services, housekeeping etc. There were a few cabinet members with whom I had a close relationship since I dealt with them on a weekly and occasionally daily basis.

Dr. Bob Wilburn was one of these, a very kind, caring, and talented man. The Governor suggested that I meet with Dr. Wilburn every Thursday morning. There was no specific topic to discuss; it was more of a chat. I was a naïve politician without a college degree and no experience in government. He would advise me how to handle any problems that arose in my department. I feel that meeting with him was the reason for what little success I had. Best of all, what is hard to believe is the fact that he treated me as an equal!

Another great Cabinet member was, James I. Scheiner, Secretary of the Department of Revenue. As a member of the Governor's Cost Reduction team, he was responsible for submitting many cost savings in his department. As an example, he submitted a savings of $743 million in improved collection of delinquent taxes by the revenue Department for the years 1979/1986. He was one of the most brilliant member of the Governor's Cabinet. I'm very happy to call him my friend.

In 1995 we made the decision to sell our home in Frackville. It was a difficult decision but it had to be made. It was a very large home with two additional buildings a guesthouse and pool house. We lived in the home for thirty-four years. At my insistence we employed a cleaning lady to work once a week vacuuming and dusting the home. She worked for us for only four weeks. While her work was satisfactory, Irene insisted that she wanted to do the work herself.

We were very fortunate to hire Mr. Albert Flail Sr., who was much more than a handyman. He was a dear friend. He had extensive grounds to take care of. He took care of the lawn, pool, and the outside buildings. He was a big help to Irene during the eight years I spent in Harrisburg. Each night when I was away, he would drive around our house in the evening to see if Irene was all right. We did not know he was doing this until after he retired. He was with us for 27 years.

The home was a perfect place to raise children. I selected a piece of ground that was next to a large forest of oak trees. A utility company owns the land behind the home which guarantees that it will stay as a forest. We were very sad to leave the home that gave us a lot of pleasure. We are very happy that my nephew and niece Tim & Carol Twardzik have purchased the home. They have three lively young sons and many young nieces and nephews to share the house and grounds with. They also share their home with their young friends and neighbors.

Our new retirement home

I am now fully retired spending my time tinkering with my antique automobiles, taking care of my tomato plants and spending a lot of time with my wife and friend Irene. During my working years, I did not spend much time at home. Now I'm spending too much time at home. Irene didn't know how good she had it!

BVG